Muchachas
No
More

In the series
Women in the Political Economy,
edited by Ronnie J. Steinberg

Muchachas No More

HOUSEHOLD WORKERS IN LATIN AMERICA AND THE CARIBBEAN

Edited by

Elsa M. Chaney

and

Mary Garcia Castro

Bibliography by
Margo L. Smith

TEMPLE UNIVERSITY PRESS
Philadelphia

Temple University Press, Philadelphia 19122
Copyright © 1989 by Temple University. All rights reserved
Published 1989
Printed in the United States of America

The paper used in this publication meets the minimum
requirements of American National Standard for Information
Sciences—Permanence of Paper for Printed Library Materials,
ANSI Z39.48-1984

LIBRARY OF CONGRESS
Library of Congress Cataloging-in-Publication Data

Muchachas no more : household workers in
   Latin America and the Caribbean / edited by
   Elsa M. Chaney and Mary Garcia Castro.
      p.   cm. — (Women in the political economy)
   Bibliography: p.
   ISBN 0-87722-571-0 (alk. paper)
   1. Women domestics—Latin America—Case studies.
I. Chaney, Elsa.   II. Castro, Mary Garcia.   III. Series
HD6072.2.L29M83 1988
331.4'816046'09—dc19   88-15577
                                               CIP

To the organized household workers of Latin America and
the Caribbean, and to their efforts to build new forms
of association through a gendered class struggle that
begins with the domestic sphere, but does not end there.

Cancíon de los Sindicatos
de las Trabajadoras del Hogar
(Perú, Song of Household Workers Unions)

Ando, ando como empleada
acompañada de tantos engaños
ay, para mí no hay justicia
hasta mis padres están explotados.

Yo no he venido a robar tu riqueza
yo no he venido a hacerme patrona
sólo he venido buscando trabajo
sólo he venido buscando justicia.

Todos me dicen que soy empleada
todos me dicen que soy muchachita
empleada pero luchadora
muchachita pero muy valiente.

Mañana, mañana, he de luchar
mañana, mañana, he de triunfar
pasado, pasado, he de triunfar
con eso, con eso, tu gozarás
todos los pobres han de gozar.

I go along, go along as a servant
So many deceptions accompany me
Ay! for me there is no justice
Even my parents are exploited.

I have not come to rob your riches
I have not come to make myself a
  patrona
I have come only looking for work
I have come only looking for justice.

Everyone tells me that I am a
  servant
Everyone tells me that I am a "little
  girl"
Maid, yes, but fighter
Girl, yes, but very brave.

Tomorrow, tomorrow, one must
  struggle
Tomorrow, tomorrow, one must win
Let bygones be bygones, one must
  win
That's it, that's it, you will rejoice
All the poor must rejoice!

Contents

Acknowledgments

The editors acknowledge, with thanks, a grant from the Ford Foundation, which enabled them to translate articles from their original languages for the English and Spanish editions of this book.

We are grateful for the many editorial suggestions of our three anonymous reviewers, and we also thank the Temple University Press staff for its assistance at every stage of the book's publication, particularly Michael Ames for his encouragement at an early point in the collection of the materials, and Jennifer French and freelancer Patricia Sterling for their always cheerful and efficient editing of the manuscript.

Introduction

A New Field for Research and Action

ELSA M. CHANEY and MARY GARCIA CASTRO

This collection is designed to give a first overview of the situation of female household workers in the Americas. Domestic workers—defined as persons who perform services for an individual or a family in the setting of a private home—account for not less than 20 percent of all women in the paid work force in Latin America and the Caribbean, according to census and labor force surveys. In many countries, the proportions of women in domestic service are much higher; depending on the country, one-fifth to one-third of the female labor force is occupied in domestic service (CEPAL 1982, 102). The percentages would be higher still if there were some way to include women who do domestic work but are not counted in the official statistics.[1]

Considering how many they are, the scant attention paid to this important sector of working women is surprising. Or, perhaps, not so mysterious when the particular characteristics of this occupation, as documented in the studies presented here, are taken into account. Among the most important and universal aspects of paid domestic labor, as reflected in this collection, are the following:

• Domestic workers engage in housework, everywhere an undervalued and depreciated activity. Housework is scarcely considered a proper occupation; it is "women's work," apparently demanding no particular training or skills, that the female was born to do. Even when housework is shared with the *patrona* (mistress), she reserves the pleasant tasks for herself, passing on the dirty and disagreeable work to her servant—and thus denigrating paid household work even further.

• Domestic workers are recruited from among poor women with minimal education who migrate to the towns and cities from the provinces of their countries. Often they are indigenous women; their

3

culture, language, dress, and race are considered inferior to those of the dominant urban classes.

• Domestic workers usually work alone or with, at most, one or two others. They have no central workplace, no common free times and holidays. Because they are so isolated, as a group they are essentially "invisible" to themselves and to society. Under these conditions, they find it hard to join together to become aware of, and to fight for, their rights. Nor have their brothers and sisters in the trade union movement been, for the most part, supportive of domestic workers' efforts to organize.

• Domestic worker organization is impeded also by the fact that household workers are not covered by ordinary legislation for manual workers. The pretexts for denying them parity with the *obrero/a* are that they do not have a common workplace, do not produce a tangible product, and are paid partially "in kind." In many countries, domestic workers do not yet have the right to organize.

• Domestic worker leaders have been deeply distrustful of those who would appear to be their natural allies: women in professional organizations and feminist groups. They distrust the former because efforts to help (and these have been infrequent) have often turned into projects to provide middle- and upper-class women with more efficient servants. They are dubious about the latter because of the ambivalence of some feminists, who do not want to alter the present *patrona/empleada* relationship on which their own freedom to carry on their work and activities depends. Nor have feminist groups, with rare exceptions, taken up the cause of domestic workers.

For these and other reasons, discussed in detail in the articles that follow, domestic workers in most countries remain among the most oppressed and neglected sector of the working class. Indeed, in a survey in Peru (Heyman 1974), women placed only two occupations lower in desirability: prostitution and begging.

And no wonder. In the descriptive pieces in Part II of this book, we follow the initiation of these women into service at a young age, their struggle for themselves and their children into their middle years, and the bleak old age they often face, after years of service, without a pension or other means of support. They live in families that are not their own, witness to an affective life that is most often denied to them. Their pay is low, averaging $30 to no more than $50 per month in most countries. There is little or no upward mobility in the occupation; even a progression from a house in a poor district to a situation in a better area appears to be more an aspiration than a calculated strategy for upward mobility.[2]

Nor does government offer them much protection. While many countries have legislation on the books in relation to work hours, days off, vacations, and social security, there typically is little or no enforcement machinery. In fact, legislation has had an unintended outcome; in Peru, for example, the provision that household help must have eight hours of rest in each twenty-four hours has been widely interpreted as a license to *patronas* to exact sixteen-hour workdays.

The co-editors of this collection became aware of the plight of domestic workers through prior research of their own. Chaney collaborated with a Chilean colleague on a study of domestic workers in Peru (Bunster and Chaney 1985); Garcia Castro (1982) and her colleagues (1981) have carried out a major research project on domestic workers in Colombia for the International Labor Office. We organized a panel at the 1983 Mexico City congress of the Latin American Studies Association (LASA), and four of the twenty-two articles in this book (Duarte, Gálvez and Todaro, Goldsmith, and Prates) were presented there. In the years since the LASA meeting, we have been searching out additional studies and decided to put together a collection when we had a sufficient number of contemporary articles based on field research and historical pieces based on primary sources. This volume comprises some of the best research that has been carried out to date. In several cases the study is the only work on domestics in that country, and not every country is represented in the collection; nevertheless, the coverage—both thematically and geographically—is broad.

In the main, scholarly work on domestic service has been a series of unconnected efforts, not based on any central theoretical concepts. Only in a few cases has there been an attempt to link findings to theory, and only the first steps have been taken toward theory building. In this collection, Duarte, Gálvez and Todaro, Garcia Castro and León, in particular, represent such efforts. Most of the articles included here represent a "first cut"; they are descriptive rather than theoretical. A new field of research first needs to establish a solid base upon which theorizing can be built. We believe that our selection of articles does this, and it is our hope and intent that the present volume will help set a new field of research on its way and that many other studies will follow. The next round should begin incorporating theoretical concerns much more consciously and systematically.

One unusual feature gives our collection special strength and authority: both the scholars and the representatives of the group studied have a voice (see Part V). This follows from the fact that two domestic worker organizers, Adelinda Díaz Uriarte of Peru and Aída Moreno Valenzuela of Chile, came to Mexico City to comment on the scholars' presentations and, in a *pequeño encuentro* (small meeting) the day following, outlined the history and situation of their organizations. Moreno's presentation was revised to become the article "History of the Household Workers' Movement in Chile, 1926–1983." We encouraged Díaz to put her material in the framework of her own life, and she wrote for this volume "The Autobiography of a Fighter."

Additionally, pioneer Brazilian leaders "Zica" (Anazir Maria de Oliveira) and Odete Maria da Conceição contributed an article on household worker organization in Brazil, while the SINTRASEDOM has written the history of its struggle to become an officially recognized union in Colombia. Our collaboration with these leaders has continued; in early 1988, we assisted representatives of domestic workers' unions of Chile, Colombia, and Peru to organize a Latin American/Caribbean *encuentro* in Bogotá, where representatives of household workers in eleven countries founded the Confederation of Household Workers of Latin America and the Caribbean.

Many chapters in this collection touch on questions and themes emphasized in the pioneer studies on the topic of domestic service and several major issues emerge from the studies carried out to date.

There is the search for a *class identity*, already set in motion by domestic workers themselves. They want recognition that they are workers, not "maids" or *muchachas* (serving girls) or *cholitas* (a depreciative term for indigenous women) or "daughters of the family." They fight for their work to be respected, for affirmation of their social role in the daily reproduction of the family unit,[3] for the right to organize, for the legislation and programs already won by other members of the working class. They want domestic service to win collectively from the state and the *patrones* the salary, regulated workday, social security, and treatment between employee and employer that characterize labor relations among all the other wage earners. These principles are common themes in the publications of the unions and associations of domestic workers in Brazil, Chile, Colombia, Mexico, Peru, and elsewhere. Domestic workers are searching for unity and are communicating among themselves; they are attempting to integrate their struggle with other sectors of the working class while retaining their relative autonomy.

Whether domestic service is *disappearing* in Latin America and the Caribbean (Chaney 1985; Garcia Castro et al. 1981) is an unresolved question. Higman's historical study of Jamaica (this volume) challenges the relationship suggested by Boserup (1970) between the decline of domestic service and industrialization. Garcia Castro, Pereira, and Prates (this volume) all call attention to the possible association between the economic crisis of capitalism in the region and the increase or decline of domestic service.

There is the question of *occupational mobility* among domestic workers, first addressed by Smith (1971) in a pioneer study of domestic service in Lima. Since then, there have been many additions to the controversy (Chaney 1985; Grau 1982; Jelin 1977; Saffioti 1978). In this volume Smith reviews the discussion and her own early research.

The relation of domestic service to *women's migration* in the region involves investigating the conditions of life in the sending areas. Systematic examinations of this question were initiated by Arizpe (1975) and Jelin (1977) in works that have become classics on the migration of women and the links to domestic service. In this collection, Colen discusses the conditions of life and work in New York City for women migrants from the West Indies, but almost all the articles presented here touch on the theme of migration.

Racism, "lack of respect," and the "asymmetry" of relations between *patronas* and workers are elements stressed in the works produced by militant household workers' organizations and trade unions. There is as well, a critique of the deficient legal coverage because the laws that exist are not applied (see particularly León, but many of the articles touch on this issue). Additional legal disabilities are encountered by migrant domestic workers in developed countries (Colen in this volume; Silvera 1983).

The *patrona/empleada relation,* with its elements of identity and antagonism, is a theme that perhaps has contributed most to analyses that go beyond the macro level and illumine our understanding of the uniqueness of domestic service as a work relation (Garcia Castro et al. 1981; Grau 1982; Saffioti 1978; as well as the articles in the 1980–81 issue of *FEM*). Colen, Gálvez and Todaro, and Pereira in this collection explore this theme from different analytic perspectives.

The *"ideology of service"* employs elements reenforcing women's subordination. Several articles explore the belief that responsibility for household chores is something "naturally feminine" and that paid domestic service is a natural extension of domestic work. The relation between domestic work and domestic service is examined in depth by León (this volume). Flora's analysis of the typology of the *fotonovela* (illustrated romance) comments on the representation of the household worker and the creation of "myths" about her which are not quite static—they do change over time as other social changes occur—but have in common that they utilize the figure of the maid to recapture the characteristics of her work and to present them as acceptable (Toussaint 1980–81; see also Smith in this volume for references to the representation of the domestic worker in the *telenovela*, or TV soap opera). Garcia Castro, Gogna, and Mohammed (this volume) also contribute to the discussion of the boundaries between ideology and reality.

The *treatment accorded domestic workers by feminists and professional women* is questioned in several of the articles appearing in *FEM* (1980–81). In this volume Duarte has systematized questions that need to be examined by the feminist movement, especially the thesis of the "double day," which does not apply to all Latin American women but does affect domestic workers and other poor women who are expected to perform a "second shift" of housework after their waged work is finished. Other chapters touch on the feminist/domestic-worker theme, notably Goldsmith, León, and Pereira.

The *heterogeneity* of domestic service and its *transformation* over time are themes particularly emphasized in the historical articles in this volume. Higman, as mentioned above, discounts industrialization as a major factor influencing the proportions of domestic workers and centers his discussion on the changes in social status of domestic workers in Jamaica which have been crucial in determining the levels of employment in this sector. Kuznesof associates the transformations—from an occupation in which (perhaps) one-half of domestics were male and some were white, to an occupation that has become "almost entirely female" and almost exclusively the domain of persons of "mixed blood and caste"—with structural changes in society. In another historical piece Graham shows how domestic service offered the possibility of greater liberty rather than less: within certain limits domestics could enjoy the plazas and streets, a privilege forbidden to the *sinhas* and *sinhazinhas* (the married and unmarried women of the upper class).

In more recent times, work relations have become more and more contractual in some cases (Gogna, Buenos Aires; Pereira, Rio de Janeiro; León, Colombia—all in this volume). In such cases as Lima, there is testimony to persisting feudal-like work relations, as shown particularly in the autobiography of the union leader Díaz Uriarte (this volume). Many of the collaborators in this collection (among them Duarte, Gálvez and Todaro, and Gogna) underscore the importance of the growing numbers of live-out domestics who have their *puertas afuera* (literally, "doors outside") in contrast to domestic workers with *puertas adentro* (doors inside) and thus are involved in more capitalistic work relations. Others who have examined this topic are Almeida e Silva et al. (1979), Chaney (1985), and Grau (1982). Opinions differ as to whether live-in or live-out positions hold more potential for fostering participation in organizations, and on the costs/benefits of each in the worker's own life, but there is agreement that day work "emotionally and personally, represents a great advance" (Gálvez and Todaro, this volume). As day workers increase in number, the question of how their work might be institutionalized through the medium of service enterprises, and what sort of work alternatives might minimize the servile elements in the relationship between workers and *patronas,* needs to be explored (Gálvez and Todaro, this volume, make a beginning in addressing this issue).

The lack of an *affective life* of their own results when domestic workers live on intimate terms within families yet are only superficially part of the give-and-take of family life with its easy banter and warm demonstrations of affection. Indeed, an affective life of their own is often proscribed for *domésticas;* many *patronas* actively work to prevent their employees from forming "liaisons," almost always considered to be negative.

The type of *remuneration,* in money or in kind, as an element that differentiates the work of the domestic and that of the mistress is a basic theme emphasizing the uniqueness of domestic service (Grau 1982; Jelin 1977). This discussion takes us back to the subject of shared characteristics between domestic work and domestic service, and the singularity of this work as a redefined precapitalist occupation, as well as the social relation of production established when it is mediated by a salary that circulates as individual income and that does not produce surplus value, as Saffioti (1978) has noted.[4]

The *domésticas'* own *struggles to organize* are represented not only in the materials in Part V but also in the contributions of Gálvez and Todaro, León, Prates, and Schellekens and van der Schoot. We are presenting here the first information, aside from the pioneering work of Gutiérrez (1983), on the associations and organizations of domestic workers themselves. This is a topic on which much more work needs to be done, since we are as yet unaware of much of the organizational activity that is taking place. In connection with the *encuentro* mentioned above, the meeting of representatives of domestic workers' organizations that took place in Bogotá, members of the organizing commission traveled to to several countries to seek out sister organizations. It is notable that in almost every country, domestic workers began to organize under the aegis of the Juventud Obrera Católica or JOC, the once radical Catholic youth movement with origins in Belgium (Cussiánovich, 1974). Since then, the conservative Spanish Catholic organization Opus Dei has made great inroads among domestic workers, and the struggle already is underway between those groups aligned with militant Catholic and/or leftist groups and those under the sway of pious organizations that attempt to persuade *domésticas* to be content with their lot in life (see Goldsmith, this volume).

The *unique orientation* of domestic workers' unions makes them at once the place for political education, the front line of the struggle for working-class rights, and the locus of the domestics' own battle for legal recognition and rights as workers. At the same time, the organization is the "new family" where they find support and solidarity in personal difficulties. Moreover, the unions are attempting to respond to the demand for training for possible intra- or interoccupational mobility and for services: placement, legal advice, recreation, even a place to stay between jobs. In the small, cramped headquarters of the Coordinadora Sindical de las Trabajadoras de Hogar de Lima Metropolitana (Coordination of Household Workers' Unions of Metropolitan Lima), four or five old mattresses piled in a corner are ready for use by members who have been fired and have no other place to go.

Finally, reflection on the *treatment given domestics in new societies*—the schools for household workers that functioned from 1961 to 1967 in Cuba (Gil, this volume); the creation of a domestic workers' union in Nicaragua in 1979 (Roffiel 1980–81)—calls attention to the complexity of the social transformation process and of ideological change.

We believe that the studies presented here will contribute toward making the situation of domestic workers better known and understood. All the themes and topics singled out above need more work and elaboration by scholars, linked as closely as possible to the organizations and associations of the domestic workers themselves. Above all, what is needed now is theoretical reflection—particularly on the nature of domestic service, a precapitalist work process lingering on as few other occupations have done; on the linkages between domestic work and paid domestic service; and on the many questions this occupation poses about prospects for female solidarity across races and classes (see Garcia Castro, this volume).

Notes

1. Kusnesof and Higman (this volume) show that not even in this hemisphere has domestic service always been an exclusively female occupation, nor has it throughout history always been classified as an inferior category of work. On the contrary, in seventeenth-century Europe, servants and apprentices (usually boys) were placed on the same footing as the children of the family (Ariès 1962, 396). Nor has domestic service always and everywhere been uniformly depreciated. Nevertheless, because in today's Latin America and the Caribbean, 95 percent of all domestic workers are women, this collection does not treat the situation of male domestics.

2. But see Smith (this volume) for another view and a long-term discussion of different viewpoints on this issue.

3. The terms "production" and "reproduction" of the labor force in this context refer to women's major responsibilities not only for bearing the world's future workers, but also for most of the household tasks that daily "reproduce" the labor power of family members, enabling them to engage in productive work.

4. Saffioti's pioneer study (1978) has until now been the definitive one in its theoretical discussion of domestic service under capitalism. The author recurs to the concept of "mode of domestic production" (Meillasoux 1981): that is, production defined by the identity between housework and domestic service. Goldsmith (1980–81), on the other hand, views domestic service as part of the "terrain of simple circulation," an idea rejected by Saffioti on the basis that domestic work does not produce a marketable good. Following this discussion, Garcia Castro (1982) emphasizes the direct relation to the product that is a function of the unique type of salary (combining remuneration in money and in goods), and the ideological implications of defining the uniqueness of domestic service in the relationship between *patronas* and *empleadas,* involving in this discussion issues that would not be found in the Meillasoux model because his whole elaboration has the spouse as its referrent. Gálvez and Todaro (this volume) also develop, by another route, the issue of the difference between the domestic worker and the *patrona,* "both dedicated to the same common task of service to the family members" but situated in an actual contradictory relationship "between the craftlike work process and the management of that process." In this collection, Garcia Castro revises her 1982 ideas and puts more emphasis on the elements of contradiction between *patronas* and *empleadas,* underscoring the importance of devoting more effort to the analysis of the material basis that sustains the relationship and pointing to the necessity of studying the role of the state in the maintenance of domestic service (a theme only suggested in the article).

Various authors accept the original proposal of Saffioti that one must consider the linkage between forms of work proper to noncapitalist modes and the capitalist mode of production, and the redefinition of both: e.g., Garcia

Castro et al. (1981). Nevertheless, Saffioti questions the use of the term "reserve army," and also she questions the mobility of paid domestic workers to industrial occupations but accepts the structural functionality of the reserve army for maintaining the development model current in countries of the Third World. Almeida e Silva et al. (1979) and Garcia Castro (1982) consider the notion of "excess work" and "relative overpopulation" as more adequate to the case of domestic workers, but they do not believe that capitalism needs a reserve army in order to maintain itself on the periphery. The debate over the appropriateness of the reserve army concept to Latin America and the Caribbean is not new, but it has not previously referred to domestic service. Saffioti's inclusion of domestic service as a "mode of domestic production" is a pioneering effort that merits careful consideration, though as she herself points out, more vigorous theoretical work remains to be done on these questions.

References

Almeida e Silva, M. D'Ajuda, Lilibeth Cardoso, and Mary Garcia Castro. 1979. "As empregadas domésticas na região metropolitana do Rio de Janeiro: Uma análise atravez de dados do ENDEF." Governo do Brasil, Fundação Instituto Brasileiro de Geografía e Estatística (IBGE). Also in *Boletín Demográfico* 12, no. 1 (1981):26–92.

Ariès, Philippe. 1962. *Centuries of Childhood: A Social History of Family Life.* New York: Vintage Books.

Arizpe, Lourdes. 1975. *Indígenas en la ciudad de México: El caso de las "Marías."* Mexico, D. F.: SepSetentas.

Boserup, Ester. 1970. *Woman's Role in Economic Development.* New York: St. Martin's Press.

Bunster, Ximena, and Elsa M. Chaney. 1985. *Sellers & Servants: Working Women in Lima, Peru.* New York: Praeger Special Studies.

CEPAL (Comisión Económica para América Latina). 1982. *Cinco estudios sobre la situación de la mujer en América Latina.* Estudios e Informes No. 16. Santiago de Chile: CEPAL.

Cussiánovich, Alejandro. 1974. *Llamados de ser libres (empleadas de hogar).* Lima: Centro de Estudios y Publicaciones.

FEM, Publicación Feminista. 1980–81. [Special Issue on Domestic Service] 4, no. 16 (Mexico, D. F.).

Garcia Castro, Mary. 1982. "¿Qué se compra y qué se paga en el servicio doméstico?: El caso de Bogotá." In Magdalena Léon, ed., *La realidad colombiana,* vol. 1, *Debate sobre la mujer en América Latina y el Caribe,* pp. 92–122. Bogotá: Asociación Colombiana para el Estudio de la Población.

Garcia Castro, Mary, Bertha Quintero, and Gladys Jimeno. 1981. "Empleo doméstico, sector informal, migración y movilidad ocupacional en áreas urbanas en Colombia." Programa Naciones Unidas, Proyecto Oficina Internacional de Trabajo sobre Migraciones Laborales, Bogotá. Final report, mimeo.

Goldsmith, Mary. 1980–81. "Trabajo doméstico asalariado y desarrollo capitalista." *FEM* 4, no. 16:10–20.

Grau, Ilda Elena. 1982. "Trabajo y vida cotidiana de empleadas domésticas en la cuidad de México: Un estudio cualitativo." In Magdalena León, ed., *Sociedad, sobordinación y femenismo*, vol. 3, *Debate sobre la mujer en América Latina y el Caribe*, pp. 167–81. Bogotá: Asociación Colombiana para el Estudio de la Población.

Gutiérrez, Ana. 1983. *Se necesita muchacha*. México, D. F.: Fondo de Cultura Económica.

Heyman, Barry Neal. 1974. "Urbanization and the Status of Women in Peru." Ph.D. diss., University of Wisconsin, Madison.

Jelin, Elizabeth. 1977. "Migration and Labor Force Participation of Latin American Women: The Domestic Servants in the Cities." *Signs* 3, no. 1:129–41.

Meillasoux, Claude. 1981. *Maidens, Meal, and Money*. Cambridge: Cambridge University Press.

Roffiel, Rosa María. 1980–81. "Informe de Managua." *FEM* 4, no. 16:93–97.

Saffioti, Heleieth Iara Bongiovani. 1978. *Emprego doméstico e capitalismo*. Petrópolis, Brasil: Editora Vozes.

Silvera, Makeda. 1983. *Silenced: Talking with Working Class West Indian Women about Their Lives and Struggles as Domestic Workers in Canada*. Toronto: Williams-Wallace.

Smith, Margo L. 1971. "Institutionalized Servitude: Female Domestic Service in Lima, Peru." Ph.D. diss., Indiana University, Bloomington.

Toussaint, Florence. 1980–81. "Otro mito de la televisión." *FEM* 4, no. 16:67–68.

PART I
Domestic Service Yesterday

1 A History of Domestic Service in Spanish America, 1492–1980

ELIZABETH KUZNESOF

Domestic service in Spanish America coincides with the beginning of Spanish colonization. Its history has been determined by such ideological factors as the corporate view of the state, the role of the patriarchal household, and the role of women in society. In addition, the slow development of domestic technology, city services, and the factory system have influenced women's employment opportunities generally, and domestic service in particular. This chapter analyzes these factors to determine the role of domestic service in the society and the social relations of production in preindustrial Spanish America, then traces the history of domestic service as an occupation within the changing economic context of the nineteenth and twentieth centuries.

The Colonial Period (1492–c. 1800)

While lineage or clan frequently determined social status in medieval Spain, in colonial Spanish America the patriarchal household soon became the primary basis of juridical identity and social control (Dillard 1976, 74–76). The new Spanish towns—Mexico City, Guadalajara, Puebla, Lima, Cusco, Santiago, Quito, Panama—were administrative centers and also, by law, the main residences for the new aristocracy of *conquistadores,* who, as *encomenderos* (agents), were entrusted with the protection, education, tribute, and labor of the Indian population of the surrounding areas. Their majestic stone houses, or *casas pobladas,* were required by law to include a Spanish wife, room for at least forty guests and military retainers, black slaves, a staff of Spanish and Indian servants, and a stable with a minimum of sixteen horses (Braman 1975, 63–64; Lockhart 1968, 21). The *casa poblada* was literally viewed as the basis for Spanish civilization in the New World. The new towns were small settlements with unstable populations, difficult communications to other Spanish areas, and generally

17

few guarantees of order. In these circumstances the crown delegated tremendous authority and responsibility to the male property owner to supervise and control the members of his residence, whether or not these persons were related to him by blood or marriage. He was to direct the economic, spiritual, social, and educational care of all persons living in his house and make restitution for any misconduct (Braman 1975, 89–91; Gakenheimer 1964, 46–47; Lockhart 1968, 21; Waldron 1977, 125).

Not only did the patriarchal household become the central unit of social control in the colonial period—an extension of the corporate view of society espoused by Roman Catholicism and the Spanish state—but Spanish authorities generally felt that women should be maintained in a position of tutelage (Lockhart and Schwartz 1983, 7–8). This policy was enforced as much as possible through residence within the patriarchal household and through the laws of marriage and inheritance. However, the policy was also enforced—and this aspect had particular importance for *mestizos, castas,* Indians, and freed blacks—by the systematic exclusion of women from all areas of economic life where they might exercise any significant control over resources. These measures were enforced through the guild system and were generally supported by the laws of the Indies (Konetzke 1947, 421–49; Ots Capdequi 1930, 311–80). Where women did involve themselves in crafts or commerce, their participation tended to be marginal, informal, or mediated through kinship with a male relative.

Even where guilds did not develop, the artisan trades were controlled through the city council, which designated their training, examinations, and types of tools; limited the number of artisan establishments in each trade; and specified what kinds of persons were allowed to work in them (Johnson 1974, 8–9). The stipulation that the only laborers allowed beyond the licensed apprentices and journeymen were the wife and children of the master indicates how the domestic sphere entered into the formal economy for the artisan class. The widow of an artisan was also frequently allowed to keep the shop and in some cases practiced the trade, though it was usually expected that she would soon marry a journeyman, who would become the new master.

Commerce was another area of considerable attraction for women, but during the colonial period commercial establishments were also governed by the city councils. For example, in Mexico City in 1816 small grocery stores, designated *pulperías,* which sold basic food stuffs at controlled prices, could not be managed by women, mixed-blood persons, or anyone without a certain capital. Women and the poor could sell from *acesorías*—small niches in the sides of buildings—but were not to deal in goods normally carried by *pulperías*. Indians, both male and female, were allowed to sell crafts and foods of their own making on the central plaza (Kicza 1979, 66–68). The system of municipal controls over crafts and commerce had the effect of either preventing female involvement in these areas or keeping their involvement minimal, indirect, and confined to nonmanagerial roles.

Employment open to women in the Spanish colonies was frequently domestic with regard to where the work was executed, the kind of labor demanded, or often—particularly in craft industries—the type of family relationship necessary to exercise the trade. The employment options available to women outside agriculture were limited and low-paid—and those options were often conditioned by and determined in the domestic sphere.

In Europe domestic service was a highly respectable occupation. For many people in preindustrial England and France, it was viewed as a stage of life rather than as an occupational choice. Tilly and Scott (1978, 20) present statistics indicating that "servants" included between 15 and 30 percent of the population aged fifteen to sixty-five in preindustrial European cities. They explain that the term "servants" was a very broad category of employment, including any household dependent performing domestic or manufacturing tasks, but most often "they were young men and women who joined a family economy as an additional member. Indeed the language used to describe servants denoted their dependent and age status. 'Servant' was synonymous with 'lad' or 'maid'—a young, unmarried and therefore dependent person."

In rural peasant families the proportion of "servants" was often higher, as the families sought to balance production and consumption, depending upon how many working-age, unmarried children they had at their disposal. For most young people, working as a "servant" functioned as a kind of apprenticeship in the period before general education systems developed. Viewed in this context, working as a servant in the New World in the early colonial period seemed like a reasonable possibility for all but the elite. Such work also had the advantage of taking place in a protected, educational, and paternalistic environment. These factors, added to the limitations on women's work in the overall colonial environment, account for much of the popularity of domestic labor.

Domestic servants were also necessary because the technology of colonial life required that most items of domestic consumption—including clothing, flour, candles, gunpowder, and many utensils and articles of furniture—be produced within the home. In addition, water and firewood had to be procured daily. The absence of contraception also meant that considerable labor was needed to care for infants, even though high infant and child mortality meant that no more than half of them would survive. Domestic servants were visible in the sixteenth century not only in the houses of the *encomenderos* but also in the houses of merchants and artisans—indeed, in almost all Spanish houses (Lockhart 1968, 159–69). Studies of sixteenth-century towns in Mexico, Peru, and Chile indicate that Spanish households might include anywhere from one to more than forty domestic servants. Their dominant race varied by location, depending upon the ethnic mix of the population; however, Indians, freed slaves, persons of mixed races or *castas*, and white women were all part of the servant population (Braman 1975, 89–91; Gakenheimer 1964, 178; Hirschberg 1976, 24–264; Lewis 1978, 165; Lockhart and Schwartz 1983, 91).

Indian women were most common as servants and were paid the least. Writing on sixteenth-century Peru, Burkett (1978, 111) discusses indigenous women who "abandoned their villages and traditional life" to serve Spaniards in the cities as domestics. Burkett argues that the decline in the *ayllu* system (the Inca system of property distribution and support based on residence and kinship), male migration to the mines, and the heavy obligations placed on widows with the tribute system for cloth, animal, and agricultural produce, made life in the traditional communities difficult and working for Spaniards in the city relatively attractive. In striking contrast to the European situation, once the Indian woman began working in a Spanish house, she was often virtually enslaved, prevented from leaving or marrying. Household servants in Peru included resident mistresses (even in the presence of a Spanish wife), as well as wet-nurses, cooks, and other helpers, including contract laborers. The contracts specified that in return for their work the servants were to receive room, board, medicine, religious instruction, two sets of woolen or cotton clothing, and a salary that ranged from 6 to 30 pesos a year (Burkett 1978, 108–11).

Freed slaves were another important category of domestic servants in the sixteenth and seventeenth centuries. In keeping with patriarchal norms, the law required them to put themselves in the employ and supervision of a Spanish master. Most of them, male and female, became domestic servants and were more highly valued and better paid than Indians (Bowser 1974, 104; Burkett 1975, 283–84). White women also worked as servants. According to Boyd Bowman (1976, 583, 596–601; 1973, 51), women made up 28.5 percent of Spanish emigrants to the New World from 1493 to 1600; most of them after 1540 were unmarried, and many were listed on the passenger rolls as *criadas*, or servants. Often they were indentured to an employer already living in the colonies, or else they accompanied an employer to the New World. After working off their passage, the female Spanish servants frequently married Spanish artisans (Burkett 1975, 93–94).

Many *mestizos*, especially the illegitimate children of Indian women and Spaniards, were raised in Spanish households. According to Lockhart (1968, 164), they "received sustenance, eduation and affection, but were seen in the light of servants." Orphans and the children of poor families might also have been included in the household on a similar basis, as was common in preindustrial Europe.

The racial mixture of domestic servants changed over time. For example, Indians were the dominant form of domestic labor in Mexico during the sixteenth century, but with legislation protecting Indians against Spanish abuses, blacks—both slave and free—became more important in the late sixteenth and the seventeenth century. By the eighteenth century most domestic servants were *castas* of mixed racial descent (Seed 1982, 587–88; Váldes 1978, 140). However, Spanish servants continued to be considered prestigious to the end of the eighteenth century. In Mexico City, women seeking employment as wet-nurses sometimes advertised in the newspapers, frequently claiming Spanish blood—probably because of the generally accepted idea that a baby would imbibe qualities of character common to an ethnic group along with its milk (Kicza 1983, 13).

Domestic service continued to be an important category of employment, particularly for women, throughout the colonial period but is sometimes hard to trace. Although Spanish colonial law was overwhelming in its detailed regulation of every aspect of economic life, the only rule concerning domestic servants was one specifying that they were under the authority and responsibility of the head of the household in which they worked. In most cases a very significant proportion of their wages was paid in kind—room, board, clothes, medical help, and general protection—a characteristic of domestic service that confounds efforts at regulation to this day.

As in studies of preindustrial Europe, the significance of domestic servants in colonial Spanish America is most apparent in studies of household composition. Research on eighteenth-century Caracas, Buenos Aires, and various areas in Chile indicates the high proportion of *allegados*, or nonnuclear dependent members of the household, frequently constituting from 20 to 40 percent of household members. Undoubtedly, many of these were servants, either orphaned or poor people charitably included in households but regarded as servants, or consciously recruited for manufacturing or domestic tasks in this preindustrial setting (Hagerman Johnson 1978a, 632, 641; Johnson and Socolow 1979, 365; Waldron 1977, 119).

The fact that many domestic servants in the colonial period were orphaned relatives, illegitimate offspring of the head of the household, or adolescent children of friends living elsewhere led to a personalized, paternalistic relationship often strengthened by bonds of ritual kinship. This characteristic of domestic servitude declined in the nineteenth century. At the same time the association of domestic service with the lower end of the class/caste/color system that so dominated Spanish American society caused a gradual alienation between employers and servants, as well as a loss of status for the occupation of domestic service.

The Nineteenth Century

With the dawn of liberalism and the political independence of almost all Spanish American governments by 1825, the position of domestic service as an employment for women was altered, though to a lesser degree than seemed to be so at the time. In the first place, ideas concerning the education of women and their roles as producers underwent a marked change toward liberalization in the eighteenth and the early nineteenth century (Lavrin 1978, 28–29); however, notions persisted of the sanctity of the family and the household, and the relative position of husband and wife. If anything, eighteenth- and nineteenth-century legal codes tended to reassert the authority of the male head over other members of the household, especially females. For example, Guy (1985, 318) suggests that from the independence period onward, the state of Argentina began to carve out a symbiotic relationship with the family through the male heads of households in local communities. In Mexico, nineteenth-century legislation gave increased importance to the corporate nuclear family—especially to the power of the male head over his wife and minor children, an emphasis that coincided with a general tendency to use property and residence as criteria for social and political privileges (Arrom 1985, 309–10).

Women's position in the labor market altered in the nineteenth century. The guild system was abandoned in most Latin American cities some time prior to 1840, partly because the new machinery could be operated by unskilled or semiskilled workers with a minimum of training. This opened the craft industries to anyone who wished to enter, and women and children were considered ideal workers because they were docile and would work for one-third to one-half the wages of men (Hollander 1974, 48; Vallens 1978, 20). Thus, formal political restrictions against women's employment were waived at the same time that demand for their labor expanded. Even in this period, however, openings for women's employment were limited to specific industries, and ideologically, the idea of women's work was more closely related to the domestic sphere than to ideals of individualism, professional development, and especially sexual equality.

The life employment patterns of women workers also must have affected the kinds of work for which women were hired. In nonindustrialized countries, women have generally begun work between the ages of ten and fourteen and have continued to work for about 50 percent of their lives, until close to death, with interruptions for marriage, childbirth, and child care. They have been most influenced in this activity by their marital status, their fertility, their class or race, and their education (Pantelides 1976).

Figures on female employment by age clearly reveal that in the nineteenth century women worked before marriage and after widowhood but seldom while married (Arrom 1977, 119). The importance of marriage as a norm for women, and ideas concerning the appropriate role for women in marriage, have had critical importance for women's options as workers. Spinsterhood was, of course, regarded with strong disapproval, denounced by one nineteenth-century Mexican as "the gangrene of the population" (Arrom 1977, 173, quoting Manuel Payno). Furthermore, those who worked were predominantly women of mixed race, black or Indian background, employed in humble occupations. In spite of the apparent expansion in the types of work being done by women in Mexico, Argentina, and Chile, nineteenth-century politicians and travelers commented on the disgrace, misery, and undernourishment of women who were being "driven to prostitution" by lack of employment (Arrom 1977, 76–77; Hagerman Johnson 1978b, 14; Hollander 1974, 19–20, quoting Manuel Belgrano).

Official policies in Spanish American governments in this period supported the idea that everyone should be able to work and that the government should not interfere in the setting of wages, prices, hours of work, or any other area of contention between industrialists and workers (Turner 1968, 169). Indeed, in the latter part of the century women were in considerable demand as industrial workers, even to the degree that vagrancy laws were used in both Argentina and Mexico to force them to take certain employment against their will. Women who headed their own households and depended substantially on a subsistence economy could be legally defined as "wayward or unemployed" and placed by the police in "decent work institutions." (In keeping with the patriarchal ethos, however—at least in Argentina—the police never used these measures against women over the objections of male relatives.) Both textile factories and bakeries in Mexico are known to have "imprisoned" women workers to prevent their escape (Guy 1985, 323; Keremitsis 1971, 186, 198; Reyna 1982, 436–37; Vallens 1978, 38). These policies clearly continued the ideology that women were properly in a situation of tutelage.

Still, domestic service continued to absorb a substantial proportion of female labor during this period; it acted as a continuation of preindustrial social and productive relationships as well as a reinforcement of the patriarchal household. The private home was seen as a "protected place for a woman to work," a "guardian of moral virtue." In Mexico an 1834 law determined that domestic servants would be subject to strict surveillance and personal control by their employers (Arrom 1977, 715). In Argentina poor women (viewed as vagrant) were placed with "respectable" families to work as domestic servants (Guy 1985, 322–23). The reluctance of the state to interfere with work performed in the home, and the ideal of home as a place of respectability, also gave employers substantial power over the lives of their domestic servants.

As in preindustrial Europe and America, domestic service in early nineteenth-century Spanish America continued to be seen as a form of education for adult life, an "ideal education for a poor girl." Josefita, the de la Barcas' little servant girl, entered domestic service in Mexico City in 1849 under her mother's conditions that "she should be taught to read, taken to church, and instructed in all kinds of work" (Arrom 1977, 123; Shaw 1975, 288).

Rural-urban migration characterized late eighteenth- and early nineteenth-century Latin America. In every case for which we have data, the urban populations in this period included more women than men. Humboldt (1811, 1:253), writing about Mexico City in 1808, attributed the disproportion to the fact that "country women came into the cities to serve in houses," a common explanation for the urban sex ratio at the time. Certainly domestic service continued to be a very popular means of handling a whole range of necessary domestic work and manufactures in a period of primitive city services when household technology was generally based on the expectation of slave labor; often there were ten or more servants or slaves in an elite household. In Mexico City and in Argentina about 60 percent of women workers were live-in domestic servants (Arrom 1977, Table 5; Hollander 1974, 29–30).

Although the idea that women of this period were attracted to the cities by jobs seems plausible, migration studies indicate that many, if not most, rural-urban migration was of the "push" rather than "pull" variety, occasioned by economic problems in the area of origin rather than opportunities in the area of destination (Hagerman Johnson 1978a and 1978b; Scardaville 1977, viii; Shaw 1975, 52; Toscano and Anaya 1975, 35–36; Higman, this volume). In some cases, domestic servants worked as families in elite households: husbands acted as porters, coachmen, and gardeners; wives and daughters were maids, and sons served as errand boys (Shaw 1975, 288). In other cases young women were either sent to the city to work as servants or else, finding themselves abandoned and without sustenance, had little choice but to migrate to the city; domestic chores were often the only skills these women possessed.

In late eighteenth- and early nineteenth-century Mexico City, most domestic servants were migrants from nearby villages (Toscano and Anaya 1975, 33–34). By 1849 over 70 percent of the migrants fell into the unskilled occupations, the majority of females into domestic service (Scardaville 1977, 64; Shaw 1975, 52); 70 percent of those listed as domestic servants in the census of 1849 resided with their employers (Shaw 1975, 288). These live-in domestics are easily traced by means of household census manuscripts to elite households near the central plazas in Buenos Aires, Mexico City, and Caracas (Arrom 1977, 41; Friedman 1976, 18; Johnson and Socolow 1979, 362–63). About one household in five had one or more servants; of these in Mexico City in 1811, 4 percent had three or more servants, and 18 percent had one or two (Arrom 1977, 41).

Nevertheless, Fanny Calderón de la Barca complained in the 1840s that servants frequently changed employment (Váldes 1978, 103, quoting de la Barca). Furthermore, Hagerman Johnson (1978b, 12–13), writing about Santiago, Chile, between 1875 and 1907, finds that the level of female migration into the city did not correspond to but exceeded the level of opportunity in domestic service. This finding is echoed by Higman (this volume); in a study on Jamaica he cites an 1865 royal commission report to the effect that "not half" of one town's domestics were employed at any one time. Those migrants able to find a permanent full-time position as domestic servants were fortunate. In Santiago—and one suspects this was also true in other Spanish American cities—most labor was part time and relatively informal. Women tended to be freelance laundresses and seamstresses: in 1907 in the department of Santiago there were only about 14,000 housemaids, but there were 12,000 laundresses and 25,000 seamstresses. So many of the very poorest women were laundresses that government officials advocated large washrooms in all tenements so that women would not have to leave their children in order to work (Hagerman Johnson 1978b, 12, quoting the 1907 census).

Live-in domestics could count on much more food and other necessities as payment in kind than nonresidential domestic laborers, who generally lived in tenements that often had as many as thirty rooms in a one-story house, with each family occupying a single room or even a corner of a room or a stairwell landing. Sanitary facilities were in the central patio, and the residents seldom ate or bathed at home for lack of facilities (Arrom 1977, 49; Toscano and Anaya 1975, 35). Many lower-class people lived in nonfamily groups in communal situations. For example, in Santiago the poor were criticized for "the horrible custom of many people of different sexes, whose habits as a general rule are terrible, living in a single room, [and] the custom of excessive hospitality, of receiving people outside the family" (Hagerman Johnson 1978b, quoting *Assemblea de la Habitación Barata*, 209–10; see also Di Tella 1973, 95; Johnson and Socolow 1979, 366). In addition to tenements or *vecindades*, lower-class housing in Buenos Aires, Santiago, and Mexico City also included single-occupant housing, *casitas*, in which a single woman might live at the margins of the city. Data on late eighteenth-century Mexico City indicate that the average period of residence in lower-class housing was four months or less, a figure that suggests extreme fluidity in lower-class residential and employment arrangements. Conditions undoubtedly became more extreme in the nineteenth century (Váldes 1978, 132).

The upswing in the economies of most Latin American cities in the late nineteenth and the early twentieth century did not benefit the lower classes, according to studies on Mexico City, Buenos Aires, and Caracas (Brennan 1978; Graeber 1977, 121; Little 1980, 14; Reyna 1982, 435–41). The constant influx of migrants from the provinces resulted in a labor surplus that kept wages low in most areas. Evidence suggests that in Buenos Aires and Chile an increasing proportion of women were acting as primary earners by the end of the nineteenth century (Graeber 1977, 121; Hagerman Johnson 1978a, 642). This situation appears to have been associated with the dissolution in many areas of the subsistence mode of production that very much favored a domestic unit based on a couple with children. The differential migration that brought more women into urban areas for industrial work and domestic service also resulted from stronger male involvement in rural extractive industries and commercial agriculture. Many women who had been joined to their mates only by consensual union found themselves suddenly alone or, even worse, the sole support of dependent children.

A frequent assumption among social scientists is that the move to the city was automatically an improvement for the migrant; however, migrants arriving in the cities faced a competitive labor market and relatively high unemployment rates as well as "disguised" unemployment and underemployment. Studies on poorhouses and orphanages in Guadalajara, Mexico City and Buenos Aires indicate the extraordinary problems of child abandonment, infanticide, homeless populations, and general immiseration of the period (Brennan 1978; Little 1980, 14–29). In Buenos Aires the result of an official government investigation, published in 1900, revealed that many of the women who abandoned or murdered their children were domestic servants in danger of losing their jobs because the employers did not want an extra mouth to feed. It was also common for the woman abandoning her child at the orphanage to be brought there by a wealthy woman who waited outside in her carriage; the poor woman then became the wet-nurse for the wealthy woman's newborn child (Little 1980, 100–103).

In summary, during the nineteenth century official government regulations concerning women's employment in Spanish American countries changed, giving women access to jobs in industry and commerce. However, ideas that women should be married and that married women should not be employed continued to be strong and were reflected in the employment patterns. Women's work was degraded both because of its temporary or occasional character and because of its association with lower-class groups of non-prestigious ethnic background. (For similar observations on Jamaica, see Higman, this volume.) Furthermore, although there appeared to be a new recognition of the individual in the legislation of Spanish American governments, there was also a reassertion of the authority of the male head over other members of the household, especially females.

This attitude effectively continued the condition of the domestic servant in a position of near absolute, unregulated subordination to the male head of household. Governments such as those in Mexico and Argentina were known to place "vagrant" women arbitrarily in positions as domestic servants to protect their morals and provide them with an education. Domestic service continued to be an important area of employment reinforced by low levels of urban services and technology, the continued paternalistic and patriarchal attitudes evinced by state actions toward women, and high levels of unemployed single female migrants willing to accept almost any form of employment and sustenance.

The Twentieth Century

Female labor participation in Latin America has followed an interesting path that can best be envisioned as U-shaped. The high levels of female participation in the labor force reported in the mid-nineteenth century, from one-third to one-half of total workers, were followed by reports in 1920 or 1930 that females constituted one tenth to one-fifth of workers. This decline has been attributed to the disappearance of small-scale domestic manufacturing—which meant that women could no longer combine production with household tasks—and to the increasing capitalization of production, which favors male employment (Madeira and Singer 1975, 490–96; Richards 1974, 337–57; Weller 1963, 60).

Data for Mexico reveal that even domestic servants, who represented the majority of female workers in Spanish America in the early nineteenth century and somewhat less than half by 1895, when employment in textiles and cigarmaking became significant, declined in absolute numbers between 1895 and 1930 (Keesing 1977, 12). According to Chaplin (1978, 98–99), the point in the U where total female employment is lowest corresponds to the point when the highest proportion of employed women in a society work as domestics; this occurs partly because of the disappearance of employment for women in agriculture, crafts, and textiles during a "transitional" period in industrialization before the expansion of the tertiary sector. Chaplin also suggests that examining domestic service in the twentieth century provides insights into the rationalization of the domestic economy, as the production of goods and services is progressively moved out of the home.

From 1895 to 1930, laborsaving technology in industry and higher wages for men resulted in a reduction of the number of domestic servants. Changes in city services such as the provision of water, gas, and garbage collection on a residential basis; the expansion in schooling; the increased emphasis on the importance of mothering and child rearing; and the development of privacy as a family value also influenced households to employ fewer domestics. Those that would have employed seven to ten in the nineteenth century began to employ only one to three, and some households stopped employing domestics entirely. Since domestic labor has no product—as Jelin (1977) has observed—it also has a highly elastic demand curve, and the economic downswing of the 1930s undoubtedly convinced many families that one luxury they could do without was domestic servants.

Female employment expanded dramatically throughout Latin America in the period from 1940 to 1970, in response to generally improved economic conditions and to sectoral changes favoring women. This is the stage most characterized by growth in the tertiary or service sector. According to Safa (1977), it is in this stage that a marked change in the class composition of the female labor force takes place, incorporating middle- and upper-class women who may have delayed entering the labor force until jobs commensurate with their status opened up. Those women entered the expanding white-collar sector, an area of growth that was much facilitated by the increase in female education in Latin America in this period. This development, in turn, enlarged the market for domestic servants, thus maintaining the responsibility for the home in the hands of women. Upper- and middle-class women were able to go to work without threatening the traditional organization of the household.

The increase in domestic labor since 1940 also can be partly explained, however, by the shrinking market for unskilled female labor outside of domestic work. For example, Chaplin (1967, 190–95) emphasizes the marked decline in women's industrial labor in Peru since 1940. The major reasons were the increase in the availability of male labor and the application of generous welfare laws that made female labor more expensive than male. This decline in industrial jobs for women means that unskilled female workers in the second half of the twentieth century have fewer opportunities, thus making even very low-paid and unregulated work attractive. In Peru from 1940 to 1961 the proportion of domestic servants in the female work force increased from 9.7 to 21.4 percent (Smith 1971, 58–63); "some young women see work as a servant—and the room, board and salary they receive—as the best or only way to finance their continuing education or the support of an illegitimate child." Most Spanish American countries have passed similar laws equalizing the industrial pay of men and women and extending maternity care and leave to women, which has led to decreased employment of women in industry in the region and expansion in the ranks of domestic servants because of an absence of other opportunities.

Even though domestic service can be viewed as the continuation of preindustrial work patterns, it nevertheless has changed with industrialization. Servant-*patrón* relationships in the twentieth century tend to be less personal, less likely to result in fictive kin connections and aid to the servant and her family than in earlier times (Smith 1971, 165). Job turnover within domestic service is heavier; nevertheless, one suspects that the servant population is less mobile between occupations than in earlier centuries.

In other words, the occupation of domestic servant has maintained an important position in Spanish American society quantitatively, but the personal dimension appears to have greatly diminished. The basically patriarchal structure of Spanish American society remains, however, and continues to support a rule of domination within particular households. Thus, a servant who complains of her *patrona* is a servant who lacks "discretion" and is not good or grateful (Nett 1966, 443). The patriarchal family favors a servant by allowing her into the household; she should indicate her gratitude by working as many hours as indicated and accepting whatever is offered without complaint. Unfortunately, the direction that Spanish American economies are taking with respect to social services, income distribution, and employment practices may mean that such an ideology and practice will become more, rather than less, the norm.

Most domestic servants are migrants, frequently utilizing the "educational" and patronage advantages of a live-in domestic situation to provide them with a transition from the provinces. Chaplin (1967, 21) describes domestic service as a "make or break" occupation in Peru, characterized by abuse and heavy turnover. Domestics either return to the provinces or leave for the factory, he says.

Other observers see less mobility among jobs. Smith (1973, 195–96) describes a pattern of about six jobs in seven years, but such "mobility" involves moves not from domestic to factory or shop work but rather to a better neighborhood with a higher salary and more privileges (see also Nett 1966, 441). Jelin (1977, 137–38) correctly observes that domestic service is a dead-end occupation, allowing for little occupational change and, most important, almost inevitably incompatible with marriage and childbearing. As was also true in sixteenth-century Peru and eighteenth- and nineteenth-century Mexico and Argentina, domestic servants today are predominantly single and under thirty years of age.

At the same time, in the 1980s the increased value of privacy, the growth of day care and nursery schools, and improved technology in the middle-class home are beginning to dampen the demand for full-time live-in domestic servants. What Chaplin (1978, 123–24) has called the "casualization" of domestic service—with more domestics employed part time for specific tasks—removes many paternalistic privileges of the live-in situation, as well as some of its oppressiveness in terms of hours and personal supervision; nevertheless, "casual" domestic labor is even less regulated and usually less secure than a live-in position, though it does permit the domestic to acquire several employers.

Everywhere in Latin America domestic service has been the most important form of female employment throughout history and has also been the least regulated of any employment. Domestic service has a historical significance that extends into the areas of gender definition, class, patriarchy, technology, the relationship of the household to the state, women's occupations, and domestic education. In the colonial period domestic servants were necessary for the primitive mode of production, which involved considerable home production. Domestic service also served as a means for educating youth in a protected environment. However, in part because of the colonial circumstances of conquest and caste/race relations, domestic service in Spanish America became an aspect of race and class subordination rather than the "stage of life" learning experience it had usually been in preindustrial Europe.

In the sixteenth century many (perhaps half) of domestic servants were male, and some were white. By the eighteenth century most domestic servants were female and predominantly of mixed blood or caste background; those who were male were also of mixed blood. Domestic service in the nineteenth and twentieth centuries has become an almost entirely female and lower-class occupation. In the nineteenth century, the patriarchal character of the state and of the family was strengthened, with domestic service providing one means of "protecting" and controlling single women. The unorganized, nonregulated nature of domestic service in Spanish American countries today is in part a historical legacy of an occupation profoundly determined by its association with the corporate, patriarchal household. The divisions of race, ethnicity, and class introduced in colonial Spanish America have resulted in the development of what was originally a respectable, transitional, educational, frequently affectionate, life-stage relationship of subordination to a family head, into a dead-end, low-status, nonregulated and often hostile condition of exploitation.

One is tempted to write that the continued importance of domestic labor is an anachronism in the modern age, a continuation of patriarchal employment practices and paternalistic educational methods. For live-in domestics it is a job in which personal life is subsumed in the work situation, in which hours are uncontrolled and marriage and children impossible. The continued demand for domestic service is strengthened by the low level of commercial services available in most Spanish American countries, and especially by the extraordinary level of polarization of income levels. The poor will often work for literally nothing but bread and a place to sleep. Ironically, in this century the efforts to equalize employment benefits for women have led to a shrinkage of available jobs and an increased willingness among lower-class women to become domestic workers.

Note

Acknowledgments: The research for this article was supported by the General Research Fund, University of Kansas in Lawrence. The author also wishes to acknowledge the helpful comments and suggestions of Ann Schofield.

References

Arrom, Silvia Marina. 1977. "Women and the Family in Mexico City, 1800–1957." Ph.D. diss. Stanford University, Stanford, Calif.

——. 1985. "Changes in Mexican Family Law in the Nineteenth Century: The Civil Codes of 1870 and 1884." *Journal of Family History* 10, no. 3:308–18.

Bowser, Frederick P. 1974. *The African Slave in Colonial Peru, 1542–1650.* Stanford, Calif.: Stanford University Press.

Boyd Bowman, Peter. 1973. *Patterns of Spanish Emigration to the New World, 1493–1580.* Buffalo: State University of New York, Council on International Studies.

——. 1976. "Patterns of Spanish Emigration to the Indies until 1600." *Hispanic American Historical Review* 56, no. 4:580–604.

Braman, Thomas C. 1975. "Land and Society in Early Colonial Santiago de Chile, 1540–1575." Ph.D. diss., University of Pittsburgh.

Brennan, Ellen. 1978. "Demographic and Social Patterns in Urban Mexico: Guadalajara, 1876–1910." Ph.D. diss., Columbia University, New York.

Burkett, Elinor C. 1975. "Early Colonial Peru: The Urban Female Experience." Ph.D. diss., University of Pittsburgh.

——. 1978. "Indian Women and White Society: The Case of 16th Century Peru." In Asunción Lavrin, ed., *Latin American Women: Historical Perspectives,* pp. 101–28. Westport, Conn.: Greenwood Press.

Chaplin, David. 1967. *The Peruvian Industrial Labor Force.* Princeton, N.J.: Princeton University Press.

——. 1978. "Domestic Service and Industrialization." In Richard Thomasson, ed., *Comparative Studies in Sociology,* pp. 97–127. Greenwich, Conn.: Jai Press.

Dillard, Heath. 1976. "Women in Reconquest Castille: The Fueros of Sepulveda and Cuenca." In Susan Stuard, ed., *Women in Medieval Society,* pp. 71–90. Philadelphia: University of Pennsylvania Press.

Di Tella, Torcuato S. 1973. "The Dangerous Classes in Early Nineteenth Century Mexico." *Journal of Latin American Studies* 5, no. 1:79–105.

Friedman, Stephen J. 1976. "The City of Caracas, 1830–1846." Ph.D. diss., University of Pennsylvania, Philadelphia.

Gakenheimer, Ralph A. 1964. "Determinants of Physical Structure in the Peruvian Town of the Sixteenth Century." Ph.D. diss., University of California at Los Angeles.

Graeber, Karl. 1977. "Buenos Aires: A Social and Economic History of a Traditional Spanish-American City on the Verge of Change, 1810–1855." Ph.D. diss., University of California at Los Angeles.

Guy, Donna. 1985. "Lower-Class Families, Women, and the Law in Nineteenth Century Argentina." *Journal of Family History* 10, no. 3:318–31.

Hagerman Johnson, Ann. 1978a. "The Impact of Market Agriculture in Family and Household Structure in 19th Century Chile." *Hispanic American Historical Review* 58, no. 4:625–48.

——. 1978b. "The Impact of the Labor Market on Women in Nineteenth Century Chile." Paper presented to meeting of the American Historical Association.

Hirschberg, Julia. 1976. "A Social History of Puebla de Los Angeles, 1531–1560." Ph.D. diss., University of California at Los Angeles.

Hollander, Nancy. 1974. "Women in the Political Economy of Argentina." Ph.D. diss., University of California at Los Angeles.

Humboldt, Alexander von. 1811. *Political Essay on the Kingdom of New Spain*. 4 vols. Rpt. New York: AMS Press, 1966.

Jelin, Elizabeth. 1977. "Migration and Labor Force Participation of Latin American Women: The Domestic Servants in the Cities." *Signs* 3, no. 1:129–41.

Johnson, Lyman L. 1974. "The Artisans of Buenos Aires during the Viceroyalty, 1776–1810." Ph.D. diss., University of Connecticut, Storrs.

Johnson, Lyman L., and Susan Migden Socolow. 1979. "Population and Space in Eighteenth Century Buenos Aires." In David J. Robinson, ed., *Social Fabric and Spatial Structure in Colonial Latin America*, pp. 339–68. Ann Arbor: University of Michigan Press.

Keesing, Donald B. 1977. "Employment and Lack of Employment in Mexico, 1900–1970." In James W. Wilkie and Kenneth Riddle, eds., *Quantitative Latin American Studies: Methods and Findings*, pp. 3–21. Los Angeles: American Center Publications.

Keremitsis, Dawn. 1971. "Development of the Cotton Textile Industry in Nineteenth Century Mexico." Ph.D. diss., University of California at Berkeley.

Kicza, John. 1979. "Business and Society in Late Colonial Mexico City." Ph.D. diss., University of California at Los Angeles.

———. 1983. "Women and Business Life in Late Colonial Mexico City." Manuscript.

Konetzke, Richard. 1947. "Las ordenanzas de gremios como documentos para la historia social de Hispanoamérica durante la época colonial." *Revista Internacional de Sociología* 18 (abril–junio): 421–49.

Lavrin, Asunción. 1978. "In Search of the Colonial Woman in Mexico: The Seventeenth and Eighteenth Centuries." In Lavrin, ed., *Latin American Women: Historical Perspectives*, pp. 23–59. Westport, Conn.: Greenwood Press.

Lewis, Leslie Kay. 1978. "Colonial Texcoco: A Province in the Valley of Mexico, 1570–1630." Ph.D diss., University of California at Los Angeles

Little, Cynthia J. 1980. "The Society of Beneficence in Buenos Aires, 1823–1900." Ph.D. diss., Temple University, Philadelphia.

Lockhart, James. 1968. *Spanish Peru, 1532–1560: A Colonial Society.* Madison: University of Wisconsin Press.

Lockhart, James, and Stuart B. Schwartz. 1983. *Early Latin America: A History of Colonial Spanish America and Brazil.* Cambridge: Cambridge University Press.

Madeira, Felicia R., and Paul Singer. 1975. "Structure of Female Employment and Work in Brazil, 1920–1970." *Journal of Inter-American Studies and World Affairs* 17, no. 4:490–96.

Nett, Emily M. 1966. "The Servant Class in a Developing Country: Ecuador." *Journal of Inter-American Studies and World Affairs* 8, no. 3:437–52.

Ots Capdequi, José María. 1930. "El sexo como circunstancia modificativa de la capacidad jurídica en nuestra legislación de Indias." *Anuario de Historia del Derecho Español* (Madrid) 7:311–80.

Pantelides, Edith. 1976. *Estudio de la población femenina económicamente activa en América Latina, 1950–1970.* Santiago de Chile: Centro Latinoamericana de Demografía.

Reyna, María del Carmen. 1982. "Las condiciones del trabajo en las panaderías de la Ciudad de México durante la segunda mitad del siglo XIX." *Historia Mexicana* 31, no. 3:431–48.

Richards, Eric. 1974. "Women in the British Economy since about 1700: An interpretation." *History* 59, no. 197:337–57.

Safa, Helen Icken. 1977. "The Changing Composition of the Female Labor Force in Latin America." *Latin American Perspectives* 4, no. 4:126–36.

Scardaville, Michael C. 1977. "Crime and the Urban Poor: Mexico City in the Late Colonial Period." Ph.D. diss., University of Florida, Gainesville.

Seed, Patricia. 1982. "Social Dimensions of Race: Mexico City 1753." *Hispanic American Historical Review* 62, no. 4:569–606.

Shaw, Frederick J. 1975. "Poverty and Politics in Mexico City, 1924–1854." Ph.D. diss., University of Florida, Gainesville.

Smith, Margo L. 1971. "Institutionalized Servitude: Female Domestic Service in Lima, Peru." Ph.D. diss., Indiana University, Bloomington.

———. 1973. "Domestic Service as a Channel of Upward Mobility for the Lower-Class Woman: The Lima Case." In Ann Pescatello, ed., *Female and Male in Latin America*, pp. 191–207. Pittsburgh: University of Pittsburgh Press.

Tilly, Louise A., and Joan W. Scott. 1978. *Women, Work, and Family.* New York: Holt, Rinehart & Winston.

Toscano, Alejandra Moreno, and Carlos Aguirre Anaya. 1975. "Migrations to Mexico City in the Nineteenth Century: Research Approaches." *Journal of Inter-American Studies and World Affairs* 17, no. 1:27–42.

Turner, Frederick C. 1968. *The Dynamic of Mexican Nationalism.* Chapel Hill: University of North Carolina Press.

Váldes, Dennis. 1978. "The Decline of the Sociedad de Castas in Mexico City." Ph.D. diss., University of Michigan, Ann Arbor.

Vallens, Vivian M. 1978. *Working Women during the Porfiriato, 1880–1910.* New York: Reed & Eterovich.

Waldron, Kathleen. 1977. "A Social History of a Primate City: The Case of Caracas 1750–1810." Ph.D. diss., University of Indiana, Bloomington.

Weller, Robert H. 1963. "A Historical Analysis of Female Labour Force Participation in Puerto Rico." *Social and Economic Studies* 17, no. 1:60–69.

2 Domestic Service in Jamaica since 1750

B. W. HIGMAN

Domestic service has been the most common form of employment for women in Jamaica throughout the twentieth century and ranked second only to agriculture in the preceding centuries. Although never as important an employer of males, domestic service performed in private households has constituted the major work experience of a significant proportion of the population. Further, it made employers-of-labor of many who otherwise never thought of playing such a role. After a steep decline in the domestic servant population of Jamaica in the immediate postslavery period, it then expanded rapidly in the late nineteenth and the early twentieth century in response to demand from the emerging bourgeoisie, and contracted again only after about 1950. But in spite of their obvious importance in the economic and social history of Jamaica, the domestics have been served poorly by historians. Sociologists and economists have been similarly dismissive, so that it is impossible to find even one paper on the history of domestic service or its contemporary social and economic significance for any part of the West Indies. For Jamaica, de Lisser's novel *Jane's Career* (1914) is the best one can point to. The reasons for this neglect are not hard to find: domestics have always been an isolated group, shut off from trade union development (and hence from "labor history"); they have never constituted a true social class, have been predominantly female and poor, and have left relatively few records for historians.

Secular trends in the employment of domestic servants have most often been explained in terms of the process of industrialization. In traditional agricultural economies only small numbers of domestics work in households other than those of their families. But industrialization and urbanization are said to create a rapid rise in the do-

This chapter appeared in Higman, ed., *Trade, Government and Society in Caribbean History 1700–1920: Essays Presented to Douglas Hall*. Kingston, Jamaica: Heinemann Educational Books Caribbean, 1983. Used with permission of the author and publisher. © 1983 The Department of History, University of the West Indies, Mona, Jamaica.

mestic service work force because they produce a servant-employing middle class and are accompanied by surpluses of unskilled labor. Hence Boserup (1970, 103) argues that "it is a characteristic feature of countries at an intermediate stage of economic development for a large number of women to be engaged in paid housework." With the maturing of industrial economies, however, the domestic work force declines even more rapidly because of the broadened employment opportunities of women, the mechanization and commercialization of household tasks, and the shrinking of the middle-class family. The service sector grows but becomes external to the household. According to this model, the relatively large proportion of household workers found in most Latin American countries today is a function of their economies being at an intermediate stage of development, a stage passed by the mature industrial economies in the later twentieth century (Branca 1975, 129–53; Chaplin 1978, 97–127; McBride 1976, 116).

This chapter tests the validity of the foregoing model in the case of Jamaica, with comparative reference to the experience of Britain and the United States.[1] It argues that the pattern of growth and decline in private domestic service over the past two hundred years was common to Jamaica, Britain, and the United States but with differences in chronology that are not easily explained by variations in the rate of industrialization.

The Domestic Service Work Force

Domestic servants are here defined as employees performing personal service within the households of families not their own in return for wages in cash or kind (or slaves compelled to perform such tasks). Although census takers were not always as precise in their definitions, the broad comparative trends cannot be disputed. Only the quality of the Jamaican data (Table 2-1) need be discussed here. The figure for 1834 is based on the slave compensation claims (which probably understated the size of the group) and estimates for the white and freedman populations—assuming none of the whites but 25 percent of the freedmen were servants (Higman 1976, 38, 276). The census data for the period 1844–1921 have been accepted by Roberts (1957, 87) with only minor modifications but have been revised upward by Eisner (1961, 155–62).[2] Eisner's adjustments are too much designed to bring

TABLE 2-1.
Numbers of Private Domestic Servants, Washerwomen,
and Seamstresses, Jamaica, 1834–1970

YEAR	DOMESTICS	WASHERWOMEN	SEAMSTRESSES
1834	38,865	—	—
1844	20,571	—	—
1861	16,253	2,586	9,714
1871	16,287	5,631	14,565
1881	14,907	8,104	14,773
1891	26,503	10,400	18,966
1911	35,701	11,715	20,340
1921	49,965	9,580	23,237
1943	70,568	3,873	17,038
1960	63,180	1,948	—
1970	43,690	—	—

Sources: Higman 1976, 38, 276; Jamaica, Department of Statistics 1844–1970.

Jamaica in line with the British pattern to be acceptable, however. A further problem with the Jamaican census data, not discussed by Eisner or Roberts, relates to the categorization of washerwomen and seamstresses. The 1834 data for slave "domestic servants" incorporated them, as did the 1844 census for "household servants." In 1861 washerwomen and seamstresses were generally distinguished and placed in the "industrial" category, but in two of the island's twenty-two parishes no washers or seamstresses were listed, and in another domestic servants were grouped with washers but separated from seamstresses (Higman 1980). From 1871 washerwomen and seamstresses were clearly distinguished in the censuses. The importance of this problem is that specialized washers and seamstresses were the first to work independently outside the employer's household but had not completed this transition by 1860. Thus, the actual rate of decline in the size of the domestic servant work force between 1834 and 1871 was somewhat less rapid than Table 2-1 indicates.

The proportion of the labor force employed in private domestic service increased steadily in the United States until about 1870 and in Britain until 1890 before falling quite rapidly (Fig. 2-1). Jamaica's secular trend differed significantly. Whereas the abolition of slavery in

FIGURE 2-1   Percentage of Labor Force Employed in Domestic Service, Jamaica, Britain, and United States, 1800–1971

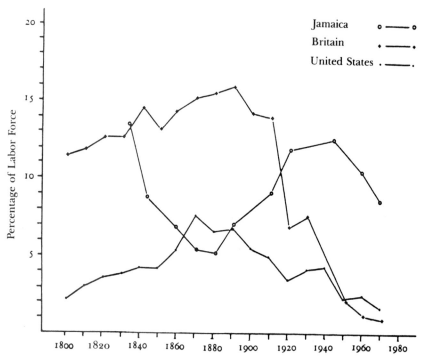

Sources: Deane and Cole 1969, 142; Great Britain, Department of Employment 1969; Higman 1976, 38, 276; Jamaica, Department of Statistics, 1844–1970; U.S. Department of Commerce 1975, 139.

the United States did nothing to prevent continued growth in the servant population, the preponderance of slaves in the Jamaican labor force meant that emancipation in 1838 was followed by a prolonged decline in the importance of employment in domestic service. After 1880, however, Jamaica's servant work force began to grow again at a rapid rate, not losing its impetus until about 1960. It is difficult to extrapolate these trends back before 1800, but it is certain that the later eighteenth century showed growth in Britain and the United States; for Jamaica the trend between 1750 and 1830 is much less certain because of conflicting economic and demographic changes. Absentee proprietorship increased throughout the period and so reduced the size of plantation retinues, and urban decline after the abolition of the slave trade in 1807 similarly reduced demand. On the other hand, the growth of the slave and free colored populations operated to increase the number of persons traditionally allocated to domestic employment.

A different perspective can be obtained by considering the size of the servant population relative to the total population (Fig. 2-2) and thus avoiding changing definitions of the labor force. Viewed in this way, the very large domestic servant population of Jamaica in the period of slavery is much more outstanding, and the twentieth-century decline can be dated from about 1930 rather than 1960. In Britain the decline in the servant population can be dated from 1870 rather than 1890, though the most rapid decline did not begin until about 1940, when domestics deserted even their traditional aristocratic employers (Cannadine 1978, 450). The United States never shared the same tradition of service, so the ratio of servants to total population was always less than in Jamaica or Britain until about 1950.

In Jamaican slave society, domestics served as the most constant reminders of the planter's prosperity and power over labor, but the superfluity of domestic slaves has often been exaggerated. In eighteenth-century Britain most noble households had thirty to sixty servants, and few had less than twenty, while the rural and urban gentry rarely had more than ten (Hecht 1956, 5; Mingay 1963, 230). Certainly some resident Jamaican planters did have the servants decried by critical observers, but by the early nineteenth century the majority had less than twenty, and it was rare for domestics to constitute more than 10 per cent of the slave labor force on large plantations (Higman 1976, 194–98; Long 1774, 281). Some planters continued to employ as many as thirty servants until the 1880s, but by that time half of the 224 sugar estates had resident proprietors, compared to the one-fifth of 670 in 1832.[3] Thus the postemancipation abandonment of estates was more important than the contraction of domestic staffs in reducing demand. The large-scale emigration of urban whites further reduced the demand for servants in the hard times that followed equalization of sugar duties in 1854.

Although the absolute decline in the size of the domestic servant labor force in Jamaica between 1838 and 1880 was largely because of the contraction in demand (reflected in falling wages), it also involved changes in supply. Before 1838 the status of domestic slaves was regarded by both slaves and masters as superior to that of field slaves, though their relative treatment was ambiguous (Brathwaite 1971,

FIGURE 2-2   Domestic Servants per 1,000 Population, Jamaica, Britain, and United States, 1800–1971

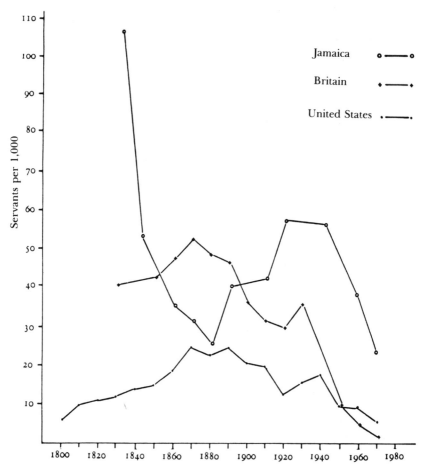

Sources: Deane and Cole 1969, 142; Great Britain, Department of Employment 1969; Higman 1976, 38; Jamaica, Department of Statistics 1844–1970; U.S. Department of Commerce 1975, 139.

155). But if this evaluation was carried over into freedom, it was complicated by the fact that recruitment to slave domestic employment depended heavily on color. Female slaves "of color" with white fathers were thought incapable of field labor and universally recruited to the house. With the decline of the estates, many of the coloreds moved to the towns, so that a relative shortage of domestics appeared in the rural areas. At the same time peasant agriculture expanded rapidly. By 1865 it could be observed that "in hiring servants, the upper classes seldom ask for any character, for the people are so independent that it is a mere matter of choice with them to be domestic servants or to labor in the field or on the family freehold." (Great Britain, Parliamentary Papers 1866, Vol. 51: 66, 127). In the towns, however, there was a surplus of domestic servants, and employers made only the stock complaints of laziness, impudence, and dishonesty. At Spanish Town, the island's capital, it was said in 1865 that "not half" of the town's domestics were in work at any given time, "not a quarter" of the washerwomen could find employment, and seamstresses had work only for the August and Christmas holidays. (*Ibid.*, 177). As well as suffering from the relative poverty of the community as a whole in the 1860s, seamstresses were affected by the large-scale importation of ready-made clothing and the introduction of the sewing machine.

The growth of the domestic servant populations of Britain and the United States in the nineteenth century has been explained by the decline of agriculture and cottage industries and the establishment of industrial capitalism, which engendered rural-urban (and transatlantic) migration and the emergence of a servant-employing bourgeoisie. Although the period of growth in Jamaica's servant population 1880–1950 shared the experience of rural-urban migration and an expanding bourgeoisie, it was by no means one of industrialization. There was some expansion in manufacturing industry in Jamaica during the period, but most of it was merely rudimentary import substitution, and the economy remained essentially agricultural. Industrial employment accounted for less than 15 percent of the labor force throughout the period (Eisner 1961, 176; Roberts 1957, 87). Factory employment had little to do with the growth of the bourgeoisie before 1950.

To a certain extent the growth of the Jamaican servant population can be explained by urbanization, which occurred independent of industrial development before 1950. There had, of course, always been a strong concentration of domestics in the towns. In 1834 the urban parish of Kingston and St. Andrew had 32 percent of the island's domestic slaves but only 8 percent of the total slave population. But Kingston–St. Andrew's domestics decreased between 1834 and 1880 in spite of the growth of the urban population. From 1880 to 1950, however, urban population growth was followed fairly closely by growth in the domestic servant work force. Yet it is important that the role of urban demand not be overstated. Between the censuses of 1881 and 1943 the rural-urban ratio of domestics changed little. In 1881 there was an average of one domestic to every forty-five people in rural Jamaica, and one to twenty-one in 1943. Kingston–St. Andrew, on the other hand, had one domestic per twenty people in 1881, and one to ten in 1943. Thus, although there was an increasing concentration of servants in Kingston–St. Andrew, there was no relative decline in the density of domestics in rural Jamaica. In order to explain the overall growth in the domestic work force, then, it is necessary to understand rural demand and supply as much as urban bourgeois development.

In 1913 H. G. de Lisser, editor of the Kingston *Daily Gleaner* and author of the first Jamaican novel to have a domestic as heroine, estimated the "middle classes" at 80,000, when the total population of the island's towns was only 120,000. Since the servant population was 40,000, de Lisser concluded that "almost everybody who has the slightest pretentions to be considered anybody employs a servant. In fact you are not respectable if you have not a servant. That at least is one law of Jamaica life" (de Lisser 1913, 53, 97). Exactly the same law applied to the middle classes of Victorian England, the employment of servants being the most obvious index of their status. In Jamaica these attitudes must have penetrated the small-farmer class as well as the urban bourgeoisie. The remnants of the plantocracy were incapable of providing scope for a growing servant population. The number of sugar factories dropped from 202 in 1880 to a mere 39 in 1930, and in the latter year there were only 19 coffee plantations and 484 livestock pens. The only area of growth was in banana plantations, which increased from 100 in 1890 to 500 in 1930 (Eisner 1961, 203). In the early 1950s Edith Clarke (1957, 150) found that in sugar estate areas domestics were employed in middle- and working-class homes, as well as in the few upper-class households, and argued that "the keeping of a servant confers status and whatever her husband's income, a married woman expects to be able to keep one." If the latter argument was an exaggeration (since there were 92,000 married women in Jamaica in 1943 but only 70,000 servants), there is no doubt that a significant number of domestics were employed in working-class households by the 1950s, both in town and country (Jamaica, Department of Statistics 1955; 1957).

The ability of the emerging bourgeoisie and the better-off working classes of Jamaica to employ domestic servants depended very much on the abundant supply of potential workers. This abundance resulted from the absence of alternatives to field labor for girls in rural Jamaica, the exhauston of the supply of land available for peasant settlement, and the rapid growth of population due to rising fertility levels. Although the wages offered domestics in the rural parishes were always somewhat less than in Kingston, this enabled a wider range of social classes to employ servants, and the wages were in any case competitive with those offered by agriculture.

It is impossible to trace in detail the fluctuations in the supply of domestic servants between 1881 and 1943, but indications can be obtained from the annual reports of the parish tax collectors, published for the years 1880 to 1939 (Jamaica, Collector General 1920–39).[4] These provide for each parish a statement of the range of wages (or an average) for field laborers, artisans, and domestics, and of the "supply" of labor for each category. These data are no doubt impressionistic, but equally there is no doubt that the supply of domestic servants in the urban area of Kingston–St. Andrew was thought to have become increasingly abundant over the period, changing from "very bad" or "bad" in the 1880s to "fair" by the 1910s to "greater than demand" in the 1930s. Also illuminating is the fact that the supply of domestics in the rural parishes fluctuated from "fair" to "good" to "plentiful" over the entire period, accounting for the relatively rapid growth in domestic employment in the countryside before 1940.

An additional index of the supply of domestics and the demand for their services can be derived from newspaper advertisements. These have the advantage of comprehending the entire twentieth century, providing data unavailable in any other source for the recent period of decline. Figure 2-3 shows the number of advertisements appearing in the Kingston *Daily Gleaner* on the first Saturday or Sunday of each year since 1910. These issues contained many more advertisements than weekday issues or other months of the year, since both employers and employees tended to make changes after Christmas. Before 1920 the advertisements were confined largely to elite domestic positions, so that the employers outnumbered the work seekers. Thereafter, apart from a brief decline in the 1940s, the supply of domestics increased steadily until 1965, when it fell away steeply. The trends were similar for male and female work seekers except that the males withdrew somewhat earlier. The pattern of advertisements suggests that demand slackened during the depression of the 1930s but expanded dramatically in the 1950s with the growth of the urban bourgeoisie. Since 1973, demand has dropped rapidly because of

FIGURE 2-3   Domestic Employment as Reflected
in Newspaper Advertisements, Jamaica, 1910–1981

Source: Daily Gleaner (Kingston). Number of classified advertisements appearing in the
first Saturday (1910–45) or Sunday (1946–81) issue in each year (3-year moving
averages).

negative economic growth and the shift to daily as against live-in and
weekly employment. Daily workers are less likely to seek jobs through
advertisement, of course. Supply ran ahead of demand in the periods
1930–35, 1946–53, and 1960–66, but demand grew rapidly while
supply fell in 1967–73—the most interesting period, since the great
decline in advertising by female domestic work seekers, while em-

ployers sought them avidly, suggests that the shift to live-out day work originated more in the preferences of the employees than in the attitudes of the employers. The same transition occurred in the United States between 1900 and 1930, and in Britain in the 1940s (A. Chapman 1953, 219; Katzman 1978, 94; McBride 1976, 113). In each case it went together with the application of electrical and other appliances to household tasks, and widened employment opportunities.

The decline in Jamaica's servant population after 1950 was, in part, a product of changes in the structure of the labor force, females under twenty years of age participating much less frequently as a result of broadened educational opportunities. It also reflected migration to Britain and the United States and the increased alternative avenues of employment in factories, commerce, and the extradomestic service industries. The shift to the day-work, live-out system meant that fewer domestics were shared by a larger number of employers. This fundamental change was facilitated by the increasing use of mechanical appliances and the declining size of the middle-class family. Although electric stoves, for example, had been available in Kingston from the early 1930s, it was not until the 1960s that they became really common (*Daily Gleaner* 1933 [January 7]; *Jamaican Housewife* 1962). On the other hand, the washing machine and the maid-of-all-work meant that washing was brought back into the household and so marked the demise of independent washerwomen as a class. But the washerwomen had already been depleted by competition from steam laundries in Kingston at the beginning of the twentieth century, at much the same date as they began to disappear in the United States (*Jamaica Times* 1907 [January 5]; Woodson 1930).

By the 1970s the servants' quarters, the adjunct of many middleclass suburban houses built in the 1950s, had come to be occupied by rent-paying lodgers. All these changes occurred in the first period of Jamaican history to see manufacturing contribute more to gross domestic product than agriculture (by 1959) and employ a larger proportion of the female labor force (from 1960) (Boland 1974, 75; Jefferson 1972, 125). It is difficult, then, to fit this trend to the thesis that the domestic servant work force reaches a peak in the intermediate period of industrialization. In Jamaica the decline appeared at the beginning of this phase, not at its end. Part of the reason for this divergence is the fact that Jamaican industrialization since 1945 has been capital-intensive, creating only a small employment base for potential servant employers, but for the very same reasons the amount of alternative employment offered potential servants has been limited. It is equally important to notice that the size of the servant population cannot be explained in terms of variations in the level of unemployment. Although no reliable series of unemployment statistics is available for Jamaica, it is at least certain that the decline in domestic service after 1960 went along with a return to the disastrously high levels of unemployment that had existed about 1940 (Jefferson 1972, 32). The surplus of unskilled labor, referred to by Boserup (1970) certainly existed in Jamaica after 1960, along with a growing bourgeois demand for servants. But the rewards and status offered by domestic service became increasingly unattractive.

Recruitment

Changes in the size and status of the servant population were associated with changes in its composition, especially in terms of sex, race, and age. Females have always been more numerous than males in domestic service in the Western world, and males were always the first to shift into other occupations. In Jamaica, females comprised about 70 percent of the domestic servants at the end of the period of slavery, but by 1890 they accounted for 80 percent and in 1960, 90 percent (Higman 1976, 194–98). As early as 1910 some 96 percent of domestics in the United States were females and 92 percent in Britain. Of greater interest is the fact that the proportion of the Jamaican labor force employed in domestic service actually declined over the entire period 1890–1970 at a rate comparable to that in Britain and the United States. Thus the growth in the domestic servant population of Jamaica after 1880 was entirely due to the increasing participation of females.

In the period of slavery Jamaica's domestics were predominantly "colored," but today they are mostly black. Exactly when this shift occurred and how the transition affected the status of the occupation is uncertain. Most colored female slaves were recruited to the master's household, while colored males spent at least their youth as domestics, before being taught skilled trades. To a certain extent the size of the servant population was a function of the rate of miscegenation and manumission. By 1834 at least 60 percent of the slave domestics in Jamaica were colored, compared to 10 percent of the total slave population (Craton 1978, 180–85; Higman 1976, 194–98). Free colored women also often worked as domestics. The preference for colored

TABLE 2-2.
Color/Ethnic Group of Jamaican Domestic
Servants in 1943 and 1960

	% DOMESTICS		% LABOR FORCE IN DOMESTIC SERVICE	
GROUP	Males	Females	Males	Females
1943				
Black	85.8	81.8	4.1	51.0
Colored	11.7	16.5	2.9	46.2
White/European	0.6	0.8	1.9	30.9
Chinese	0.2	0.1	0.9	12.9
East Indian	1.7	0.8	2.5	21.6
Total	100.0	100.0		
1960				
African	86.9	85.5	0.3	30.5
Afro-European	8.3	10.9	0.2	20.2
European	0.2	0.1	0.0	3.3
Chinese/Afro-Chinese	1.3	0.1	0.3	2.1
East Indian/Afro–East Indian	1.9	1.1	0.2	11.6
Other	1.4	2.3	0.1	20.3
Total	100.0	100.0		

Source: Jamaica, Department of Statistics 1844–1970, Censuses 1943, 1960.

servants, established during slavery by the whites who remained the principal employers of the declining work force until about 1870, probably persisted, and the occupation was to some extent hereditary. As the colored came in turn to predominate in the emerging servant-employing middle class at the end of the nineteenth century, so they gave way to the black domestic (see Spinner 1894, 22). By 1943 the female servant work force was representative of the racial composition of the Jamaican population, but the balance had shifted firmly toward black women by 1960 (Table 2-2). In terms of the labor force's racial components, there was a very definite withdrawal of white, Chinese, and colored females from domestic service between 1943 and

1960 as clerical and commercial employment opportunities opened up on a racially selective basis.

Domestic service has always employed large proportions of young people. Under slavery this was less true because occupations tended to remain fixed through life, especially for females, but in free populations domestic service was often only a brief period of employment prior to marriage. This pattern fit Britain much better than Jamaica or the United States, where the black domestic remained in service after marriage, reflecting differences in family structure and the role of women in economic provision. Thus, male domestics in Jamaica were even more heavily concentrated in the younger age groups than females, whereas the reverse was true in Britain and the United States. While the age distribution of Jamaican male domestics varied little between 1890 and 1960, much greater changes occurred among females. When domestic service was at its peak in Jamaica (1943), the age distribution of the employed females was similar to that for Britain and the United States at comparable stages of development (1911 and 1890). Broadened educational opportunities removed many young girls from the Jamaican labor force between 1943 and 1960, increasing the average age of domestics somewhat.

All of these changes in the sex, age, and race of domestic servants reflected changes in the process of recruitment. Under slavery, domestics were recruited from the master's own slaves or were purchased or hired. As applies to the entire history of domestic service, personal contact was most important in this process, though advertisements did play a role by the early nineteenth century. In Jamaica, newspaper advertisement became important only after 1930. The advertisers stated their preference and qualifications very precisely. Employers placed most emphasis on servants being youthful and from the countryside; after 1950 they stressed the willingness to live in. Domestics put the emphasis on the desire for part-time or day work after 1950. They often mentioned color (particularly when they could describe themselves as white, fair, clear, brown, or half-Chinese) until about 1955, suggesting again that domestic employment retained the somatic preferences established under slavery well into the twentieth century. Employment agencies emerged in Kingston in the 1920s but remained of minor importance in the recruitment of servants.

The long-term trend in domestic service in Jamaica, Britain, and the United States has been toward a generalization of functions. The extent of specialization depended on the total size of the servant population relative to the number of employing households, of course, so specialization survived longer in Jamaica then in Britain (with the exception of aristocratic households), and longer in Britain than in the United States. The typical household staff of the Jamaican planter in the late eighteenth century seems to have approximated fairly closely that of the English gentry with comparable incomes (of about £5,000 sterling per annum). Edward Long, writing in 1774, claimed that the typical planter had a household staff of twenty slaves, comprising a butler, two footmen, a coachman, a postillion, a helper, a cook, an assistant cook, a key or store keeper, a waiting maid, three house cleaners, three washerwomen, and four seamstresses, plus a nursemaid with an assistant for every white child in the family (Long 1774, 281–82; see also Burnett 1977, 156; Senior 1835, 28). Few changes occurred in this pattern before emancipation.

Although model household staffs were frequently described throughout the nineteenth century for Britain and the United States, as a part of the considerable literature that developed to guide the middle-class mistress unaccustomed to employing servants, no such literature ever emerged in Jamaica because until the end of the nineteenth century the servant-employing class was a long-established group and because the "servant problem" was never an issue. No doubt some Jamaican mistresses read Mrs. Beeton, but increasingly her advice must have seemed unrealistic. By the 1950s, however, newcomers to Jamaica had to be introduced to "the custom of the country," which differed from the employment of a single maid-of-all-work by then typical of Britain and the United States. In 1952 it was said that the family occupying a house on a plantation could expect to find among their live-in staff a gardener, a yard boy, a butler or butleress, a laundress, a housemaid, and a cook (E. Chapman 1952, 92). In the suburbs of Kingston the ideal household staff was said to be two women with no specialized functions, a gardener (who might also wait at table) and perhaps a part-time laundress. As well as the much smaller staffs, compared to the period of slavery, there was a shift to dependence on at least some live-out workers and away from those whose functions were most obviously ceremonial, and males were confined almost exclusively to the outdoor staff.

Similar evidence of the decline in specialization can be found in the newspaper advertisements. In 1930 only 6 percent of women offering their services in the *Daily Gleaner* named a single, generalized function; in 1950, 7 percent. But by 1970 some 56 percent did so; in 1980, 88 percent.[5] The following designations disappeared from the advertisements between 1930 and 1970: butleress, washerwoman, chambermaid, pantrymaid, lady's maid, pastry cook, housemaid. On the other hand, the terms general worker, day worker, general maid, and domestic helper appeared first in the 1950s and then rose to overwhelming dominance.

Income and Standard of Living

The personal character of domestic employment and recruitment, the rarity of written contracts, and the tendency to mix cash and kind payments all make it difficult to establish the real income and standard of living of servants. Katzman (1978, 303), in his study of the United States, despairs of reconstructing any more than general trends before 1900, while A. Chapman (1953, 217) contends that for Britain 1920–38 "estimates of average annual earnings are pure guesswork." The case of Jamaica is no less problematic. Estimates of average weekly wages—or, more often, the range of wages—are available in the *Jamaica Bluebooks* from 1840 to 1938 but with many gaps before 1870. How these estimates were arrived at is unknown, and often they were repeated unchanged year after year. Data found in the Jamaican Collector General's *Annual Report* for 1880–1939, discussed above, give wage levels by parish but suffer from the same limitations. After 1940 the only published series is an index covering the period 1943–51 for Kingston (Jamica, Department of Statistics 1947). From 1951, newspaper advertisements are the only systematic source available.

Figure 2-4 presents the available data in the form of annual earnings (current money). The Jamaican estimates are based on weekly wages cited in the *Bluebooks* (1840–1938) or offered by advertisers in the *Daily Gleaner* (1940–75). Also shown are wages paid to the cook at King's House, the governor-general's residence, between 1962 and 1972, and the minimum wage order of 1975. The British data are derived from annual earnings estimates, though their ultimate origin lies in weekly rates found in newspaper advertisements. The United States data for 1900–1975 are based on annual earnings, but those for the nineteenth century derive from weekly wages. Since there are no reliable estimates of the average number of weeks worked per annum, or the number of domestics occupied in each income category, it is assumed here that domestics worked forty-eight weeks each year in all periods (see A. Chapman 1953, 217) and, for Jamaica, that the

FIGURE 2-4   Annual Average Money Wages of Private Domestic
Servants, Jamaica, Britain, and United States, 1820–1975

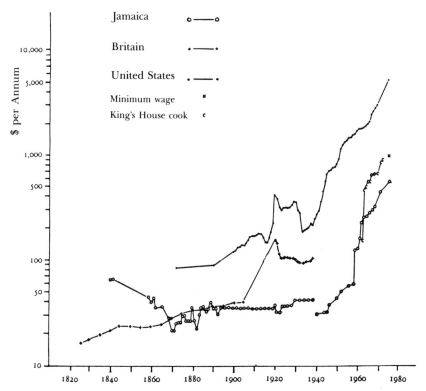

Sources: Burnett 1977, 160–64; A. Chapman 1953, 218; *Daily Gleaner* 1940–75; *Jamaica Bluebooks* 1840–1938; Jamaica, Collector General 1962–72; Katzman 1978, 306; U.S. Department of Commerce 1975, Table D 739.

Note: $1.00 Jamaican = £0.50 sterling.

average wage was the midpoint of the range given in the *Bluebooks.* Although these assumptions are not entirely arbitrary, it is probable that they tend to inflate the Jamaican wage rates, relatively, in some periods.

The money wage data presented in Figure 2-4 have been converted to indexes and related to the available price and cost-of-living indexes to produce the real wage estimates for domestics presented in Table 2-3. The latter show that the trends observed in money wages for

TABLE 2-3.
Estimated Real Wages of Domestic Servants, Jamaica,
Britain, and United States, 1850–1970

YEAR	JAMAICA	BRITAIN	UNITED STATES
1850	115	57	—
1860	—	45	—
1870	60	54	49
1880	—	72	—
1890	96	96	69
1900	100	100	100
1910	100	—	125
1920	—	116	115
1930	91	196	141
1940	95	—	138
1950	70	—	217
1960	120	—	277
1970	250	—	317

Sources: Wage data in Figure 2–4; cost-of-living/consumer-price indexes in Eisner 1961, 377; Jefferson 1972, 73; Mitchell 1971, 474; Taylor 1964, 73; and U.S. Department of Commerce 1975, 210.
Note: Index: 1900 = 100.

Britain and the United States did in fact mean substantial increases in real wages, except that the boom around 1920 was an illusion and that the depression of the 1930s was not as harsh as might have been supposed (since the domestics were somewhat sheltered). In Jamaica the decline in wages between 1840 (when the real wage index must have exceeded 150) and 1870 is confirmed as a real decline in the standard of living of domestics. The improvement in 1870–90 was also real, but the gains made in money wages between 1890 and 1950 were insufficient to prevent a further decline in real wages. The increases in money wages in the 1960s did mean substantial gains in real wages, as did the minimum wage order of 1975.

The wages of domestics were always highest in the United States. Although the British closed the gap somewhat by the 1930s, and Jamaica after 1950, the average U.S. domestic still earns seven times as much as the Jamaican. Of more interest is the fact that Jamaican domestics received higher wages than their British counterparts over the period 1840–70 (see Craton 1978, 311–13; Hall 1959, 217). It was not until the 1890s that British observers began to remark on the low rates of servants' wages in Jamaica, and it was only in the twentieth century that the difference became a commonplace (Emigrants' Information Office 1894, 26). But by 1920 it could be said that "taking things all round, householders in the West Indies may consider themselves very fortunate as regards domestic service, especially if they compare themselves with those in England or America" (Cundall 1920, 73).

The long-term trend in Jamaican domestics' money wages was by no means one of steady improvement. At the time of emancipation domestics were paid more than field laborers but less than artisans. Between 1838 and 1870 the wages of all three groups declined significantly. Between 1870 and 1900, however, the money wages of domestics and artisans rose again, while those of field laborers continued to decline. This relative improvement occurred in the early period of expansion of the servant population and may to some extent account for that expansion. After 1900 servants' wages improved little until the 1930s but retained their position relative to those of field laborers and artisans. In fact the increasing seasonality of agricultural employment meant some gain for the domestic servant sector. Although money wages increased quite rapidly after 1940, the domestics lost ground, lacking the advantages of unionization. Between 1943 and 1951 the money wages of employees in all industries in Kingston doubled, but the increase for domestics was only 58 percent (Jamaica, Department of Statistics 1947). In 1954, Maunder's survey of Kingston found that domestics earned an average of 28 shillings per week, making them the lowest paid of all groups except male handicraft workers (Maunder 1960, 118–22; see also Orde Browne 1939, 74–97). During the 1960s domestics probably improved their position relative to other unskilled workers, especially those in agriculture (Jefferson 1972, 37–38). The first minimum wage order to affect domestics, introduced in 1975, established a rate of $20 per forty-hour week, plus 75 cents overtime (*Jamaica Hansard* 1975–76, 192).

Servants also received income in kind. Most important were the provision of housing and food. In Victorian England these expenses were often greater than the servant's money wages. Although there were great differences in the quality of housing and food provided, according to the wealth and status of the employer, during the nineteenth century most domestics in Britain and the United States were better off in these respects than the majority of the working classes. As in the eighteenth century, British servants not housed with their employer were given "board wages" to cover the cost of housing and food. A similar practice was followed in Jamaica, where town slaves received "board wages" and had to seek their own shelter and food (*Columbian Magazine* 1797, 3:8; Long 1774, 2: 282). On the plantations only two or three domestic slaves were fed entirely by the masters, but the others received leftovers from the great house, distributed by the head waiting man (Senior 1835: 29). Thus Jamaican house slaves may have eaten better than the field slaves, and they certainly received more goods in the annual handouts. After emancipation the elite status of domestics meant that many were not required to pay house or ground rents (Great Britain, Parliamentary Papers 1839, Vol. 35: 73). But by the 1890s most Jamaican servants other than nursemaids were expected to provide their own food even if they lived in. They were given "findings," food items meant to supplement those purchased out of their money wages, but this practice tended to vary according to the wealth of the employer (Aspinall 1912, 149; E. Chapman 1952, 93; Jamaica, Institute of 1895, 30). By the 1930s almost half of the servant's wages were needed to buy food (E. Chapman 1938, 10; West India Royal Commission 1945, 219).

In Jamaica, as in Britain and the United States, the long-term tendency was toward dependence on money wages and away from income in kind. In 1942 almost one-third of Jamaican female domestics were described in the census as "unpaid family workers," but less than 2 percent by 1960. One reason for this change lay in the decline of the "schoolgirl" system, which had emerged at the end of the nineteenth century when rural mothers sought domestic rather than agricultural work for their daughters. According to de Lisser, when a girl reached twelve years of age her mother would seek out a mistress "willing to give food, clothing and shelter to the child in exchange for her simple services" (de Lisser 1913, 99; 1914). The mistress, "a 'white' or 'colored' lady, or a brown 'female,'" taught her schoolgirls how to "cook, clean, wash and to do other household work in an indifferent manner." When she reached seventeen or eighteen, said de Lisser, the schoolgirl looked for wage-earning employment and was thenceforth styled a "domestic servant" (see also *Daily Gleaner,* January 6, 1940). The schoolgirl received all her income in kind apart from a little pocket money intended to deter theft.

Wages of male domestics were generally double those of females in

Jamaica, Britain, and the United States until 1920 at least. In 1884, for example, the *Jamaican Bluebook* gave male wages as 10 to 15 shillings per week, and female as 4 to 8 shillings. In 1942 there were actually more male than female domestics earning more than 20 shillings weekly, in spite of the preponderance of females in the work force in Jamaica. Beyond these differences by sex lay a whole scale of wage rates that reflected accurately the internal hierarchy of the domestic staff. To some extent, then, the slow rise in domestics' wages in the early twentieth century might have been a result of the withdrawal of highly paid males, the declining demand for top-ranking servants, and the dominance of the maid-of-all-work, rather than of deterioration in the wages paid each category.

There is no doubt that domestics worked longer hours than any other occupational category in nineteenth-century Britain and the United States. This is why factory and clerical employment proved so attractive in spite of the competitive wages offered by service. For Jamaica, the nineteenth-century position is less certain. House slaves were at the continuous beck and call of their masters, but just how many hours they worked and whether they received Sunday or Saturday holidays when these were given to field slaves is not clear. After emancipation, however, it was complained that even offers of doubled wages could not induce servants "to forego their practice of claiming Saturday as a holiday" (Great Britain, Parliamentary Papers 1866, Vol. 51: 219). In 1925 Jamaican domestics worked an average of seventy-four hours per week without receiving any overtime pay, twenty hours more than workers in any other occupation. This level remained virtually unchanged until 1960 at least, while hours were reduced in other occupations (*Jamaica Bluebook* 1925, 394; 1945, 311; Jamaica, Department of Statistics 1943–51). In 1960 the majority of domestics still worked six to seven days per week. The minimum wage order of 1975, however, made a significant impact on the length of the working day and week of servants, along with the shift to live-out and day-work systems.

Jamaican domestic servants lack the benefits that have accrued to workers in unionized industries since 1938. The Masters and Servants Law, passed in 1842 to control a newly emancipated labor force, stayed on the books until 1974, whereas its British equivalent was repealed in 1875.[6] But the legal framework was always of minor importance in determining the welfare of the domestic; even the most recent Jamaican legislation cannot effectively restrain the power of the employer to terminate employment without notice, or refuse holidays or sick-leave pay, for example. The employer's word has always been overwhelming in any contractual dispute.

In industrializing Britain and the United States, domestics enjoyed a relatively good standard of living though under harsh conditions of work. There, the decline in domestic service had less to do with the level of earnings or the cost of employing servants than with changes in income distribution and the structure of society (Stigler 1956, 94–96). The low status attributed to domestic service after about 1920 derived not so much from the standard of living it offered as from the conditions of work and social relations it entailed. In Jamaica, by contrast, the standard of living of servants actually deteriorated when service came to dominate female employment in the first half of the twentieth century. Yet as late as 1922 it could be said that "in Jamaica the house-servant ranks high in the social scale" (Gaunt 1922, 139). If the long-term trends in the standard of living of Jamaican domestics have been identified correctly, it follows that the low status evaluation of service must be dated from about 1930. In part, this deterioration was a product of the changing social status of the servant-employing classes. The relative social and economic position of Jamaican servants was really good only when they constituted a quasi-caste, in the period 1750–1850.

The Social Architecture of Service

If household work was first and foremost a means of earning a living for the free domestic, it was also the most personal of all forms of work and led to the most intimate contact and confrontation between classes and races. Because she or he penetrated the boundaries of the employer's private world, a whole set of rules had to be established to ensure that the servant's position within it was clearly defined and demarcated.

Servants were defined in English law throughout the nineteenth century as dependents of their employers, and servants and women were the last social groups to be enfranchised (McBride 1976, 15; Marshall 1949, 10). In the eighteenth century, and to a lesser extent in the nineteenth, employers exercised the power of corporal punishment over free adult servants as well as children and slaves (Burnett 1977, 165; Hecht 1956, 79). But overall legislation was relatively unimportant in defining the nature of social relations in the isolated and private world of servanthood. The servant was constantly reminded of his or her position within the household. Modes of address helped to establish the hierarchy: the employer was to be addressed by servants as Mr./Mrs. So-and-so, whereas employers would call upper servants by their surnames and lower servants by their first names.

Modes of dress also helped to define the servant's position. So long as master and servant were of different ethnic groups, of course, the social inferiority of the servant needed little symbolic emphasis. Whites serving whites and blacks serving blacks, however, had to be marked off more definitely. Livery for men and uniforms for women, or even incongruous combinations of garments, were forced on servants for this reason. In large establishments the upper categories of servants were allowed to approach more closely the dress of their employers, emphasizing their role as the mediators of authority. Livery was worn by some domestics in Jamaica during the slave period, but whether it was abandoned earlier or later than in England (c. 1870) is not certain (Brathwaite 1971, 155; Stewart 1808, 188). Employers' concern about servants' dress extended beyond the workplace. It was a stock complaint that servants loved finery and wasted their substance on clothing; when the servant's dress imitated that of the master or mistress, this was seen as proof of "arrogance." Thus employers, particularly those from the middle classes, often restricted the amount of cast-off clothing they gave servants, to avoid encouraging "vanity." In England the emergence of the bourgeoisie as the chief servant-employing class went together with an increasing rigidity and uniformity in the dress of domestics and hence a deterioration in their status (Burnett 1977, 171; McBride 1976, 25, 59, 95). Whether a similar trend occurred in Jamaica in the first half of the twentieth century, when the employers became increasingly colored, black, and middle-class and the servants increasingly black, has not been established.

Although the nature of domestic work made it impossible for employers to establish prohibited zones within the household, the servant's penetration could be rationalized or ritualized. The physical closeness of the servant could be ignored. Thus the U.S. slave Henry Bruce recalled vividly that he was "called as a boy to the side of his unclad mistress in her bedroom merely to pour additional water for a bath" and that she seemed aloof, hardly aware of his presence (Owens 1976, 115). In the same way, Jamaican slave masters talked at table of rebellion, plots, and abolition as though oblivious to the slaves who waited on them or brushed mosquitoes from their shins beneath the tablecloth. White Jamaicans behaved similarly in the days preceding the disturbances of 1938, loudly insulting and downgrading the Negro race in general at dinner parties and in the presence of their own servants, whom they regarded as "nonpeople" (Cargill 1979, 94). The servant, on the other hand, had to show deference by always standing when the master or mistress entered the room and by shuffling backward out of the room.

Most house slaves in the United States lived in huts near the Big House or in the slave quarters, but some slept in the same room as the master, "supplying nightly needs as they arose" (Owens 1976, 108). In England the Tudor servant often slept outside his master's door, but by the seventeenth century separate quarters were common, and by the nineteenth aristocratic houses had extensive servants' wings, containing the entire domestic hierarchy. The typical English servant in the period 1870–1920, however, lived in the attic or cellar of an urban middle-class dwelling, often having to share a bed, or, in the poorer households, slept in the kitchen or corridor (Franklin 1975, 211–39; Girouard 1978; McBride 1976, 50; Marshall 1949, 13).

In Jamaica the domestic slave living on a plantation was quartered near the great house or in the slave village. In towns, both in Jamaica and the United States, domestic slaves occupied rooms within their master's house or a separate building on the same lot. This pattern of building a separate range of "servants' rooms" continued in Jamaica until the middle of the twentieth century, even after the kitchen had been moved inside the house. In 1913, de Lisser described them as "small boxes as a rule, and built at about 30 or 40 feet away from the house," furnished by the servants themselves, two servants generally sleeping in one room.[7] After about 1950, as the live-in system declined, servants' rooms were generally built into the main structure of Jamaican bourgeois houses, but rarely given direct access to the main house, so that the servant had to cross a clearly defined neutral zone before penetrating the private world of the employer. Marjorie Hughes described one of these as "a single bleak room about six feet by nine, well separated by a back-patio from the rest of the house" and containing a bed, washbasin, and water closet; the main house having "three Gracious Living jacques-de-luxe, pale-blue, pale-pink, pale-green" with matching lavatory paper (Hughes 1962, 19). A hundred years earlier, in 1850, when water closets were still a rarity in Jamaica, the "better houses" were said to have two privies, one for the household and one for the servants; these, with their separate entries, were "under one roof, and built over one cess-pool or pit" (Jamaica, Board of Health 1852, 101). This mode persisted in rural Jamaica well into the twentieth century. Although the servant's task was to protect the household from dirt and disorder, emptying the chamber pots each morning and washing the dirty dishes after dinner, she could not be allowed to use the same toilet seat or the same knives and forks. As argued by Mary Douglas (1970) in *Purity and Danger,* such attitudes to pollution and purification must be understood in terms of their social/ritual functions rather than as having anything to do with ideas about hygiene. Servants had to be constantly reminded of their place.

Private balls and dinners were the stage for the most elaborate ritual demonstrations of social distance, reaching the level of dramatic performances. In 1830 Lady Nugent ordered a fete for the servants at Government Penn, near Spanish Town, and she "began the ball with an old negro man . . . exactly the same as I would have done at a servants' hall birthday in England." Meanwhile, "the gentlemen each selected a partner, according to rank, by age or service." But later, Lady Nugent was told by white women present that her act had reduced them almost to fainting and a flood of tears, "for in this country, and among slaves, it was necessary to keep up so much more distant respect" (Wright 1966, 156). In 1932 Lady Stubbs offended Jamaican society similarly by attending her chauffeur's wedding. But in this case one of her defenders pointed out that "in the Old Country the true nobility is marked by the courtesy which those in its charming circle shew to their dependents" (*Daily Gleaner,* November 18 and 22, 1932). Probably, the continued middle-class domination of servant-keeping in Jamaica meant that the social distance between master and servant, reflected in ritual observance, narrowed more slowly there than in England.

Conclusions

The argument that domestic service rose and fell along with the growth and maturing of industrial society, as an economic mechanism, has been criticized even for the North Atlantic (Branca 1975, 130; Katzman 1978, vii). So it is perhaps not surprising that it fits Jamaica poorly, in spite of the universal claims made for the model. What is less expected is the failure of urbanization to account for the Jamaican pattern and the uncertain role of unemployment levels. The persistence of the dual economy in Jamaica has meant that the levels of living afforded by the modern sector, with its unionized labor force, have raised the reserve wage below which potential domestic servants prefer to remain unemployed, even in the absence of a welfare state. To this extent, industrialization has operated to reduce rather than increase the supply of servants.

Changes in the social status attributed to domestic service have been crucial in determining the level of employment. The coincidence of status and material welfare was never complete. In Jamaica, slave domestics were selected on the basis of their higher status in the racially determined social hierarchy, and this was reflected in relatively high real wages immediately after emancipation. Declining wages and the emergence of the new bourgeoisie as the major servant-employing class led to a deterioration in the status of the servant which was not to be reversed by the combination of improved wages and high unemployment levels in the last fifteen years, the era of Black Power, Democratic Socialism, and government intervention.

Although the strictly ceremonial functions of domestics diminished greatly after emancipation, the servant's role in giving "dignity" to Jamaican households remained of central importance to those of the middle class who believed "that they should supervise labour, but not do the work themselves" (*Jamaica Times* 1932; *Report of the Middle Class Unemployment Committee* 1941, 5). While servants increasingly came to perform productive economic functions within the household, a whole set of rules had to be formulated to establish clearly the servant's place within it. Economic and social change, together with political ideology, were perhaps equally important in determining the acceptability of these rules within particular societies and hence the evaluation given to domestic service independent of the material returns it might offer.

Notes

Acknowledgments: I wish to thank Patricia Branca, Erna Brodber, Stanley Engerman, Howard Johnson, and Merle Johnson for their comments on an earlier version of this paper.

1. For Britain, see Burnett 1977; Davidoff 1974, 406–28; Hecht 1956; McBride 1976; Marshall 1949. For the United States, see Gallman and Weiss 1969, 287–381; Katzman 1978; Stigler 1946.

2. Eisner's figures diverged from the census trend only between 1871 and 1881, where she found a decrease "improbable."

3. Report of the Royal Commission to Enquire into the Public Revenues 1884; see also Higman 1976, 13–14; Musgrave 1880, 10.

4. See also Jamaica, *Collector General, Governor's Report on the Bluebook* 1880–1939, (the *Bluebooks* were statistical reports of the colonial government).

5. Based on advertisements appearing on the first Saturday or Sunday issues of each year.

6. 5 Vic. cap. 43, amended 1940 (cap. 387); see also Davidoff 1974, 406.

7. De Lisser 1913, 103; see also Daisy E. Jeffrey-Smith's letter in "Jamaica Memories," 1959 (Jamaica Archives, File 7/12).

References

Aspinall, Algernon E. 1912. *The British West Indies*. London: Isaac Pitman.

Boland, Barbara. 1974. "Labour Force." In G. W. Roberts, ed., *Recent Population Movements in Jamaica*, pp. 56–93. Kingston: Committee for International Coordination of National Research in Demography (CICRED).

Boserup, Ester. 1970. *Woman's Role in Economic Development*. New York: St. Martin's Press.

Branca, Patricia. 1975. "A New Perspective on Women's Work: A Comparative Typology." *Journal of Social History* 9:129–53.

Brathwaite, Edward. 1971. *The Development of Creole Society in Jamaica, 1770–1920*. Oxford: Oxford University Press.

Burnett, John. 1977. *Useful Toil: Autobiographies of Working People from the 1820s to the 1920s*. Harmondsworth, Eng.: Penguin Books.

Cannadine, David. 1978. "The Theory and Practice of the English Leisure Classes." *Historical Journal* 21, no. 2:445–67.

Cargill, Morris. 1979. *Jamaica Farewell*. Secaucus, N.J.: Cinnamon Books.

Chaplin, David. 1978. "Domestic Service and Industrialization." *Comparative Studies in Sociology* 1:97–127.

Chapman, Agatha. 1953. *Wages and Salaries in the United Kingdom, 1920–38*. Cambridge: Cambridge University Press.

Chapman, Esther. 1938. *The Truth about Jamaica*. Kingston: West Indian Review.

———. 1952. *Pleasure Island*. Kingston: Arawak Press.

Clarke, Edith. 1957. *My Mother Who Fathered Me: A Study of the Family in Three Selected Communities in Jamaica*. London: Allen & Unwin.

Craton, Michael. 1978. *Searching for the Invisible Man: Slaves and Plantation Life in Jamaica*. Cambridge, Mass.: Harvard University Press.

Columbian Magazine (Kingston). 1797. Vol. 3, no. 8.

Cundall, Frank. 1920. *Jamaica in 1920: A Handbook of Information for Intending Settlers and Visitors*. Kingston: Institute of Jamaica.

Daily Gleaner (Kingston). 1910–81.

Davidoff, Leonore. 1974. "Mastered for Life: Servant and Wife in Victorian and Edwardian England." *Journal of Social History* 7, no. 4:406–28, 446–59.

Deane, Phyllis and W. A. Cole. 1969. *British Economic Growth, 1688–1959.* Cambridge: Cambridge University Press.

De Lisser, H. G. 1913. *Twentieth Century Jamaica.* Kingston: Jamaica Times.

———. 1914. *Jane's Career: A Story of Jamaica.* London: Heinemann.

Douglas, Mary. 1970. *Purity and Danger.* Harmondsworth, Eng.: Penguin Books.

Eisner, Gisela. 1961. *Jamaica, 1830–1930: A Study in Economic Growth.* Manchester, Eng.: Manchester University Press.

Emigrants' Information Office. 1894. *General Information for Intending Emigrants to the West Indies.* London: Emigrants' Information Office.

Franklin, Jill. 1975. "Troops of Servants: Labour and Planning in the Country House, 1840–1914." *Victorian Studies* 19 (December): 211–39.

Gallman, Robert E., and Thomas J. Weiss. 1969. "The Service Industries in the Nineteenth Century." In Victor R. Fuchs, ed., *Studies in Income and Wealth,* 34:287–381. New York: Columbia University Press.

Gaunt, Mary. 1922. *Where the Twain Meet.* London.

Girouard, Mark. 1978. *Life in the English Country House: A Social and Architectural History.* New Haven, Conn.: Yale University Press.

Great Britain, Department of Employment. 1969. *British Labour Statistics Yearbook.* London: Department of Employment.

Great Britain, Parliamentary Papers. 1839. "Copies of Any Communications Addressed to the Secretary of State by the Agent for the Island of Jamaica," Vol. 35.

———. 1866. "Papers Relative to the Affairs of Jamaica," Vol. 51.

Hall, Douglas. 1959. *Free Jamaica, 1838–1865.* New Haven, Conn.: Yale University Press.

Hecht, J. Jean. 1956. *The Domestic Servant Class in Eighteenth-Century England.* London: Routledge & Kegan Paul.

Higman, B. W. 1976. *Slave Population and Economy in Jamaica, 1807–1834.* Cambridge: Cambridge University Press.

———, ed. 1980. *The Jamaican Censuses of 1844 and 1861.* Mona, Jamaica: University of the West Indies, Department of History.

Hughes, Marjorie. 1962. *The Fairest Island.* London: Victor Gollancz.

Jamaica, Board of Health. 1852. *Report by the Central Board of Health, of Jamaica.* Spanish Town, Jamaica.

Jamaica Bluebooks. 1840–1945. Kingston: Government Printing Office.

Jamaica, Collector General. 1880–1939. *Estimates of Government Expenditure.* Kingston: Government Printer.

———. 1920–39. *Annual Reports.* Kingston: Government Printer.

——. 1962–72. *Governor's Report on the Bluebook*. Kingston: Government Printer.

Jamaica, Department of Statistics (previously Central Bureau of Statistics; currently Statistical Institute of Jamaica). 1844–1970. Censuses of Population.

——. 1943–51. *Quarterly Digests of Statistics*. Kingston: Department of Statistics.

——. 1955. *Household Expenditure Survey, 1953–4*. Kingston: Department of Statistics.

——. 1957. *Rural Household Expenditure Survey, 1956*. Kingston: Department of Statistics.

Jamaica Hansard. 1975–76. New Series 1.

Jamaica, Institute of. 1895. *Jamaica in 1895*. Kingston: Institute of Jamaica.

Jamaica Times. 1907. January 5.

——. 1932. April 2.

Jamaican Housewife (Kingston). 1962. 1 (Winter).

Jefferson, Owen. 1972. *The Post-War Economic Development of Jamaica*. Kingston: Institute of Social and Economic Research, University of the West Indies.

Katzman, David M. 1978. *Seven Days a Week: Women and Domestic Service in Industrializing America*. New York: Oxford University Press.

Long, Edward. 1774. *The History of Jamaica*, Vol. 2. London: T. Lowndes.

Marshall, Dorothy. 1949. *The English Domestic Servant in History*. London: Historial Association.

McBride, Theresa Marie. 1976. *The Domestic Revolution: The Modernization of Household Service in England and France, 1820–1920*. New York: Holmes & Meier.

Maunder, W. F. 1960. *Employment in an Underdeveloped Area*. New Haven, Conn.: Yale University Press.

Mingay, G. E. 1963. *English Landed Society in the Eighteenth Century*. London: Routledge & Kegan Paul.

Mitchell, B. R. 1971. *Abstract of British Historical Statistics*. Cambridge: Cambridge University Press.

Musgrave, Anthony. 1880. *Jamaica: Now and Fifteen Years Since*. Kingston: Royal Colonial Institute.

Orde Brown, G. St. J. 1939. *Labour Conditions in the West Indies*. London: HMSO.

Owens, Leslie Howard. 1976. *This Species of Property*. New York: Oxford University Press.

Report of the Middle Class Unemployment Committee. Kingston. 1941.

Roberts, G. W. 1957. *The Population of Jamaica*. Cambridge: Cambridge University Press.

Senior, Bernard Martin. 1835. *Jamaica, As It Was, As It Is, and As It May Be.* London.

Spinner, Alice. 1894. *A Study in Colour.* London.

Stewart, J. 1808. *An Account of Jamaica.* London.

Stigler, George Joseph. 1946. *Domestic Servants in the United States, 1900–1940.* Occasional Paper N. 24. New York: National Bureau of Economic Research.

———. 1956. *Trends in Employment in the Service Industries.* Princeton, N.J.: Princeton University Press.

Taylor, LeRoy. 1964. *Consumers' Expenditure in Jamaica.* Kingston: University of the West Indies, Institute of Social and Economic Research.

U.S. Department of Commerce. 1975. *Historical Statistics of the United States.* Washington, D.C.: Bureau of the Census.

West India Royal Commission. 1945. *West India Royal Commission Report.* London: His Majesty's Stationery Office.

Woodson, C. G. 1930. "The Negro Washerwoman, A Vanishing Figure." *Journal of Negro History* 15, no. 3: 269–77.

Wright, Philip, ed. 1966. *Lady Nugent's Journal.* Kingston: Institute of Jamaica.

3 Servants and Masters in Rio de Janeiro: Perceptions of House and Street in the 1870s

SANDRA LAUDERDALE GRAHAM

In Rio de Janeiro in 1872 a Portuguese goldsmith and shop owner had occasion to testify in court that a young slave woman, Belmira, had been sent to his shop by her owner to fetch a pair of earrings for her master's daughter. The jeweler went on to say that he supposed that "Belmira is not a virgin"; it was "enough for her to go out on the street [for him] to presume this." According to her owner, she frequently went out to do shopping and even to sell fruit and vegetables. A neighbor recalled seeing Belmira serve as companion to the daughter on her strolls and excursions. By her own account, Belmira was "17 years old more or less, single, and employed in domestic service."[1]

Neither the reason for the case nor Belmira's eventual fate concerns us here. Rather, what are we to make of the fact that a woman could be judged sexually experienced merely because, in the performance of household errands, she left her master's house alone? The jeweler did not think it necessary to explain or elaborate his remark, and in the course of the proceedings no one questioned him. Those who heard his testimony apparently found his statement intelligible and plausible. We can also note that, in contrast, the master's daughter did not venture out unaccompanied, either to fetch her own earrings or for diversion. Being free and socially more valued, and perhaps younger, she counted on the services of a slave, barely more than a girl herself, for protection.

The usual distinctions drawn between house and street, illustrated by the description of the slave Belmira, were recognizable to both servants and *patrões* within a commonly shared culture. For servants, however, house and street could represent quite different meanings. It is worthwhile to discover these different significances.

Imagine, then, the city of Rio de Janeiro as residents knew it

67

around 1870. As the capital it held the palaces of royalty. There the members of parliament, cabinet ministers, councillors of state, higher court judges, and fiscal officers conducted the everyday business of government. As Brazil's principal port, the city dominated the nation's commerce. The great coffee barons and their factors funneled coffee through Rio de Janeiro warehouses to supply the rich Atlantic trade. In exchange, European luxury goods entered Brazil to satisfy the expensive tastes of a local elite. The major export firms established there, together with local and foreign banking houses, made Rio the financial hub of Brazil. There the wealthy resided, either permanently in splendid mansions or intermittently in townhouses, overseeing their interests.

Slavery endured and would endure until 1888. Despite an effective end to the African slave trade in the 1850s, a thriving internal trade shifted slaves from northern provinces through Rio de Janeiro to the coffee plantations of the Paraíba Valley and western São Paulo. In Rio itself the slaves, divided nearly equally between women and men, numbered about 50,000, or one-fifth of the city's population (Brazil, Directoria Geral de Estatística 1873–76, 58).

Thus, for all its power and wealth, Rio de Janeiro presented another, shabbier workaday aspect. Among a population in 1872 of 275,000, few held rank as judges, senators, or property owners of consequence; many more filled minor bureaucratic posts; but most others—men or women, free poor or slaves—performed physical labor in order to survive. And most working women labored as servants.

In 1870 a city census considered 63 percent of working-age free women as engaged in some identified and gainful occupation, as well as 88 percent of the slave women (Tables 3-1 and 3-2). The few women with "professional" occupations included midwives, nuns, teachers, and those skilled at a craft; the liberal professions—law and medicine—and public service were closed to them. A scattering of women engaged also in commerce, probably as market or street vendors; men or young boys were preferred as shop clerks or cashiers, although a few foreign women did own dressmaking shops. Somewhat more commonly, women worked in the manufacture of textiles and clothing, in the tanning and hat industries or in boot and shoe factories. Factory jobs, an alternative for few, could absorb only a small portion of working women.

Principally, then, women who worked had little choice but to hire out as domestics: cooks and house servants; *amas de leite* (wet-nurses) or *amas*

TABLE 3-1.
Working Women as a Percentage of Women of
Working Age, Rio de Janeiro, 1870–1906

	1870		1872		1906
	FREE	SLAVE	FREE	SLAVE	
Working	63	88	58	89	49
No declared oc-cupation	37	12	42	11	51
Total	100	100	100	100	100
(N)	(45,018)	(16,217)	(58,667)	(16,501)	(208,879)

Sources: Brazil, Directoria Geral de Estatística 1871, Mappas A–K, n.p.; 1873–76, 1–33; 1907, 174–317.

secas ("dry" nurses), who looked after young children; laundresses or women who only starched or ironed; pantry maids; mucamas, personal maids or chambermaids; and seamstresses. Even the women, especially slave women, who sold vegetables or sweets on the street typically doubled as house servants during part of the day, as Belmira did. In the 1870s servant women represented about 16 percent of the total population in Rio de Janeiro's urban parishes.[2] We can think, then, of Rio as a city where as many as 30,000 free and slave women labored as domestics.

The emphatic presence of servants meant that domestic life in nineteenth-century Rio de Janeiro included not only family members—those connected through ties of blood and kinship—but a larger company of the household. By cultural preference and in fact the household often included servants, either slaves or free persons or sometimes both, who served as live-in household members or as day workers (Table 3-3).[3] "Household" defined a set of social relationships among persons who by race and birth occupied markedly unequal social positions.

A paternalistic culture set the terms within which the male head was invested with authority and responsibility over all members of the household. It remained for dependents to return obedience appropriate to their place either as wife, children, other kin, or servants. Portuguese custom had long established the husband and father as

TABLE 3-2.
Working Women by Occupation, Rio de Janeiro,
1870–1906 (in percentages)

	1870		1872		1906
	FREE	SLAVE	FREE	SLAVE	
Domestic service	61.0	90.0	68.5	91.6	76.0
Dressmaking	—	—	25.5	8.3	—
Manufacturing	31.0	9.1	—	—	19.0
Commercial	3.0	.1	1.2	.02	1.0
Professional	2.0	—	1.8	—	3.0
Property owning	2.0	—	2.8	—	1.0
Agricultural	—	.2	.2	.1	—
Odd jobs	1.0	.4	.4	—	—
Total	100.0	100.0	100.0	100.0	100.0
(*N*)	(28,537)	(14,347)	(33,886)	(14,672)	(101,496)

Source: Brazil, Directoria Geral de Estatística 1871, Mappas A–K, n.p.; 1873–76: 1–33;
1907, 174–317.
Note: Percentages do not total 100% due to rounding.

the undisputed head of family, the *cabeça de casal*. By that authority he
legally administered family property, both his own and that of his wife
and minor, unmarried children; he granted or withheld permission to
marry to minor children or even to a widowed daughter. Nor could
he refuse to exercise the powers that custom and law decreed for him,
for only with his death could such authority legally pass to his wife or,
with regard to minor children, to a guardian (Almeida 1870, liv. 1, tit.
LXXXVIII, par. 6; liv. 4, tit. XCV, nn. 2, 5; liv. 5, tit. XXII).

　　More important, paternal authority did not end with the circle of
immediate family but extended to the full membership of the household. The *amo*—the head of household and master—possessed by
Portuguese law the right to castigate physically his "servant, follower,
wife, child, or slave" (Almeida 1870, liv. 5, tit. XXXVI, par. 1; Filgueiras 1876, art. 14, par. 6). At the same time, nevertheless, the head
of household was expected to assure protection to the honor of ser-

TABLE 3-3.
Declared Servants in São Cristovão Households, 1870

SERVANTS IN HOUSEHOLD	HOUSE- HOLDS	% OF HOUSE- HOLDS WITH SERVANTS	CUMULA- TIVE %	% OF ALL HOUSE- HOLDS
1	110	44.0	44.0	7.1
2	55	22.0	66.0	3.9
3–5	48	19.0	85.0	3.4
6–8	25	10.0	95.0	1.8
9–11	9	4.0	99.0	.6
12–13	2	1.0	100.0	.1
Total	239	100.0	100.0	17.0

Source: Brazil, directoria Geral de Estatística 1870.

vant women. Any man who attempted to sleep with or marry a servant without permission from her *patrão* risked banishment—or death. The law stated the more severe penalty if she had served "within doors," the less if she served "outside the house" (Almeida 1870, liv. 5, tit. XXIV). Servant women then, lived as household members, subject to the authority of its head.

Contemporaries used interchangeably the words *familia, morada,* and *fogo* to indicate a household: "all those persons who habitually occupy a dwelling, both those who properly constitute a family as well as free dependents and slaves"; or "a certain number of persons who, by reason of kinship relations, subordination, or simply dependence, live in a dwelling or part of a dwelling, under the power, direction, or the protection of a *chefe* . . . and with a common economy."[4] As elaborated by Brazilian usage, "household" had come to refer simultaneously to family and dependents, a dwelling place, a distinct economic grouping, and paternal authority.

The Brazilian notion of household itself fit within a larger conceptual frame bounded by the competing images of *casa e rua*, house and street (Freyre 1961, I: 33–48).[5] By contemporary understandings, "house" represented private and protected space, contrasted with the public, unpleasant, even dangerous places of "street." The known and orderly ties of blood kin belonged to the house; less lasting or temporary relations, those that involved choice, were associated with the street. "House" distinguished and separated family from the anonymous, coarse, and disorderly society that was seen to belong to public squares, shops, and streets. Describing an area of danger or risk and another of safety and protection, notions of house and street transformed simpler physical places into culturally mapped zones, thereby indicating what behavior could be expected and what behavior would be appropriate.

In practice, the boundaries between house and street took several forms. Physically, a walled garden filled with trees and fragrant flowers might set a villa apart from the noise or dirt that waited outside. In older, more settled parishes a merchant and his family might occupy the floors above a ground-level shop or warehouse; thus a vertical boundary separated what was below and public from what was above and private. In modest houses without even a veranda to separate house from street, wooden shutters could at least be closed (Burmeister 1853, 47; Kidder and Fletcher 1879, 27, 163).

The boundary between house and street had not only a spatial but a temporal quality. The commerce of the street was a daytime matter wherein all classes of persons might transact business, earn their livelihood, enjoy the company of their fellows, or merely come and go. After dark, however, the commercial and social life of the street officially ceased, and persons were expected to return home. To mark that hour the church bells tolled—at ten o'clock in summer, nine in winter—for half an hour "in order to call home the citizens" and to warn slaves off the street with a curfew. After that time anyone "on the street without clear reason" was subject to jail or fines. Artisans or laborers were allowed to carry tools on the street only during the day; "after the Ave-Maria" or tolling of the bells, tools became weapons and were prohibited (Almeida 1870, liv. I, tit. LXV, par. 14, n.3; Baretto and Lima 1942, 3:102–3; Rio de Janeiro, Câmara Municipal 1870, tit. IX, par. 20).[6]

Recognition that street and house encompassed vastly different social spheres produced double distinctions between sex and class. Brazilian men might enjoy "the easy fellowship of the street and plaza . . . where they discussed politics . . . and transacted business," but women of good family who went out into the street—even during the daytime—went accompanied by their maids, in effect taking with them the protection of the house in the person of a servant. Women frequently strolled in the Passeio Público in the cool late afternoon with their children and servant women. But one young widow could not take the sea baths her doctor prescribed, because as she explained, she "had no person of trust to accompany her" (Ewbank 1856, 89–91; Freyre 1922, 612; Kidder and Fletcher 1879, 88–89; Rebello 1886, 188). The image of women shielded from the vulgarities or dangers of the street had value precisely because it distinguished women of position from those with lesser means, who faced the risks of the street alone.

This distinction between house and street not only identified women of different social classes but further set apart servant women of roughly the same class. As escorts or companions, maids "knew the streets"; other servants were engaged with the express condition that they would "not go out on the street." One household in 1870 kept three female slaves occupied with the "service of the house" and sent their one male slave out to perform the "service of the street" (Brazil, Directoria Geral de Estatística 1870, HH 548).

If masters confined some servants to interior work because the world outside would either harm or tempt them, not all servants needed or warranted such regard. Sexually experienced women—as perhaps Belmira was—were assumed able to cope with the street. Thus Brazilian households, following older Portuguese tradition, continued to distinguish those who "served behind doors" from those who "served outside the house."[7] By that difference a family might apportion the protections it offered and the demands it made.

Despite the mental ordering of city life into competing zones of danger or risk on one side and safety or protection on the other, the fact remained that Rio de Janeiro households functioned precisely because of daily contact with the street. Since neither a sewage system nor piped water served the city's homes, householders relied instead on their servants to carry water, to launder at public fountains, to empty waste at nearby beaches. Families sent servants out daily to shop because as city dwellers they neither produced the bulk of their daily goods nor, in the tropics, could they store significant quantities or varieties of food supplies. Since few families could afford the luxury of enough servants to reserve some exclusively for indoor work, most servants routinely crossed back and forth between house and street. Servant women were required, as their protected mistresses were not, to face and cope with the apparent hazards of bargaining at public markets, making their way through congested and filthy streets, and withstanding the implied sexual insults or transgressions posed by male society.

If, however, we attend to the servants' own experience of the world outside the house as they perceived and encountered it, I think the zones of danger and safety were or could be reversed. For those servants the spaces beyond the house came to be broken down into familiar, perhaps wearily familiar, landscapes of particular streets and *praças*. Dirty, noisy streets where all manner of shops, private residences, warehouses, and public buildings crowded together became ordered by them according to the private meanings they assigned. Servants shared among themselves and all those whose labor similarly took them out on the streets—vendors and porters, for example—the city as a place of known sounds, smells, and images. Individually, servant women could establish a favorite way from house to fountain or market, knowing well its landmarks and the distances from place to place.

Work that took servants out into the street allowed for a more diverse and more egalitarian social world. Away from the surveillance of an ever watchful *dona da casa*, women might expect to encounter other servants similarly embarked, or to meet friends or lovers briefly at some prearranged time and place. Household shopping meant repeated contact with vendors who, like servant women, were slaves or belonged among the city's free poor. In those public places social bonds among equals could be established, tested, enjoyed and individual identities formed.

Washing at the fountain or at *cortiço* laundry tanks and queuing up to fill water jugs were social occasions. Drying or bleaching clothes in the sun spelled a long wait for laundresses, enough time to wash their own clothes or tend their children, brought along to the washing place or left to run about in a courtyard. Washing afforded the chance for camaraderie. For a span of hours or a full day, women were freed from the need to behave deferentially, to move silently about. The fountain site rang with their talk and their labors. Water carriers who waited at a fountain or street-corner spigot enjoyed the time to chat or flirt (Backheuser 1906, 109; Ewbank 1856, 94; Kidder and Fletcher 1879, 174).

From the many barefoot women who hawked *quitanda* (produce) from baskets securely balanced on their heads, house servants purchased peaches, pineapples, onions, or greens. One vendor, her hands strong and rough from work, sold giblets from a case she carried strapped around her neck (Costa 1938, 1:128; Kidder and Fletcher 1879, 167).[8] For the most part, though, servants bought from the men who filled the ranks of vendors.

Either way, they traded in more or less aggressive situations where they bargained for good prices, ever watchful that they received quality. Marketing demanded a certain cunning and strategy. If a servant hoped to save small change for herself aside from what she returned her mistress, or to avoid her ready accusations, she had to bargain hard. Common background did not necessarily ensure against shady dealings by those vendors who would sell dear, if not out-and-out cheat the unwary. Servants risked buying meat or bread weighed on falsely balanced scales (Carvalho 1901, 45; Kidder and Fletcher 1879, 172).[9] Alert servants kept an eye out for bread baked from putrid flour or for decomposing meat, exposed overlong to sun or transported in slow wagons, covered only with a dirty cloth. Even the most inexperienced knew to avoid bad fish, kept in barrels of salt water; their smell was foul enough to cause vomiting.[10] Hence, a servant woman responsible for taking home perishables that would meet a *dona's* critical standards searched out reliable sellers who knew she meant business. If assertive and quick to discern quality, she could then confidently enjoy dealing in a predominantly male world.

So, too, servant women managed to conduct private lives, at least partially separate and independent from the houses where *patrões* dominated, lives that placed them within the larger society of the city's working poor. They participated in the friendships, the troubles, and the celebrations of neighborhood that affirmed a common background of poverty, race, or kinship. Contrasted with the lives of the well-off of the city, who were screened from common view in their closed carriages, walled mansions, or fine churches, the private lives of the poor belonged to more public and accessible places: tavern or corner shop, tenement or *cortiço*.

The numerous live-out laundresses and seamstresses who did work for several households took slum life for granted. Other servants, like Antonia Mendez, maintained a double life. Antonia worked as live-in servant for a family in the distant suburb of Tijuca; at the same time she rented a room on the Campo de Sant'Ana, which she agreed to share with her lover, Salvador. Energetically, with planning and careful savings, Antonia arranged a private life even though she could get to her rented room to see Salvador "only every eight days or so."[11] Even slave women sometimes achieved separate lives. Maria Joaquina lived on her own, with "license from her master." From her work as a laundress she returned to her owner in cash a portion of what she earned, keeping the rest to support herself (Brazil, Directoria Geral de Estatística 1870, HH 1058).

For servant women, then, "street" could signify a measure of freedom, self-assertion, or the company of lover, kin, or friends, while the supposedly protected space of "house" meant the restraining and watchful presence of *patrões* and even, of course, punishment. For them, danger could lie within the house rather than outside its walls. For their part, Rio de Janeiro *patrões* located their authority within the domain of *casa*. Slavery, coupled with older Iberian notions of the household, meant that *patrões* exercised over free and slave servants dominance that was both personal and private. By the 1880s householders believed their authority to be less secure. They had come to identify social disorder with disobedient servants and, far more alarmingly, to identify house servants—especially wet-nurses—as the carriers of dreadful disease. They insisted that the times called for the regulation of servants as well as firmly enforced measures of public health. But because such measures would require transferring what had long been exclusively personal powers to public officials, householders refused, despite their alarm; they preferred the risk of diseased or disrupting servants to any diminishing of their own jurisdiction over daily domestic life.[12]

No expression of the distinctions between house and street that mapped the meanings of social life matched the rowdy annual display of pre-Lenten *carnaval*. For masters and mistresses, "house" signified control, authority, a secure and stable domain where sex, age, and particularly blood ties ordered all relations. To "street" belonged connotations of uncertainty, movement, novelty (Da Matta 1981, 70), and during *carnaval* the poor publicly and triumphantly declared dominance over the street as their own place.

For those whose patterns of daily life routinely belonged to the street, *carnaval* did not invert the ordinary but rather celebrated and exaggerated it. By their celebrations common people bestowed on their way of life a legitimacy usually denied it; they converted streets to festive and glittering places, decorated with tree branches, flags, and lanterns suspended from posts. They ridiculed ordinarily perceived dangers with the play of water syringes and flour bombs. People jammed into the city's commercial center or gathered for fireworks in the Largo da Constituição, or cheered the acrobat who "went through the streets performing feats." Brass bands, individuals in fancy dress, or full-scale processions heightened with more movement, color, and sound the usual commotion of the street (Barreto and Lima 1942, 2:197, 305; *Revista Illustrada* 1884, 4–5; *Rio News* 1883, 2).[13] Not in the street to toil in the service of others, for three whole days the poor ruled by their brazen, gaudy presence. For common people—

and servants among them—during *carnaval* "street" remained street, only more so—exaggeratedly, excessively so.

Similarly, *carnaval* did not disrupt but rather affirmed the established understandings of "house." "More secluded" persons (the phrase indicated privilege) retained their suspicions about the polluting street; they watched processions from upstairs windows or vestibules, protected from jarring and unruly crowds. The rich did not join street festivities but conducted their own celebrations—indoors. At hotels or at private clubs, "the best families" hosted luxurious balls where in sumptuous costumes they masqueraded safely among those they could count as equals, despite their masks (Morais Filho 1946, 179–95; Rios Filho 1946, 330; Toussaint-Samson 1883, 77). The special time of *carnaval*, then, displayed and confirmed the usual notions that ordered everyday life.

House and street—competing conceptualizations. For servants they carried reversed or contrary meanings from those that *patrões* understood. The meanings that servant women derived from their experience formed part of the self-awareness by which they set themselves apart from *patrões* and the households where they labored.

Belmira and the jeweler each recognized distinctions between house and street—but not the same distinctions.

Notes

1. Côrte de Apelação, Acção de liberdade pela Belmira por seu curador, réu, Francisco da Veiga Abreu, Rio de Janeiro, 1872, Arquivo Nacional, Rio de Janeiro, Seção do Poder Judiciário, Maço 216, N. 1740, fls. 41, 33v, 21.

2. Throughout this chapter, the city of Rio de Janeiro refers to the urban parishes. In 1870 and 1872, they were Sacramento, São José, Candelaria, Santa Rita, Santo Antonio, Espirito Santo, Engenho Velho, São Cristovão, Gloria, Lagôa; by 1906, they further included Gavea, Engenho Novo, Santa Tereza, Gambôa, Andarahy, Tijuca, and Meyer.

3. In the parish of São Cristovão, 239 families, or 17 percent of the 1,404 households, positively identified servants who worked and lived in their households. Yet the census certainly undercounted the overall number of households with servants: at least another 392 households included free dependents or slaves, among them 323 working-age slave women for whom no occupations were recorded. Surely many of them worked in their masters' homes as domestics. Further, servants who worked by the day but did not live

in would not have been counted by the census taker as belonging to their employers' households (Brazil, Directoria Geral de Estatística 1870).

4. Brazil, Directoria Geral de Estatística (1871, 4); Brazil, Laws, statutes, etc., Decreto 4856, 30 December 1871, Regulamento, cap. I, art. 3, par. 1; Rio de Janeiro, Câmara Municipal 1870: Secção Segunda, Policia, tit. IX, par. 3.

5. Freyre first suggested the competing images of "house and street." I have drawn on the elaborations of the concepts for contemporary Brazil of Da Matta (1981, 71–75).

6. For an example of a slave accompanied on the street because it was past curfew, see 6º Distrito Criminal, Furto de escravo, réu, Severiana Mariana Maria da Conceição, Rio de Janeiro, 1882, ANSPJ, Caixa 1736, N. 5191, fl. 10v.

7. For examples, see Almeida 1870, liv. 5, tit. XXIV; Brazil, Directoria Geral de Estatística 1870, HH 548; *Correio Mercantil* 1872, agósto 28; 1877, julho 25).

8. In São Cristovão, thirty-two free women and eight slave women worked as *quitandeiras* (Brazil, Directoria Geral de Estatística 1870).

9. Proposals for regulating the sale of bread in Câmara Municipal, Rio de Janeiro, 1861 and 1892, Arquivo Geral da Cidade do Rio de Janeiro, Commercio de pão, 1841–1907, Cod. 58-4-36, fls. 38, 129; Câmara Municipal, Rio de Janeiro, 10 março 1879, ACG-RJ, Infracção de Posturas, Sacramento 1870–79, Cod. 9-2-35, fl. 29.

10. Sociedade Cosmopolita Protectora dos Empregados em Padarias, Rio de Janeiro, 22 dezembro 1902, AGC-RJ, Commercio de pão, 1841–1907, Cod. 58-4-36, fl. 145; Junta Central de Hygiene Pública a Câmara Municipal, Rio de Janeiro, 10 abril 1864, Director do Matadouro Público a Câmara Municipal, Rio de Janeiro, 30 novembro 1881, AGC-RJ, Carnes e matadouros . . . serviço sanitario, 1853–1909, Cod. 53-4-10, fls. 30–30v, 76; Secretaria, Ministerio da Justiça, Consultas, Conselho de Estado, Secção de Justiça, Rio de Janeiro, 25 julho 1881, Arquivo Nacional, Rio de Janeiro, Seção do Poder Executivo, Caixa 558, Pac. 3; Honorio Hermeto Leite Campos a Câmara Municipal, Rio de Janeiro, 5 março 1877, AGC-RJ, Mercado da Candelaria, 1870–79, Cod. 61-2-17, fl. 40.

11. Delegacia de Policia da 9ª Circumscripção Urbana, réu, Salvador Barbará, Rio de Janeiro, 1899, ANSPJ, Caixa 1069, N. 50, Fls. 2–4, 6, 7v, 8–9v.

12. For examples of proposed work contracts and regulations, see Propostas . . . 1884–1906, AGC-RJ, Serviço Domestico, Cod. 48-4-56, and Projectos de posturas . . . 1884, 1885, 1888, 1891, 1896, AGC-RJ, Serviço Domestico, Cod. 50-1-47; concerning the regulation adopted and then canceled, see Rio de Janeiro, Câmara Municipal, 22 novembro 1888, and remitted to Minsterio do Imperio, 17 dezembro 1888, AGC-RJ, Serviço Domestico, Cod. 50-1-45, fls. 2, 3; Consulta, Conselho do Estado, Secções Reunidas de Justiça e Imperio, Rio de Janeiro, 5 agosto 1889, AGC-RJ, Serviço Domestico; Projectos de posturas e pareceres do Conselho d'Estado sobre o serviço

domestico no Rio de Janeiro 1881–89, Cod. 50-1-43; Brazil, Ministerio da Justiça 1882, 195–97; Rego 1872, 170–75; Figueiredo 1876, 498–504; Francisco Rebello de Carvalho a Câmara Municipal, Rio de Janeiro, 31 julho 1884, AGC-RJ, Instituto municipal de amas de leite, 1884–85, Cod. 41-1-40, fls. 3–5; Projecto de organização do pessoal medico da Câmara Municipal, and Exame de carnes-verdes, estabulos de vaccas e serviço de amas de leite, 1884, 48-4-3; *Mãe de Familia* 1880, 2–3; Moncorvo Filho 1903, 167–73.
13. See also requests to Câmara Municipal [1875?], AGC-RJ, Carnaval, Cod. 40-3-86, fls. 2–3.

References

Almeida, Candido Mendes de. 1870. *Código Philippino; ou, Ordenações e leis do reino de Portugal, recopilados por mandado d'el-rey D. Philippe I. 14. ed. segundo a primeira de 1603 e a nona de Coimbra de 1824. Addicionada com diversas notas . . . por Candido Mendes de Almeida.* Rio de Janeiro: Instituto Philomathico.

Backheuser, Everardo. 1906. *Habitações populares.* Rio de Janeiro: Imprensa Nacional.

Barreto, J. F. de Mello, and Hermeto Lima. 1942. *História da polícia do Rio de Janeiro: Aspectos da cidade e da vida carioca, 1831–1870.* 3 vols. Rio de Janeiro: Editora "A Noite."

Brazil, Directoria Geral de Estatística. 1870. Arrolamento da população do Municipio da Côrte (São Cristovão), MS, Instituto Brasileiro de Geografía e Estatística, Rio de Janeiro, Departmento de Documentação e Referência.

———. 1871. *Relatorio apresentado ao Ministro e Secretário d'Estado dos Negocios do Imperio pela Commissão encarregada da direcção dos trabalhos do arrolamento da população do Municipio da Côrte a que se procedeu em abril de 1870.* Rio de Janeiro: Perseverança.

———. 1873–76. *Recenseamento da população do Imperio do Brazil a que se procedeu no dia 1º de agosto de 1872.* Rio de Janeiro: G. Leuzinger e Filhos.

———. 1907. *Recenseamento do Rio de Janeiro (Distrito Federal) realizado em 20 de setembro de 1906.* Rio de Janeiro: Officina da Estatística.

Brazil, Ministerio da Justiça. 1882. *Relatorio.* Rio de Janeiro: Ministerio da Justiça

Burmeister, Karl Hermann Konrad. 1853. *Viagem ao Brasil através das províncias do Rio de Janeiro e Minas, visando especialmente a história natural dos distritos auridiamantiferos.* Traduzido por Manoel Salvaterra e Hubert Schoenfeldt. Biblioteca História Brasileira 19. Rpt. São Paulo: Martins, 1952.

Carvalho, José Luis Sayão Bulhões. 1901. *A verdadeira população da cidade do Rio de Janeiro.* Rio de Janeiro: Jornal do Commercio.

Correo Mercantil (Rio de Janeiro). 1872. agósto 28.

——. 1877. julho 25.

Costa, Luiz Edmundo da. 1938. *O Rio de Janeiro do meu tempo.* 3 vols. Rio de Janeiro: Imprensa National.

Da Matta, Roberto. 1981. *Carnavais, malandros e heróis: Para uma sociologia do dilema brasileiro.* 2d ed. Rio de Janeiro: Zahar.

Ewbank, Thomas. 1856. *Life in Brazil; or A Journal of a Visit to the Land of the Cocoa and the Palm.* Rpt. Detroit: Blaine Ethridge Books, 1971.

Figueiredo, Carlos Arthur Moncorvo de. 1876. "Projecto de regulamento das amas de leite." *Gazeta Medica da Bahia,* pp. 498–504.

Filgueiras, [José Antonio de] Araújo. 1876. *Código criminal do império do Brasil.* 2d ed. Rio de Janeiro: Laemmert.

Freyre, Gilberto. 1922. "Social Life in Brazil in the Middle of the Nineteenth Century." *Hispanic American Historical Review* 5, no. 4: 597–630.

——. 1961. *Sobrados e mucambos, decadência do patriarcado rural e desenvolvimento do urbano.* 2 vols. 3d ed. Rio de Janeiro: José Olympio.

Kidder, Daniel P., and James C. Fletcher. 1879. *Brazil and the Brazilians Portrayed in Historical and Descriptive Sketches.* 9th rev. ed. London: Sampson Low, Marston, Searle & Rivington.

Mãe de Familia (Rio de Janeiro). 1880. janeiro, pp. 2–3.

Moncorvo Filho, Arthur. 1903. "Exames de amas de leite do 'Dispensario Moncorvo.'" *Archivos de Assistencia a infancia* 2, nos. 10–12: 167–73.

Morais Filho, Alexandre José Melo. 1946. *Festas e tradições populares do Brasil* (1888). 3d rev. ed. Anotado por Luis da Camara Cascudo. Rio de Janeiro: Briguiet.

Rebello, Eugenio. 1886. "Da vida sedentaria e de seus inconvenientes anti-hygienicos." *Revista de Hygiene,* Setembro, pp. 184–88.

Rego, José Pereira. 1872. *Esboço historico das epidemias que tem grassado na cidade do Rio de Janeiro desde 1830 a 1870.* Rio de Janeiro: Nacional.

Revista Illustrada. 1884. 9, no. 373:4–5.

Rio de Janeiro, Câmara Municipal. 1870. *Código de posturas da Ilma: Câmara Municipal do Rio de Janeiro e editaes da mesma Câmara.* Rio de Janeiro: Laemmert.

Rio News (Rio de Janeiro). 1883. janeiro 24, p. 2.

Rios Filho, Adolfo Morales de los. 1946. *O Rio de Janeiro Imperial.* Rio de Janeiro: Editora "A Noite."

Toussaint-Samson, Adele. 1883. *Une Parisienne au Brésil avec photographies originales.* Paris: Paul Ollendorff.

PART II
Domestic Service Today:
Ideology and Reality

4 Domestic Workers in Buenos Aires

MÓNICA GOGNA

It has been repeatedly emphasized that there are few studies of the different types and conditions of employment in domestic service. This chapter—which is essentially exploratory and descriptive—is part of current attempts to respond to the need for such research.

In addition to relying on information from other sources—existing studies of domestic employees, secondary data, classified ads, and some accessible life histories—a substantial part of what follows is based on interviews with domestic workers, carried out in an attempt to reconstruct their migratory and work histories while obtaining information about their employment.[1] The interviews were set up through personal contacts and two institutions connected to domestic employment: the Sindicato del Personal Doméstico de Casas Particulares (Union of Domestic Personnel in Private Homes) and Orientación para la Jóven (Orientation for Young Women); the latter, linked to the Catholic Church, is in charge of receiving young migrants in railroad stations and later placing them in homes.

Domestic service is the principal work alternative for women of the lower classes in Latin American cities, especially for migrant women. But domestic service is not like any other kind of work. The nature of this occupation—where it takes place, how it is paid (by monetary and nonmonetary means), the work relations it generates (contractual and at the same time requiring living in close quarters), and the existence of different ways of carrying out the tasks (which lead to clearly differing living and working conditions)—justifies a deeper discussion of the topic.

This article is a synthesis of my thesis for a degree in sociology (Universidad del Salvador, Buenos Aires, 1980).

TABLE 4-1.
Domestic Service Workers by Sex and Percentage of
Female EAP, Argentina, Various Years

YEAR	TOTAL	MEN	WOMEN	% IN FEMALE WORK FORCE
1947	400,499	23,927	376,572	30.5
1960	346,126	11,758	336,653	20.5
1970	538,550	11,400	527,150	23.0
1980	576,356	9,186	567,170	20.6

Sources: Recchini de Lattes 1977, Cuadro 2.4, 2.7; Argentina, Instituto Nacional de Estadística y Censos (14 years and older, 1947, 1960, 1980; 10 years and older, 1970).

Some Statistics and Regulations

The census of 1980 counted 2,756,000 women in the economically active population (EAP) in Argentina, of whom 21 percent were employed as domestics. Almost half of these (49 percent) resided in greater Buenos Aires; a little more than 20 percent lived in the homes where they worked.

The proportion of domestics in the total female work force is similar to the proportion registered in two previous censuses; it has fallen from the higher rates registered at the turn of the century (see Table 4-1).[2] But even though the relative weight of domestics in the service sector has diminished since 1947 in favor of "more dynamic" categories of work, they still represented in 1980 12 percent of employees in this service sector (Argentina, Ministerio de Trabajo 1985, Table 3).

As in other Latin American countries, these workers tend to be young women (almost 60 percent are under thirty-four), to have had little formal instruction (see Tables 4-2 and 4-3), and to be migrants: in 1970, 53 percent of recent internal migrants worked as domestics; 63 percent of migrants from bordering countries and 35 percent of the established migrants did so, but only 5 percent of the area's natives (Marshall 1977). The inclusion of the "residence" variable (Table 4-4) allows for discrimination among different work arrangements that the term "domestic servant" lumps together: the very

TABLE 4-2.
Domestic Service Workers by Age,
Argentina, 1980

AGE	NUMBER	%	CUMULATIVE %
14–19	125,034	22.0	22.0
20–24	85,399	15.1	37.1
25–34	119,983	21.2	58.3
35–44	100,016	17.6	75.9
45–54	82,159	14.5	90.4
55–64	42,064	7.4	97.8
60+	12,515	2.2	100.0
Total	567,170	100.0	100.0

Source: Argentina, Instituto Nacional de Estadística y Censos 1982.

young woman; the unmarried woman (88 percent of female live-in domestics are in this category [Argentina, 1980 Census of Population, Table 3. Unpublished]) who migrated from the family farm and sends part of her salary home; the adult who has her own family and enters into domestic service as a means of rounding off the family income or, if she is head of household, as her livelihood.

TABLE 4-3.
Domestic Service Workers by Level of
Formal Education, Argentina, 1980

LEVEL	NUMBER	%
None and incomplete primary	317,355	55.1
Complete primary	205,944	35.7
Incomplete secondary	43,600	7.6
Complete secondary	7,941	1.4
Higher, including university	1,516	0.3
Total	576,356	100.0

Source: Argentina, Instituto Nacional de Estadística y Censos 1982.
Note: Women constitute 98.4 percent of this occupational group.

TABLE 4-4.
Female Domestic Service Workers by
Age and Work Modality, Argentina,
1980 (in percentages)

AGE	LIVE-IN	LIVE-OUT	TOTAL
24 and younger	56.9	31.8	37.5
25–44	26.2	42.0	38.4
45–64	13.5	24.2	21.8
65 and older	3.4	2.0	2.3
Total	100.0	100.0	100.0
(*N*)	(126,541)	(440,269)	(567,170)

Source: Calculations based on unpublished data from the Argentine Census of 1980.

The norms that regulate work relations in domestic service are found in two 1956 law decrees (Nos. 326 and 7979) that specify who is to be considered a domestic worker and therefore eligible to receive the benefits of the statute:

> The present law decree is valid in the whole national territory for work relations of employees of both sexes who serve within the domestic sphere and do not produce profit or economic benefit for the employer, not being applicable to those who serve for less than a month, work less than four hours a day or less than four days a week for the same employer. [Law decree No. 326/56, Art. 1]

These decrees also determine the legal obligations and rights of the employees and employers, and establish for the Federal District[3] five work categories whose salaries can be set freely as long as they are above the minimum wage determined in each case.[4]

The law recognizes the following rights of domestic employees: a weekly rest period of twenty-four uninterrupted hours or, if this is not possible, two half-days weekly; a continuous vacation period yearly, paid at the established rate (according to years worked); a yearly bonus; and pension. For live-in domestics the decree establishes a daily rest period of three hours between morning and afternoon work, paid sick leave up to thirty days a year, and minimal conditions for room and board.

This legislation also creates an authorized body, the Council on Domestic Labor, to adjudicate individual conflicts that arise from the work relations that it regulates and to determine the different categories of domestic service personnel. The council is a division of the National Administration of Employment Services, Ministry of Labor. Domestic service workers are excluded from laws that regulate work contracts, accidents, family salary, overtime pay, and maternity leave.

In relation to the topic of social security, since December 1975 contributions to social services and a pension fund are mandated by law for all domestic workers in a dependency relation: that is, those who work at least four hours a day for at least four days a week. This law applies only to the Federal Capital and the greater Buenos Aires area.

Besides pension, social benefits include only medical assistance to the member and her family group. The employer contributes an amount equal to 4.5 percent of the domestic's pay; the employee contributes 3 percent of the same. All other domestic workers must contribute to the benefit fund of independent workers. (There is no information available about the number of domestics covered.)

Access to Employment in Domestic Service

It is possible to obtain employment in domestic service in a home in Buenos Aires in several ways: personal contacts, employment agencies, newspaper ads, and worker's exchanges—including the special "domestics' market" that functions in the Plaza Primera Junta; there, as in some suburbs of the Federal Capital and greater Buenos Aires, employees and *patronas* meet publicly, without intermediaries, to arrange a work contract.

In describing domestic service in Mexico City, Arizpe (1976, 638) points out that "these jobs are sought after and offered through personal contacts." A study of domestic employees in Chile reveals that the family usually acts as an employment agency in the first stages of a work history (Alonso et al. 1978). In Buenos Aires research on migrant families reveals that 81 percent of the interviewed migrants (30 percent of whom worked as domestics) had obtained employment through "particularistic means," which probably refers to the connection of primary groups (family, friends) that "are the best way of placing young women in work roles" (Puigbó n.d., 4).

The employees I interviewed also used personal channels in most cases. As Nicolasa puts it, "One recommends another, asks someone or other."

> INTERVIEWER: And what about the way to secure jobs?
>
> NICOLASA: Ah, one is always recommended.
>
> INTERVIEWER: You never had to use an agency or the newspaper?
>
> NICOLASA: Never, there were always people. People who recommend me or ask me if I have a little time left over, and when I don't, then I recommend someone else.

Doorkeepers, too, often act as intermediaries:

> The doormen busy themselves a lot with the working girls; were it not for them many would not have any work. [Nicolasa]
>
> I am searching, bah, looking, for now. I have only asked the residence manager there to help, the doorman, he will know of something, because I want to change my situation. [Adela]

Employers, of course, rely on personal contacts because of their need for some kind of reference; trust is one of the requirements most demanded for this kind of employment. For the workers, the advantages of using personal contacts are the ease of access to employers and that it works. Moreover, the personal connection often works as a "control." Relatives, friends, or neighbors do not lose interest in the fate of the worker once the position has been arranged. This is true of Nelly (age twenty-five), who obtained her job through the intermediation of a neighbor to a friendly family:

> The one who brought me to the *señora* talked to her after fifteen days or so had passed. The lady says she asked: "And how is Nelly?" "She is very well," my *patrona* answered. Then she said: "Yes, because if she is not well I will take her from this house to another one."

Sometimes, however, the commitment to the network can become an obstacle:

> There are persons who charge for their travel, but I have terrible luck; I ask for travel money and they do not want to give it to me. I do not know whether they refuse because they think me a fool or because I have been recommended by so-and-so.
>
> They say to me: "But so-and-so did not tell me; I can't [pay any more]," and in order not to let down the person who recommended me, I answer: "It is all right, Señora."

These examples, in which the intermediary seems to "threaten" alternatively the employer or the employee, reveal the double edge of the personal relationship. But the relation can also be difficult for the intermediary, as is suggested by the reticence of some persons interviewed to become a channel of access.

Besides personal channels, some interviewees have used parishes, newspaper ads, or the labor union to obtain work. In the Union of Domestic Personnel in Private Homes, a work exchange functions. Every morning a job exchange brings together a large number of women of all ages who form groups—those who work "by the hour," those that work "half a day," and those who want live-in situations—to wait for requests. When potential employers telephone to ask for hourly workers, the requests are made public by shouts of "one for Callao, 1:00 P.M."; "For cleaning and ironing, quickly"; "For cleaning, active." Those interested present themselves to the person in charge, who, after verifying that the applicant's dues are paid up, gives her the address where she is to go and the registration of the union. In the case of live-ins, the employers generally come to the labor union premises to make the arrangements personally.

Job exchanges are also found in various institutions, public and private: parishes, municipalities, and so on. One interviewee, for example, explained: "In the municipality [of Berazategui] there is a young lady who reads the want ads of the newspaper *El Sol* of Quilmes. That is how I got the job."

Job exchanges connected to the Catholic Church offer this service free and other benefits as well, ranging from permission to study at the Orientation for Young Women to membership in the social security system, and scholarships from various educational institutions in the parish of San Cayetano. In the latter, the employee can take advantage of these benefits after she presents a form signed by the employer indicating agreement.

Classified ads and employment agencies are also channels of access to domestic service. Generally, ads are used to contact live-in employees and those who live out but work an eight-hour day; agencies offer not only these sorts of personnel but, fundamentally, people who work by the hour. Though I have no detailed information about the functioning of employment agencies, it is possible to distinguish at least two kinds: in one case the domestic works for the agency, which pays her a monthly salary and sends her to different houses; in the other case the agency only arranges contacts for placement and receives a percentage of the pay for whatever hours the domestic is hired to work.[5]

Which women use agencies most often? What are the advantages and disadvantages with respect to other means of obtaining employment? What control mechanisms do the agencies employ? These questions have not yet been answered in what has been written about this occupation.

Classified ads are the most impersonal means of access analyzed. Still, references—that is, information from former employers (name, telephone number) that can be used to verify the honesty of the candidate—can serve as a substitute for the intermediary, especially in the case of live-in domestics.

To summarize: although kinship, friendship, and neighborliness—determining factors for entering the informal sector—are important channels of access, there are also other channels in which, as in other occupations, the existence of a process of contracting and certain formal norms are clearly visible.

Qualifications

Frequent allusions to the ease of entry to domestic employment suggest that this occupation does not require special qualifications or training. But household workers point out that requirements do exist:

> All they ask is that you know how to work, that you be honest and trustworthy. That the *patrones* can leave the house with their minds at ease. If they have kids, that they feel you really

like kids, or that you will not mistreat them. That is all they ask for.

These requirements are concerned not only with the ability to do certain tasks but with social and human relations. Trust is a fundamental requirement, especially when a stable relationship is desired in a live-in situation.

The classified ads demonstrate that in the live-in modality—given a potentially long period of living closely together—requirements are much more rigid and "references" have a fundamental role in the mechanisms of contracting for these services. The formulas that most often head the list of conditions in these ads include "with references," "useless to apply without known references," "with documents and references." Next in importance are knowing how to cook, sometimes an age requisite, general competency, previous experience, and "a good appearance."

In regard to what is involved in the strict fulfillment of domestic tasks, my interviews confirm that "for the young woman who comes to the city, entering a middle-class home means getting accustomed to a variety of artefacts and habits that correspond to a life style not previously known to the migrant" (Jelin 1976:14). Nelly, for example, recalling her early days in Buenos Aires, makes a comparison: "There [Paraguay] it was very different. Here one must do everything well. There it was a big house, and it was sufficient to throw buckets of water; here [an apartment in Buenos Aires] one has to be careful the water does not fall below."

Sometimes, one person is in charge of training the new worker. When Elsita left her position as a live-in domestic in order to get married, she brought in to take her place one of her sisters, who was fifteen years old. They were together for a week. In that time Elsita taught her sister the domestic tasks that would be expected of her: the use of various cleaning tools and the polishing machine, the correct method of cleaning windows, and the like. "It is very different," she says. "At home one does not really know how to clean the floor . . . the floor is just dirt!" In other cases the training takes place on the job, and it is influenced by all the tensions of living together and of adapting to a new situation.

Nelly recalls that it was difficult for her to get accustomed to her job. In Paraguay they had told her, "They ill-treat the girls and do not feed them well, they shout at them for any reason." As a result she was very nervous, and that was why the things she did turned out poorly.

Furthermore, there was a backlog of work; she ate little and did not sleep well:

> The first Saturday that I went out I finished working at 2:30 P.M., took a shower and left on the run . . . I did not want to spend one more minute there. Seriously. In the train I fell asleep. I think two weeks went by, and I did not want to be there. Because afterward the mistress of the house said to me: "Look, you do not have to go out every Saturday. If you want you can sleep here; no one will bother you." But I could not wait until Saturday to leave the house. On Saturday I would get up earlier so I could finish my work earlier. I did not feel well. It seemed to me—I don't know—that I bothered them, it seemed to me.

As Elsita points out, "at first one gets very tired"; afterward, "you are better organized," and progressively one "manages well."

The qualifications that have to do with technical ability, then, are acquired during the working career—a career that leads from home to home.

The Work Day

The length of the workday and the diversity of tasks that must be performed by household workers vary a great deal, depending basically on the kind of work and the nature of the employing family: the number and age of its members, their purchasing power (is there another person who helps with the work?), whether the employer works outside the home or not (what responsibilities are assumed by the employer?), and so on.

Obviously, live-in housework implies an extensive work schedule, but for those who do hourly housework, travel to and from the job may considerably lengthen the workday. Because of the special characteristics of Buenos Aires (upper- and middle-class groups live in the central part of the city, the lower classes in the suburbs), many of the persons interviewed spent three hours daily travelling to and from their workplaces.

Comparisons spontaneously made by those interviewed indicate that live-out domestic service offers a more flexible schedule than live-in employment or other occupations but that live-in domestic service seems to offer a comparatively greater flexibility of tasks. María, for example, points out that if she does not finish something one day, she can do it the next, whereas a friend who works by the hour "has to do in a day two general housecleanings; she ends up burned out."

The work that has to be done varies, for the live-in domestic, from the extreme of "everything" to a lesser diffusion of tasks with specified omissions. Some classified ads illustrate the diversity:

Active girl for a small family. No washing. No cooking.

Active girl, live-in. All services.

Live-in maid, to cook and do other chores; there is other help.

Live-in girl, all kinds of work but no cooking.

Sometimes, though rarely, the classified ads for live-out employees also specify the tasks to be done:

Girl, eight hours cleaning.

Mature woman, 8:00 A.M. to 5:00 P.M., without washing or ironing.

Girl with references, to take care of a baby and for domestic chores.

A third kind of schedule is that of the live-out domestic who works for several different employers. Even though this is not "work in a family house," strictly speaking, here as an illustration is a workday of one of the persons interviewed:

Yesterday I got up a little later, it was 5:30 A.M. I worked in the pharmacy from 8:00 A.M. to 12:00. I do all the cleaning. At 11:45 A.M. I change my clothes to go to my other job. It is around the corner; there I cook. The day before I will leave something prepared for the next day so I can meet my schedule. I cook, clean the kitchen, wash the dishes, and mop the floor. I finish at 3:30 P.M. From there I go to the house of this man from whom I have now accepted employment. I clean his apartment. It is small, and I have it all cleaned up (it took me a week to do it first). From there I go home and throw myself on the bed for a while. Well, this morning at 4:00 A.M. I began my rounds again. Now . . . I must go cook and from there to the man's apartment, and then to the doctor, and afterward I will arrive home.

Compensation

The first difference between the two basic types of domestic service is related to compensation. Live-in domestic service is paid monthly; for live-out domestic service there is a variety of possible arrangements: by the hour or day or week or month, with or without travel money, and so on.

In selecting among these, workers use the criterion of necessity ("I need money every day," says Rosa, a head of household with three small children) or of convenience: "I only work by the month," says Adela. "I do not work by the hour; it is not to my advantage. I am too quick. That way I would be asking for handouts in the subway, because I can do the same work, but in less time." Of course, this option is limited by the convenience of the other contracting party.

The amount of compensation varies a great deal. Younger household workers in their first jobs are the worst paid, though the worker may not notice this fact because of her youth and because her pay is much greater than what she got in her home province for similar kinds of work. Or she may be compensated by a nonmonetary benefit (beyond food and shelter) such as permission to study.

Such benefits may take various forms. It is interesting to note how Isabel's parents value their connection to her employers:

> Isabel is working for a lawyer. She takes care of the children on weekends. She now says she will work all week. The lawyer does not pay her much, but it is something: one has a friendship, a useful friendship, someone to consult on any matter, for any problem or doubt. Isabel told me the lawyer was going to take care of the documents for the children. Free of charge, all the paper work. All of it.

In addition, there are more traditional forms of nonmonetary compensation: "She promised she would dress her [Manuela]. 'Yes,' she said, 'do not worry; I will pay her something, but I will buy her clothes.' And she wants her to study." "Bonuses" of this kind are usually related to the live-in modality of housework but sometimes also occur in live-out domestic service.

Of course, partial payment in shelter and food makes a difference between the compensation of live-in employees and "eight-hour" workers, because their monetary income is practically the same.[6] Food is not generally provided for live-out workers; if it is, in effect it raises the nominal weekly or monthly salary.

Finally, various mechanisms are employed in practice to readjust salaries.[7] The following dialogue illustrates, from the perspective of the household workers, some situations related to raises and wage comparisons:

> INTERVIEWER: More or less every two months they raise your salary?
>
> MANUELA: Yes, I am satisfied with these people. They are not tight, they offer me raises.
>
> INTERVIEWER: You also work in family homes? . . . And you are getting the same pay?
>
> PATRICIA: Yes, the same.
>
> INTERVIEWER: But do you have to work more to get this pay?
>
> PATRICIA: I have to ask, she doesn't. It's funny. I do not like to ask. She is lucky; when prices rise, she gets a raise. I have to ask. Sometimes they give me a dirty look.
>
> INTERVIEWER: But do they generally give in to your request?
>
> PATRICIA: Yes, they do.
>
> INTERVIEWER: How often do you ask for a raise?
>
> PATRICIA: I . . . well, after she does [laughter].
>
> INTERVIEWER: So you use her as a reference point!
>
> MANUELA: Yes, I tell her they raised me, then she asks.
>
> PATRICIA: And afterward I go with the story to my sister-in-law, and so it goes. . . .
>
> MANUELA: The other day I ran into your niece, the one I sent to work there. I told her: "Ask them 3,500 pesos now," because if she does not ask for it, they are not going to give it

to her. And now almost everybody is paying 4,500 pesos an hour.

INTERVIEWER: And you, how do you find out how much they are paying in Palermo?

MANUELA: Because I have a friend there.

PATRICIA: It also comes out in the papers, in the classified ads: "So much is offered."

Sometimes the question of a raise is more awkward than for either Manuela or her cousin Patricia, and the difficulty may become a reason for leaving the job.

Job Stability and Instability

It is conventional wisdom to say that domestic servants have high mobility: in other words, they often change jobs. Making claims with respect to this issue is beyond the scope of this discussion, but we can observe some of the causes that frequently lead to a change of jobs and suggest that the issue of job stability be analyzed in close relation to the nature of the occupation.

Like those studied in Chile (Alonso et al. 1978), the interviewees in Buenos Aires basically change jobs in order to obtain a better salary: "I don't care if I have to start at 10:00 A.M. and leave at 3:00 P.M., so as to be able to go to another job, or at 4:00 P.M., but I want to leave that woman. I don't care about the schedule. I need more money."

The household worker is also interested in having an easier workday and in being treated better. Another worker explains the reasons her friend Vilma made a change:

> Well, sometimes it is because of the irresponsibility of the employer, let us say . . . work conditions, and the injustices one has to endure. . . . Later Vilma left that house. For starters the *patrona* treated her formally; in other words, she placed a barrier directly between them: you in your place and I in mine. Then she did not trust her as she should, because—for example—here in this house, I go to the market, bring things; they give me a cashier's slip, but I never give it to my *patrona* be-

cause she would not accept it. Instead, I write things down: so much at the meat market, so much at the bakery. Well, Vilma's *patrona* was not like that. She had to have: cookies, so much; lettuce, so much; everything in detail, and afterward the *señora* would not let Vilma do the sums; she had to do them to see if they were well done. In other words, there was no confidence.

In the study of Chile previously cited, a relationship between "work modality" and "change of house" is highlighted: there is a greater chance that the employee contracted as a live-out domestic will leave her job than the person contracted as a live-in (Alonso et al. 1978, 418). Surely this correlation can be explained: not living in the workplace gives the work relation a more contractual character; there are fewer ties in that relation and fewer of the benefits that sometimes accompany residential domestic service: assistance in the case of sickness, permission to study—the leftovers of some of the advantages that the role of servant traditionally had in respect to other types of work (Coser 1973).

Nevertheless, favorable labor market conditions can produce a high rate of job change among live-in domestics as well. Specifically, in regard to residential domestic service, it has been suggested that beyond personal situations and the motivations expressed by the actors themselves, job instability is linked to characteristics inherent in the occupation itself (Coser 1973; Davidoff 1974); from this perspective, the move from one job to another appears to be a mechanism designed to preserve the worker's independence. On the other hand, my collected material suggests that in domestic service, "horizontal mobility" typifies the passing of individuals through the occupation (Becker 1952).

The job history consists, then, of a series of changes—which do not imply upward mobility—in the search for a more satisfactory position: that is to say, a job in which the basic problems of this kind of occupation are attenuated. Even if the accessible positions are similar in rank, they are not identical in everything: it is evident that some family homes are preferred to others as workplaces in relation to pay, length of the workday, and/or personal treatment. Consider as an example the experience of Manuela who came to Buenos Aires when she was fifteen. In the first home where she was employed she was "not comfortable"; she suffered a lot and was sorry she had left her province. Through her sister she found another situation where she did find herself "at home"; she remained there for nine years—until she married and became a housewife and mother.

The experiences of some of the persons I interviewed, as well as the results of other studies, highlight the fact that in addition to material improvements (salary and work conditions), with each change the household worker accumulates experience in managing the relationship with the employer.

The Work Relation

References to the complexity of the relationship between domestic employees and their *patrones* are frequent in the domestic service literature, as well as a certain concern about the effects that conflicts produce in their protagonists and, more specifically, the effect of the continuous interaction with persons from whom they work on the development of household workers' class consciousness and future experiences (Arriagada 1977; De Barbieri 1975; Jelin 1977; Rutté García 1976).

Generally, this set of problems is presented in terms of "paternalism." The notion designates a face-to-face relation between employer and employee—or between superior and inferior in a work group—in which (using technical terms taken from Talcott Parsons) elements of particularity, diffusiveness, and affectivity are present (Coser 1973; Dore 1973).

"Diffusiveness" implies a work relation that is not limited to the specific exchange of work and money but in some way affects the total individual. It also refers to the existence of employer initiatives to improve the well-being of the employee in such circumstances as sickness or financial crisis, initiatives that are counterpart of the employee's loyalty.

Because of the close and prolonged period of living together, in domestic service—unlike other occupations in which the work is highly independent of personal relations with this or that client—the "particularistic" elements have a fundamental role. "Particularism" conveys the idea that, unlike other occupations, the job performance is not independent of the personal characteristics of the client and the relation with him/her. "Affectivity" refers to the existence of a social and human relation that exceeds the impersonal ties of purely contractual relations between the parties.

These concepts emphasize an important element of the relation, derived from daily contact in an environment that belongs to the family and is socially defined as private. Nevertheless, this perspective appears to ignore the fact that there can be more conflicts in this contact than in purely contractual labor relations and that, given the asymmetry, the relationship contains as many elements of hostility as of identification. Hence, the identification of the employee with the employer will always be full of tension and social distance, an aspect of the interpersonal relation clearly perceived by the household workers:

> There is a difference; we are from a lower class. Now *why* we never studied interests no one. It is simply the fact that one is a servant. Then one belongs to the lower circle, because one does not have a culture. [Adela]

> Some people, even though here they are civilized, treat one as a . . . she is a servant; she is not the same as us. [Nelly]

Without disregarding the conflictive aspects of this complex relation, let us return to the concepts mentioned before. They help to explain certain things that can form part of the relationship, especially in residential domestic service.[8] The following remarks illustrate what seems to constitute an extreme case:

> When I started working for her she [the *patrona*] told me, no, it [permission to study] was impossible because she was a university professor, and all those things. Later, after four months had passed here—of course they started to like me— then she said to me that the *señor* has said to her, that they had talked it over. . . . She offered me permission to finish my studies. . . . They are very cordial, because there is respect and trust, because if they did not have trust, they would not talk to me, right? We talk about everything. Including about the youngsters, when they were young. Things which if they were about somebody else, I would not be interested in or care about! But they tell me everything.

Elements of "affectivity" or "particularity" are clearly seen; the interchange exceeds purely contractual ties. In effect there are certain "favors": "Here they can visit me. . . . If it is a friend of mine they do not have problems. In this way things that do not seem to have any importance, do." And there is a certain corresponding reciprocity: "Even Saturdays, which is my day off, I buy things for the *patrona* because I know she takes it into account. I don't mind losing half an hour of my time." The interviews show that this sort of tie can continue even after the work contract ends, permitting the possibility of returning to that job in case of need.

However, reference to these particularistic aspects of the relationship does not negate the observation that the work relation is becoming progressively more contractual. Probably the growing importance of the live-out modality, the conditions of the labor market, and the effect of other employment opportunities and other work experiences (among other factors) explain the change summarized by one interviewee:

> When I worked as a live-in, I did not have regular rest periods. Today there is a law; some obey it, others don't, but if you do not like it . . . there are a lot of job openings. You go somewhere else. You have a greater chance of changing jobs. Before, this was not the case. We were a bit like slaves: we were slaves of the job, of the *patrones*, of everything. But not now, thank God. In this sense there has been a change. . . .
>
> I say there is a change, but it is the people who have changed. . . . The girls do not take, do not stand for, what I took and bore. Today, if they do not like something . . . because they do not have a washing machine, if they do not have a polishing machine, they do not go to work. They ask them what days they can go out, how many days off, if there any children. Most of them do not want to work where there are children. Now, it is different. I see it today through the many girls who are protesting.

This sort of relation, which is established or broken independent of the personal characteristics of the clients and in which the household worker determines her conditions (Does she have a washing machine? Which are the days off?), does not invalidate that other sort presented above. Both realities exist. They are part of a plurality of relationships that have to do fundamentally with (a) the work modality (working "by the hour" is more independent; a live-out job is more similar to a live-in job); (b) personal characteristics of the employee (age, education, other work experience); (c) the type of employer (if the employer works outside the house, the domestic has greater leeway and can also be indispensable); and (d) the social context of the relation. When Adela speaks of this more contractual relation "today, here" in Buenos Aires, she probably refers to differences—and not only at the level of pay—from domestic service in the interior of the country.

Concluding Comments

This chapter has described ways in which women from the lower classes enter the urban labor market. Today's reduction of industrial activity allows us to hypothesize that the incorporation of women into the labor force will continue to take place to a great extent through domestic service.

This discussion has gone beyond the characterization of domestic service as "informal employment," demonstrating that it includes a diverse number of situations in which the "degree of formalization" varies. I have also redefined some questions. For example, it is more significant to view requirements in terms of their duality (compe-tence/confidence) than in terms of the low level of qualification that this occupation requires relative to others. Further, I have tried to include in my characterization of domestic employment the temporal dimension and, especially, the perspective of the workers themselves which reflect the complexity and assymetry of this special work rela-tion.

Nevertheless, there are important aspects of this relationship still to be investigated. First, there is the issue of unionization, which is influ-enced by the isolation of this work and the kind of tasks that it in-cludes. Despite the difficulty of obtaining information about union membership among domestic workers, it is clearly far from massive. What are the characteristics of the existing unions? What are their demands, and what services do they offer? These are questions that must be answered in other studies.

Second, given the high percentage of live-out domestic servants, it becomes pertinent to analyze the conflict between work and home. How do these women manage to fulfill their own household duties, especially the care of their children? Not even the members of unions have access to child-care centers. A first look at this issue indicates that they sometimes resort to other women of their own families, who be-come the primary care providers for the children. But the resolution of the problem is always based on overburdening the household worker and requiring her do the same kind of work at home that she does on the job.

A final comment with respect to the legal situation. As demanded by the Multisectorial Meeting of Women on March 8, 1985, and supported by the recently constituted Coordinating Committee of Labor Union Women (which brings thirteen unions together), we urgently need in Argentina a reform in the contract work law that will give domestic employees the same kind of rights as the rest of the work force.

Notes

1. An interview guide—based on a few preliminary interviews, the theme of the informal sector, and knowledge of studies about other occupations—included a list of the principal items about which information was to be collected. To obtain information about the workday, the technique called "yesterday" was used; it consists in registering retrospectively "the use of time" of the day before the interview (Mueller 1978).

2. In 1895, workers in domestic service represented 42 percent of the female labor force. Their internal composition reveals that by far the greatest number were concentrated in less-skilled work within an already unskilled group (Kritz 1978). The proportion of women in domestic service in relation to the female labor force was 38 percent in 1914 (Zurita 1983, Table 2).

3. The Federal District is the "capital city"; greater Buenos Aires incorporates additional districts.

4. Category 1: instructors, preceptors, governesses, housekeepers, companions, and nurses. Category 2: specialized cooks, specialized supervisors, valets, specialized nurses, valets and doormen in private homes. Category 3: cooks, servants, child-care givers in general, auxiliaries for all types of work, helpers, gardeners, and watchmen. Category 4: apprentices of all sorts from fourteen to seventeen years of age. Category 5: all personnel who live out.

5. Only one of my interviewees had used this channel of access: "The *señor* across the street has an agency. He charged the *patrona* but not me because he knew me. Now I don't know whether he charges or not."

6. In August 1980, as announced in the classified ads, both work modalities were paid around 700,000 to 900,000 Argentine pesos a month, according to the tasks they performed (the exchange rate at that time was 1,910.50 Argentine pesos to the U.S. dollar). The net salary of an industrial worker for that month was 1,413,000 pesos (Argentina, Instituto Nacional de Estadística y Censos 1982). (A clarification that has to do with the "pecu-

liarities" of the Argentine economy of those days: one result of the official policy of overvaluing the U.S. dollar was that it had less purchasing power in Argentina than internationally.

7. At the beginning of 1984 the Ministry of Labor, when it set pay scales for rural and domestic service workers, established that these should be revised monthly at the rate of 4 percent according to the salary policy of 1980 (*Clarín*, January 30, 1980).

8. This is so because some circumstances favor a certain amount of integration with the employing family: age and previous experience of the employee (migration, lack of other relationships), treatment of the children, etc.

References

Alonso, Pablo, María Rosa Larraín, and Roberto Saldías. 1978. "La empleada de casa particular: Algunos antecedentes." In Paz Covarrúbias and Rolando Franco, eds., *Chile: Mujer y sociedad*, pp. 339–442. Santiago de Chile: UNICEF.

Argentina, Instituto Nacional de Estadística y Censos. 1982. *Censo Nacional de Población y Vivienda, 1980*. Buenos Aires: INEC.

Argentina, Ministerio de Trabajo y Seguridad Social. 1985. *La terciarización del empleo en la Argentina: El sector del servicio doméstico*. Buenos Aires: Ministerio de Trabajo.

Arizpe, Lourdes. 1976. "La mujer en el sector de trabajo en Ciudad de México: Un caso de desempleo o elección voluntaria?" *Estudios de Población* (Asociación Colombiana para el Estudio de la Población) 1, no. 2: 627–45.

Arriagada, Irma. 1977. "Las mujeres pobres en América Latina: Un esbozo de tipología." In Instituto Latinoamericano de Planificación Económica y Social (ILPES), *La pobreza crítica en América Latina*, pp. 270–301. Santiago de Chile: Comisión Económica para América Latina (CEPAL).

Becker, Howard. 1952. "The Career of the Chicago Public Schoolteacher." *American Journal of Sociology* 57, no. 5: 470–77.

Clarín (Buenos Aires). 1980. January 30.

Coser, Lewis A. 1973. "Servants: The Obsolesence of an Occupational Role." *Social Forces* 52, no. 1: 31–40.

Davidoff, Leonore. 1974. "Mastered for Life: Servant and Wife in Victorian and Edwardian England." *Journal of Social History* 7, no. 4: 406–28, 446–59.

De Barbieri, M. Teresita. 1975. "La condición de la mujer en América Latina: Su participación social; antecedentes y situación actual." In Comisión Económica para América Latina (CEPAL), *Mujeres en América Latina:*

Aportes para una discusión, pp. 46–87. México, D.F.: Fondo de Cultura Económica.

Dore, Ronald. 1973. *British Factory—Japanese Factory: The Origins of National Diversity in Industrial Relations.* Berkeley: University of California Press.

Jelin, Elizabeth. 1976. "Migración a las ciudades y participación en la fuerza de trabajo de las mujeres laginoamericanas: El caso del servicio doméstico." Buenos Aires: Centro de Estudios de Estado y Sociedad.

Kritz, Ernesto. 1978. "Ensayos sobre los determinantes de la participación en el mercado de trabajo argentino." Mimeo.

Marshall, Adriana. 1977. "Inmigración, demanda de fuerza de trabajo e estructura ocupacional en la área metropolitana argentina." *Desarrollo Económico* (Buenos Aires) 17, no. 65: 3–37.

Mueller, Eva. 1978. "Time Use Data." University of Michigan, Ann Arbor, Population Studies Center. Mimeo.

Puigbó, Raul. n.d. "Migración de las jovenes del interior a Buenos Aires." Publicación interna de la Orientación para la Jóven, Buenos Aires.

Recchini de Lattes, Zulma. 1977. "Participación de las mujeres en la actividad económica en la Argentina." Centro de Estudios de Población (CENEP), Buenos Aires. Mimeo.

Rutté García, Alberto. 1976. *Simplemente explotadas: El mundo de las empleadas domésticas en Lima.* 2d ed. Lima: Centro de Estudios y Promoción del Desarrollo (DESCO).

Zurita, Carlos. 1983. "El servicio doméstico en Argentina: El caso de Santiago de Estero." Santiago del Estero: Instituto Central de Investigaciones Científicas, Universidad Católica de Santiago del Estero. Documento de Trabajo.

5 What is Bought and Sold in Domestic Service? The Case of Bogotá: A Critical Review

MARY GARCIA CASTRO

When the article "What is Bought and Sold in Domestic Service: The Case of Bogotá," was published in 1982,[1] I was concerned to highlight the sex/gender identity relation between *patronas* and *empleadas,* a dimension I believed would lead to an understanding of the specificity of domestic service vis-à-vis other occupations.[2] What became clear was that an analysis of domestic service in terms of the most commonly used economic indicators alone—productivity, hours worked, and the cost of buying and selling labor power—would not yield the requisite criteria.

I recognized that because it does not generate exchange value, domestic service would be considered unproductive. In addition, its continued existence could be explained generically in terms of the unequal and mixed development characterizing Third World countries where different types of productive activities are associated with and overdetermined by the imperatives of capital. Many Latin Americanists consider the subsistence peasantry and the activities of the urban informal sector to be modified expressions of precapitalist survival strategies.[3] These activities, as well as paid household work, are frequently considered to be "survival strategies of the poor" and ways to guarantee the reproduction of the labor force. My previous article, however, argued that these analyses have failed to take into account one specific element—the domestic labor that is the analog of domestic service—essential to an understanding of the special case of domestic service. Domestic labor and domestic service are concrete expressions of the sexual division of labor, of a particular cultural logic—the sex/gender culture—which decrees that women's work is not a socially important contribution to the reproduction of the species and does not guarantee its welfare.

The present essay is a critical revision of these theses. It attempts to delineate the relation between the sex/gender culture and class relations in the context of paid domestic service. Several conclusions follow from refocusing the discussion in this way. On the one hand, at a given level of abstraction, it is accepted that a sex/gender identity does exist between *patronas* and *empleadas*. They might have common interests; alliances might be developed between them with regard, for example, to the redistribution among household members of those tasks not limited by the sexual division of labor. They might also agree about the need for state-supplied collective services that reduce the domestic work load. On the other hand, I am skeptical about the possibility of a harmonious contract based on identity of interests and real equality: that is, whether or not it is possible to eliminate the element of subordination in the *empleada-patrona* relation.

When they stress the need for class organizations, the professional associations and domestic service unions, such as the Sindicato Nacional de Trabajadores del Servicio Doméstico or S I N T R A S E D O M (National Union of Household Workers) of Colombia, argue that the "natural" contradictions between *patronas* and *empleadas* will not be resolved at the level of personal relations but must be defined at an institutional level, as a class conflict, and with the participation of the state (see S I N T R A S E D O M 1980).

In the empirical base used for the original article, what stands out very clearly are the structural limitations of Colombian development: the lack of employment opportunities for poor men and women.

The following sections give a general idea of how many domestics work in Bogotá, highlight some aspects of their daily lives, and stress the ideological framework within which *patronas* and *empleadas* relate. In order to analyze the various elements that affect the way domestic service labor power is bought and sold—a central analytic point—the discussion focuses on the issue of wages for domestic service as a key indicator.

How Many Domestic Workers Are There in Bogotá?

In 1980, according to official statistics, about 20 percent of the female labor force in the seven largest cities in Colombia[4] worked as *puertas adentro* (literally, "doors inside"): that is, live-in or resident domestic workers.[5] In Bogotá around 17.4 percent of the population, or

108,182 persons, performed this kind of labor; of these, 98.9 percent were women.

Another type of domestic worker is the *por días* (daily), *puertas afuera* (literally, "doors outside"), or nonresident domestic. A worker in this category provides a service in the house of the employer family but does not live there. A third type is the *empleada por oficios* (literally, "employee by tasks"), or specialized worker, who comes to the house only to do certain chores, such as laundry. According to sources interviewed, although all these categories are expanding, official statistics underestimate the actual numbers.[6]

The information on domestic service gleaned from government household surveys refers only to resident *empleadas*. In the subgroup of the four largest cities surveyed in 1977,[7] almost 20 percent of the female economically active population (EAP) was engaged in this type of domestic service. A survey in the same cities carried out in 1977 by the Centro de Estudios sobre Desarrollo Económico (Center for Economic Development Studies) at the Universidad de los Andes (University of the Andes), or CEDE-UNIANDES, made it a point to include nonresident domestic service. This study indicates that the combination of the two modes of domestic service accounts for 28.5 percent of the female EAP (see Table 5-1). The inclusion of dayworkers and the methodology used in the CEDE-UNIANDES survey account for the discrepancy between its data and those of the government survey. The time frame employed was longer than in the official study, which included only people resident in the house during the previous week; the CEDE-UNIANDES survey asked about "the ten months prior to the time of the survey." Moreover, all the workers in each household were interviewed (Rey de Marulanda 1981, 116).

According to the statistics gathered by the Hollis Chenery Employment Mission for the Colombian government (Londoño de la Cuesta 1985), the index of domestic service employment in the four main cities dropped from 117 to 92.5 for 1976–81, only to recover in 1981–84, rising from 92.5 to 112.5 with its highest point in 1983, at 116. The statistics also show that the domestic service employment index (men and women included) as of 1982 rose above that of factory and other wage workers (see Fig. 5-1). The period 1976–78, when the numbers of people engaged in this occupation showed a sharp decline, corresponded to a cycle of economic recovery and expanded employment opportunities for urban workers (López Castaño et al. 1982). In 1980 Latin America began to feel the effects of the world

TABLE 5-1.
Workers by Sex and Occupation, Four Cities of Colombia, 1977
(in percentages)

OCCUPATION GROUP*	WOMEN	MEN	INDEX OF DIFFERENTIALS†
Professionals, technicians, educators, artists	10.4	11.1	−6.3
Directors, supervisors	2.5	8.6	−70.9
Office employees, finance agencies and companies	13.8	10.8	27.8
Businesspeople, service managers-owners	5.9	5.7	3.5
Business salespeople (direct contact with public)	17.8	8.4	199.9
Street vendors	2.6	5.4	−51.9
Resident and nonresident domestic workers	28.5	—	—
Police and security forces	.2	4.3	−95.3
Direct workers, factory workers	9.7	24.4	−60.2
Overseers, foremen, laborers, electricians, conductors	3.4	18.1	−81.2
Artisans	5.2	3.3	57.6
Total	100.0	100.0	
(N)	(1,097,880)	(1,516,120)	

Source: Rey de Marulanda 1981, 70 (for Bogotá, Cali, Medellín, and Barranquilla).
*Reclassification of International Classification of Occupations (ICO) of the International Labor Organization, prepared by Center for Economic Development Studies, Universidad de Los Andes, Bogotá.
†[(Proportion of women − proportion of men) ÷ proportion of men] × 100.

FIGURE 5-1   Employment Index by
Occupational Position and Activity Level in Four
Cities of Colombia, 1976–84

Household Workers +━━+

GNP   o━━o

Factory Workers   •━━•

+ Self-employed Workers ━━━

Source: Data from the "Hollis Chenery Employment Commission" for the Government
of Colombia, cited in Londoño de la Cuesta, 1985.
Note: The cities are Bogotá, Cali, Medellín, and Baranquilla. Index 1980 = 100.

economic crisis. The period from 1983 to 1985 is considered one of
deep economic recession. According to Fernando Urrea, self-employed workers show an atypical tendency: while the sector expands
during periods of economic growth as well as during periods of recession, wage workers increase at a greater rate during the growth cycles;
self-employed workers increase in times of recession.[8]

This suggests that a correlation may exist between the performance
of the domestic service sector and the pattern of economic cycles as a
whole. It also undermines the hypothesis that domestic service in Colombia is tending to disappear—a thesis defended during the government of Turbay Ayala (Garcia Castro 1982).

A possible explanation for the growth of the sector during periods of recession is that many women opt to work as live-in domestics when they or their husbands are unable to find employment in other sectors. On the other hand, demand for domestic employees rises, according to the various sources interviewed, during periods of economic growth, another possible explanation for the fact that during these periods the domestic service sector tends to increase at simple replacement rates.

The majority of the sources consulted also agree that the supply of resident domestic workers dropped off in 1981, while the supply of daily and by-task *empleadas* rose, and the activity itself underwent a certain amount of reorganization. It became more common for a single employee to perform all the domestic service work, whereas work had previously been spread out among two or three. According to one unionized domestic: "Yes, live-in work has declined because there was so much discrimination. Because of the discrimination, and because many domestics left their jobs. Live-ins are decreasing, but there are more are day workers, and we have to do everything."

Who Are the *Empleadas* and Their *Patronas?*

Female migrants predominate in both resident and nonresident domestic service: about 85 percent of the women in residential domestic service in Bogotá in 1977 were migrants. The majority of those interviewed came from rural areas, from families of smallholders or agricultural laborers.

The average age of native Bogotá residents working as live-in domestics is between thirty and forty; that of the more recently arrived migrants (who have lived in Bogotá for up to five years) fluctuates between fifteen and twenty.

A study sponsored by the Departamento Administrativo de Bienestar Social or DABS (Administrative Department of Social Welfare) of the City of Bogotá in 1980 included 1,771 women employed as day workers. The study shows that day workers are older, on average, and have been urban residents for longer periods than other workers. Although a large proportion are single (68.7 percent), the majority register one or more liaisons (common-law or other). Day workers have an average of two children, and those with common-law spouses have in most cases been left to fend for themselves.

Motherhood is largely incompatible with resident domestic service. The response of a twenty-three-year-old domestic to the question "When did you decide to become a day worker?" makes this point:

> When my daughter was born. I had to quit my job because I was pregnant. I thought that it wouldn't be a good idea to work such long hours, and I didn't want to live in with my daughter . . . the family doesn't treat the child well when you live in; they aren't very nice to you (the mother) either, because they think that you have to do what you are told (they have more power over you) if you have a child. And the child has a lot of restrictions also. It is quite an undertaking to have a child in a big house, where you have no rights except to a room or a patio.

Only three of every ten households in Bogotá employ live-in or daily domestic workers, and in the majority of these, the wives and/or female household heads work outside the home. However, the majority of the *patronas* who work outside (60 percent) also perform domestic labor in their own homes.[9]

Approximately seven of every ten homes that employ a day worker are upper-middle or upper class; approximately eight of every ten homes that employ live-in domestics belong to those same classes.[10]

The fact that *empleadas* are concentrated in the homes of the middle and upper classes indicates how relative is the thesis (Garcia Castro 1982) that associates domestic service with the reproduction of the labor force: the classes with limited ability to sustain the cost of the components of reproduction do *not* employ domestic service. If the majority of households that do employ domestic service ceased to do so, at most their lifestyle would change, or the wife or female head of household would no longer be able to participate in the labor market. The reproduction of the labor force, however, would not be at risk. This is a subject that calls for further study.

The relation between domestic service and the reproduction of the labor force is clearer in households where the woman is the only or principal breadwinner, in working-class households, and where the *empleada* herself is the sole provider. According to the interviews we conducted and to other studies, in many cases almost 50 percent of the empleada's salary goes to maintain her family of origin, usually in the rural areas.

Training or Indoctrination?

Domestic workers usually have little formal education. In 1980 an estimated 75,000 women working as live-in domestics in Bogotá were illiterate or had not finished primary school (Gobierno de Colombia, Departmento Administrativo de Bienstar Social 1980).

The majority of the live-in domestic workers who take part in training courses go to lay-religious institutions such as the Opus Dei.[11] Generally between fifteen and twenty years of age, these *empleadas* are recent arrivals from the countryside and are often taken to training centers by their *patronas*. Because the lay-religious centers are committed to maintaining the institution of domestic service, they manipulate the ideological framework of the workers, promoting the ethic of servitude. (See the material on the San José Center in Part V of this book, and the notes on the study courses in these centers in the article on SINTRASEDOM, Chapter 19, Appendix B).

Interviews with *empleadas* who take courses at the centers illustrate the extent to which they have internalized this ethic:

> Q: What are your employers like?
>
> A: They are very religious, very upright people. They have been good to me, they call me their elder daughter. . . . I don't have any complaints about this family.
>
> Q: Do you like to work in domestic service?
>
> A: Yes, because I have learned to appreciate the work and, more than anything, because I get training at the [Opus Dei] center. That is the main thing, because they teach us about the work, and how to do it more easily. And above all, because we do it more efficiently, or rather we don't waste any time, and because our employers respect us more.

That interviewee was twenty-two years old; the next was eighteen.

> A: Household work seems fine to me, because it is very convenient, especially for women. I think it was work that the Virgin did, too. I think that we must follow her example, and do it well, out of love for her.
>
> Q: Where did you learn to feel that way about your work?
>
> A: I learned to love the work when I came here [Opus Dei].

> Here they talk a lot about housework, and we learn to appreciate it, to like it more.

These centers tend to promote a conservative work ethic and a sex/gender ideology patterned on traditional models. According to Gladys Jimeno: "The approach to sex in the centers is very restrictive; marriage is portrayed as the only institution where sexuality is acceptable. If an *empleada* has had sexual relations without being married, she is said to have 'fallen' and will set a bad example to the others" (Garcia Castro et al. 1981, 200).

The domestic workers union SINTRASEDOM runs a training program that is committed to imparting basic formal education, knowledge of labor legislation pertaining to work-related demands, and the promotion of occupational mobility. Since SINTRASEDOM was founded, these objectives have been gaining the support of a variety of organizations including the Teachers Union, labor union consultants, religious groups having a liberation theology orientation, and private associations. Fewer than 5 percent of the domestic workers were unionized in 1980, however, and even the most active groups never had more than fifty members at a time, whereas the Opus Dei centers in Bogotá enroll an average of 350 students a year, more than five times the number of *empleadas* who attended union courses in 1980 (fewer than sixty; see Chapter 19 for an analysis of the factors limiting union participation).

Among other things that limit domestic service organizing, SINTRASEDOM leaders point to the *empleada's* denial of her occupational status and the *patrones'* resistance to the unionization of their *empleadas*. Members of the SINTRASEDOM leadership made the following observations during interviews:

> The *patrones* don't want the union to be approved because it works against their interests; it gives us some bargaining power. That's why they pressure domestic service employees to stay away from it.
>
> The *compañeras* [in this case, nonunionized domestics] don't really know what a union is; they haven't had their consciousness raised about the fact that we need an organization—they aren't really interested. What usually happens is that the *patrón* makes them afraid of it, which is too bad since they don't know how to get out and find out for themselves. . . . Sure, they are more likely to listen to the *patrón*

than to someone who does the same kind of work they do. That is the main reason why the majority of the *compañeras*— although they would like to or need to join the union, or are oppressed—are unlikely to do so, because they are afraid of the *patrón*.

SINTRASEDOM and other labor organizations are fighting to have domestic workers recognized as workers in their own right. When the government refused to grant the union legal recognition in 1981, however, only the Secondary School Teachers Union protested the decision, despite the fact that SINTRASEDOM had always supported the causes of workers in other sectors. At that time, leaders of the workers' centrals (city-wide, regional, and national offices of labor unions) frequently voiced the sentiment in interviews that domestic *empleadas* were not productive workers and hence not part of the working class. During this period the union was consulting the María Cano Union Institute (ISMAC), which was also advising other unions and defending the principle that the domestic service sector is a part of the working class.

Through a concerted outreach campaign, SINTRASEDOM has gradually won the recognition and support of the other unions. Yet although it marched with other workers' groups in the 1983 May Day Parade, SINTRASEDOM still had to fight to have domestic workers themselves recognize it is a necessary organization. This is a struggle that becomes entangled with the female domestic worker's personal search for identity—an identity that is affirmed, according to the SINTRASEDOM leadership, when the worker no longer allows herself to be designated "part of the family." Clearly, this is an easier matter for the day worker. The following exchange took place in an interview with unionized day workers:

Q: As a dayworker, do you think that you'll be able to earn as much as a live-in like Lucía? She earns 2,000 Colombian pesos a month, and you earn 4,000, plus you get lunch and breakfast.[12] In terms of money, she doesn't have to pay rent, transportation, food, and uses a lot fewer clothes. So what makes you want to live out, when you lived in before?

A: It's a lot more peaceful. If I get home a bit late, there's no problem. So I'd rather work fixed hours and have some free time. I don't think freedom can be bought.

Another *empleada* argued:

> No one is going to pay if you get sick; you have to buy your
> own medicine, food, everything, and no one will look after
> you. That is the financial drawback. But you feel more
> relaxed because you have more freedom. You can go wherev-
> er you want at night without having to ask anyone's permis-
> sion. You can get home whenever you like, and no one will tell
> you off.

Such testimony indicates the price women must pay when they opt
for a less subordinated work regime. This option, however, may often
be more onerous, since many of those who are day workers are also
mothers and household heads and must look after their children.

Domestic Service Wages

The question of wages constitutes a central point of the debate on the
specificity of domestic service. The evaluation of wages paid to a live-
in domestic worker is complex. As a capitalist instrument that regulates how labor power is bought and sold, the wage is linked to a series
of economic indicators among which are productivity, hours worked,
the amount of goods required to fill the family food basket, and the
components necessary for the daily reproduction of the labor force
(of the individual and his or her family). These elements alone, however, do not enable us to determine the wage of a live-in domestic
worker.

The productivity of the live-in domestic worker cannot, for
example, be measured by the relation between the employee and the
product. The products prepared by an *empleada* materialize in her
presence, in the course of her routine duties: food preparation, housework, laundry, child care, and so on.

Likewise, the calculation of hours is specific to this type of work. In
Bogotá in 1977 approximately 78 percent of the women engaged in
live-in domestic service worked more than a fifty-six-hour week. It can
be argued that the "hours worked" indicator does not have the same
significance for domestic workers as it does for female factory workers, white-collar workers and self-employed female workers, because
the *empleadas* may have more flexibility in the way they schedule their

tasks. A counterargument can be made, however, that the live-in domestic does not have her own psychosocial space, since her workplace is the home of the *patrones* and she is always on call; given that, the time when her labor is *potentially* at the service of the patron is actually work time.

Because a part of live-in domestic wages is in kind, it is frequently argued that these workers receive higher real wages than other occupational categories (Saffioti 1978). The fact that the wage rate as well as the quality of the services provided by the *patrones*—that is, the constituents of the in-kind wage: a room, clothes, food, medical-dental care, medicines—depend upon the good will of the employers further reinforces the ties of dependency between *empleadas* and *patrones*. Because the in-kind wage is considered a gift, and not a type of salary proper to the social relation of this mode of labor, payment in kind is an obstacle in the *empleada's* becoming aware of her class situation.

Heleieth Saffioti (1978) considers that even if domestic *empleadas* do receive higher real wages than other workers, this should not be a justification for the low cash wage they actually earn. Because there is no fixed pay for this kind of work, they may be paid very low wages. Rates are often determined by a series of factors such as migration, age, literacy level, and the class situation of the *patrones*. In the interviews carried out, it was found that the salaries of live-in *empleadas* varied from 1,000 to 4,000 Colombian pesos per month; wages lower than 500 pesos were also recorded, as was child labor—generally unpaid. According to an interview with a SINTRASEDOM member: "The women who come from the country are paid less, given more to do, sometimes not allowed out, refused any type of benefits, and don't know what is going on. It is much better for the *patronas*, because the girls don't know enough even to ask for their days off."

Most of the domestic service associations are calling for a fixed minimum cash wage and demanding that the in-kind salary not be factored into its calculation. They allege that the in-kind salary should be analyzed not only as part of the worker's individual consumption but as an integral part of the labor process of the live-in domestic: that is, of the way the social relation is established between *patronas* and *empleadas*, this being a point that sets domestic service apart from domestic work. On the other hand, it is argued that the low price of domestic service, as well as the unpaid domestic work performed by the *patrona*, contribute to reduce the everyday social cost of reproducing the labor force and to maintaining middle- and upper-middle-class lifestyles.

The fact is that the state does not provide for a series of basic needs; it does not provide workers with food, laundry, child care, or recreation services. The private sector provides these services at high prices. The "activities of the informal sector take up a space that large capital has no interest in occupying" (Corchuelo and Urrea 1980, 15). The same is true for paid domestic service. To the extent that the state's role as a provider of collective urban services is deficient, the provision of these services and the low price paid for them are significant factors in the general wage-fixing process for other sectors.[13] According to Francisco de Oliveira (1972, 30):

> Likewise, some types of strictly personal services that are provided directly to the consumer or within the family itself, reveal a disguised form of exploitation that reinforces the accumulation of those services. An infrastructure the cities simply don't have, and a base of capital accumulation that clearly doesn't exist at this time, are prerequisites for the deprivatization of these services. Only industrial laundry can replace home-based laundry, in terms of cost, and this would compete with the low salaries paid to domestic employees. The private chauffeur who takes the children to school can only be replaced by an efficient collective transportation system. Compared with a middle-class North American, a Brazilian of the same class who earns an equivalent cash income enjoys a better lifestyle, one that includes all the personal services provided within the family and relies on the exploitation of female labor.

Karen Giffen (1980) argues along the same lines:

> With respect to the redistribution of income represented by domestic service, it is useful to compare the situation of upper-class professional women in the U.S. and in Salvador (Bahia-Brasil). For North American women with relatively high incomes: "The expenses associated with having two careers, such as paying a private child-care service, are very high. . . . In some cases, or at some points of her career, the wife now has to pay for the privilege of working in the market."
>
> Research on female doctors, lawyers, engineers and archi-

tects in Salvador, on the other hand, showed that the total cost of engaging a live-in domestic *empleada* was equivalent to, on average, 10 percent of the *patrona's* salary.

Patronas we interviewed in Bogotá, in professional positions similar to those cited by Giffin, usually pay their *empleadas* less than 5 percent of the combined monthly household income of the *patrones*.

The wage analysis also enables us to affirm the hypothesis that the low wage levels of domestic workers cannot be explained *only* in terms of the supply side, or by the relation between domestic work and paid domestic service, or by the lack of social recognition or even recognition by the women themselves (*patronas* and *empleadas*) of the importance of the product of this work or service. What stands out are the structural factors, such as the reduced number of wage-work alternatives for the popular sectors, in particular for women, and the need to consider the social meaning of domestic service in the development or underdevelopment model of countries such as Colombia.

The Ideological Framework

I suggest that domestic work fits into an ideological framework, shared by domestic workers and their employers alike, that conditions and legitimizes the low wages paid in domestic service. The particular way domestic work is perceived and the low value assigned to it are factors that contribute to the determination of the wage paid in the contractual agreement between *patronas* and *empleadas*.

For nonunionized female domestic workers, in contrast to unionized workers, salary is not the most important factor in appraising their employment. Most frequently voiced is their demand to be "well treated."[14] The fact that the *empleada* values "good treatment," however, does not mean she is conforming to the cultural impositions of a "patriarchal" society or a sex/gender cultural system that exists only in the realm of ideas.

For one thing, she spends most of her time in the workplace; the workplace is her "home," the space where she sustains not only affective relations but her economic survival as a wage worker. Moreover, she tends to compare her present working conditions to her former (often negative) experience in the rural areas.[15] According to one migrant live-in domestic worker: "I like domestic work, because in the first place I hate staying at home [in the countryside] because of my father, because those people [in the rural area], I don't know whether it is because they are ignorant. . . . He [the father] is a very stupid person who doesn't think, who has very bad thoughts.

In many cases, the domestic work carried out by the *ama de casa* is considered different from that performed by the *empleada;* the differences are based on subjective factors rather than on rational criteria or quality of the work. One *patrona,* herself a secretary, said in an interview, "It [the work done by the *empleada* and by herself] isn't the same; there is no love in it."

The socioeconomic conditions of the employer family are reflected in the labor relations with the domestic employees. Upper-class families maintain a markedly paternalistic attitude toward their *empleadas* and, although the class discrimination is more pointed, treat them more considerately than do employers of other strata.

According to Bertha Quintero (in Garcia Castro et al. 1981, 125), "Women from middle-class families who have small children, but who do not necessarily work outside the home, feel that they absolutely must have a domestic *empleada*—not to look after the children directly but to do the rest of the housework." In fact, the social stratum of the household influences the way *patronas* and *empleadas* distribute domestic tasks. Domestics perform child care for all classes of *patronas,* under the direct supervision of the wife-mother, but for the most part they are relegated to the more routine and heavier tasks. Quintero (Garcia Castro et al. 1981, 130) says:

> The attempt is made, although not always in a direct manner, to have the woman who works as a live-in domestic break all affective ties to her former life and become the property of her new "family". . . . Although they think of her as "one of the family," she has more duties and fewer rights. For instance, she can't get sick. If an *empleada* gets sick, she is often given her vacation ahead of time, so that she might return to work fully recovered.

Sometimes *empleadas* find that the households where they work are more repressive than those they left in the rural areas. From an interview with a *patrona:*

> Q: You said that you hire domestic workers who don't have male friends and don't go out. Does this mean that you think an *empleada* who works for you shouldn't have sexual relations?

A: That's right, unless you don't know what's going on. Because it becomes a problem, especially when everyone else in the house knows that she has been sexually involved, and she loses their respect.

Although the *patrona-empleada* relation is clearly asymmetric, it must be examined in all its complexity, not just as a direct reflection of class antagonisms. In the case of the labor relation of paid domestic service, class antagonisms are bound up with mutual identification,[16] with the *patrona*'s frustration at having to transfer something so personal—something that is *her* job, "serving her own"—to someone else, and with the *empleada*'s frustration at being unable in turn to serve her own household.

It is significant that the majority of domestic *empleadas* interviewed refer to the "lady of the house." The husband is viewed as more understanding and more considerate, although more often absent. Yet few *patronas* mention the fact that employing a domestic is associated with their husbands' expectations about domestic standards.

The game of antagonisms and identities is also played out in the way the sexuality of the *empleada* is classified by the employers. The Colombian psychologist Alvaro Gavíria Villar (1974), who conducted a clinical study with paid household workers in Bogotá, found that like children, domestic *empleadas* are treated as asexual beings by their employers. They are allowed to go out (particularly those who are younger) only between certain hours and may not receive male (and in many cases female) guests in their rooms. Said one *patrona* who engages a twenty-four-year-old *empleada*, "If I find out that she has a boyfriend, I will fire her. It sets a bad example, and there is always the danger of disease."

Analysis of the control over the domestic *empleada*'s sexuality would require another article analyzing how the *patrona* experiences her own sexuality, often with the same kind of frustration and self-control she attempts to impose on her domestic workers.

What Is Bought and Sold in Domestic Service?

In the case of Bogotá, it appears that the declining growth rate of the residential domestic service sector during certain periods does not necessarily indicate that domestic service is on the way out. The sector's performance reflects that of other social phenomena. Domestic service is particularly sensitive to the behavior of the economy, and some indexes show that it may tend to recuperate in times of crisis. The statistical underestimation of the number of day workers and by-task workers—subgroups that are expanding—affects the inferences on the performance of this sector in Colombia. The decline or disappearance of domestic service in underdeveloped capitalist countries would be contingent upon the advent of other social changes and the availability of sufficient employment alternatives for women of the popular sectors.

I must insist that women do not freely choose to engage in paid domestic service; rather, given the limited alternatives available, those who perform domestic service in Colombian society are left with no option. Women who work in the domestic service sector are the youngest, the oldest, or the more recently arrived migrants; among poor women they are the group that has the least professional training: that is, their ability to compete in an inelastic labor market, at the level of the formal sector, is minimal. Another reason domestic service is imposed on the poor woman is that its identity is many-faceted: it is at once a job and a shelter; it is a family and an activity that adapts readily to the "feminine personality."

The salient feature of domestic service, like domestic labor, is that it is performed by women, a social category that participates not only in the daily reproduction of the labor force but also in the biological and ideological reproduction of the species. However, the live-in *empleada*, in contrast to the day worker, is unable to realize her potential for biological reproduction in the house of the employer family and is thus restricted to the reproduction/restoration of the labor force and the reproduction/restoration of social relations. Such ambiguities demand that the feminist debates on sex/gender culture include analysis focusing specifically on the dimension of class relations and antagonisms. It must be borne in mind that such a culture materializes via specific situations, overdetermined by the class positions of the persons concerned.

It is no coincidence that the organized movement of domestic workers emphasizes a viewpoint challenging the notion that alliances with *patronas* and between women of different social classes—in other words, in different positions of power—are viable. Given the basic goal of the movement to do away with the ideology that the *empleada* is a "daughter of the employer family," it is necessary for the *empleada* to establish an identity that will distinguish her from the other woman, the *patrona*, "the other."

The union insists on this point: that when the *empleada* identifies herself as a member of the working class, she has chosen a specific identity as a person, as a social being endowed with the potential to transform the labor relations as they are immediately experienced: that is, their precapitalist features. She has chosen to identify herself as a social being with the potential to participate with other oppressed people in the struggle to transform the society into one without *patrones* and *empleadas*.

What is bought and sold in domestic service is not simply the labor power of an *empleada* or her productive work and energy; it is her identity as a person. This is the most specific feature of domestic service.

Notes

1. The article that I critique here was published in León (1982). I owe certain points that are developed in the present article to discussions with Elsa Chaney and Magdalena León. Manuel Piñeiro edited the Spanish version. Both articles, the one published in 1982 and this one, are based on research on domestic service in Colombia carried out under the auspices of the International Labour Office (ILO); see the final report in Garcia Castro et al. (1981).

Various sources of the Gobierno de Colombia, Departmento Administrativo Nacional de Estadística, were consulted for the ILO study, including *encuestas de hogar* (household surveys) for 1977, 1978, 1979, and 1980, as well as the census of 1973. The household surveys were carried out in Colombia's seven largest cities. I also have used special tables from the study coordinated by Ayala and Marulanda (1982). Interviews also were conducted with 10 *empleadas* in the directorate of the Sindicato Nacional de Trabajadoras del Servicio Doméstico (SINTRASEDOM; National Union of Household Workers), 120 nonunion *empleadas*, 15 directors of employment agencies and training schools for domestic service workers, and 30 *patronas*.

Readers should make allowance for the fact that since this essay is part of a larger study, the information is here presented in an abbreviated and simplified form, and some of the reflections are not fully developed.

2. "Sex/gender" is an expression that means, from a feminist perspective, the extraction of gender from the sociocultural definition accorded to each sex. According to Rubin, (1975, 157): "Every society has ways of organizing economic activity. Sex is sex, but what is considered as sex is also culturally

determined and obtained. All societies also have a sex/gender system—a set of rules under which the natural material of human sex and procreation is shaped by human and social intervention, and satisfied in a conventional way."

3. There is considerable debate on the informal sector in Latin America. According to López Castaño et al. (1982, 171): "Since the ILO legitimized it, the term continues to evoke other, older ones such as 'hyper-urbanization,' 'terciarization,' 'hypertrophy' of a set of non-useful activities, 'marginal,' 'urban poverty,' etc. We have proceeded to estimate, from two alternative perspectives, the volume of informal employment. The first measurement considers as 'informal,' self-employed workers, unpaid family helpers and domestic service workers. . . . Second, we took the total employment figures and subtracted 'protected employment' as given by the Social Security Institute; what remained was total employment excluded from social security, which could be termed 'unprotected employment.' "

4. The seven cities are Bogotá, Cali, Medellín, Barranquilla, Bucaramanga, Pasto, and Manizales.

5. The official statistics do not consider the heterogeneity of domestic service, which encompasses the daily *empleada,* the by-task *empleada,* and the specializations of the live-in *empleada:* children's nurse, cook, housekeeper, etc. According to a document of the Departamento Administrativo Nacional de Estadística (1977b, 79), "Wage workers in domestic service are those workers in personal service engaged as domestic employees in private households who live in the house where they work." As a result, neither nonresident domestics nor those who are classed as "unpaid family helpers" are considered.

6. Those interviewed were members of the directorate of SINTRA-SEDOM, directors of domestic service employment agencies (private and official), technicians of the Departamento Administrativo de Bienestar Social of the City of Bogotá, and lay and religious agencies and institutions involved in training and service.

7. Bogotá, Cali, Medellín, and Barranquilla.

8. I am indebted to Fernando Urrea for his comments on recent trends in domestic service.

9. The data used to document this section are from Ayala and Rey de Marulanda 1982.

10. The Employment and Poverty Study (CEDE-UNIANDES) used surveys from the Departamento Administrativo Nacional de Estadística to categorize the neighborhoods of Bogotá into six different levels: low-low, medium-low, lower-middle, middle, upper-middle and upper (Rey de Marulanda and Bonilla 1980).

11. The Opus Dei is a lay religious order with branches in various parts of the world. It was founded in Spain in 1928 and is commonly known as the "Santa Mafia." Considered ultraconservative, it does not accept the conclusions of Vatican II. Its propaganda is virulently anti-Communist, and it upholds orthodox church doctrine on abortion, clerical celibacy, and other tradi-

tional teachings. According to Paulo Martinechen (quoted in Nascimiento 1972), "Opus Dei endeavors to recreate a Christianity that is a throwback to the Middle Ages; to transform the mentality of the people who assume leadership roles in the society." Through formal education and courses, Opus Dei directs the recruitment of the technocratic political and economic elites. Using similar techniques in Latin America, it indoctrinates young people of peasant and worker origin. It has schools for domestic workers throughout the world.

12. In 1981 the exchange rate for the U.S. dollar was 50 Colombian pesos.

13. According to Heleieth Saffioti (1978, 10): "A characteristic of domestic employment, like all individually provided services, is that it allows for a certain redistribution of national income. In this sense, it helps delay the crisis of surplus value."

14. A study conducted in Bogotá (Llinas 1975) shows that the wages paid domestic service workers often do not determine how long they stay in a particular household. The following reasons were given for staying: they were well treated (51 percent); they did not know Bogotá (13.8 percent); they had an obligation (12.5 percent); good wages (9.0 percent) and other reasons (7.7 percent).

15. See Jelin (1977) for a pioneering reflection on the intrinsic relation between rural-urban migration and domestic service. For the case of Colombia, see in Garcia Castro (1979) an analysis of the migration of women, working conditions in the rural area, and the reasons rural women give for migrating.

16. The literature on domestic service emphasizes the *empleada*'s effort to imitate the *patrona*'s style. SINTRASEDOM has researched this pattern of behavior. A study conducted by the Juventud Obrera Católica (Young Catholic Workers) referred to this research: "Without realizing it, [the domestics] imitate the patrona's style: they use the same shampoo, the same soap, the same type of clothing. . . . among the girls who work in middle-class households, it is common to 'look for a boyfriend in a different class,' and to 'study to get ahead and have the same comforts' [as the *patrona*]. . . . Those who work in upper-class houses tend to imitate less because of the greater class gap between themselves and the *patrones*" (JOC 1980).

References

Ayala, Ulpiano, and Nohra Rey de Marulanda. 1982. *Empleo y pobreza*. Bogotá: Centro de Estudios sobre Desarrollo Económico, Universidad de los Andes.

Corchuelo, Alberto, and Fernando Urrea. 1980. "Algunas anotaciones metodológicas sobre los mercados de trabajo en las zonas urbanas." Programa de las Naciones Unidas, Proyecto Oficina Internacional de Trabajo sobre Migraciones Laborales, Bogotá. Mimeo.

Garcia Castro, Mary. 1979. "Migración laboral femenina." Programa de las Naciones Unidas, Proyecto Oficina Internacional de Trabajo sobre Migraciones Laborales, Bogotá. Mimeo.

———. 1982. "¿Qué se compra y qué se paga en el servicio doméstico?: El caso de Bogotá." In Magdalena León, ed., *La realidad colombiana*, vol. 1, *Debate sobre la mujer en América Latina y el Caribe*, pp. 92–122. Bogotá: Asociación Colombiana para el Estudio de la Población.

Garcia Castro, Mary, Bertha Quintero, and Gladys Jimeno. 1981. "Empleo doméstico, sector informal, migración y movilidad ocupacional en áreas urbanas en Colombia." Programa Naciones Unidas, Proyecto Oficina Internacional de Trabajo sobre Migraciones Laborales, Bogotá. Final report. Mimeo.

Gavíria Villar, Alvaro. 1974. *El servicio doméstico: Un gremio en extinción.* Bogotá: Editorial Controversia.

Giffen, Karen. 1980. "A mulher na reprodução da força de trabalho: Serviço doméstico pago como estrátégia familiar de sobrevivência." Paper presented at the 32d Congresso de la Sociedade Brasileira para o Progresso da Ciência, Rio de Janeiro. Photocopy.

Gobierno de Colombia, Departamento Administrativo de Bienestar Social. 1980. "Estudio socio-económico laboral de los empleados a domicilio en el servicio de empleo del distrito." Alcaldía Mayor de Bogotá. Mimeo.

Gobierno de Colombia, Departamento Administrativo Nacional de Estadística. 1973. *XIV censo nacional de población, muestra de avance.* Bogotá: DANE.

———. 1977a. *Encuesta de hogar, primer trimestre, Etapa 14.* Bogotá: DANE.

———. 1977b. "Clasificación socio-profesional para Colombia." DANE, Bogotá. Mimeo.

———. 1978. *Encuesta de hogar, primer trimestre, Etapa 18.* Bogotá: DANE.

———. 1979. *Encuesta de hogar, primer trimestre, Etapa 22.* Bogotá: DANE.

———. 1980a. *Encuesta de hogar, primer trimestre, Etapa 26.* Bogotá: DANE.

———. 1980b. *Encuesta nacional de hogares—manual de conceptos básicos y recolección* (EH-29). Documento No. 11. Bogotá: DANE.

Jelin, Elizabeth. 1977. "Migration and Labor Force Participation of Latin American Women: The Domestic Servants in the Cities." *Signs* 3, no. 1: 129–41.

JOC (Juventud Obrera Católica). 1980. "Empleadas del hogar." JOC, Baranquilla, Colombia. Photocopy.

Llinas, Mario Alberto. 1975. "Introducción al servicio doméstico en Colombia." Tesis, Universidad de los Andes, Bogotá, Facultad de Ingeniería.

Londoño de la Cuesta, Juan Luís. 1985. "Evolución reciente del empleo y el desempleo urbano." *Economía Colombiana* 7:171–73.

López Castaño, Hugo, Oliva Sierra, and Marta Luz Henao. 1982. "El empleo en el sector informal: El caso de Colombia." In *La problemática del empleo en Colombia y América Latina,* pp. 171–204. Medellín: Universidad de Antioquia, Centro de Investigaciones Económicas.

Nascimiento, Augusto. 1972. "A traves del cursillismo, el Opus Dei concreta su penetración en Brasil." *La Opinión,* 30 de septiembre.

Oliveira, Francisco de. 1972. "Economía Brasileira: crítica a razão dualista." Estudos de Centro Brasileiro de Análise e Pesquisa (CEBRAP), No. 2.

Rey de Marulanda, Nohra. 1981. *El trabajo de la mujer.* Centro de Estudios sobre Desarrollo Económico, Documento 063. Bogotá: Universidad de los Andes.

Rey de Marulanda, Nohra, and Elssy Bonilla. 1980. "El trabajo de la mujer y los medios de comunicación." Universidad de los Andes, Centro de Estudios Sobre Desarrollo Económico, Bogotá. Photocopy.

Rubin, Gayle. 1975. "The Traffic in Women: Notes on the Political Economy of Sex." In Rayna R. Reiter, ed., *Toward an Anthropology of Women,* pp. 157–210. New York: Monthly Review Press.

Saffioti, Heleieth Iara Bongiovani. 1978. *Emprego doméstico e capitalismo.* Petrópolis, Brazil: Editora Vozes.

SINTRASEDOM (Sindicato Nacional de Trabajadores del Servicio Doméstico). 1980. "¡Basta ya! . . . de ignorarnos." SINTRASEDOM, Bogotá. Mimeo.

6 Where Is María Now? Former Domestic Workers in Peru

MARGO L. SMITH

If we are to believe *Simplemente María*, the *telenovela* (soap opera) popular in Peru in the late 1960s,[1] the life of María Ramos after her servant career ends is ultimately rosy. She first endures the hardships of migration from the provinces to the capital city, works as a domestic servant, and is fired from her job after the birth of her child. When a kind male schoolteacher befriends her, she gets a basic education and becomes a seamstress. Then she skyrockets to fame as a glamorous, world-class couturier in Paris and marries her former schoolteacher in a highly publicized Lima wedding.

The early episodes in María's life reasonably capture the servant situation. Domestic servants in Latin America are largely migrants from provincial areas of the country to the major cities; they are usually young; they have few years of formal education and few, if any, urban job skills. Their employers and others often take advantage of them and/or treat them badly. It is not unusual for servants to get pregnant while they are employed; however, they never end up as world-famous couturiers married to schoolteachers. What happens to them?

From 1967 to 1970 I conducted an in-depth ethnographic study of female domestic service in Lima, Peru, and in 1982 a brief follow-up study.[2] The most controversial aspect of that research (Chaney 1977) has been my contention (Smith 1973) that work as a servant in Lima provides for these women one of the few available economic means of survival and the opportunity for urban exposure; therefore, a middle-aged former servant and her children might have a "better" life, from their point of view, then if she had stayed in the province of her birth. That is, the woman might experience "upward social mobility within the broad spectrum of the lower class" (Smith 1973, 193).

Domestic service in Peru is a temporary career for most women

---

A version of this paper was presented at the eleventh annual Third World Conference, Chicago, 1985.

who work in this occupation. Some 68 percent of the servants enumerated by the Centro Arquidiocesano de Pastoral in Lima's residential districts in 1967 (unpublished) were between fifteen and twenty-nine years of age. A closer examination of this age distribution shows a marked increase in participation at age fifteen, a peak at eighteen, and a sharp decline after age twenty-two. In fact, about 49 percent of all servant women were included in this eight-year age span (Smith 1971, 65–66).

At the conclusion of their careers as primarily live-in servants, the women are known to pursue a variety of alternatives (Smith 1971, 393–404): they return to their provinces of origin, work as live-out servants such as laundresses,[3] become street vendors, pursue other economic activities, or drop out of the work force to be full-time housewives and mothers. Rarely do they become factory workers; Villalobos and Mercado (1977) found only three *obreras* (blue-collar workers) who had previously been domestics. Schellekens and van der Schoot (1984, 60–61) do not eliminate the possibility that some former servants become prostitutes, but they do not have any data on this for Peru. We do not know the frequency with which servants pursue one or more of these activities.

Since the long-term life histories of large numbers of former Peruvian servants—which would shed light on this question—have yet to be done, the remainder of this chapter examines the relationship between servants and street vendors,[4] and reports on my follow-up interviews in 1982 with women who had been servants between 1967 and 1970.[5] The former servants who become street vendors make essentially a lateral socioeconomic move; their lives remain economically precarious, but they no longer have the social stigma of being servants. Those who become housewives improve their socioeconomic situations to some degree, depending on their health, the number of children they have, and particularly the occupation of their husbands; they do not need to work outside the home and see that their daughters are educated so that they will not have to enter domestic service. Only a few either remain working as servants or have jobs identified with the middle class.

Servants and Street Vendors

One interdisciplinary study of working mothers in Lima, conducted in 1975–76, focused on domestic servants (Chaney 1977), street vendors (Mercado 1978; Villalobos and Mercado 1977), and industrial workers. Chaney and Mercado suggest that a Lima woman's career as a domestic is often followed by a career as a street vendor. Mercado (1978, 7), for example, concludes that "la vendedora ambulante actual a su llegada a Lima, encuentra la mayor posibilidad de trabajo en el trabajo doméstico" ("On her arrival in Lima, the street vendor of today finds the best employment opportunity in domestic service").

In a composite profile put together by Chaney (1977, 2), the eighteen-year-old domestic gets pregnant, loses her job as a result, and is unable to find another job in housework because she has an infant; three months later, "in desperation," she begins a new career as a street vendor. Employment options are few for former servants.[6] In fact, Mercado (1978, 28) did find that 57 percent of her sample of street vendors (twenty-four of forty-two cases) had become domestic servants on their arrival in Lima from the provinces—where, apparently, they had worked as domestics or in agriculture, or had been unemployed prior to their migration to Lima.[7] However, such a career progression is oversimplified in that it ignores the other alternatives mentioned above, which servants are known to pursue. Furthermore, the servants and vendors seem to come from somewhat different, though slightly overlapping, populations.

To examine in more detail the relationship between women who work as domestics and women who work as street vendors, I have compared the available demographic data for the two groups: the predominance of women in the two occupations; their age and place of origin; the occupation of their fathers; the women's level of education and marital status; and their age on arrival in Lima. Unless otherwise specified, the data in the accompanying tables are taken from my analysis of approximately 2,000 servants in a 1967 household survey (of the census of the Centro Arquidiocesano de Pastoral cited above) and from a 1976 census of more than 61,000 Lima street vendors (cited in Mercado 1978).

Women are in the majority in both occupational categories; however, domestic service is almost exclusively a female occupation, with nearly 90 percent of all domestics being women, whereas only slightly more than half of Lima street vendors are women (Table 6-1). Among street vendors, women sell primarily prepared foods (70 percent of such vendors are women) and edible agricultural products (also 70 percent).

There is little in domestic service that prepares one for a career as a street vendor. The prepared foods sold by street vendors generally

TABLE 6-1.

Domestic Servants and Street Vendors by Sex, Lima, 1970s

SEX	DOMESTIC SERVANTS				STREET VENDORS	
	Smith		National Census		Mercado	
	N	%	N	%	N	%
Male	240	12.0	9,072	10.5	28,260	46.1
Female	1,760	88.0	77,071	89.5	33,083	53.9
Total	2,000	100.0	86,143	100.0	61,343	100.0

Sources: Smith 1971, 62 (Cols. 1, 2); República del Perú 1972, 476 (cols. 3, 4); Mercado 1978, 12 (cols. 5, 6).

are not the same foods servants cook and serve in the home. However, most domestic servants probably develop a network of acquaintances among street vendors whose wares they purchase. In addition, domestic servants can learn the interpersonal skills for successful interaction with both employers and other servants, the customers of the street vendors.

Table 6-2 presents the two occupations according to age. The domestic servants are substantially younger: about three-quarters of the servants are under thirty; 64 percent of street sellers are over thirty. In the case of *ambulantes,* more than one-fifth are forty-five years of age or older, whereas only 5 to 6 percent of domestic servants are in the older age group. This is consistent with Mercado and Chaney's hypothesis; however, less than 40 percent of the servants are teenagers (Smith 1971, 65), a finding inconsistent with Chaney's composite.

The women who work in both occupational categories are predominantly migrants to the capital city from other parts of the country, at least 90 percent of the domestic servants and 80 percent of the street vendors. Table 6-3 includes the five places of origin cited most frequently in the studies of domestics and street vendors. Eight departments and metropolitan Lima, are listed; with the exception of Lima, all are Andean rather than coastal or Amazonian departments. Furthermore, four of the six departments are located in the southern Peruvian highlands: Apurímac, Arequipa, Ayacucho, and Cusco. The

TABLE 6-2.
Female Domestic Servants and Street Vendors by Age, Lima, 1970s
(in percentages)

| | DOMESTIC SERVANTS | | STREET VENDORS | |
AGE	Smith	National Census	Street Vendors Census	Mercado*
15 and younger	4.6	5.9	.9	—
15–29	68.4	76.6	35.1	50.0
30–44	10.5	12.1	42.8	42.0
45 and older	4.5	5.5	21.0	8.0
Unknown	12.0	.1	.1	—
Total	100.0†	100.0	100.0	100.0
(*N*)	(1,760)	(77,071)	(33,083)	(50)

Sources: Smith 1971, 65 (col. 1); República del Perú 1972, 476 (col. 2); Mercado 1978, 23 (col. 3); Mercado 1978, 20 (col. 4).
*This sample has a more compacted age distribution because only mothers with children under the age of ten years were included.
†Tables do not total 100% due to rounding.

occupational distribution of migrant women from these departments raises several questions. Why are so many street vendors from Ayacucho, while the largest group of domestic servants comes from Ancash? Are special factors operating, perhaps similar to those cited by Arizpe (1977, 34–35) for the Mazahua migrants' attraction to street vending in Mexico City? Are there distinctive characteristics of Cusco which account for the apparently dramatic increase in Cusqueñas among domestic servants between 1967 and 1975 (as shown in columns one and two of Table 6-3)?

Although women in both occupational categories are most likely to be migrants from Andean departments, their family backgrounds—as reflected by the occupation of the women's fathers—are somewhat different (Table 6-4). Farming or raising livestock are the most prominent work activities for the fathers of both servants and street vendors; however, 54 percent of street vendors come from such families, compared with only 42 percent of domestics. The rest of the street vendors in Lima are most likely to come from families in which the father was also a street vendor; servants, from families in which fa-

TABLE 6-3.
Female Domestic Servants and Street Vendors by Origin, Peru, 1970s
(in percentages)

PLACE OF ORIGIN	SERVANTS	SERVANTS	VENDORS
Ancash	11.0	10.6	7.6
Apurímac	6.9	6.4	9.1
Ayacucho	8.6	8.5	16.7
Cusco	8.0	14.9	8.2
Junín	6.5	6.4	9.5
Lima	8.6	4.2	17.2
Callao	—	—	.9
Metropolitan Lima	9.3	—	—
Arequipa	5.5	8.5	3.0
Other	35.6	40.5	27.8
Total	100.0	100.0	100.0
(*N*)	(1,760)	(50)	(33,083)

Sources: Smith 1971, 84 (col. 1); Chaney 1977, 25 (col. 2); Mercado 1978, 15 (col. 3).

TABLE 6-4.
Fathers of Female Domestic Servants and Street Vendors, Lima,
1970s (in percentages)

OCCUPATION	SERVANTS	VENDORS
Agriculture or livestock	41.9	54.0
Street vendor	1.8	18.0
Obreros	24.9	10.0
Barber, policeman, driver, other	10.7	10.0
Petty merchant	6.8	—
Not known	8.9	8.0
No response	5.0	—
Total	100.0	100.0
(*N*)	(1,760)	(50)

Sources: Smith 1971, 88 (col. 1); Mercado 1978, 22 (col. 2).

TABLE 6-5.
Female Domestic Servants and Street Vendors by Level of Education,
Lima, 1970s (in percentages)

LEVEL	SERVANTS	VENDORS
Illiterate	4.9	35.0
Primary, incomplete	68.6	36.7
Primary, complete	18.3	16.8
Secondary, incomplete	7.7	8.4
Secondary, complete	—	1.8
Other	.5	.2
Not known	—	1.1
Total	100.0	100.0
(*N*)	(1,760)	(33,083)

Sources: Smith 1971, 72 (col. 1); Mercado 1978, 13 (col. 2).

thers were employed as *obreros* (factory, construction and other types of manual workers). A significant proportion, 8 to 9 percent of both groups, did not know the occupation of their fathers, probably because they had been abandoned or orphaned at a young age.

The level of education of the women in both occupational groups is roughly comparable, as shown in Table 6-5. What appears to be a dramatic distinction between the two groups in the categories of "illiterate" and "incomplete primary" may reflect a distinction in how the data were gathered more than a meaningful distinction in literacy skills: the servants were asked to what grade they had attended school. Only those who were illiterate *and* who had not attended school would have appeared in the "illiterate" category. However, the literacy skills of the 37 percent who had attended only through the third grade (Smith 1971, 72) might be poor or forgotten. Nevertheless, both domestic servants and street vendors have very limited formal educations. Only 8.2 percent of the servants and 10.4 percent of the street vendors have had more than a primary education.

The available information on marital status (Table 6-6) of the women working as servants and street vendors is also consistent with Mercado and Chaney's hypotheses. Only 8 percent of the domestic servants are or have been married or are living in consensual union. In contrast, nearly 67 percent of the street vendors are married or living

TABLE 6-6.
Female Domestic Servants and Street Vendors by Marital Status,
Lima, 1970s

STATUS	SERVANTS	VENDORS
Single	90.0	20.1
Married	5.4	48.9
Widowed	1.6	8.1
Divorced	1.0	.4
Separated	—	4.4
Consensual union	—	18.0
Not known	2.0	.1
Total	100.0	100.0
(*N*)	(1,760)	(33,083)

Sources: Smith 1971, 66 (col. 1); Mercado 1978, 14 (col. 2).

in consensual union, and an additional 13 percent are widowed, divorced, or separated.

The data most inconsistent with Chaney's hypothesis are those dealing with the servant or vendor's age upon her arrival in Lima. If migrants become servants first and then later become street vendors—that is, if they are members of the same population—then the age at migration should be the same for both groups. However, as can be seen in Table 6-7, the women who work as domestics arrive in Lima at a much earlier age than do the women who work as street vendors: 80 percent of the domestic servants arrived in Lima before the age of twenty, whereas only 11.7 percent of the street vendors had arrived by that age. Furthermore, Bunster and Chaney (1985) found that their servant mothers had arrived in Lima and were working at the median age of only twelve years. In short, women who end up working as servants appear to migrate to Lima at a younger age than do women who end up working as vendors.[8]

Finally, the number of people in each occupational category does not clarify the relationship between servants and vendors. In 1972 the Peruvian national census enumerated more than 77,000 women working as domestic servants in Lima; conservatively, it can be speculated that at least an additional 150,000 Limeñas have worked as servants although they no longer do so. The 1976 census of street ven-

TABLE 6-7.
Female Domestic Servants and Street Vendors by Age of Arrival
in Lima, 1970s (in percentages)

TOTAL	SERVANTS	VENDORS
Under 9	9.5	.1
10–14	28.6	2.0
15–19	41.9	9.6
20–24	12.3	15.0
25–29	3.5	16.6
30–35	—	18.9
36–44	4.2	22.1
45 and over	—	15.7
Total	100.0	100.0
(*N*)	(1,760)	(29,236)

Sources: Smith 1971, 94 (col. 1); Mercado 1978, 16 (col. 2).

dors included slightly more than 33,000 women, certainly an under-
count.[9] In fact, there is no accurate count of either servants or vendors; both groups are more numerous than they appear in the statistics. Nevertheless, if we accept an estimate of either 100,000 *ambulantes* (Grompone 1981, 108) or 109,500 (Flores Medina 1981, 4,
10–11), that is still only approximately two-thirds of the population of
former servants.

The largest group of street vendors may have been domestic servants in the past, but what factors select some domestics and not others to become street vendors? It is more than just age and marital
status; moreover, women working in the two occupations reflect differences in their place of origin, family background, and age at migration to Lima. How meaningful these differences are remains to be
investigated. What has happened to those servants who do not become street vendors?

The 1982 Interviews

In 1982, I had the opportunity to return briefly to Lima, primarily to
participate in a conference on Andean women but also hoping to

gather additional data to supplement my previous research. Since domestic service in Peru is largely a relatively short-term career for women, representing one of the earlier full-time occupations of their adult lives, what do servants do after this stage in their lives? Although I had attempted to gather data on this topic during my previous research, the information remained more elusive than I liked because of the very low status of the servant occupation: that is, women were reluctant to admit that they had previously worked as domestics. Consequently, in 1982 my goal was to locate and interview as many of my informants from 1967–70 as possible. What had happened to them in the twelve to fifteen years since I had seen them last? Were their lives "better" than before? How had domestic service changed during this period?

The changes in domestic service have been less than I had anticipated (Smith 1973, 204). Private employment agencies for servants that had flourished during the late 1960s had been eliminated in accordance with an International Labour Organization provision. Only a few remained under a grandfather clause. Sociologists working in the area of labor and employment suggest that there is more demand for servants than supply.[10] As a result, prospective servants interview prospective employers, expecting color television and permission to study as regular job benefits. At the same time, employers seem to be more concerned about hiring an honest person. In addition, there appears to be an increasing percentage of servants doing *cama afuera* (live-out) work.[11] All of these changes have the potential to revise domestic service dramatically.

My field notes are peppered with three other observations. The servants seem to "look better" in terms of having cleaner, crisper, better-fitting clothing and uniforms. In addition, the servants' territory within the home is furnished with more modern appliances (in the kitchen and laundry) and more comfortable furnishings (in their rooms). Probably most important is that half the servants I interviewed were notably more assertive in their conversation and less willing to let the anthropologist direct the discussion. Nevertheless, the essential nature of being a household servant does not seem to have changed substantially.

During the time available in 1982, I was able to locate six women who had been servants during my earlier investigation in 1967–70 and to have lengthy informal interviews with four of them. Four of the six are housewives, unemployed outside the home (including one who has returned to the provinces); one still works as a servant; and one works in the office of a medical laboratory. This is not a random sample, nor is it entirely representative, if only because it does not include any who have worked as a street vendor, a known subsequent economic activity of many former servants (Mercado 1978). Neither does it include any live-out servants[12] such as laundresses. Here are their updated profiles.

Señora M. had worked for three middle-class households in the same family for at least nine years. While she was working in one of the households, she gave birth to a son but continued working for the family until the boy was about six years old. Then she married, quit her job, and returned to a small city in the *selva* region. She has one toddler and is again pregnant. Because of the illnesses of her younger son and herself, the family is selling its land in Tingo María and returning to Lima. The husband is a construction worker but does not yet have a job lined up in Lima. While the family is reestablishing itself in the city, she and the children will be living with a brother-in-law in a low income area of Surquillo (a district of Metropolitan Lima). She has reactivated her ties with her former employers to request money and clothing for the family but is not looking for a job.

Señora M.M. is a housewife. She had a five- or six-year career as a servant prior to her marriage and quitting her job. One of her employers had promised to set her up in a small shop selling meat, but never did so. When her first child died as an infant, she was so grief-stricken that she took a job as a servant for a European family and lived with them for a year in Europe before returning to her husband in Lima. Since then she has had two children and is determined not to have any more because they are so expensive. Both children are in elementary school. Her husband had studied accounting at a Lima university, but dropped out before graduating. He works at two low-level white-collar jobs. They are building their own brick home in a new lower-income development in Metropolitan Lima. Her home is more completely furnished than those of her mother or sisters; it has indoor plumbing, a refrigerator, a gas stove, and television. She proudly displays an album full of the photographic *recuerdos* of a few vacations she and her husband and children have taken around Peru. When the back bedrooms of the house are completed, one of the front rooms will be converted into a small store for her to operate, the same goal she had spoken of in 1969. She complains about the plight of the poor in Lima, a group with which she identifies.

Señora P.M. is also a housewife. She had a servant career for about four years prior to her first pregnancy, during which she quit her job to marry a long-distance truck driver. She has had four children and has not worked outside of the home since her marriage. For a while the family lived in squalid rented rooms in an inner-city tenement; now they live in the husband's hometown along the coast north of Lima. The family has endured very serious economic hardship but seems to be recovering slowly. She would like to return to Lima to live because she thinks life is "better" there.

Señora F. still works as a servant, a trusted *ama de llaves* (housekeeper) for an affluent family. She has been employed by three households in the same family for more than thirty-five years. Starting as the teenaged *ama* caring for the two young daughters of her employers, she has improved her position to the point of being completely responsible for managing the household on a daily basis, and she supervises the work of two other servants. Approximately thirty years ago, right after her marriage to a cabinetmaker, she worked as a market vendor for about a year but returned to domestic service in response to her former employers' (and marriage godparents') appeal. She and her husband have been separated for many years, and she has been entirely self-supporting. For several years she worked half-days in the knitting factory owned by her brother-in-law, in addition to her employment as a servant, in order to earn more money, but she no longer does so. In the mid-1960s she purchased a small apartment for herself in a modern low-income building in Lince, a modest, middle-income neighborhood of Metropolitan Lima; she is now purchasing a second unit there for one of her nieces, a single mother. Her living conditions in the home of her employer are much more comfortable than they were in 1970; as her employer prospered economically, her situation also improved. She has no children but has contributed to the support of her six nieces and nephews.

Señorita C. was raised by her aunt, a *cama afuera* servant, with whom she lived. As she grew up and completed a high school education, she became the live-in upstairs maid for the same affluent family for which her aunt worked. She did not socialize with other servants, and all of her friends were from a nonservant population. Within a year of her high school graduation she became engaged to a Peruvian whose family owned a fish farm near Miami, Florida. She moved there for about a year and learned some English but did not marry after all. She returned to Lima and since then has been a bilingual secretary in the office of a medical laboratory. She continues to live in the servants' quarters with her aunt (who is now a live-in domestic) and vacations annually in such places as Iquitos, Peru, and Buenos

Aires, Argentina. She is dating a chronically ill Danish jeweler, against the wishes of her aunt who views such a prospective husband as a potentially poor provider. She has no children.

Señora B. worked for two North American families during her career as a servant. She and her husband have built a two-story brick house in Comas, a low-income neighborhood which began as a squatter settlement. Both of her daughters have attended a local university in Lima; one is now a nurse.[13]

Among these former servants, two—the wives of the construction worker and the truck driver—find themselves in precarious situations. Their lives are "better" only in the sense that they are no longer stigmatized by the occupational label of servant and that their families manage to make ends meet without the mother's needing to earn an income. Their living conditions are not as good as they were when the women worked as servants, however. The situations of the remaining four servants, on the other hand—their housing, furnishings, clothing—have visibly improved since 1970. The wife of the white-collar employee and the single office worker have much more prosperous and economically secure lifestyles than their sisters do. (The two sisters of Señora M.M., who had also been servants, are housewives in towns outside of Lima. The three younger sisters of Señorita C. never entered domestic service. Two are still at home with their parents; the third is struggling to get by as a young, single working mother.) However, none of these six former servants can be considered middle class.

Conclusions

The data are not yet sufficient to permit definitive conclusions. Bunster and Chaney (1985) appropriately note that servants who become street vendors are making essentially a lateral socioeconomic move. Their lives might well continue to be economically precarious. Neither career is very remunerative or secure. However, vending is valued because self-employment generally is viewed positively, because it is *not* domestic service,[14] and because it can be more compatible with the care of young children. The lives of those servants who become housewives may or may not improve, depending on their health, how many children they have, whether or not they remain in Metropolitan Lima, the occupation of their husbands, and the like—factors not related to their previous work as servants. However, with respect to the two housewives who remained in Lima and who had daughters (Señora P.M. and Señora B.), it is reasonable to conclude that none of their daughters will ever have to work as servants as their mothers did. This fact certainly represents some degree of upward mobility within the broad parameters of the Peruvian lower class.

Domestic service is the most common occupation for working women not only in Peru but in all of urban Latin America. In spite of the number of major social science investigations of domestic service in Peru during approximately the past fifteen years,[15] none has completely answered the questions surrounding the destiny of former servants. What is needed is a large number of detailed life histories of former servants that follow them over a long period of time as they enter and leave various occupations and sectors of the labor force, raise their children, and eventually become grandmothers.

Notes

1. It was also popular elsewhere in Latin America and among Spanish-speaking audiences in North America.

2. Most of the results of this research have been published (Smith 1973; 1975; 1978) or otherwise reported (Smith 1971; 1980; 1982). Travel funds for the 1982 study were provided by the Pathfinder Fund and Northeastern Illinois University.

3. Bunster and Chaney (1985) found that among these working mothers, laundresses earn a higher income and work fewer hours per week than do live-in servants, although they recognized that the work is very arduous.

4. This section is a revised version of Smith 1980.

5. This section is a revised version of comments prepared for the *Pequeño Encuentro* on domestic service that followed the 1983 Latin American Studies Association meeting in Mexico City.

6. Elsa M. Chaney, personal communication.

7. This is supported by a Peruvian migration study published in 1967 (in Smith 1971, 96).

8. Chaney (personal communication) suggests that "the older age of street vendors might be explained by the fact that women who are older already have children, and thus go directly into street selling because they cannot get (and do not want) household jobs if they have family responsibilities."

9. Grompone (1981, 108) notes that when families with several members were vendors, most frequently only one was counted. Furthermore, the municipal police were actively involved in the census.

10. Abel Centurión, personal communication. Also see Schellekens and van der Schoot 1984, 23.

11. Bunster and Chaney (1985) found that more than 50 percent of their servant mothers worked as live-outs.

12. In addition, see the autobiography of Adelinda Díaz Uriarte in this volume. She worked as a live-in *empleada doméstica* in the late 1960s and continued working on a *cama afuera* basis in 1983 and after.

13. William Howenstine, personal communication.

14. Only begging and prostitution are viewed as occupations with lower status.

15. Figueroa 1974, Young 1985, and Hammond 1985, as well as those cited previously.

References

Arizpe, Lourdes. 1977. "Women in the Informal Labor Sector: The Case of Mexico City." *Signs* 3, no. 1: 25–37.

Bunster, Ximena, and Elsa M. Chaney. 1985. *Sellers & Servants: Working Women in Lima, Peru.* New York: Praeger Special Studies.

Chaney, Elsa M. 1977. "Agripina: Domestic Service and Its Implications for Development." Mimeo.

Figueroa Galup, Blanca. 1974. *La trabajadora doméstica (Lima, Perú).* Lima: Asociación Perú-Mujer.

Flores Medina, Rosa. 1981. "Características de la mano de obra femenina en Lima Metropolitana: Análisis de las diferencias salariales." In Perú-Mujer, *Investigaciones acerca de la mujer en el Perú.* Lima: Asociación Perú-Mujer. Mimeo.

Grompone, Romeo. 1981. "Comercio ambulante: Razones de una tercera presencia." *QueHacer* 13 (noviembre): 95–109.

Hammond, María Elena Mujica de. 1985. "Women in Peru: Domestic Individuals and Domestic Service." Master's thesis, University of Birmingham, England.

Mercado, Hilda. 1978. "La madre trabajadora: El caso de las comerciantes ambulantes." Centro de Estudios de Población y Desarrollo, Lima, Serie C, No. 2. Mimeo.

República del Perú. 1972. *Censos Nacionales, VII de Población, II de Vivienda, Departamento de Lima,* vol. 15. Lima: Oficina Nacional de Estadística y Censos.

Schellekens, Thea, and Anja van der Schoot. 1984. "Todos me dicen que soy muchachita . . . trabajo y organización de las trabajadoras del hogar en Lima, Perú." Ph.D. diss., Catholic University of Nijmegen, Netherlands.

Smith, Margo L. 1971. "Institutionalized Servitude: Female Domestic Service in Lima Peru." Ph.D. diss., Indiana University, Bloomington.

———. 1973. "Domestic Service as a Channel of Upward Mobility for the Lower-Class Woman: The Lima Case." In Ann Pescatello, ed., *Female and Male in Latin America*, pp. 191–207. Pittsburgh: University of Pittsburgh Press.

———. 1975. "The Female Domestic Servant and Social Change: Lima, Peru." In Ruby Rohrlich-Leavitt, ed., *Women Cross-Culturally: Change and Challenge*, pp. 163–80. The Hague: Mouton.

———. 1977. "Construcción residencial y posición social del servicio doméstico en el Perú contemporáneo." In Jorge E. Hardoy and Richard P. Schaedel, eds., *Asentamientos urbanos y organización socioproductiva en la historia de América Latina*, pp. 363–75. Buenos Aires: Ediciones S I A P.

———. 1980. "Women's Careers in Lima, Peru: Domestic Service and Street Vending." Paper presented at the annual meeting of the American Anthropological Association.

———. 1982. "Perspectives on Domestic Service." Paper presented at the Congreso de Investigación acerca de la Mujer en la Región Andina.

Villalobos, Gabriela, and Hilda Mercado. 1977. "La madre trabajadora en los sectores populares: El caso de las obreras industriales y vendedoras ambulantes." Mimeo.

Young, Grace Esther. 1985. "The Myth of Being 'Like a Daughter': Domestic Service in Lima, Peru." Master's thesis, University of Chicago.

7 Domestic Service in the Latin American *Fotonovela*

CORNELIA BUTLER FLORA

Domestic service is the modal occupation for women in Latin America. Income inequality and a growing integration into a capitalist economy have meant that for many women of humble origins, domestic service is the most direct way of entering the cash economy, of becoming financially independent and perhaps upwardly mobile socially. But they do so at the risk of being tied into a very rigid and at times degrading occupational structure.

The reality of work as a domestic servant or maid involves long hours, low pay, and lack of respect. Domestic service patterns have shifted rapidly in the last decade, however, as other employment opportunities for women have emerged, particularly with the shifting locus of light manufacturing. At the same time a change in ideology as to what is acceptable work for women has had its effect on the dual goals of labor force participation for women: income and independence.

The image of domestic service is important because it influences the conditions that women will accept and their willingness to seek either their rights as domestic workers or other employment options. That image, the mythology surrounding the work of domestic service, is perpetuated in many ways. The most important is through oral tradition, the kind of information women give each other through informal networks. But the mass media also feed upon the popular mythology and contribute to it as women define the options appropriate for them.

The *fotonovela*—captioned photographs telling a story, usually a love story—is a form of mass culture aimed primarily at the social class of women who enter domestic service and thus an excellent way of monitoring the images of domestic service that enter the popular consciousness. According to the publishers of *fotonovelas*, they are

---

A version of this chapter appeared in *Studies in Latin American Popular Culture* 4 (1985).

143

generally aimed at working-class women in urban areas. In fact, many such publishers whom I have interviewed in Mexico, Colombia, Venezuela, and Chile have stated explicitly that maids constitute one of their major readership categories. Although they often speak with derision, they told me that they aim their product at the sort of woman they imagine maids to be.

How are maids presented in the various genres of *fotonovelas* that have emerged over the years? What are the implications of these images? Maids are a very important social group throughout Latin America, both for working-class women—for whom domestic service is one of only a few employment options—and for middle- and upper-class women who depend on maids to maintain their class status and, increasingly, their own ability to enter the labor force. Yet maids represent a minority of the female images portrayed in *fotonovelas*.

In the *fotonovelas rosa* that were dominant during the 1960s and early 1970s, only 8 percent of the heroines in twenty-six examples from that period were maids (Flora 1973, 73). Generally, these maids were the heroines because their goodness and dedication led the hero to notice them and to contrast their sweet and pure nature to that of the wicked upper-class woman to whom he had previously been linked; thus, the millionaire would choose the maid as his true love. Despite her proclaimed humble circumstances, she often seemed to have the same wardrobe, the same physiognomy, and the same educational level as her more prestigious rival. Their marriage (somehow, she was never set up in a *casa chica* as a mistress, the more common pattern of interclass sexual liaisons) showed that social class was not important to love and happiness in the world of romance, which is devoid of the reality of class divisions.

Maids occasionally appeared in the background of these stories as well, serving a drink or opening a door. Their presence provided an ambiance of affluence and the comfort through passive service that men of substance—doctors, lawyers, businessmen—needed in order to pursue their more important ends in life.

The early *fotonovelas rosa* reinforced one of the most popular myths surrounding maids, that of social mobility. In one a young girl, daughter of a good family in reduced circumstances for reasons of family misfortune, must economically defend herself in some way. Seeking a respectable livelihood, she enters domestic service as a live-in helper. However, her live-in chores are never solely those of a maid—cooking, cleaning, and being on call twenty-four hours a day to attend the capricious wishes of a large and demanding family; instead, she is a more specialized domestic helper, a practical nurse or a nanny. Her downward social mobility is a temporary decline in fortune, her entry into domestic service something not dishonorable but noble. The young woman is presented as willing to sacrifice herself for the sake of maintaining the honor of her family. The work is not degrading to her but uplifting for the materially rich but spiritually impoverished family for whom she invariably works, people who lack the basic human values that this woman of reduced circumstances, present as a domestic servant once removed, is able to provide.

That image of women in domestic service also stressed the *temporary* status of being a maid. It suggested that domestic service was simply a short period of servitude leading almost naturally to achieving not only one's previous social status but an even higher one. Marriage to the handsome, wealthy, previously unhappy male head of household would always result.

Upward social mobility, particularly a two-generational pattern, was portrayed in a number of the *fotonovelas rosa*. Perhaps an archetypical story is represented in the *Corín Tellado* series, published in Spain in 1975, called "Tengo que respetarla" (I have to respect her). The heroine is Natalia, the daughter of a maid who died in giving birth to her. The wealthy family with whom she lives took her in as a poor, motherless babe and raised her as part of the family, educating her as befits a child of high social class and allowing her to be the close companion of their own children. Natalia is a particularly close friend of the daughter, Glenda, who is the same age, and friends also with the three handsome sons. At seventeen she has emerged as a beautiful woman who is pursued by all the young men around, particularly the two younger sons of the family. However, she systematically refuses their advances and maintains herself alone and aloof. She knows there is a contradiction between her friendship with them and her actual place in the household. She keenly senses the circumstances of her humble birth and thus devotes her time to helping the two other servants, Isa the cook and Claudina the maid. She says to Isa in a moment of confidence, "The fact that I don't wear a uniform doesn't mean that I am not simply another servant in this household."

The women's sensitivity to social class differences is much more highly tuned than that of the men. The young men in the family invite Natalia to parties and urge her to attend, but the mother and Glenda, once Natalia's bosom friend, emphasize her separateness. Whenever they have company, the mother always thinks of a pretext for Natalia to leave the family table, where she usually dines, and eat in the kitchen with the servants in order not to cause embarrassment. The embarrassment is not Natalia's manners, because she has been educated to fit in, but the mother's need to explain who this girl is and why she is there. Thus, education has removed what might be viewed as visible social class differences. The only differences that are left, in this story at least, are the prejudices of upper-class women, who have traditionally upheld social position and its symbols in upper-class families (Lomnitz and Pérez-Lizaur 1979, 165–67).

The mother sums it up very well: "The bottom line is that Natalia is only the daughter of poor Susan." She comments on the situation to her older son, Max, who is a doctor in the rural community where they maintain their luxurious ranch: "I'm concerned because Tom wants to take Natalia to the party the Harrises are giving, as if she belonged to our group." When Max asks if this displeases her, she says, "It is just that I am concerned about Natalia. I prefer that we cut the thing off now before she suffers. Everyone knows that Nat is the child of our dead housekeeper." That knowledge alone is apparently enough to mean that the girl will be abused and not taken seriously.

The prejudices displayed by the women, basic to the maintenance of social class separations, are also seen in terms of protecting the powerless by denying them access to situations of potential exploitation. The evils of social class divisions that separate the child of the maid from her "betters" in social interaction are also seen as protecting her from the kinds of suffering that may emerge. As the story progresses, it is clear this cross-class exploitation eventually can be sexual exploitation.

The other maids in this story do not have the education or the bearing of Natalia. Claudina, the maid who serves the household when Natalia is not doing so, is shown to be a rather frivolous young woman concerned more about seeing her soap operas on television than with doing her job; Natalia accuses her of "always dreaming fantasies." However, it is Claudina's passion for fantasies that causes her to ask Natalia to serve Max, the doctor, his milk—and thus begins a relationship that ends in Max's finding her out walking in the cold and rain and, inevitably, having sexual relations with her. She is unable to resist, ostensibly because of the passion of the young man and her awakening reciprocal feelings. But her inability to resist is also caused by her powerless position within the family. Having forced his sexual attentions on a "maid," however, Max is embarrassed; both are humiliated and pretend it didn't happen. Both are overcome by feelings of guilt because of inappropriate behavior.

Finally, of course, the differences in social class are overcome: Max and the whole family realize the error of rejecting a person solely on the basis of social origin when Natalia becomes ill as a result of her exposure to the cold and damp. Each family member recognizes his or her error in being blinded by social class prejudice, and Max declares that he intends to marry Natalia as soon as possible. All are delighted by his choice.

The subtleties of cross-class relationships are made clear in the presentation. The servants, including Natalia, always speak of the family by titles: *Señorito, Jóven, Señorita,* or even, when referring to the matriarch, simply *ella,* "she." In contrast, the family indicates its lack of respect for the maids by calling them by their first names or nicknames.

As its title indicates, the story revolves around respect—who deserves it and why. *Buen trato* (good treatment) within the domestic situation is represented by it. True love overcomes a whole social class order that has generated lack of respect for the identity and even the sexual integrity of the domestic servants. Natalia's body is violated by the oldest son of the household because of a momentary lowering of respect, but his basic good character and his intrinsic high respect for her allow such intimacy to lead to an honorable conclusion. In Spanish *fotonovelas,* an honorable conclusion is immediate marriage and the more egalitarian intimacy of husband and wife, as marriage confers the husband's class status on the wife. That change in status is ultimately accepted by the rest of the family as something natural, just, and indeed desired by all, as the threat of losing Natalia through either death or departure has made it clear to them that they truly care for her and would be very lonely without her.

The *fotonovela rosa* is now a subject of historical interest rather than a current image of domestic service in Latin America. It has evolved into forms that present more explicit sex, more violence against women, and more realistic day-to-day problems. The first of the three major genres to have emerged is the *fotonovela suave,* the "soft" *fotonovela,* which deals with more realistic plot situations but contains little explicit sex and violence. The characters are primarily middle class in middle-class settings. The second is the *fotonovela roja,* which treats working-class settings and involves much more sex and much more violence. The third is the *fotonovela picaresca,* which presents graphic sex for its own sake. (For more on this typology, see Flora 1980a; 1980b; 1982.)

In the *fotonovela picaresca,* maids are often portrayed simply as objects of sexual exploitation. A favorite ruse is to present a young man, sexually inexperienced, who manages to have simultaneous affairs with a beautiful maid and her beautiful mistress (naturally, in such cases the husband is old and sexually unattractive). The erotic nature of maids is assumed, as is the notion that maids are always available and willing. The sharp focus on maids as mere sexual objects is particularly insidious because discussion with sellers make it clear that these *fotonovelas* are bought primarily by young men—often middle-class young men in households in which female domestic servants are an important reality. It could be argued that the *fotonovela picaresca* adds to the vulnerability of those women by depicting them as sexually available because of their powerlessness within the household, and desirous of sex because of their libertine nature, which, according to this view, is not held in check by middle-class norms of female purity.

The *fotonovela roja*, in contrast, makes clear that norms of purity are not unique to the middle class; in fact, it reinforces the importance of virginity to poor women. Virginity is the currency with which to negotiate escape from servitude. The *fotonovelas roja* and *suave* both emphasize the tragedy that sexual relations can hold for domestic servants, particularly when forced on them because of powerlessness.

The multiplication of genres has increased the variety of images of maids. The *fotonovela roja* and *suave* stress the congruence of economic and sexual vulnerability and the tragedy that the two intertwined can have on a young woman's life. The *fotonovela suave* implies that there is still the chance for a young woman of humble origins— one who is either a maid or is treated like a maid in the family that takes her in because of pity—to overcome her lack of education through her beauty and purity and ultimately to marry the boss or to marry above herself in social standing. In the *Foto Romance fotonovela* "Adversidad" (Adversity), published in Mexico in 1980, a beautiful, poor relation who works as a servant within her aunt's house is taken advantage of sexually by her cousin's fiancé. However, she ultimately overcomes her sexual and economic degradation to marry the boss of the cousin's fiancé, who had the good sense to fire the man who violated and continued to harass her. As a servant she was sexually vulnerable, unable to resist; indeed, in her innocence she enjoyed the sexual liaison as long as it lasted. Fortunately, she is able to find a wealthy male protector who enables her to break out of the unhealthy, exploitative relationship and substitute for it a pure and, needless to say, more lucrative relationship in marrying him. The *fotonovela suave*, then, shows the maid's sexual vulnerability but also ways to rise above it.

Such happy endings are not typical in the *fotonovela roja*. This genre also presents love across social class barriers—for example, the rich child of a family may love a family servant—but here the rich parents are shown as unable to accept the relationship. Interestingly enough, this occurs for male as well as female servants. In "Basura humana" (Human garbage), the servant is male. (This story, one of the *Los Adolescentes* series, was filmed on location in Vera Cruz, Mexico.) Elena, the heroine, is of very high social position and living a life of luxury. She falls in love with Julian, the son of family servants, who is now the family chauffeur. Julian reciprocates and determines to marry her. Elena assures him that her father is very democratic and will accept their love for what it is; Julian has doubts that he will be accepted as a son-in-law—and with good reason. Although the father pretends to accept Julian, he really is thoroughly opposed to the marriage and diabolically plots to destroy the relationship by arranging a fake medical examination and the prescription of a medicine that will poison Julian and destroy his brain.

The evil plot proceeds as planned except that Julian does not immediately die; Elena discovers what is going on and intervenes. She determines to remain with him despite the physical debilitation that he has undergone. Dealing with Julian's increasing inability to function causes the couple's economic situation to go from bad to worse. Elena resorts first to housework and eventually to prostitution in order to support her true love. Ultimately, they die of hunger, but they die together. True love does not protect them from the condemning eyes of the world, but it is made clear to us, the readers, that their death is the ultimate triumph of true love. There is no happy ending, but there is a romantic ending. The son of the maid *can* find love and happiness, if not riches, in the arms of the daughter of the householder.

The parents of rich young men can be equally cruel, as they are in "Una cualquiera" (A tramp), also in *Los Adolescentes*. Marcos, the son of a rich family, falls in love with the family maid, Analía, who is simple and genuine, not self-indulgent and uncontrolled like the women of his own class. Just as Elena, because of her social class, was able to force her sexual attentions on Julian, Marcos is able to force sexual relations on Analía. But because of her simpleness and purity (she resists at first) true love is born, and the couple is determined to marry. As a result the parents fire Analía, and the father explains to Marcos, "I understand that you like women, son, but it is really not very fitting to mix with the servants. You see you've not done her any good, and she's left without work."

But his parents have underestimated their son's dedication to her: when she leaves, he goes with her. Having abandoned the parental mansion, the lovers are penniless, but their love continues. Still, the parents persist in attempting to separate them. As a result, Marcos suffers a heart attack and loses his will to live. The parents convince Analía that it is not good for Marcos to be with her, and so, even though she is expecting his baby, she selflessly fakes sexual betrayal to separate him from her for his own good: she persuades another young man to be caught in bed with her so that Marcos will leave her. With the jolt of the separation Marcos again becomes ill and can only be saved by Analía. Meanwhile, realizing she cannot live without him, she kills herself; Marcos, without Analía, dies. Both in their own ways have been faithful, so true love triumphs—but only in death, not in life.

While domestic servants are economically and sexually vulnerable to their masters, which make them objects of exploitation, they are also feared because of the symbolic power of downward social mobility that intimacy with them implies. They are feared and hated by their employers because of their class position and the threat it implicitly carries. The maid's sexual availability, whether voluntary or involuntary, is a major theme in many of *fotonovelas roja,* but the authors, mainly male, present unequal sexual intimacy not in terms of exploitation but in terms of the natural order of the universe. Thus, having sexual relations with the employer is depicted as one of the accepted working conditions, like wearing a uniform, having every other Sunday off, and scrubbing the toilets.

Maid-employer sexual relations are often used as a plot vehicle in order to heighten problems between the couple around whom the main story is built. In these cases, the maid neither seeks out sexual relationships nor is able to resist when they occur, although she will often point out to the man that she doesn't understand why he is coming to her when he has a young and beautiful wife. In this case, both the maid and the wife can be seen as victims of men's insatiable desire not only for sex but for the power implicit in the quantity of sexual partners. Maids are assumed to be semilegitimate sources of sexual variety, whether they desire it or not.

Maids are also a source of evil in many of the stories, both *fotonovela suave* and *fotonovela roja.* In the *suave,* the evil maids generally are older women who either rob or attempt to murder the older men they work for. The boss is either a good and trusting man of whom the maid takes advantage, or he has promised things to the maid that he has not delivered, and she becomes evil because of his actions, seeking vengeance for his abuse.

In the *fotonovela roja* the evilness of maids is intrinsic and highly related to their sexuality as opposed to their reduced financial situation. In the Mexican "La ladrona" (The thief) in *Los Atormentados,* the maid Olivia, deliberately uses her sexuality with the son, Fabián, to get what she desires: she seduces him, luring him to her room (a male version of the sexual liaison, as a man wrote the story line). In Olivia's room Fabián realizes that many of the things that have been disappearing in the household have been stolen by her. He castigates her for it, but Olivia explains that she only steals because his family has a lot of things and she has very little—she *needs* those things. She also has been selling her body in order to get the money she has so desired, which has been denied her by her class origins. Her thievery leads them deeper and deeper into trouble: Fabián is driven to theft himself in trying to stop Olivia from stealing. Olivia dies as they are fleeing from a robbery.

The fact of being a maid is equated with the reduced economic circumstances that lead to Olivia's immorality. That she drags down a decent young man is shown as tragic—even more tragic than her own death, since her immorality is presented as almost natural, given the setting.

In an issue of *Adolescentes* called "La ama de llaves" (The housekeeper), the maid's wickedness is even stronger and more closely linked to sexuality. The young man of the household, David, has just lost his young wife in a car accident. The maid, Rocio, who has loved him from afar since he was a boy, comforts him sexually, hoping that he will turn to her as he always has. David is quite willing to use Rocio sexually but is unwilling to love her. Being independently wealthy, he goes around the world seeking some sort of release and finds it in a fine, pure young woman, Irene, whom he marries and brings back to the household. Rocio, wildly jealous, poisons the young wife, then confesses the murder to David as she offers herself to him. The new widower, naturally provoked, hits the maid with a lamp, which electrocutes her. The story ends with David looking over her body; the caption reads: "As a sleepwalker, he remained looking at the woman who had raised him since he was a child, although never understanding him. That infamous passion had destroyed four lives." He slowly dresses himself, asking, "But why, why?"

Rocio, the domestic servant, harbored illusions of overcoming class restrictions through love (here confused with sex), living in the same fantasy world as Claudina, who watched all the *telenovelas* (soap operas). Rocio desired a love relationship with the master of the house but was unable to understand the social separations that meant such love could never be. While David willingly turned to her for sex, it was clear he would never love her, which was what she ultimately desired.

In contrast to the voluptuous maid whose base instincts, both sexual and material, lead to destruction, another type of maid presented in the *fotonovela roja* is the domestic who represents the wise spirit, the essence of good and wisdom that saves the household from itself. While maids as spirits of evil dress in mini-skirts and low-cut blouses and spend a lot of time running around in bikini panties and uplift bras, the maid as wise spirit is sixty-five or seventy (an age at which other working women should be retired and comfortably living on a pension), dresses modestly and acts piously in order to try to turn away evil from the household.

The most striking case of the good-spirit maid confronting evil appears in "Pecado de juventud" (Sin of youth) in the fotonovela series *Pecado Mortal,* published in Mexico. María, the seventy-year-old maid, is happily serving Carlos and Teresa in an upper-middle-class household. They clearly adore each other in their house full of birds and flowers, guarded by a faithful dog and María. A beautiful young woman, Selene, unexpectedly arrives on the scene in short shorts and a blouse cut to the navel, claiming to be the daughter of Carlos. Selene is the spitting image of Zayda, Carlos's lover in his youth, whom he lost when he was suddenly called back to the city after they had established a sexual relationship. We discover that Selene has really come to get vengeance on the household. Like her mother before her, she is a witch, but only the elderly maid observes that the birds die, the flowers wither, and the dog disappears in the presence of that woman.

One evening María witnesses Selene in the kitchen declaring a pact with the devil and working evil charms on the food in order to kill her father's present wife, Teresa. María, of course, is not surprised; even on meeting Selene she had declared, "I feel that she will bring only tragedy and disgrace to this house. The *señor* and the *señora* should not have such faith in her." Selene uses her hypnotic powers to charm Carlos, to draw her father from the marital bed and into hers; hypnotized, he cannot help himself. But María, praying, goes to her room and grabs a crucifix from over her bed, rushes to the couple about to enter a very intimate embrace, and places the crucifix on Selene's chest. That brave and pious action suddenly returns the husband to himself, and Selene disappears in a cloud of evil-smelling smoke. The wisdom, religious faith, and quick action of the maid as a good spirit have saved the household from the evil powers that constantly attack a marriage. It is clear that María has maintained her powers of good because of her great religious faith. The story ends with her saying, "Let us give thanks to God, Our Lord, who reigns forever and ever."

Sometimes, the maid as good spirit cannot totally save the situation, but she can point out the error of the ways of other characters who are economically but not spiritually her betters. Another story of the *Pecado Mortal* series called "Amor equivocado" (Mistaken love) has Rebeca giving up her fiancé, René, for the less desirable Jaime and playing false to both. Her faithful maid, Luchita, tries to counsel her to behave better and advises René to find someone else. Both René and Jaime ultimately leave Rebeca, Jaime because he is married, and René because he cannot live without her or with her betrayal. Then he kills himself in a car crash, thinking "Perhaps I am a coward, but I can't find another way out." Lucita tells Rebeca, "Neither you nor he would ever have been happy, knowing that you had destroyed other lives." Through her counsel, she attempts to bring Rebeca back to the straight and narrow path of purity and respect for others that Lucita's goodness and wisdom represent.

Domestic service in the *fotonovela suave* and *roja* is used as an indicator of both degradation and reduced economic circumstances. When couples are fighting or there are problems, one very strong statement the woman can make is, "I am not your servant." And the greatest sacrifice she can make for her husband when their circumstances are reduced is to offer to work as a servant. In one issue of *Los Adolescentes* called "El Gigolo," Raúl, the handsome but faithless young man, entices Christina, the daughter of a good family, to marry him. He, the thorough heel, refuses to earn a living, so she offers to go out and work as a maid. He offers instead to set her up as a prostitute. A wife almost never becomes a prostitute as a sacrifice, only under coercion—but Raúl, we discover, had previously earned money as a pimp.

Christina, furious at the dishonor he suggests, grabs a handy dagger and plunges it into her husband's chest. Her parents had thrown her out because of Raúl and the dishonor of her marriage to him. But the story asserts, "When a decent girl gives herself to a man, it is a lifelong commitment." A servant may be only a step above a prostitute in terms of economic degradation, but the heroine sees domestic service as worlds apart from prostitution in terms of sexual and human degradation.

Most of the domestic servants presented in these stories are live-in maids, which makes them very vulnerable sexually as well as economically. However, a number of the *fotonovelas roja* deal with women who—because of reduced circumstances, generally due to the husband's alcoholism—become day maids or go out to do washing. Such economic degradation would never occur if a good man were around to defend them. Still it is clear that the problems of day maids are economic, not sexual; they usually avoid the double exploitation of the live-in maid. Yet if the woman is young and beautiful, and particularly if there have been problems in her past, sexual vulnerability is carried over into day work.

In one of the issues of *Casos de la Vida* called "El morboso" (The morbid one), published in Mexico, a young woman named Amelia is hiding out with her brother after he steals a car and murders the owner. She seeks work as a maid to earn some money for them. Rodrigo, the old man for whom she works, follows her and finds out the true story of her brother's escape from justice. By threatening to turn her brother over to the police, he forces her to have sex with him. She becomes pregnant, and they marry. It is clear that Amelia does not love Rodrigo; she is only staying with him to try to save her brother. In retaliation, Rodrigo abuses her physically as well as sexually and economically. Amelia dies in childbirth.

When her mother, Concha, comes from the countryside to try to find her children, she and Rodrigo encounter each other in the hospital. Through their discussion Rodrigo realizes that he is not only Amelia's husband but her father as well: he had seduced Concha when she was a young servant and had left her pregnant with the baby whom he ultimately raped and caused to die. His tendency to abuse women, to take advantage of them sexually and economically, has led to consecutive tragedies.

Upward social mobility for the daughter or grandchild of maids still occurs, however, particularly in the *fotonovela suave*. In the *Foto Romance* series published in Colombia but produced in Mexico, "Error de juventud" (Error of youth) shows rich people as basically good and able to overcome their prejudice against individuals of a different class origin. Doña Mercedes, a rich matriarch, is presented in her luxurious house contemplating a life that is totally happy except for the memory of an unpleasant incident eleven years before. She castigates herself, saying that because of her pride she has ruined the life of a young girl. We learn that this girl was the *novia* (fiancée) of her son Andrés. Doña Mercedes had refused to accept the relationship because the young girl was the daughter of a servant; unable to face this threat to her social class, she had sent her son abroad. Although they did not know it when the son left, the girl was pregnant and died in giving birth.

Unknown to the family, María, now the day maid in the household, is the servant who was the mother of the *novia*. She has been raising her grandson, Andresito (little Andrés) to be upright and strong. She has told Mercedes and Andrés much about her grandson, of whom she is very proud; he attends school in the morning, sells lottery tickets in the afternoon, and does his homework at night. When the child comes to the household and meets Andrés (his father), who is now engaged to a woman of an even wealthier family than his own, Doña Mercedes suddenly recognizes Andresito as her grandson and determines to tell her son the truth. Andrés is shocked but forgives his mother. They determine that they must take in both the child and his grandmother and try to right the wrong that was done.

When Andrés tells his fiancée, Paula, she is willing to welcome the child as part of her household, but her parents refuse to accept a lower-class grandchild. They lock Paula into the house and refuse to let her see Andrés. Andresito, meanwhile, charms everyone by his grace, intelligence, and liveliness. He even invents a way to rescue Paula: he sneaks into the house and changes clothes with her, allowing her to escape. When he is discovered by the gardener and chauffeur, he is beaten soundly but eventually makes it back home. He announces, "They say that mothers suffer much when they have a child. It is only fair that I suffer a little bit in order to have you as a mother. Isn't that so?" All are happily reunited, and again it is affirmed that social class is unimportant. Love—both between men and women and between children and parents and grandparents—is able to overcome all obstacles.

The *fotonovela suave* retains the romantic notion that love conquers all, with happy endings the rule. Like the *fotonovela rosa,* it shows that servants' relations with people outside their social class can lead to love fulfilled and economic problems resolved. The *fotonovela roja* is more pessimistic.

In the sample of 150 *fotonovelas* randomly chosen from among the most popular sold in Mexico, Colombia, Peru, Chile, and Argentina between 1979 and 1981, about 20 percent included maids in the cast of characters, especially in the *fotonovelas roja,* which dealt heavily with sex and violence. During that period the dominance of the *roja* was very strong, despite attempts in Mexico to censor their explicit sexuality.

The consistent pessimism in the *roja* about the chances that live-in domestic servants can ultimately find either economic independence or sexual integrity can be seen as reinforcing the trend toward work by the day. The shift away from live-in work has been quite marked in the past decade. Improved economic conditions in some countries gave women other options of employment, and the *fotonovelas*—by focusing on the strong negative aspects of live-in domestic service, particularly the sexual vulnerability and possible sexual degradation, and by presenting domestic work as something of last resort rather than an opportunity for upward social mobility—helped provide the basic ideological superstructure that made manifest the actual conditions of work as a maid.

Interestingly enough, none of the *fotonovelas* stresses the hard, physical labor that maids do; instead, they emphasize the threat to the integrity of the person implicit in the role of domestic servant. That integrity is assaulted sexually, economically, and by lack of respect from others. In terms of ideology, the personal integrity of the woman, more than the hard physical labor or low pay, can be seen as a motivation for women to seek any other sort of employment than that of domestic service.

There is little difference in the proportion of *fotonovelas suave* and *roja* currently featuring domestic servants: 15 percent of the *fotonovelas suave,* show maids, compared to 16 percent of the *fotonovelas roja.* There *is* a big difference depending upon where the *fotonovelas* are produced: only those from Mexico show maids who have a major part in the story *because* of their situation as maids. In those stories, the status of domestic servant makes a difference in the development of the plot. None of the *fotonovelas* produced in Colombia and only one from Venezuela show any domestic servants, and none of these has a maid as a principal actor in the plot.

Seventy *fotonovelas* were analyzed from the Southern Cone (Argentina, Chile and Uruguay)—the majority published in Argentina, although all of them were produced in Italy, then translated and published in Argentina at a very large profit to an ever increasing number of publishing firms. Maids appear in 10 percent of these; however, in only one does the maid have an important role in the plot. In the others, she is either part of the background—simply someone who opens doors, answers the phone, or relays information—or the narrator. Or she may have a very small role as a good spirit who sees that evil is occurring and acts as a Greek chorus trying somehow to stop or at least make less extreme what clearly is destined to happen. All the good-spirit maids are elderly and often heavy, in sharp contrast to the ravishingly beautiful heroines. In one case a male servant, the gardener, plays the good spirit role.

The good spirit in the *fotonovelas* from the Southern Cone has a much less active role than those portrayed in the *fotonovelas roja* produced in Mexico. The one exception among the seventy analyzed is in a series of medium circulation, *Ideliofilm,* called "Reflejos del ayer" (Reflections of yesterday). It was published by one of the original major *fotonovela* houses in Buenos Aires, Editorial Abril, translated from the Italian, and was purchased in Chile.

In "Reflections of yesterday," we are introduced to Mercedes, who describes herself as "beautiful, rich, and nevertheless more alone than ever." Laura is her maid, also young and beautiful—but clearly not rich. Mercedes is constantly pursued by young men seeking her fortune and not loving her for herself. Determined to unmask them, she announces to her suitors that she is very ill and has only a few months to live. The two rich suitors ask to marry her immediately. The poor suitor, Ricardo, dramatically leaves, presumably overcome with grief, but it is clear that he has something going with the maid as well as the mistress. Laura and Ricardo are plotting to get the fortune of Mercedes, although Ricardo is faithless even to his accomplice.

Little by little each of the suitors is unmasked and shown to be after Mercedes for her money. Still, she loves Rick, the poor one. Eventually, not only do she and Rick declare their eternal love, but the other two suitors find romance with women of their own economic level. Only Laura is left alone—the worst of fates in *fotonovelas* Her economic vulnerability as a maid allowed her to be used by a man seeking access to another woman. The maid is important to give him advantage in the love story, but her fate is not supposed to be of concern to the reader. Her social station leaves her out as a main character, although she is shown in almost one-quarter of the photos.

Live-in employees do at times appear in the Southern Cone *fotonovelas* as evil presences. In one such story the live-in help is not a maid but a private secretary working with a male accomplice who attempts to seduce her young and beautiful employer. The secretary cooperates with him to steal jewels and money from her mistress. Like the maid in "Reflections of yesterday," the private secretary loses her man. But in this case, because she is of higher social status, another man appears to take his place. The private secretary can achieve love; the maid cannot. The secretary is able to interact socially with the mistress and her friends, in sharp contrast to the maid, who is totally left out. The maid has less ability to defend herself in the exclusive social circles so often portrayed in the *fotonovela* of the Southern Cone.

In Mexico, Central America, and the Andean region, *fotonovelas* cost less than a pack of cigarettes and are recirculated through neighborhood rental businesses; in the Southern Cone they are more expensive. In Chile, the few that have managed to survive the economic crisis are aimed at a more middle-class audience. Data from the Lord Cochran publishing company show that after the 1973 military coup, the declining purchasing power of the working class vis-à-vis the middle-class meant a very rapid decline in sales of *fotonovelas* compared to a much more modest decline in the sale of middle-class women's magazines such as *Paula* and *Vanidades*. This suggests that the more peripheral role of maids in the Southern Cone *fotonovelas* reflects a class bias in the readership, as well as the lack of acquisitive power of women who are maids.

Since the publishers in Argentina choose from the total Italian production, one can argue that the Southern Cone *fotonovelas* reflect to a degree the customs and desires of Southern Cone countries, based on what the publishers believe will sell. The people interviewed in Buenos Aires at Editorial Abril thought that the majority of their readers were people in the provinces but of a higher educational level than ordinary domestic servants. The portrayal of domestic servants also may represent the changing educational levels of young women in both Italy and the Southern Cone countries, where there are options other than being a maid when the economy improves.

Domestic service continues to be presented as an option for women in *fotonovelas*, but it is shown as a poor option, superior only to prostitution and begging. Domestic service is decreasingly depicted as a mechanism of social mobility and increasingly as a vehicle for exploitative cross-class relations, both sexual and economic. Even when maid-master love occurs, class prejudice condemns the lovers to a hideous death. The solution to the problem of exploitation is death— never collective action. Fatalism is emphasized by not confronting the situation.

In Southern Cone *fotonovelas*, maids form part of the background, indicating the social status of the major characters. Only for domestics, particularly elderly ones, who serve as protectors from the evil that constantly threatens true love, is sexual and economic vulnerability not an issue. Sexual vulnerability is avoided by age, and economic vulnerability is ignored: the dear little old lady remains with the household as a domestic servant out of love and loyalty, not economic necessity. When the economic vulnerability of the maid is mixed with her sexual aggressiveness (almost always in stories written by men), the maid herself becomes the evil spirit threatening the peace of the upper-middle-class household.

The shift in *fotonovela* genres since 1970 eliminates hope from the maid's role and provides no new positive images with which working-class women would wish to identify. The negative images more accurately reflect the position of the domestic servant in society.

References

Flora, Cornelia Butler. 1973. "The Passive Female and Social Change: A Cross-Cultural Comparison of Women's Magazine Fiction." In Ann Pescatello, ed., *Female and Male in Latin America,* pp. 59–86. Pittsburgh: University of Pittsburgh Press.

——. 1980a. "Women in Latin American Fotonovelas: From Cinderella to Mata Hari." *Women's Studies: An International Quarterly* 3, no. 1:95–104.

——. 1980b. "Fotonovelas: Message Creation and Reception." *Journal of Popular Culture* 14, no. 3:525–34.

——. 1982. "The Fotonovela in Latin America." *Studies in Latin American Popular Culture* 1:15–26.

——. 1985. "Maids in the Mexican Photonovel." *Studies in Latin American Popular Culture* 4:84–94.

Lomnitz, Larissa, and Marisol Pérez-Lizaur. 1979. "Kinship Structure and the Role of Women in the Urban Upper Class of Mexico." *Signs* 5, no. 1:164–168.

8 Domestic Workers in the Caribbean

PATRICIA MOHAMMED

That there is a negative value placed on housework and household workers in the Caribbean is painfully clear. For instance, the Industrial Relations Act (1972) of Trinidad and Tobago decrees that "household workers" are not workers under the law; therefore, they do not come under the protection of labor laws designed to look after the interests of workers in this country. Significantly also, in all the territories of the Caribbean, the gross national product and national income accounts do not include the value of household work and related activities.

Granted, there are numerous difficulties in trying to impute a monetary or social value to housework; whether paid or unpaid, it is viewed as "non-work." Additionally, it is assigned a negative and very often demeaning status in the hierarchy of work roles. The domestic worker therefore automatically has low status in a society whose definitions of social class rely on occupational classification.

Of even greater concern is the fact that domestic labor comprises some of the most repetitive, tedious, unfulfilling, and unrewarding tasks; that it is normally carried out in isolation from other workers; and that women constitute the large majority of domestic workers. These workers are among the most exploited in the labor market today.

There are several reasons why such low value is attached to housework. Most of us do not understand that domestic labor is basic to the society and, in fact, involves the reproduction of daily life itself. Who has sifted through the details of the housewife's day, the early morning chaos of rushed breakfasts, unmade beds, unswept floors, mountains of wash, trips to shops and markets—all this tied in perhaps with the unceasing demands of young children? Such are the activities that

This chapter appeared in Patricia Ellis, ed., *Women in the Caribbean* (London: Zed Press, 1987). Reprinted with permission of the author and the Women and Development Unit (WAND), University of the West Indies, Barbados.

161

are dumped into the laps of the domestic worker. This kind of work, repeated over and over, becomes monotonous, mindless, uninspiring. And at the end of it all the meals have been eaten, the house is untidy, and clothes are soiled; no evidence of productive labor remains to show the effort that has gone into it.

"Work" as we know it has come to be associated with labor outside the home, done for a wage or salary, where the mental or manual labor that has gone into it remains concretely evident. Under the present economic system a high value is placed on skills training, and education and rewards are naturally higher in those areas where skilled or trained labor is in lower supply. Therefore, housework, which requires little formal training, is given a very low rating. In addition, the skewed and highly distorted value system of our postcolonial societies continues to place white-collar occupations and interests far above those not requiring formal education.

Why are most domestic workers women? Housework has historically been assigned to women as their domain of work, an assignment that has come to be accepted in many cultures throughout the world. This relation of household tasks to women evolved out of the interplay between women's biological makeup—that is, their capacity to reproduce the society and thus the labor force—and the demands of the economy to produce surplus goods and services for the survival and reproduction of the society. It is not, as is popularly believed, the "natural" domain of women. Traditionally though, this cultural assignment has withstood many generations, and women are prepared from early childhood, through the socialization process within the family, for the roles of housekeeping and child rearing. Within the formal education system this tradition continues, for implicit in their training is the view that they are to become good mothers, wives, and housekeepers, while men are prepared for the roles of breadwinners in the family.

In the history of Caribbean society, however, the majority of women have carried a double role, economically supporting their families as well as performing all the daily household chores. With the shift from agriculture to industrialization, women who formerly worked as unskilled laborers in agriculture were forced into the new labor market, many of them unprepared for the kinds of skills now demanded of the labor force. Many women must thus seek employment in the only area in which they are "trained"—that of the domestic service. With the expansion of the education system, the state, and the private sector, more job opportunities have become available to women, but here they are faced with a continuing battle to compete for jobs with the male labor force.

In the more developed and larger economies of the Caribbean, such as Trinidad and Jamaica, more jobs outside the home have become available to women. Hence, more employed women in these countries require domestic help, and as a result there is greater demand for domestic servants among the upper and middle classes in these societies. The availability of jobs as well as the dire need for employment shift women from rural to urban communities, from the smaller to the larger Caribbean islands, and from the Caribbean itself to such countries as the United States and Canada.

A significant point to note about this shift of labor is that it involves many young women between the ages of eighteen and twenty-five. Their need to find and retain a job sometimes places these women in very vulnerable positions. They accept jobs under unfair and possibly highly exploitative conditions. A large proportion of unskilled workers makes for greater supply than demand and thus for an easily expendable labor force. This partly explains the kinds of wages and oppressive conditions faced by domestic workers.

The available statistics on occupational and industry groups in the Caribbean give an indication of the extent to which women dominate domestic service. The category usually described as "service worker" refers largely to domestic servants. In this category in Barbados in 1960, 69 percent of the workers were female; the proportion had fallen to 65 percent by 1970.

Harewood (1975) argues for Trinidad and Tobago that there was an increase in the number of domestic servants employed in this country between 1946 and 1960, with this category being the largest source of employment for female labor. More than one-third of the women employed in domestic service in 1960 were from the neighboring Commonwealth Caribbean islands.

For Jamaica, Boland (1974, 75) notes that "the most significant changes (in industry) have been experienced by the Service Industries and, in particular, the Personal Services which continue to employ many more women than men." Boland points out that according to the censuses of 1946, 1960, and 1970, the service sector consistently has been the largest single employer of female labor, accounting for over half of the female labor force. The number of males actually employed in domestic service in 1960 was 6,841; females numbered

69,157 in this year. By 1970 the number of males in domestic service had fallen to 4,293, females to 43,690.

The decrease in the absolute number of women employed as domestic servants was balanced by an increase in female employment in such other service areas as health, community, and education. It is interesting to note that these are areas in which women in Caribbean society have tended to predominate over time, as changes have occurred in both technological developments and social attitudes to women's work outside the home. They are, noticeably, areas that are deemed female-oriented and are spinoffs from tasks carried out in the domestic sphere.

Working Conditions

A study carried out by the Housewives Association of Trinidad and Tobago HATT (1975) yields some vital and formerly undocumented information on the conditions under which domestic workers are employed.[1] Although this study was done in Trinidad, the similarities between the islands make the findings relevant also to the situation of domestic workers in the other regions of the Caribbean. The HATT study was carried out in two phases: the first involved preliminary research into the conditions of domestic workers; the second, a sample survey of selected household workers and selected households.

The study identified four types of household workers: live-in, whole-day, half-day, and part-time servants. The duties performed by these workers ranged from general housework such as cleaning and washing to specialized services such as child care and ironing. Some of the workers questioned in the survey were found to be working very long hours: over 50 percent worked more than eight hours per day. Sleep-in workers tended to work the longest hours, sometimes more than twelve a day (25 percent of the respondents). Further, 32 percent worked six and a half to seven days a week; 29 percent worked five and a half to six days a week.

Domestic workers are given no protection against sickness, maternity, or old age disabilities, and their low wages make it impossible for them to provide adequately for such needs on their own. At the time of the survey in 1975, the average weekly wage for household workers was $15 TT.[2] At that time there was no legally stipulated or informally accepted minimum wage for domestic workers; rather, wages and other conditions of work were determined in a private agreement between employer and employee, and benefits to the worker, if any, depended on the generosity of the individual employer. One of the strong recommendations at the conclusion of the study was the "need for minimum wages and conditions of work to be fixed, to be accepted and used by the community on a voluntary basis in the first instance, but eventually as part of legislation providing for minimum wages and conditions of service for all workers" (HATT 1975).

Several other important findings emerged from this study. Live-in domestic workers complained of inadequate accommodation and of improper and discourteous modes of address from their employers and employers' offspring. In some cases, there were stringent and unhealthy restrictions on the visitors they were permitted to have. On the other hand, employers complained of dissatisfaction with the service provided by household workers and the abuse of privileges extended to them.

An interesting picture emerges of the entire domestic employee/employer relationship in the society. Despite the obvious and growing dependency of working and professional women on the services provided by domestic workers and, obversely, the need for many women to find employment as domestic servants, there exists a strong element of distrust between employer and employee, rooted in the class differences between these women. This is especially curious in the light of the particular work situation of the domestic employee, which implies a certain level of intimacy and confidence between employer and employee.

The proposal by Minimum Wages Board appointed in 1979 that minimum wages for domestic workers be set at $45 TT weekly generated a spate of letters to the media in Trinidad and Tobago. The exchange gives a clear indication of the sentiments existing on both sides. The *Trinidad Guardian* (May 16, 1979) carried a letter written by one disgruntled female employer who suggested that domestic servants were already overpaid and overindulged. She viewed domestic servants as "sly, lazy and overpaid" and was especially condemnatory of the theft of costly items by maids. She was also vehement about the quantity and cost of the food consumed by domestics at their place of work.

A reply to this kind of censure, as well as to the proposal of the Minimum Wages Board, was published in the same newspaper (June

25, 1979) and captioned "A Maid's Eye View." This long letter by a particularly outspoken and articulate domestic servant, Eliza Olli-vierre of Port-of-Spain, asserted that the wages proposed by the board were below those already received by maids and were highly unre-alistic in the light of the cost of living. She was scathing in her com-ments on the treatment meted out to domestic workers at the hands of their employers, and on the practice of some more fortunate mem-bers of the society of hiring a maid purely as a status symbol when in economic terms they cannot actually afford one. Other letters and articles in the daily newspapers of the same period expressed the view that many domestics are expected to work extra time for no extra pay (*Trinidad Express,* June 12, 1979), as well as being underpaid and un-derprotected. One article noted that the latter problems are especially severe in Guyana.

Recent Developments in Legislation

Over the years since the HATT study, the plight of household work-ers has been given special consideration in several of the Caribbean territories. As already hinted, in Trinidad and Tobago this has taken the form of the establishment of a Minimum Wages Board to propose fair wage and working conditions. According to legislation that came into effect in January 1980, household assistants were to be paid a weekly wage of $55 TT during 1980 and $70 TT during 1981 for a forty-four-hour work week, spread over six days.[3] For the first time the working hours of this category of worker were stipulated. Even living-in and receiving meals was to have no bearing on the stipend proposed by the board. Another first in the conditions of household workers was that they were to enjoy public holidays as all other citizens.

By 1982 domestic employees in Trinidad were represented by their own union, the National Union of Domestic Employees (NUDE), run solely by women and headed by Clotil Walcott, a long-time fighter for women's rights. Walcott had organized a group of domestic em-ployees and had been agitating for several years before the union gained recognition in 1982. NUDE is now very vocal in the cause of domestic employees in Trinidad and Tobago.

The situation of domestics in Barbados is less favorable. The one piece of legislation that exists for their protection is the Domestic Employees' Hours of Duty Act. This law states that a domestic servant should not work more than eight hours a day except by special agreement with the employer and sets a fine of $25 BDOS for the employer who breaks this regulation.[4] By 1982 there was still no legislation fixing a minimum wage for domestic employees.

In Guyana there is little or no legal protection existing for domestics. By 1979 Guyana had enacted no minimum wage agreement for domestic workers; in fact, the minimum wage for other categories of work—$11 G per day—did not apply to domestic workers.[5] It is useful to note the history of the domestic workers' struggle in Guyana. As far back as 1922 the labor union led by Hubert Critchlow was agitating for improved working hours and minimum wages for domestics. In 1948 the colonial government appointed a committee to look into the working conditions of domestics and persons in the catering trade. Women militants such as Janet Jagan attempted to get domestics unionized, and finally the Domestic Workers' Union became a registered body. In the 1970s and 1980s, however, this union has been defunct. *Women Speak* (1983) reported that the Conference on the Affairs and Status of Women in Guyana (CASWIG) was examining Guyana's labor laws as they relate to domestic workers and hotel and restaurant employees.

In Jamaica, a minimum wage rate of 75¢ J per hour was proposed for household workers by the Jamaican Trade Union Council to the National Minimum Wages Board. Subsequently, a minimum wage stipulation put forward by this board was enacted in 1978. At another level, efforts are being made by some Jamaican women in SISTREN, a working class women's theater group, to highlight the conditions of domestic workers in Jamaica. Two of their staged plays, *Domestick* and *QPH*, focus on and pay tribute to "women's work."

St. Kitts, like Trinidad and Tobago and Jamaica, also has a minimum wage for domestic servants, in 1974 at 60¢ EC per hour with the additional agreement that the total wages should not be less than $20 EC per week.[6]

While the situation of domestic workers appears to be a grim one in the Caribbean at present, it is encouraging that some attempt is being made to organize these employees, to raise public consciousness about the value of housework and household workers, and, at the state level, to inquire into their wages and working conditions.

Recommendations for Relief

Four major areas especially bedevil the situation of domestic workers. The first relates to the attitudes held both in the society at large and by employers that domestic servants are less deserving of respect than other workers and that housework is non-work. There must be a change in attitudes toward housework itself and to the labor performed by domestic workers. This can be initiated by greater employer consideration to household assistants with regard to overtime, accommodations, and the like.

The second area relates to wages. Payment should in the first instance be commensurate with the jobs performed by the household worker. Those who set minimum wages should also be cognizant of the fact that domestic workers have families to support and need to survive under the same cost-of-living conditions suffered by the employer class.

Third, support services for domestic workers are nonexistent. While they are employed to look after other people's children, they must utilize uncertain and makeshift arrangements, such as relying on aged relatives, to care for their own. Proper day care or nursery facilities should be provided inexpensively.

Finally, in the area of union organization, there is every need for domestic workers in all the Caribbean territories to become organized. Lessons must be learned from countries that have already gained union recognition. So far we have seen that the gains won among domestic workers were made through the efforts of working women themselves. This suggests that any organization among domestic employees has to be spearheaded by the women, especially women of the working class. They can best articulate their grievances and propose solutions in their own interests.

Notes

1. HATT no longer functions in Trinidad.
2. In 1975 the official exchange rate was $2.30 TT to $1.00 U.S.
3. In 1980–81, $2.42 TT = $1.00 U.S.
4. In 1982, the year in which this legislation was promulgated, the exchange rate was $1.20 BDOS = $1.00 U.S.
5. The exchange rate in 1979 was $3.74 G = $1.00 U.S.

6. The Eastern Caribbean dollar (EC) was on a par with the U.S. dollar when this article was written.

References

Boland, Barbara. 1974. "Labour Force." In G. W. Roberts, ed., *Recent Population Movements in Jamaica,* pp. 56–93. Kingston: The Herald, Ltd., for the Committee for International Coordination of National Research in Demography (CICRED).

Harewood, Jack. 1975. *The Population of Trinidad and Tobago, World Population Year 1975.* Paris: Committee for International Coordination of National Research in Demography (CICRED).

HATT (Housewives Association of Trinidad and Tobago). 1975. *Report of the Employment Status of Household Workers in Trinidad.* Port-of-Spain: HATT.

Trinidad Express. 1979.

Trinidad Guardian. 1979.

Women Speak. 1983. No. 11 (July).

9 "Just a Little Respect": West Indian Domestic Workers in New York City

SHELLEE COLEN

Who are the West Indian women pushing white children in strollers through the park or waiting to pick them up in front of schools in the predominantly white and wealthy sections of New York City? Who are the less visible West Indian women cleaning other people's city apartments and suburban houses? How did they come to do this work? What motivates them to leave their homelands? What are their relations with the women who employ them and with the children they care for? What are their experiences as migrants, child-care and domestic workers, mothers, and members of their own families? What do these experiences mean within the contested domain of reproduction?

These questions stimulated the anthropological fieldwork I am conducting among West Indian (English-speaking Afro-Caribbean) women in New York City currently or previously employed as private child-care and domestic workers. These women arrived in New York as recently as four months before this writing (1985) and as long ago as 1968. They are all mothers; their children reside either with them in New York or with kin or friends in their home countries. The women range in age from their late twenties to late forties, with most in their early to mid-thirties.[1]

This article addresses a few of these questions. It relates them to an abbreviated history of domestic work in the United States and then focuses on aspects of the asymmetrical relations of domestic work that these West Indian women experience in New York.

This article is based on my doctoral dissertation research in progress. It shares data and analysis with the forthcoming dissertation and with my article "With Respect and Feelings: Voices of West Indian Domestic Workers in New York City," in Johnnetta B. Cole, ed., *All American Women: Lines that Divide and Ties that Bind*, pp. 46–70 (New York: Free Press, 1986).

The interaction of gender, class, race, place in a world system, and migration texture each woman's experience of private household work in New York.[2] Weaving these experiences together exposes the failure of the public/private paradigm and illustrates the continuous inter-penetration of the falsely dichotomized public and private realms (see Kelly 1979; Rapp 1978). In the contested domain of reproductive activities, their experiences clearly demonstrate that having and caring for households and children is stratified and has differential meanings according to sex, class, race, and location in a world system. Motherhood and the double day look different across town and across oceans.

Migration and Domestic Work

Migration and domestic work are part of an international solution to women's problems of carrying out their responsibilities for themselves and their kin within a world economic system. The articulation of the English-speaking Caribbean into that system creates the conditions for this migration. The legacy of colonialism, dependent development, and multinational domination have structured economies in which un- and underemployment abound, educational and occupational opportunities are few, and inflation exacerbates an already low standard of living. In this context, non-elite West Indian women bear the bulk of the financial and other responsibilities for themselves and their children. As Bolles (1981, 62) states, West Indian women emigrate as an "alternative employment strategy." Although the women interviewed all were employed before leaving their homelands, their employment was not steady, offered little upward mobility, and paid wages that were insufficient to support themselves and their children. They cite responsibility for their children as the primary motivation for migration. Most also speak of "helping out" mothers and other kin. They all knew friends or family who had migrated to England, Canada, or the United States, and they shared a cultural expectation that one migrates to "better oneself."[3] The persistent ideology of "opportunity" drew them to the United States. In New York, they work for educational and occupational advancement and to provide basic consumer items for themselves and their families. Immigration policies often separate them from those for whom they provide. Paradoxically, to be good mothers, women leave their children and migrate.

For most West Indian women in New York, legal permanent resident status, obtaining a "green card," is the prerequisite to their desired upward mobility. Only with a green card can they further their education, advance occupationally, or send for and educate their children. While a few of those interviewed arrived with green cards (having been sponsored by close kin), most came on visitor's visas—which they overstayed, thereby becoming undocumented. Although spouses or certain close relatives with permanent resident status or U.S. citizenship and some employers (such as hospitals that recruit registered nurses) sponsor West Indian women, for many, employer sponsorship in domestic and child-care work is one of the few paths to legal status.[4] Many without green cards know before migrating that their first step will be domestic work. As Dawn Adams[5] remembers from St. Vincent, "When you're at home, you hear that you do babysitting in order to get sponsored."

The Labor Department and the Immigration and Naturalization Service (INS) have several requirements for employer sponsorship in domestic work, including proof of a shortage of documented workers available to do the same work at the "prevailing wage." Most women must go through the procedure as live-in domestic workers. For them, the 1985 prevailing wage in New York City was just under $200 for a work week of forty-four and a half hours. The law does not require that a worker receive the prevailing wage before the green card is granted; it does, however, require that workers be paid the current minimum wage.

While these and other guidelines on working conditions exist, neither the Labor Department, the INS, nor any other agency monitors compliance. This can lead to a form of state-sanctioned, indenturelike exploitation; the worker is obligated to stay in the sponsored position until the green card is granted (often two or more years) in spite of any abuses to which she may be subjected. As Judith Thomas, a Vincentian mother of four says, women "really pay their dues."[6]

For most, domestic work means stepping down the occupational hierarchy. Two women had previously taught school; one had also been a policewoman. Several had been clerical workers or administrative assistants in government or private corporations. Others had done factory work, postal work, agricultural work, higglering or petty marketing, and service work in the tourist industry. Most of these women did not do paid domestic work at home, although many of their mothers had done so (Mohammed, this volume). Joyce Miller from Jamaica says, "Housekeeping for pay back home is the last resort." Ironically, in New York it is the first step.

Private household work is central to the experiences of many West Indian women in New York. While other occupations are increasingly available to West Indian women, they are open primarily to legal residents. Immigration policies direct undocumented women to meet the increased demand for child-care and domestic workers in the "gentrifying" urban and suburban neighborhoods where working mothers with young children can afford to hire them. A primary means of employment for undocumented West Indian women, private household work employs women with green cards as well. High demand makes it an easy first job to land. In some cases, legal status and training and/or experience in other occupations prior to migration are insufficient to overcome employers' demands for local experience and references. Confronting the racial, sex, and, in some cases, age discrimination prevalent in hiring and other employment practices, some women with green cards work in private households for reasons that include a preference for working with children, families, or the elderly and the possibility, in some cases, of somewhat autonomous working conditions.

The "Sponsor" Job

Most women describe sponsored jobs, especially live-in ones, as "the worst." Exploitation takes the form of abysmal pay and long hours and may involve isolation from kin, friends, community, and anyone outside the work environment. In 1977 Joyce Miller worked seven days a week and was on call twenty-four hours a day, taking care of three children and a large house while being sponsored for only $90 a week. When she took a day off to see her immigration lawyer, that day was deducted from her salary.

"You come from a good job [at the post office] back home and end up here being a housekeeper . . . and only because you need the job and only because you need a sponsor. And the worst part of it is you've got to live in." Loneliness, demoralization, and exhaustion from fifteen-hour or longer workdays are often intrinsic to the job. Monica Cooper paid several times her normal bus fare to "get out" of her suburban live-in job and come to New York during a snowstorm on her day off. As she says, "There's no way on earth I'm going to have a day off and stay in there."

Adjusting to domestic work is difficult. Dawn Adams found "missing my children" and "cleaning someone else's house" the hardest things to accept. Marguerite Andrews, a thirty-three-year-old former schoolteacher, recently arrived from St. Vincent, supports four children at home on her child-care and domestic worker's salary. Although she had an "understanding" employer, she found it difficult to move from the relative autonomy and high status of teacher—receiving respect from students, parents, and the community at large—to taking orders to clean up after others.

> She's not bossy or anything like that. But within myself I figure I should be more, I can't explain. . . . I should be, I don't like to use the word "maidish," but I should put myself all out to do everything. But you know this will have to take some time.

Marguerite Andrews was not used to the "subservient" aspect of the work. Now her expanded understanding of hierarchy from below has given her a new perspective on domestic workers at home, where she herself had employed a helper. She tells of an incident in which one of her sons left his clothes in a trail on the floor, and the woman she had hired to clean for her family refused to pick them up and wash them with the other clothes. When the son ordered the woman to do so, saying that she was paid to clean up after him, Marguerite had agreed that this was part of the job. Now, she sees it differently. She speculates on how she would feel if her employer and the child she takes care of were to treat her as she and her son treated the woman who worked for them.

On the sponsored job, the material and emotional exploitation potentially present on all domestic jobs is exacerbated by the workers' dependence on their employers for green cards; this can leave them vulnerable to employer manipulation and less likely to quit an intolerable situation. While employers vary in their treatment of workers, some employers clearly take advantage of new immigrants' lack of knowledge of local conditions and their isolation from those who might "enlighten" them. One undocumented worker was threatened with being reported to the INS for expressing her dissatisfaction. Although some quit sponsored jobs, workers are unlikely to do so because of the resultant loss of time and energy toward obtaining the green card. Workers remain beholden to employers until the card is granted, and in spite of the exploitation, are grateful to their employers for sponsoring them.

Beyond the material exploitation and the difficult adjustment to lower-status domestic work, the central issue discussed by all the women is the lack of respect shown to them by their employers. This lack of respect, embedded in the asymmetrical relations of domestic work in the United States, deeply disturbs West Indian women and shatters their cultural expectations about social behavior. Combined with the slow-moving INS bureaucracy and the high legal costs of obtaining the green card, these relations make the "sponsor" job period a trying one. Joyce Miller remembers her experiences as a domestic worker being sponsored for her green card:

> People don't understand how hard it is to get here. And we try to explain to them. It's terrible. And you think of all you go through. You go through all this paperwork and go through the lawyer and pay so much money and you get this blooming little piece of card, green paper. It's not even green. The day when I got it I said, "This is IT?" They should have a better system than this.

A History of Domestic Work in the United States

West Indian women's child-care and domestic work experiences appear unique, but in the context of the history of domestic work in the United States, it is clear that they bear similarities to other women's experiences deriving from both the structural aspects of domestic work and the recurring relationship between domestic work and migration (see Clark-Lewis 1985; Dill 1979; Glenn 1980). In the United States the history of domestic work has several strands and is differential according to region and rural/urban location. In the southern states before the abolition of slavery, African and Creole house slaves performed much of this work. Indentured servants also did domestic work prior to the American Revolution, supplanted afterward by predominantly rural "help." With the expansion of an urban middle class, migration—both rural to urban and international—became an important factor in the nineteenth-century recruitment of rural women to domestic service. The post-Emancipation migration of black women from the South to the North constitutes a major strand in this history. The related shift from live-in to live-out to day work is another.

From pre-Revolutionary times until the mid-nineteenth century, hired "help" was a major source of domestic labor, especially in rural areas. The helper was sent by her parents to work alongside other household members as a step between her parents' home and marriage. Those who "helped" were members of the community known to the employing household and were considered social equals, dining at the family table (Dudden 1983, 1–43; Katzman 1978, 98).

Urbanization, industrialization, and the expansion of a middle class transformed help to domestic service, performed on a live-in basis by a predominantly white migrant population of rural, native-born young women. Now, the worker and the employer were strangers, brought together by advertisement and agencies; increasingly, the employer supervised rather than shared the work. "Help" remained an institution in rural areas for a much longer time (Katzman 1978, 98–99). As native-born white women found other work, got married, or otherwise left the domestic work force, white immigrant women, primarily Irish, German, and Scandinavian, took their places in the domestic work force between 1840 and 1900.[7]

Several trends culminated in the situation in which black women, who, as house slaves, had performed the bulk of the domestic work in the South, came to constitute a major segment of the domestic work force in northeastern cities as well (Hamburger 1977, 23; Katzman 1978, 204–22). Black women were the domestic work force in the South, first as slaves and then, after Emancipation, as domestic workers on a predominantly live-out basis. Blacks became a service caste; as many have noted, to be a servant meant to be black, and vice versa (Davis 1981, 90, 93). Soon after the Civil War black women escaping oppressive conditions in the south began migrating north to work, often as domestics.[8] Between 1900 and 1920 a decline in the immigration of groups formerly supplying domestic workers, as well as expanded opportunities in manufacturing, sales, professional, and clerical work for white native-born and immigrant women, contributed to a decline in the percentage of women in the labor force employed in domestic work in the North and created demand for private household workers there. When large numbers of blacks came north in the great migration during and after World War I, there were few employment opportunities for black women other than private household domestic and laundry work. The women of the first sizable West Indian migration, occurring in the years following World War I, faced the same limited employment alternatives. By the 1920s black women were the single largest group in domestic work in northeastern cities as well as in the South (Katzman 1978, 222, 273). As the same author notes (1978, 72, 93), "Within a hundred years [1820–1920] the image of the household servant had changed from rural 'help' to the Irish 'biddy' of the nineteenth century to the black 'cleaning woman' of the twentieth"; domestic service, a major form of women's employment in the nineteenth century, by the 1920s was "an occupation statistically unimportant among all but black women" as it became a "predominantly black occupation" in many urban areas (see Davis 1981; Hamburger 1977; Lerner 1973).

Although some black women lived in, most preferred to live out. Their preference, along with labor-saving devices and smaller urban dwellings helped to transform domestic work from predominantly live-in to predominantly live-out work by the end of World War I (Clark-Lewis 1985; Katzman 1978, 95; Scott 1982, 182). Day work (in which a worker is employed regularly on given days by different employers) gained acceptance as well. Unlike many domestics, the majority of black workers were mothers supporting themselves and their children and struggling to arrange adequate child care (Almquist 1979, 54–55). During the depression of the 1930s, black women (native-born and West Indian) without regular employment waited on street corners in white neighborhoods, seeking through the "slave market" a few hours of domestic work (Lerner 1972, 229–31; P. Marshall 1981a, 6). During World War II, many black women found other, more lucrative employment, but after the war most had returned to domestic work when their wartime jobs disappeared or reverted to men and white women. Day work was prevalent after the war.

The antiracist struggles of the Civil Rights movement, the increase in clerical jobs, and an expanding service sector outside private household work provided black women for the first time with significant opportunities; many moved out of domestic work in the 1960s and 1970s to predominantly "pink collar" jobs in the service sector and clerical fields. In 1960 one-third of all employed black women were private household workers; by 1970, only one-seventh were. However, though constituting only 11 percent of the female labor force in 1970, black women accounted for half of private household workers

(Almquist 1979, 53; Dill 1979). Many older women remained in the field; many younger black women never entered it.

The "new" immigrants, arriving in the United States after 1965, predominantly female and Third World (Mortimer and Bryce-Laporte 1981), have filled some of the openings in domestic work. While different U.S. regions draw from different immigrant populations (for example, women from Mexico, El Salvador, and Guatemala form part of the domestic work force in California), immigration has again become a factor in domestic work. Neither West Indian immigration nor West Indian women working in domestic work are new (Gordon 1979; P. Marshall 1981a, 1981b; 1983; Reid 1939). What is new is the unprecedented number of West Indian women migrating to New York since 1965, many having left their own children behind, and doing domestic work for their green cards. Immigration policies that separate West Indian women from their families steer them to work in others' households at a time when the reproductive domain is in crisis—in part because women's paid labor force participation increases without significant concurrent changes in expectations about who bears the responsibility for child care and other reproductive labor within households by gender or between households and the state.

Asymmetry and Respect

The asymmetrical social relations of domestic work in the United States are grounded in and reinforced by hierarchical relations of class, gender, race, ethnicity, and migration. Dominant/subordinate relations of class, low wages, low status, a lack of contracts or formal agreements, little job security, low levels of unionization, its dead-end character (one must move out to move up), and other features locate this work at low levels of capitalism's service sector. Housework and child care are assigned to women by a gender ideology that trivializes the work as natural and unskilled and devalues both the work and those who perform it (Howe 1977).[9] Although women and men most often jointly employ domestic workers, the sexual division of labor structures these dominant/subordinate interactions so that the primary interaction is between employee and female employer. The ideological construct which separates public from private interferes with the recognition that domestic work, performed by women in homes, *is* work. Hence much of it is in some ways "invisible." Domestic work is often assigned to racially or ethnically distinct groups who are accorded low status in an ideological context that turns difference from those in power into inferiority. Conversely, performing this disdained work reinforces low status.[10] Further, when domestic workers are foreign born or "alien," they are more easily perceived as "other" which, in employers' eyes, increases the perceived distance between them.

As working-class, immigrant women of color, West Indian women enter into these asymmetrical relations around which domestic work in the United States is structured. Although the material manifestations of this asymmetry—exhausting, repetitive, seemingly invisible tasks; long hours, low pay, etc.—are problematic, what every woman cited as the major source of dissatisfaction is the way this asymmetry is manifested in the employer's attitude and behavior, specifically in the lack of respect shown to her.

The tension between domestic work's status as wage labor in the cash nexus and its highly personalized nature and location in the household permeates relations between workers and employers. The contradictory themes of intimacy and depersonalization appear in most of the interviews about domestic work. On the one hand, women speak of the intimate involvement in and knowledge of the employing household. Their job responsibilities include much of the maintenance, management, and care of wide-ranging aspects of this "private realm," from feeding people and (as one woman says) "cleaning their dirt" to dealing with the particularities of their personalities. Childcare activity involves emotion work (Hochschild 1983) whether performed for love or for money. The worker provides "mothering," nurturance, guidance, training, and care, both physical and affective. Employers depend on workers to free them for activities outside the home. On the other hand, having involved a worker in intimate aspects of their lives, employers rarely acknowledge either the degree to which this is the case or their dependence on the worker. Rather, many depersonalize the relationship, distance the worker from themselves, and sometimes dehumanize her in a variety of ways that workers experience as lack of respect.

Depersonalization, dehumanization, and lack of respect are played out in a variety of areas, including, most obviously, shelter, food, clothing, and names. Some women who live in must share their rooms with the children for whom they are responsible, affording them virtually no privacy. Even those who have their own rooms must sometimes take children with them at night if they wake and need feeding or comforting.

Eating is a materially and symbolically important arena for dehumanization and lack of consideration. Workers often are not allowed enough food. One woman who works from five to sixteen hours at a stretch is left only enough food to prepare for the employer's child but not enough for herself. And of course she cannot leave the children or take them along to the store to buy herself food, especially at night, even if she has the money to do so. Other women speak of the inadequate quantity or quality of the food provided, considering the heavy physical work they do. One woman who is employed for a live-in, five-day week is frequently questioned about "missing" items after she fixes her own meals. Lesser problems arise from the different foods, cooking styles, and seasonings used by their employers. The classic situation, however, is the one in which a live-in worker is distanced by not eating at the table with the rest of the household. Joyce Miller says of this practice:

> I have to eat after they finish eating. . . . And then I eat in the kitchen. There are a lot of people who do that because they want us to know that we are not equal. You are the housekeeper. I think the only reason why I was in their house is to clean. . . . Like olden days. . . . That's the part I hate. I hate that part because it's showing me a lot of things. You need things from me, but when it comes down to sitting at the table with you, you are going to show me separation there. I just don't like it.

She contrasts this experience with a former situation in which, although underpaid for her long hours living in, she was always included at the table. In fact, Joyce says, "If I went to sit by myself, they said, 'No, no, no. You've got to come right here to the table.' . . . That was something she try to do all the time. That's one thing with her she was great about. I never feel left out."

Uniforms represent a similar show of dominance, distancing, and depersonalization. Although they may provide some women with a convenient mode of dress that allows them to preserve their own clothes for "after work," they deny workers their individual identities and unmistakably identify them as servants. The women I interviewed do not like wearing uniforms and avoid doing so whenever possible.

Asymmetrical first-naming behavior symbolizes dominance and disrespect as well. While workers are called by their first names, a few of them are requested to call their employers Mrs. or Mr. As West Indian women they find this asymmetry particularly insulting and troubling: naming has more status significance in their home cultures than in New York, and most would be called Miss or Mrs. by all but elders, kin, or colleagues of the same age and status back home. Many protest being referred to as "the girl" or "the maid."

In this highly personalized relationship, workers are rarely without ambivalence toward employers. Employers display a range of behaviors. Some wrong the worker in myriad ways; others are more fair and helpful. For workers, even "understanding," "good people to work for," whom "you can talk to," "have their faults." One employer, described as "willing to help" and with "feelings," volunteered to continue to pay her employee for full-time work even though the woman was to begin college in the morning hours while the child she cared for attended nursery school. When discussing some problematic aspects of this "good" employer's behavior, the worker said, "Nobody's perfect." In airing complaints about employers whose behavior is particularly exploitative, workers often insist that "she has her good side." The highly personalized context of domestic work colors the inherent contradictions of employer and employee and exacerbates the effects of the lack of respect that is shown for domestic work and for those who perform it.

The low esteem in which domestic work is held—more than the tasks themselves—and the attitudes stemming from this lack of esteem are often the "worst part." Many of the women are proud of being good housekeepers, but as Beverly Powell from Jamaica says:

> When people look down on you for cleaning up their messes, then it starts hurting. The worst thing is when they look at you as stupid, or maybe stupid but as a damn fool. You should treat people exactly as how you want to be treated. We can't all be doctors or lawyers; someone has to clean up the dirt. . . . I'm a hard worker. I want just a little consideration. If I'm paid $1,000 for work but treated like dirt, it will pay the bills, but forget it.

For West Indian women like Beverly Powell, the relations of respect are particularly problematic because they contrast sharply with West Indian codes of and expectations about social behavior which pivot on the concept of respect. West Indian communities are structured according to particular forms of cultural duality and patterns of respect-based social ranking (Barrow 1976; Durant-Gonzalez 1976; Sutton 1976). Dominant cultural notions of stratification in which status is accorded on the basis of such factors as education, occupation, and wealth are crosscut by a more egalitarian system of reputations and ranking based on the concept of respect. Notions of respect guide an individual's social interaction and form the basis for reputations, which in turn are the basis for the indigenous system of ranking (Barrow 1976, 108, 113). Individuals behave in prescribed ways that indicate self-respect, and respect for others. The reciprocal nature of respect—that one gives respect and in turn receives it—is central to this system. The indigenous value system places importance on life cycle, kin relations, marriage, motherhood, and other aspects of behavior. Bearing, raising, and being responsible for children earn women adult status and the community's respect which can be augmented by caring for other kin or non-kin children (Durant-Gonzalez 1976, 1982). Therefore, in their own communities these women are accorded a high level of respect deriving from both the dominant and the internal systems. They are respected on the one hand as teachers, civil servants, or clerical workers and on the other hand (even women for whom those avenues are closed) as adult women, as mothers responsible for their own and other's children, as, in some cases, married women, and as individuals who behave with self-respect and respect toward others. West Indian women in the United States are insulted by the disrespectful and dehumanizing treatment they receive from people whose children they raise.

As housework passes from woman to woman, it remains unacknowledged in a variety of ways that lead workers to feel taken for granted and resentful. Monica Cooper tells of her employers' habit of undressing and leaving their clothes on the floor where they step out of them instead of placing them in the available hampers. Resenting this behavior, she once left the clothes on the floor until the following day, staging a one-day strike. When she spoke with her employer about it, Monica was told that it was part of the job; the employer "always picked up after her husband . . . that's the way he is, and she accepted him like that. Since she doesn't want to pick . . . up, I'm sure she hires somebody who will pick . . . up for her." Judith Thomas states that "you shouldn't walk all over people just because you are paying them." Joyce Miller reports that "some of them don't even talk to you. They never one day ask you how you're feeling or anything else." This statement stands in sharp contrast to the way ideology is used to manipulate the worker when she is told that she is "one of the family." Even though their own families are often ignored by employers, household workers clearly are not members of the employers' family. Family ideology, sometimes used to explain why people have to sacrifice for one another, is turned around to induce people who are *not* in the family to do things that may be exploitative. As Joyce Miller states,

> Whenever they want you to give your all in their favor or anyway to feel comfortable to do what they want you to do, they use the word "we are family." That's the one I hate. "You are one of the family." That's not true. . . . If you're one of the family, do not let me eat after you.

The manipulation of family ideology is nowhere clearer than in child care. Many women enjoy child care and prefer it to housework. They place a high value on child rearing; child care commands greater respect; and the potential for reciprocal tenderness can be rewarding. Emotional care-giving to children who are not one's own, however, can lead to emotional exploitation and vulnerability. Employers expect workers to be "like mothers" to their children, but not to usurp the employers' positions. The thought and care that workers put into tending the children, as well as the responsibility they feel for them, is obvious in conversation. Several speak of loving the children, and Dawn Adams says she felt embarrassed when "her" four-year-old child misbehaved in public: "You know it's not my child, but I take care of her and I love her. I've been with her since she was three months old. And when she did it, I was embarrassed myself." Yet the children are not always disciplined when they are rude or disrespectful to the employee. One woman was humiliated by a jealous parent when the child, after being scolded by the parent, ran to the worker—who was then ordered to go to her room. Some women state that their relationships with the children kept them on a job they might have left sooner. I spoke with Beverly Powell the weekend after she left a job in which for four years she had cared for a child, then eight years old. Her sadness about leaving the boy, who sometimes called her "mommy," was exacerbated by her fear that she would not be able to keep in touch with him because of the unpleasant relations that had developed between herself and his parents. Many women, however, do periodically visit their former charges.

The contradictions of these relations are further mirrored in relations of trust. The employers entrust the care of the children to the employees, yet may accuse them of stealing. Monica Cooper, who had worked for a family for four and a half years, told of how her employers had entrusted her with the care of their two children when they took their Caribbean vacations. Yet when she gave her two-weeks notice before leaving the job, "all of a sudden . . . they couldn't find this and they couldn't find that . . . now that I'm leaving, they're going to miss a [gold] chain and they're going to miss a slip." Such contradictions demonstrate that personal service work, which often resembles activities that women in their own families do for love, is in fact embedded in capitalist wage relations.

Asymmetry and Juggling Work and Family

The asymmetrical relations that characterize domestic work also have their impact on the ways in which these women juggle their paid work and their kin and household responsibilities. Balancing these tasks is stressful for most women under current conditions, but particularly so for the West Indian domestic worker. Her responsibilities and her employer's limited acknowledgment of her life off the job contribute to her difficulties. She must balance her time, money, and emotions.

Time is constantly being juggled. Often there are demands to stay late or stay over (when employers travel or during summer when children are not in school) and unpredictable schedule changes (when employers come home at 11:00 P.M. instead of 8:30 as promised). Such demands mean less time for the employee's own household, changes in her personal plans, and often dangerous late-night subway rides. In the interviews, there is evidence of a lack of consideration for the workers as human beings with lives, plans, and responsibilities outside their jobs. A household worker's own child care is a major problem when her job keeps her late or she is obliged to be away for days. The contradiction of separation from one's own family to care for another's is expressed by several women who say, "It's okay for them to ask me to stay extra time because they have their family together, but what about me?" or "They don't think that I have MY family waiting for me."

Juggling money is particularly problematic. Salaries vary by legal status or between live-in and live-out work; however, all are low and difficult to stretch to support the two or more households for which West Indian domestic workers are responsible—their own in New York and those of kin in the Caribbean. Women send remittances in money and barrels containing food, clothing, and other basic nonluxury goods either unavailable or exorbitantly priced at home to children, parents, and other kin. Remittances generally amount to a large proportion of the worker's income, up to a half for those who live-in. Lawyer's fees for the green card, added to remittances, can account for between 30 and 80 percent of a woman's salary. Substantial medical bills burden some, as their jobs rarely provide medical insurance. Many take on an additional part-time domestic or child-care job to cover their expenses. Women balance limited budgets between their material needs in New York (of which rent is a major expense) and the needs and demands from home. Since these are often in stark contrast to the material wealth of the households in which the domestic worker is employed, she must balance, as well, the many material and social worlds through which she passes, at some emotional cost.

Emotional juggling takes many forms and often revolves around children. Women forced to leave their children and kin behind speak of the many nights when—feeling isolated from family and friends, recalling unpleasant incidents in their workdays, or, most often, missing and wondering about their children—they've cried themselves to sleep. Missing their children leads some women to treat their employers' children as substitutes for their own. As Joyce Miller says, "Just 'cause I was lonely, I gave them all I have." The contrast in the material goods and other things to which the two sets of children have access disturbs some women.

Whether her children are in the United States or in the Caribbean, the domestic worker must contend with difficult child-care arrangements. While close kin most often keep a child, both mother and children may experience separations as stressful, no matter how carefully mothers try to provide. Child care in New York often takes a large proportion of a worker's salary but may afford her little control over quality of the care. Mothers of school-age children have legitimate concerns about the safety of their children in the often dangerous areas in which many must live. Caring for other women's children for pay, the household worker also juggles her life to care for her own for love.

Determination and Coping

Visions of their families and futures empower West Indian women to cope with and to resist the pressures and exploitation that confront them. The women in this study are strong, determined, secure, and confident—qualities that enable them to adjust to all that migration entails, including domestic work. Their determination to obtain green cards, to reunite with and provide for their own children, and to achieve their educational and occupational goals propels them. Letters from home saying "We couldn't make it without you" encourage them further. A double consciousness permits them to operate in their employers' households, yet maintain their own identities deriving from their own systems of respect operative in their home countries and in their communities in New York.

On the job, workers employ strategies such as defining their own tasks and airing grievances, admittedly easier to do when one has a green card or "good" employers. Some refuse to perform certain tasks, such as cleaning floors on their hands and knees. Marguerite Andrews maintains her five-day live-in work schedule by rarely returning on Sunday night; if she does, no matter how late she arrives, her five days become six. Quitting is an option when all else fails.

Still, no individual on-the-job strategies can remove the structural problems of domestic work. Unionization of domestic work, as other documents in this book make clear, would begin to do so. Unionized workers can demand regular hours, adequate wages, and medical and other benefits; they can define tasks, set standards for appropriate employer behavior, force acknowledgment of the need for their services, and command respect for themselves. Although domestic workers' unions have existed in the United States for over a hundred years, it is clear that breaking the isolation of domestic work and organizing women is as urgent now as ever.

For the West Indian workers that I interviewed, it is their social world and activities beyond the job that sustain and nourish them.

They actively seek out kin and friends for companionship, support, and pleasure. They find familiar patterns of respect and identity in their reconstituted West Indian communities. Dawn Adams's conversations in the park with other workers recall descriptions of a former generation of West Indian domestic workers talking with each other around a kitchen table after work to "reaffirm self-worth" and to "overcome the humiliations of the work day" (P. Marshall 1983, 6). Women in these networks share information about jobs (private household or otherwise), strategies for coping on and off the job, immigration law and lawyers, schools, and the like. They exchange services such as child care, hair grooming, sewing, or grocery shopping. Church and other community group activities as well as cocktail sips and christenings provide meaning, dignity, and relaxation. Cousins and friends as well as religious beliefs support many women through the "hard times." As one says, "You never pray so much as when you're doing domestic." For many, education is a meaningful path to the future. All but the most recent migrants have attended school since leaving their homelands, sacrificing their nights and weekends to further their education. After their high school equivalency exams, many study in fields such as health care and business, seeking to facilitate employment outside domestic work.

Some remain in private household work indefinitely; with green cards and training, they often find "good" working conditions and employers as child-care workers or home health aides. For others, however, the green card means the freedom to leave private household work. Some leave immediately; some change employers to obtain better pay or conditions, but wait to leave until they have completed schooling or until their children arrive in New York. Many who leave are employed in business, clerical, or health care or other service jobs. Although these are often sex-segregated "pink collar" jobs (Howe 1977), their attraction lies in the working conditions, benefits, and increased respect they command. After years at her sponsored job and an additional year at another domestic job, Joyce Miller is now a bookkeeper in a Manhattan real estate office. Dawn Adams became a bank teller (beginning study toward a business and management degree at a local college at the same time) in anticipation of her children's arrival. She cites regular hours, medical and dental coverage, regular raises, and the potential for promotion as crucial factors in her choice. Judith Thomas, who spent her weekends becoming certified as a practical nurse, plans to switch to a job with medical benefits for herself and her children as soon as possible after they arrive. Domestic work itself may be a dead end, but for some its a stepping-stone to the green card and to other employment.

Conclusion

The experiences of these West Indian domestic and child-care workers are both profoundly structural and historically specific. Discussions about the asymmetrical relations, the intimacy and depersonalization, and the lack of respect could have been uttered by and about Irish immigrant women a hundred years ago or, even more likely, by black women migrants to the North sixty years ago and by Salvadoran women today. Yet the experiences of these West Indian women—shaped by gender, class, race, migration, and history—are distinct.

The current conditions of underdevelopment in the Caribbean, resulting from a long history of Caribbean articulation into an international capitalist system, create the need for women to migrate in pursuit of "opportunity," educational and occupational, in order to support themselves and their families. On arrival in New York, they move into the expanding service sector of the urban United States in private household child-care and domestic work. Immigration policies, through which the state addresses labor needs, direct undocumented women into an indenture-like period of domestic work in order to obtain legal status. Their place in a world system determines how these mothers work to care for their own families. Their experiences blur the lines defining "public" and "private" and demonstrate the continuous interpenetration of these falsely dichotomized realms.

West Indian domestic workers' labor frees their employers for other activities, but both the workers and the tasks are held in low esteem. Their sex, color, and position as migrants further influence attitudes and behavior shown toward them in a society suffused with and structured by class and gender hierarchies, racial ideologies, and stratification by national origin. For them, respect is the central issue.

While many women have stressful family responsibilities to bear, the highly stratified nature of child care and household maintenance in this system is quite striking. Hired to help shoulder the domestic tasks of other women, they withstand long separations from their kin and juggle their own child-care and household responsibilities across neighborhoods and across oceans. Their strength, determination, and networks of support empower them to cope, resist, and move toward their goals.

Notes

Acknowledgments: I want to extend my deepest thanks to the women who gave their precious time to speak about their lives. This article is for them. I am extremely grateful to Elsa Chaney for her patient and painstaking editing. In addition, I thank Rayna Rapp for her editorial wizardry, and Deborah D'Amico-Samuels, Mindie Lazarus-Black, Michael Landy, and Helen Evers for their encouragement and suggestions on an earlier draft of this article.

1. I am conducting extended, open-ended interviews and life histories. Generally they take four or five sessions, each lasting at least two hours, at either the woman's home or at her place of employment. In addition, I have had many informal conversations in a variety of contexts with most of the women. The information in this article, written in 1985, represents data from the first ten sets of interviews conducted in 1984. I have also spoken with "experts" ranging from immigration lawyers and Department of Labor and Immigration officials to employment agencies and personnel from a variety of agencies and offices that provide services to the West Indian community. I will continue to conduct fieldwork with more West Indian immigrant women. In addition I will interview employers of West Indian child-care workers in New York and conduct fieldwork in St. Vincent with female kin who foster migrants' children.

2. While it is impossible to assess how representative these experiences are in relation to those of the New York female West Indian population as a whole, U.S. Immigration and Naturalization Service data and the 1980 U.S. Census indicate that a large number of West Indian women are employed in private household work with and without legal status. Due to the inadequacies in these data (the former only accounts for those who become legal residents in a given year while the latter rarely includes the undocumented and often undercounts the documented), the actual number of West Indian women employed in domestic work in New York must exceed the official one.

3. Labor migration has been central to West Indian history since slavery. Recent migrations are influenced by the labor needs reflected in the immigration policies of receiving countries (see D. Marshall 1982 for overview). England's post–World War II economy employed many West Indians who migrated in the 1950s until the 1962 English laws restricted immigration (see Davison 1962; Foner 1978 and 1979; Philpott 1973; Prescod-Roberts and Steele 1980). Canada opened up its immigration policies in 1962, resulting in increased West Indian immigration, but 1980 modifications limited nonwhite immigration (see Henry 1982). Responding to a shortage of private house-

hold domestic workers, the Canadian government began recruiting West Indian women for domestic work in Canada in 1955 under the "Domestic Scheme." Although policy has changed from automatically granting landed immigrant status to providing only temporary employment visas to fill labor shortages, and though West Indian women pursue a variety of occupations in Canada, these policies have brought hundreds of West Indian women to Canada each year to do domestic work (see Henry 1968, 1982; Silvera 1983). West Indian immigration to the United States had been on the increase since 1962, but the Immigration Act of 1965 and subsequent laws established policies that ushered in a large, predominantly female West Indian migration (Mortimer and Bryce-Laporte 1981). While these policies had several sources and diverse effects, the opening up of new and traditional service sector work and the need of U.S. businesses for cheaper labor, which undocumented and new legal immigrant workers often provide, are factors worth noting. In discussing the female majority of the West Indian migration to the United States between 1967 and 1969, Dominguez (1975, 13) states that since 1967 an "inordinately high percentage" of immigrant visas issued to "citizens of Barbados, Jamaica, and Trinidad and Tobago, has gone to private household workers who are, for the most part, female." Private agencies have recruited West Indian women for domestic work in the New York area since the late 1960s. Others, not recruited directly, have migrated knowing that achieving permanent resident status was relatively easy as domestic workers. This migration also included professionals, clerical workers, and others including many nurses (Dominguez 1975, 14; Gordon 1983, 13; interviews).

4. The official category for immigration purposes is "domestic worker" of which "housekeeper" and "child monitor" are two subcategories. When used alone in this paper I intend that the term domestic worker include both. "Private household worker" encompasses child-care and domestic workers as well as other in-home workers such as home health aides who care for the elderly or infirm. While not covered in this study, many West Indian women in New York work as home health aides. Most of the women with whom I spoke were hired primarily as child-care workers and secondarily as housekeepers. Without green cards, women do more housework (whether as live-ins or as day workers) even when child care is their main responsibility. With green cards they are more likely to live out and to define their work as child care to the exclusion of most other heavy housework; in some of these cases employers hire undocumented women to do the bulk of the cleaning on a day-work basis.

5. In order to protect their privacy, pseudonyms have been used for the women involved, and a few details of their experiences have been modified.

6. "Paying their dues" does not always insure success: Joyce Miller estimates that 15 percent of the women who return to their home islands for their final green card interviews face the cruelty of being detained up to several months or denied the card entirely due to improper processing of their

papers or failure of their medical exams (often because of such conditions as high blood pressure).

7. The 1900 U.S. Census showed that 60.5 percent of the Irish-born working women, 61.9 percent of the Scandinavian, and 42.6 percent of the German were domestic workers (Katzman 1978, 49). It also showed that 56.8 percent of the employed Japanese-born women were domestic workers; in 1920, domestic work was still listed as the largest field of non-agricultural employment for Japanese women (Glenn 1980, 440).

8. Various agencies sponsored the migration of southern black women, recruiting them to do domestic work in northern white homes. The Freedman's Bureau, a government agency, did so in 1866 and 1867. Similarly, private agencies established an indenture-like system of "justice tickets" in which they bought a worker's passage that she then "worked off" in the isolation of a live-in domestic job (see, e.g., Hamburger 1977, 23; Katzman 1978, 204–5).

9. Also note the rather large body of literature available on the nature of housework and the "housework debates," including Dalla Costa and James 1972; Gardiner 1975; Glazer-Malbin 1976; and Strasser 1982.

10. See Spellman (1981, 51–54) on racism, sexism, and somatophobia (the fear of bodies and bodily functions often associated with and symptomatic of sexist and racist assumptions that women and certain "races" are identified with bodies, "more body-like," and should therefore be assigned the physical care of others).

References

Almquist, Elizabeth McTaggart. 1979. *Minorities, Gender, and Work.* Lexington, Mass.: Lexington Books.

Barrow, Christine. 1976. "Reputation and Ranking in a Barbadian Locality." *Social and Economic Studies* 25, no. 2:106–21.

Bolles, A. Lynn. 1981. "'Goin'Abroad': Working Class Jamaican Women and Migration." In Delores M. Mortimer and Roy S. Bryce-Laporte, eds., *Female Immigrants to the United States: Caribbean, Latin American, and African Experiences,* pp. 56–84. Research Institute on Immigration and Ethnic Studies, Occasional Papers No. 2. Washington, D.C.: Smithsonian Institution.

Clark-Lewis, Elizabeth. 1985. "'This Work Had A' End': The Transition From Live-In to Day Work." *Southern Women: The Intersection of Race, Class and Gender.* Working Paper 2. Memphis, Tenn.: Memphis State University, Center for Research on Women.

Dalla Costa, Mariarosa, and Selma James. 1972. *The Power of Women and the Subversion of the Community.* Bristol, Eng.: Falling Wall Press.

Davis, Angela Y. 1981. *Women, Race, and Class.* New York: Vintage Books.

Davison, R. B. 1962. *West Indian Migrants: Social and Economic Facts of Migration from the West Indies.* London: Oxford University Press.

Dill, Bonnie Thornton. 1979. "Across the Boundaries of Race and Class: An Exploration of the Relationship between Work and Family among Black Female Domestic Servants." Ph.D. diss., New York University.

Dominguez, Virginia R. 1975. *From Neighbor to Stranger: The Dilemma of Caribbean Peoples in the United States.* New Haven, Conn.: Yale University, Antilles Research Program.

Dudden, Faye E. 1983. *Serving Women: Household Service in Nineteenth-Century America.* Middletown, Conn.: Wesleyan University Press.

Durant-Gonzalez, Victoria. 1976. "Role and Status of Rural Jamaican Women: Higglering and Mothering." Ph.D. diss., University of California, Berkeley.

———. 1982. "The Realm of Female Familial Responsibility." In Joycelin Massiah, ed., *Women and the Family,* pp. 1–24. Women in the Caribbean Project, Vol. 2. Cave Hill, Barbados: University of the West Indies, Institute for Social and Economic Research.

Foner, Nancy. 1978. *Jamaica Farewell: Jamaican Migrants in London.* Berkeley: University of California Press.

———. 1979. "West Indians in New York City and London: A Comparative Analysis." *International Migration Review* 13, no. 2:284–97.

Gardiner, Jean. 1975. "Women's Domestic Labor." *New Left Review* 89 (January–February): 47–71.

Glazer-Malbin, Nona. 1976. "Housework: A Review Essay." Signs 1, no. 4:905–34.

Glenn, Evelyn Nakano. 1980. "The Dialectics of Wage Work: Japanese-American Women and Domestic Service, 1905–1940." *Feminist Studies,* 6, no. 3:432–71.

Gordon, Monica. 1979. "Identification and Adaptation: A Study of Two Groups of Jamaican Immigrants in New York City." Ph.D. diss., City University of New York.

———. 1983. *The Selection of Migrant Categories from the Caribbean to the United States: The Jamaican Experience.* New York Research Program in Inter-American Affairs, Occasional Papers No. 37. New York: New York University, Center for Latin American and Caribbean Studies.

Hamburger, Robert. 1977. "A Stranger in the House." *Southern Exposure* 5, no. 1:22–31.

Henry, Frances. 1968. "The West Indian Domestic Scheme in Canada." *Social and Economic Studies* 17, no. 1:83–91.

———. 1982. "A Note on Caribbean Migration to Canada." *Caribbean Review* 11, no. 1:38–41.

Hochschild, Arlie Russell. 1983. *The Managed Heart: The Commercialization of Human Feeling.* Berkeley: University of California Press.

Howe, Louise Kapp. 1977. *Pink Collar Workers: In the World of Women's Work.* New York: Avon Books.

Katzman, David M. 1978. *Seven Days a Week: Women and Domestic Service in Industrializing America.* New York: Oxford University Press.

Kelly, Joan. 1979. "The Doubled Vision of Feminist Theory: A Postscript to the Women and Power Conference." *Feminist Studies* 5, no. 1:216–27.

Lerner, Gerda. 1973. *Black Women in White America.* New York: Vintage Books.

Marshall, Dawn I. 1982. "The History of Caribbean Migrations: The Case of the West Indies." *Caribbean Review* 11, no. 1: 6–9, 52–53.

Marshall, Paule. 1981a. "Black Immigrant Women in Brown Girl, Brownstones." In Delores M. Mortimer and Roy S. Bryce- Laporte, eds., *Female Immigrants to the United States: Caribbean, Latin American, and African Experiences,* pp. 3–13. Research Institute on Immigration and Ethnic Studies, Occasional Paper No. 2. Washington, D.C.: Smithsonian Institution.

———. 1981b. *Brown Girl, Brownstones.* Old Westbury, N.Y.: Feminist Press.

———. 1983. "From the Poets in the Kitchen." In Paule Marshall, *Reena and Other Stories,* pp. 3–12. Old Westbury, N.Y.: Feminist Press.

Mortimer, Delores M., and Roy S. Bryce-Laporte, eds. 1981. *Female Immigrants to the United States: Caribbean, Latin American, and African Experiences.* Research Institute on Immigration and Ethnic Studies, Occasional Paper No. 2. Washington, D.C.: Smithsonian Institution.

Philpott, Stuart B. 1973. *West Indian Migration: The Montserrat Case.* London: Athlone Press.

Prescod-Roberts, Margaret, and Norma Steele. 1980. *Black Women: Bringing It All Back Home.* Bristol, Eng: Falling Wall Press.

Rapp, Rayna. 1978. "Family and Class in Contemporary America: Notes Towards an Understanding of Ideology." *Science and Society* 42, no. 3:278–300.

Reid, Ira de Augustine. 1939. *The Negro Immigrant, His Background, Characteristics, and Social Adjustment, 1899–1937.* New York: Columbia University Press; rpt. New York: Arno Press, 1969.

Scott, Joan Wallach. 1982. "The Mechanization of Women's Work." *Scientific American 247,* no. 1:166–87.

Silvera, Makeda. 1983. *Silenced: Talks with Working Class West Indian Women about Their Lives and Struggles as Domestic Workers in Canada.* Toronto: Williams-Wallace.

Spellman, Elizabeth V. 1981. "Theories of Race and Gender: The Erasure of Black Women." *Quest: A Feminist Quarterly* 5, no. 4:36–62.

Strasser, Susan. 1982. *Never Done: A History of American Housework.* New York: Pantheon.

Sutton, Constance R. 1976. "Cultural Duality in the Caribbean." *Caribbean Studies* 14, no. 2:96–101.

PART III
Questions for Feminism

10 Household Workers in the Dominican Republic: A Question for the Feminist Movement

ISIS DUARTE

The feminist movement in the Dominican Republic, as is probably the case in other Latin American and Caribbean countries, is characterized by middle-class activism and limited participation among the popular sectors. Despite recent efforts to promote the so-called Coordinator of Women's Organizations, the movement is fragmented into small groups.

The debate engendered by this embryonic feminist movement provided the context for a study of domestic service. This chapter presents the hypotheses and preliminary results of that research project, which explores the relation between women of the middle class—*pequeña burguesía*—and those in domestic service in terms of women's struggle for greater social and particularly gender equality.

Is the Double-Day Thesis Relevant?

The thesis of the "double day" is frequently cited by sectors of the feminist movement to interpret the way women workers are exploited.[1] This thesis maintains that women are more exploited than men: because of their gender, women engage in a unique combination of wage work and unremunerated domestic labor. The latter includes socializing children and caring for the men: husband, brothers, father.

In a debate that took place in 1981 on International Women's Day, I suggested that the thesis of the working woman's double day was a very mechanical generalization in capitalist countries, imported from the feminist movements of the European capitalist countries where

197

the means of production are more highly developed (Duarte 1982a). As a theoretical category, therefore, the double-day thesis could hinder, rather than contribute to, our clearer understanding of the situation of working women. This is the case for female industrial workers in the Dominican Republic's export processing zones—"free zones"—and for domestic workers.

Preliminary studies conducted in 1981 showed that the degree of exploitation of female free-zone workers bears little relation to the concept of the double day (Corten and Duarte 1981). This analytical framework does not lead to an understanding of the working conditions of these women, the majority of whom are young, single, or separated, and living with their families.

The proletarianization of women in the free zones is characterized by a particular type of factory discipline and mode of exploitation. For an important sector of the women, this allows personal exemption from many domestic chores, which are carried out by other female household members: mothers, sisters, other female relatives (Corten and Duarte 1983). Factory exploitation tends to separate or "liberate" women wage workers from domestic work rather than overload them with it. Since a high percentage of women industrial workers do not live with their children, they are also freed from the socialization function. The concept of the double day cannot, therefore, be used to interpret the situation of these workers, as it would not reflect the characteristics of their exploitation.

Neither does the concept of the double day allow us to determine how much overtime is put in by women who work in paid domestic service. As demonstrated below, the majority of domestics in the Dominican Republic "live in," which means that they both live and work in someone else's house. Compared with a factory worker, a domestic service worker does, in fact, work a double day but not as the term is understood in the concept cited. Moreover, the proportion of domestic workers who do not socialize their own children is even higher than that of the factory workers in the free zones; children of domestic service workers are usually raised by their grandmothers or other relatives. It is necessary to develop other concepts to analyze the problematic of domestic service workers, other frameworks that will allow us a better understanding of their difficult working conditions.

As I propose below, the domestic service sector exempts the *pequeña-burguesa* woman from the double day, or at least significantly diminishes its effects. Domestic service performs a fundamental function in societies such as ours, one that distinguishes us radically from the "advanced" capitalist countries: it "liberates" the middle-income women who work outside the home from most domestic chores, including child care. And it thereby liberates those women from the double day.

The *pequeña-burguesa* woman struggling for social and gender equality pays a very high price for her liberation, however: the fact that she is in a position to employ a domestic worker reinforces, rather than challenges, patriarchy and the subordination of women in the society. In the first place, a new chain of hierarchical subordination is established in the family: husband/wife/domestic worker. On the social plane this contradicts women's struggle for equality, since it places the *pequeña-burguesa* woman in a position of protagonist-executor in relation to the subordination of another woman. Second, the material and objective conditions that allow domestic tasks to be redistributed within the family, regardless of gender or age, will not develop as long as middle-class women can transfer most of the household tasks to domestic service. In effect, the very presence of the domestic worker discourages the collaboration of male household members, children, and teenagers. The fact that domestic service is available, therefore, reaffirms *machismo* and patriarchy in the heart of the family.

These reflections suggest that the double-day thesis as an analytic tool is more useful for interpreting the situation of *pequeña-burguesa* women and proletarian women in advanced capitalist countries. Domestic service has been gradually phased out in those countries, as domestic chores—food preparation laundry, and the like—become reorganized in a capitalist mode. Yet in spite of the wide use of household appliances, women's exploitation increased, a phenomenon that *can* be interpreted as a double-day situation. The phasing-out of the paid domestic worker in those countries creates objective conditions that are more favorable for the struggle against patriarchy and against the relegation of domestic chores to women. One must ask whether or not the greater relative progress of the feminist movement in the more developed countries is related to those more favorable objective conditions.

Reflection on the relation between domestic service and the middle class led to the idea of a study that would not only research the living and working conditions of household workers (their legal, ideological, and consumer situation) but also clarify to what extent this service provided to the *pequeña-burguesa* woman in societies such as ours constitutes a hindrance at the everyday level in terms of middle-class so-

cial struggle. This touches on a particularly important and contradictory aspect for women working in the feminist movement for gender
and social equality. The study has not yet been completed, and this
article does not focus on the entire problematic. The hypotheses and
preliminary data presented below are based on a subsample of domestic workers employed in middle-class households, included in a
survey conducted in July 1983.[2]

The Female Labor Force and Domestic Service

How significant are domestic workers in the urban female labor force
in the Dominican Republic? In 1970 women accounted for only 26
percent of the total economically active population (EAP); in 1981
female participation rose to 31 percent of the EAP, with a greater
degree of participation in urban areas: in 1981 the urban labor force
was 36 percent female (República Dominicana, ONE 1983).[3] Incorporation of women into the urban EAP took place essentially through the
tertiary sector; eight of every ten workers in this sector are female,
providing primarily "community, social, and personal services" (55 percent of the total urban female EAP in 1980). Of these, one-half belong
to the occupational group "household workers" (Table 10-1). In short,
domestic service is proportionally the most important activity within
the female EAP: 27 percent of the total. Moreover, 96 percent of all
household workers are women.

Income levels of household workers are the lowest in the country.
In 1983, in the capital city of Santo Domingo, incomes averaged $62
D.R. monthly.[4] Disaggregation of income by gender, however, indicates that male domestic service workers earn almost three times as
much ($158 D.R.) as females ($56 D.R.). In accordance with current
legislation, an "in kind" payment is added to the monthly wage to
justify the fact that the income of household workers is 100 percent or
more below the national minimum wage of $125 D.R. Article 246 of
the Labor Code provides: "There being no conflicting agreement,
payment of domestic workers includes, over and above cash salary,
room and board of standard quality. Room and board provided to
domestics shall be regarded as equivalent to 50 percent of the cash
salary received." The cash and in-kind salary combination accounts

TABLE 10-1.
Economic Activity of Urban Population 15 Years of Age and Older, Dominican Republic, 1980 (in percentages)

ECONOMIC ACTIVITY	TOTAL	WOMEN	MEN
A. Not Economically Active	45.8	63.7	24.7
B. Economically Active	54.2	36.3	75.3
Employed	79.3	73.9	82.3
Unemployed	20.7	26.1	17.7
Dismissed	58.0	43.0	70.6
New Workers	42.0	57.0	29.4
C. Economically Active, Tertiary Sector	60.1	78.6	51.6
Personal and Community Services	20.2	55.5	30.0
Household Workers*	8.9	27.0	0.5

Source: ONAPLAN 1980 (summary elaborated by Isis Duarte).
*The proportion of women within the household worker group is 96.1 percent.

for the fact that most domestic workers in the Dominican Republic "live in": they are *puerta cerrada* (literally, "closed door") or *con dormida* ("with sleep") employees. It is also important to stress that this form of service is differentiated from other types of work in that those employed in a private home do not receive social security—to which, paradoxically, women who carry out similar tasks in a business or commercial environment are legally entitled.[5] Live-in domestic service has profound implications for living and working conditions: it means that the domestics' hours are unlimited (they are supposed to be available on a round-the-clock basis); their living space is segregated from that of the employing family; and they are prevented from socializing their own children. This specific type of service also favors the assimilation of certain values and a given ideology: *asistencialismo*, or welfare mentality, plus certain consumption patterns, and so on. Moreover, the very nature of live-in domestic work prevents domestic workers from organizing.

 This specificity is what distinguishes domestic workers from other occupational groups and defines the essentially "servile" character of the occupation. Like the serf, the domestic (and I believe the comparison is valid) is in the power of the family (or of the *ama de casa*, mistress of the house) for whom she works.

Hypotheses and Preliminary Results of the Research Project

Migration History and Previous Employment

Significant population movement took place in the Dominican Republic during the period between 1950 and 1980; a large sector of the agricultural labor force was displaced into nonagricultural activities and became concentrated in the cities, principally in the capital, Santo Domingo. Two indicators express this process; the urban population grew from 24 percent of the total in 1950 to 52 percent in 1981, while the active agricultural labor force was reduced to only 31 percent in 1981 (República Dominicana, ONE 1955, 1966, 1975, 1983).

This transformation from a rural to an urban population affected women in a particular way. Women not only increased their participation in the labor force (as shown above) but established specific migratory and occupational patterns. Three particular patterns have been identified since 1960.

First, women "escaped" from the small family farm and become proletarianized within the rural zone as temporary agricultural labor (being employed during the fruit harvest, for example). This tendency is demonstrated in a decline of 10.5 percent in the number of women classified in "agricultural and related" occupations as unremunerated "family workers," while the number of female wage workers rose by 13 percent between 1960 and 1970 (República Dominicana, ONE 1966 and 1975).

Second, after the insurrection of April 1965, women migrated to the United States to work, becoming employed in factories outside the country (see Pessar 1982, among others).

Finally, and most markedly during the decade of 1970–80, women migrated to cities within the Dominican Republic and found employment in nonagricultural occupations, for the most part in free zone industry and domestic service.

The geographic and occupational mobility of the labor force is related to structural processes analyzed in other texts. "Expulsion" of the agricultural labor force is related to three factors: expansion and limits of the agricultural sector, monopoly ownership of farmland, and pauperization of the *campesina* (peasant) economy (Duarte 1980, pt. 2.4). The concentration of the migrant population in the large cities, particularly Santo Domingo, is also related to capitalist expansion (Duarte 1983). Finally, the proportion of immigrants among the urban female population is higher than among males. With regard to the two largest cities, "56 percent of the migrants to Santo Domingo and 57 percent . . . to Santiago are women" (Ramírez 1978).

In the study, two hypotheses are linked to the migratory history and working situation of women before their incorporation into urban domestic service. The general hypothesis proposes that the rural household structure allows women to emigrate more easily than men, for two reasons: first, because women are involved at a more secondary and marginal level in the strictly agricultural tasks on the family farm; second, because the option of domestic service provides women with more immediate possibilities of incorporating themselves into wage work in the city. A secondary hypothesis, related to the previous one, proposes that the pauperization of the peasant population affects women first: women are expelled to the city to work in domestic service. The following data from the study are related to these two hypotheses.

Domestic workers, like the majority of the urban labor force in the country, are migrants: 85 percent of those in Santo Domingo were born outside the city. Their migration pattern also runs true to form: 82 percent migrate directly from their place of birth to Santo Domingo, a trend also registered in the "relative overpopulation" of the urban informal sector (Duarte 1980).

What distinguishes this sector, and what we wished to establish, is that as a result of the household division of labor in the rural zones, women are expelled before men. The answers to the question, "Who in the family arrived first to work in the capital?" reveal that 64 percent of the first arrivals were women and only 36 percent men.

Data in Tables 10-2 and 10-3 are intended to illustrate the hypotheses described and to contribute to reflection on why this migration pattern has evolved. The main previous source of income for households of women who have migrated to become domestic workers is "agricultural and related" (86.5 percent), and most of these are peasant households (69 percent). According to the survey, the primary agricultural work is generally performed by the fathers and brothers of the interviewees. Of the tasks considered primary, 80 percent are performed by men, 15.7 percent by both men and women, and only 4.3 percent by women alone (Table 10-2).

Of the total sample, 91 percent of the women indicates that their

TABLE 10-2.
Family Members by Principal Employment before Household Worker's Migration, Santo Domingo, 1983 (in percentages)

PRINCIPAL EMPLOYMENT OF FAMILY MEMBERS		RELATIONSHIP WITH HOUSEHOLD WORKER OF EMPLOYED FAMILY MEMBERS		SEX OF EMPLOYED FAMILY MEMBERS	
Small farming	68.8	Father	32.1 ⎱	Masculine	80.0
Agricultural work	10.6	Father and brothers	40.0 ⎰	Masculine and feminine	15.7
Animal husbandry, fishing, and related activities	7.1	Father and other relatives	10.7		
Sales	5.0	Sisters	5.7	Feminine	4.3
Other activities	8.5	Husband	5.0	Masculine	—
		Other relatives	6.5	Masculine and feminine	—
Total	100.0		100.0		100.0
(*N*)	(141)		(140)		(140)

Source: Duarte, Tactuk, and Fortuna 1983.

TABLE 10-3.
Household Workers by Prior Employment and Present Job
Responsibilities, Santo Domingo, 1983 (in percentages)

PRIOR EMPLOYMENT		PRESENT JOB RESPONSIBILITIES		
	Total (N = 160)	All Tasks	Two Types of Tasks	Only One Type of Task
Unemployed	66.3	65.6	71.7	60.9
Employed	33.7	34.4	28.3	39.1
Farmer	30.0	23.8	46.7	22.2
Household worker	31.0	47.6	20.0	22.2
Laborer	17.0	9.5	20.0	22.2
Sales	22.0	19.1	13.3	33.4
Totals	100.0	39.2	31.9	28.8

Source: Duarte, Tactuk, and Fortuna 1983.

first job in the capital had been as household workers, a percentage that does not vary with "rank" (degree of skill) or the present category of the interviewee.

Finally, to complete the profile of the migratory history and previous employment situation, two out of every three household workers interviewed say that they had been "unemployed" before entering domestic service in Santo Domingo. Unemployment rates during this phase were slightly higher—71.7 percent—for those who "do two types of work" than for those who are more "specialized" and do only one type of work—60.9 percent (Table 10-3).

Working Conditions

To the working conditions mentioned earlier must be added the explicit form of segregation characteristic of the servile nature of domestic service. Domestic workers

> have a roof over their heads but are not members of the household; they live in servants' quarters. They are also distinguished by their workplace, their mealtimes, the types of

food they eat, and, in upper class households, by their style of dress: the uniform.

Although domestic workers live in the family house, they may not use the space and environment of the house for social occasions such as visits from family and friends. Indeed, it is expected that a domestic worker's meeting place is the fence or the street corner. [Duarte et al. 1976, 96]

Data from our 1983 sample largely reflect the income levels registered by the official labor force survey for the city of Santo Domingo in the same year: almost half of all household workers earn less than $60 D.R. per month (see note 4). In our sample, those over the age of twenty-four earn more cash income than those who are younger. This slightly higher income could be attributed, however, to differences in rank. In our sample, the largest proportion, by far, of domestics (81.8 percent) is less than thirty years old (Table 10.4). Although data matching income to job responsibilities still are not available, the same table shows that a higher percentage of specialized workers (who do only one type of work) is found among those who are twenty-five and older (60.9 percent). A preliminary conclusion is that specialization gained by experience (years spent in the particular work activity) commands a higher direct salary. Nevertheless, inquiries not related to the

TABLE 10-4.
Workers by Age and Responsibility, Santo Domingo, 1983
(in percentages)

| | | JOB RESPONSIBILITIES | | |
AGE	TOTAL (N = 165)	All Tasks	Two Types of Tasks	Only One Type of Task
19 and younger	15.1	18.7	12.7	13.0
20 to 24	36.4	45.3	34.6	26.1
25 to 29	30.3	17.2	40.0	37.0
30 to 34	11.5	9.4	9.1	17.4
35 to older	6.7	9.4	3.6	6.5
Totals	100.0	38.8	33.3	27.9

Source: Duarte, Tactuk, and Fortuna 1983.

TABLE 10-5.
Household Workers by Benefits Received
during Past Two Years, Santo Domingo
(in percentages)

BENEFITS	% (N = 165)
Weekly day off	82.4
Free time during workday	79.0
Several days' leave without loss of pay	53.3
Holiday gifts	49.0
Other gifts	48.0
"Double" salary*	37.0
Payment of medical bills	35.2
Time to study	30.3
Yearly paid vacation	20.1

Source: Duarte, Tactuk, and Fortuna 1983.
*"Double" salary is supposed to be paid when the domestic
worker agrees to work on her day off or a holiday.

survey show that income is not significantly differentiated according
to rank.

Over and above income, the division into three categories is relevant in terms of workload and heterogeneity of the tasks performed.
Clearly, in terms of the physical and mental effort of coordination and
organization expended, the worker who is expected to perform a
wide range of tasks (cooking, cleaning, washing, ironing, and looking
after the children) does more than the domestic who is responsible for
only two types of chores (cooking and washing, or cleaning and ironing) or the more specialized worker who has only one chore (cooking,
or looking after the children).

With regard to the indirect wage, Table 10-5 shows the "benefits"
generally received by our domestic worker interviewees during the
two years prior to our survey. These data apply to benefits granted
only in some households, not in all. The same table shows clearly that
no indirect wage is consistently paid: only 37 percent of the sample
received double-time pay for working on holidays or their specified
days off, despite the fact that 73 percent had worked in only one or
two households during that period and had they been working in

other, nonservile, relations, would have been entitled to a double-time bonus (usually paid at year's end). Likewise, only 20.1 percent of the total sample received annual paid vacation time. It is common for the *amas de casa*, however, to give their household workers a holiday bonus that corresponds to part of their salary (49 percent do so), or some other perquisite such as clothing or food, if they have been employed for some time (48 percent).

In terms of working hours, the Labor Code states:

> The workday of domestics is not restricted to fixed hours, but they must be allowed at least nine uninterrupted hours of rest between every two consecutive working days. [Article 247]
> They shall have one period of rest every week, from 2:00 P.M. until the hour work is normally begun on the following day. [Article 248][6]

Table 10.5 does show that household workers have made some "gains" extending beyond labor legislation. In fact, 79 percent say that they have free time during the day, and 30.3 percent use their time to study. However, 17 percent say that they have "never had a weekly day off" in all the time they have been employed.

The data show that approximately half of the domestics surveyed work seventy-two hours or more per six-day work week: in other words, four hours more per day than is usual for industrial workers. It would appear, then, that the service provided by domestic workers should be calculated in terms of tasks performed rather than daily or weekly work hours; the essential characteristic of this occupational group is the demand for its round-the-clock availability and submission. It should be understood that Article 247 of the Labor Code is still in full force (although live-in workers sleep less than nine hours a night), but the extent to which the domestic must be available at all hours depends on the "benevolence" or tolerance of the *ama de casa*. It is not an accident, as we shall see later on, that domestic workers generally choose "good treatment" as a principal condition of employment (see Table 10-8).

In sum, what characterizes the working conditions in domestic service is the combination of work by assigned tasks, the unlimited working hours, and the demand for almost absolute availability and submission. Another factor in the situation may be the "despotic" behavior of the *ama de casa* and/or other family members. Domestic workers compensate for these kinds of working conditions by changing jobs or by temporarily withdrawing from domestic service for certain periods during the year. Of all the domestics surveyed, 42 percent had worked for less than one year at their present place of employment. They change jobs seeking to be "well treated" rather than better paid. Another survival strategy to make up for the exhaustion brought about by the working conditions and lack of paid annual vacation is for domestics to change jobs at the end of the year after spending the Christmas holidays at home.

Most household workers in the Dominican Republic live in (and suffer the consequences), as noted above. Also, within our specific sample (which covered diverse strata of the *pequeña-burguesía*) most domestic workers are "maids-of-all-work": the majority of the homes surveyed employ only one domestic worker (61 percent) (Table 10-6). These two characteristics combine to produce the type of household worker most commonly found in the Dominican Republic: the live-in maid-of-all-work—in other words, the one who puts forth the greatest physical and mental effort in terms of the number of tasks accomplished and coordination-organization of labor.

Table 10-6 also shows how the number of workers employed in a household vary in relation to the marital situation and number of children of the *ama de casa*. Approximately 85 percent of the *amas de casa* who have either no children or no husband/companion employ only one domestic; those who are both wife and mother tend to employ more domestics (whose duties include looking after the husband and children).

These data, although very limited, are related to the discussion introduced at the beginning of this chapter: domestic service permits the *pequeña-burguesa* woman who is employed outside the home to escape the double day, or at least lightens its burden for her. The full sample selected will demonstrate this idea more clearly, since one criterion for selecting households was whether women were employed outside the home (see note 2), but complete data are not yet available.[7]

Labor Relations, Values, and Levels of Consumption

As stated above, the study is centrally concerned with describing the characteristics common to household workers who reside in the houses where they work. Their situation as live-in domestics is the essential

TABLE 10-6.
Number of Household Workers by Employer's Marital Status and Number of Children, Santo Domingo, 1983 (in percentages)

NUMBER OF HOUSEHOLD WORKERS	TOTAL (N = 333)	EMPLOYER'S MARITAL STATUS			NUMBER OF EMPLOYER'S CHILDREN			
		Wife Alone*	Mother Alone†	Wife and Mother‡ (subtotal)	One	Two	Three	Four
One	61.0	84.6	84.4	57.3	66.7	68.7	47.0	53.8
Two	31.0	15.4	15.6	33.3	26.7	20.9	47.0	33.0
Three	8.0	0.0	0.0	9.4	6.6	10.4	6.0	13.2
Totals	100.0	4.0	9.6	86.4	13.5	20.1	25.5	27.3

Source: Duarte, Tactuk, and Fortuna 1983.
*Woman separated from husband, no children.
†Woman separated from husband, with children.
‡Woman living with husband and children.

factor conditioning the labor relation; it facilitates the assimilation of certain values and effectively prevents this important sector of the female labor force from organizing. More concretely, the live-in situation favors the development of welfare-providential (*asistencialista-providencial*) labor relations between the domestic and *ama de casa* and creates certain expectations among the household workers (also stimulated by the mass media) with regard to the patterns of consumption and personal care (clothes, cosmetics, hair care, and so on) typical of the *pequeña-burguesía*. Finally, the nature of live-in domestic service hinders development of a consciousness of their needs that would induce workers in this sector to organize for a solution to their problems.

The questionnaire asked household workers about the different ways they dispose of their income. About 90 percent of the sample purchase consumer goods for personal use, while only about 13 percent acquire durable consumer goods (furniture, appliances, and the like) on credit. What stands out is the fact that one-quarter of the women spend part of their income on "entertainment"; 30.9 percent allocate part to savings; and 19.5 percent use a portion to finance their studies. It is also significant that domestics support members of their own families: 47.7 percent spend part of their income on their children and the majority—78.1 percent—send a portion to their parents.

Disaggregation of the data by the number of children domestic workers have shows significant differences in personal consumption habits and income use. Table 10-7 shows the workers' principal uses of income during the month prior to the survey, according to number of children. While the purchase of personal consumer items continues to predominate at a general level (37.2 percent), more than half of the women surveyed use most of their income to support children, parents, and other relatives. The distribution of her income is clearly differentiated according to whether or not the domestic worker has children. Of the half that do not have children, 57 percent use most of their income for purchase of personal consumer items, in contrast to only 18 percent of those who do have children. Of those workers with and without children, 67.3 percent and 29.7 percent, respectively, contribute to the support of family members.

In short, the propensity to "superfluous" consumption and the "demonstration effect" in the context of the *pequeña-burguesa* household where the domestic is employed tend to be operative only when a domestic does not have children. Consumption patterns among fe-

TABLE 10-7.
Household Workers by How Income Is Used and Number of Children, Santo Domingo, 1983 (in percentages)

PRINCIPAL USE OF INCOME	TOTAL (N = 304)	NO CHILDREN	HAVE CHILDREN	NO. OF CHILDREN			
				One	Two	Three	Four+
Help child (children)	30.0	0.0	58.3	54.4	54.7	68.0	62.4
Help parents	16.1	27.0	5.8	8.8	—	16.0	—
Help other relatives	3.0	2.7	3.2	1.7	4.8	4.0	3.1
Buy personal consumer items	37.2	57.4	18.0	23.0	23.8	8.0	9.4
Buy consumer durables	2.6	1.4	3.8	1.7	4.8	4.0	6.3
Savings	2.0	2.0	1.9	1.7	—	—	6.3
Studies	1.6	1.4	1.9	1.7	2.4	—	3.1
Entertainment	2.6	5.4	0.0	0.0	—	—	—
Other	4.9	2.7	7.1	7.0	9.5	—	9.4
Totals	100.0	48.7	51.3	18.8	13.8	8.2	10.5

Source: Duarte, Tactuk, and Fortuna 1983.

TABLE 10-8.

Household Workers by Most Important Condition of Work and Job
Responsibilities, Santo Domingo, 1983 (in percentages)

MOST IMPORTANT WORKING CONDITIONS	TOTAL (N = 163)	JOB RESPONSIBILITIES		
		All Tasks	Two Types of Tasks	Only One Type of Task
Good treatment	71.8	71.4	71.7	72.3
Good salary	19.6	15.9	20.8	23.4
More free time	8.6	12.7	7.5	4.3
Totals	100.0	38.7	32.5	28.8

Source: Duarte, Tactuk, and Fortuna 1983.

male workers in the country's industrial free zones are similar (Corten
and Duarte 1983).

Apart from working conditions and the *ama de casa*–domestic
worker relationship, the project attempted to explore the values, preferences, and level of consciousness found among those working in
this sector. Asked "What do you believe is most important for a household worker?" 71.8 percent of the interviewees answered, "To be well
treated"; just under 20 percent specified higher wages, and only
about 9 percent "more free time" (see Table 10-8). These data indicate
that her relationship with the *ama de casa* is more important for the
domestic than salary or working hours. There are, however, slight
variations according to rank or specialization level of the worker: a
larger percentage of maids-of-all-work prefer to have more free time;
of the specialized workers, a better salary.

Table 10-9 shows to which sector, class, or social situation the domestic worker would choose to belong if she had the option. Almost
half would choose "to marry a good man and not have to work" (46.7
percent). If she had to work, her first choice would be "to find work in
a factory" (29.7 percent); her second, "to become independent and
self-employed" (12.7 percent). Only as a last resort would she look for
a better position in domestic service (10.9 percent). Once again, however, the response varies according to the category of the domestic
worker. More than half of those who carry out a full range of tasks
have a marked preference for a "good husband" and place less value
on factory work—the reverse of the valuation expressed by the more

TABLE 10-9.
Household Workers by Aspirations and Present Job Responsibilities,
Santo Domingo, 1983 (in percentages)

| | | JOB RESPONSIBILITIES | | |
ASPIRATION	TOTAL (N = 165)	All Tasks	Two Types of Tasks	Only One Type of Task
Secure other household work with better salary	10.9	9.3	5.7	18.8
Find job as factory worker	29.7	18.8	34.0	39.6
Become self-employed	12.7	18.8	11.3	6.2
Marry a good man and not have to work	46.7	53.1	49.0	35.4

Source: Duarte, Tactuk, and Fortuna 1983.

specialized workers, of whom 39.6 percent would prefer to work in a factory; 35.4 percent to make a good marriage and not work; and 18.8 percent to make a better wage as a domestic.

Still in the context of working conditions, domestics were asked who they thought could be most helpful in resolving their problems. The answers are revealing: 46 percent think that the "government" could or should resolve them; 37 percent say that their employers should improve the situation; only 17 percent think that they themselves, the domestic workers, should do something to solve their problems. Given the working conditions analyzed above, this group—despite the fact that it is the smallest proportion of the sample—is not insignificant.

Domestic Work and Socialization of Children

The working conditions of domestics are incompatible with pregnancy and the socialization (upbringing) of children, the problematic encompassing the production and biological-social reproduction of the next generation. Our preliminary analyses suggest that the domestic service sector shows a lower fertility rate and uses birth control methods more frequently than other sectors. The data also indicate that domestics who become pregnant customarily leave their work for a period that may last until the child is two years old; thereafter, it is raised by its grandparents.

Domestic service, therefore, tends to separate women from their sociobiological function, as the following indicators confirm:

- 81.8 percent of workers in the sample are less than 30 years old;
- 75.9 percent have neither husband nor companion, either because they never married (39.2 percent) or are separated/divorced 36.7 percent);
- 50 percent have no children;
- of those who are separated or divorced, 16.4 percent are childless and 42.7 percent have only one child;
- only 5.2 percent of workers' children are under two years of age.

Our data indicate how the situation of domestic workers relates to the production and socialization of their offspring. We find that only 15 percent of the children are cared for by their mothers, the domestic workers themselves. These are mainly domestics who do not live in but reside outside the house where they are in service and/or wash and iron several days a week, returning to their own homes at the end of the day. Of all the children, 62.2 percent are brought up by their grandparents and 11.6 percent by their fathers, with other relatives (8.7 percent) or non-relatives (3 percent) caring for the rest.

As indicated above, only 5.2 percent of the workers' children are under two years of age, indicating that an insignificant number of household workers in the Dominican Republic have children in this age group. The large proportional increase found in the following statistics tends to confirm this: 34.9 percent of the children are in the two-to-five age group, and an equal percentage in the five-to-ten age group; the proportion declines again in the over-ten age groups.

These data support the hypotheses noted earlier: the domestic worker leaves her job during the gestation period and does not return to work until her child is about two years old. From this time on she leaves the child to be raised by grandparents, or other relatives, and returns to work. What should be noted here is the interesting valuation placed by this sector of domestic workers on maternal care during a child's first two years, an aspect worth serious psychosocial analysis.

The household worker not only is unable to bring up her own children after they reach age two but in the majority of cases also must live geographically separated from them. This contrasts sharply with her attempt to care for the children during their first two years. Fully 66 percent, or two of every three children of domestic workers, live outside the city of Santo Domingo, mostly in the rural areas. Of the one-third who do live in the capital, only 15 percent live with their mothers.

In short, the children of domestics, after they reach age two (and in some cases before) are socialized by other relatives, mainly their grandparents, in the rural areas. Thus, with regard to the mother-child relationship, the problem involves both geographical separation and exclusion from day-to-day maternal care and influence.

Conclusions

Unfortunately, the conclusion of this preliminary reflection on the relation between the feminist movement and domestic service cannot be a recommendation to strive for the elimination of domestic service altogether. Although it is true that this sector labors under the worst working and living conditions relative to other sectors, it is also true that domestic service is the most important source of employment for the female labor force in the Dominican Republic, as it is in other countries in the region.

The domestic worker is the most subordinated of all female wage workers, and her presence in the household contradicts the anti-patriarchy struggle of the *pequeña-burguesa* woman. Yet the existence of domestic workers is a product of structural conditions that individual humanistic desires are powerless to affect. It is incumbent upon the feminist movement to challenge the socioeconomic and cultural conditions that maintain this particular form of servitude in capitalist societies such as ours. Taking on the cause of household workers is important not only because domestic service is a large and subordinated sector but because the private and isolated nature of her working and living conditions makes it very difficult for the worker herself to articulate her needs and situation.

Notes

1. See Larguía and Dumoulin (1976), in particular the section relating to "visible and invisible work" and "the second work day." In this essay, I do not attempt to carry out a theoretical criticism; my aim is to invite more discussion and analysis of the conditions of exploitation of women who, in certain occupational categories, are not linked to the problem of the "double day" in the usual sense.

2. In 1975 several of us already had suggested some of the ideas developed in this research (see Duarte et al. 1976). A quota sampling system was employed and 370 interviews carried out. Of these, a subsample of 165 cases is used here (with some exceptions). The questionnaire asks for information on the structure of the employer's household. One of the criteria for establishing the quota system was the employment situation of the *amas de casa*, who were then divided into three categories: (a) not employed in wage work; (b) working for a wage from the home; (c) employed outside the home. The sample includes three categories of domestic service that are assumed to imply a "division of work" related—among other things—to the socioeconomic situation of the family where the domestic is employed and, to a lesser extent, to family size: (a) maid-of-all-work; (b) the domestic who performs two particular tasks; (c) the worker who carries out only one task.

Besides using secondary sources, the entire project involved in-depth interviews and life histories, as well as interviews with employers belonging to the middle class. The questionnaire administered during the fieldwork was prepared with the help of Pablo Tactuk and Carmen Fortuna. The work done to date was carried out with the participation of students in Sociology II of the undergraduate program in economics at the Universidad Autónoma de Santo Domingo, as an experimental pedagogical project that attempts to combine lectures and research. Under the supervision of the author, students participated in the construction of the hypotheses and the design of the questionnaire; one group participated in the fieldwork as well.

3. Moreover, if we take into consideration only the female labor force, we find that 63 percent lived in the urban area and only 37 percent in the rural area in 1981 (República Dominicana ONE, 1983). However, most of the specialized labor force surveys that allow us to estimate the future extent of this tendency were carried out after 1980. The question is whether this is a real tendency or simply a redistribution of the EAP that does not significantly affect women's total proportional participation. The two main studies are República Dominicana, ONAPLAN 1982 and 1983.

4. The exchange rate for July 1983 was $1.00 U.S. = $1.60 D.R., making the salary equivalent to about $40 U.S.

5. According to the 1896 Social Security Law currently in force, domestic workers are included in mandatory social security, which would allow this

important sector of the female labor force access to this form of indirect salary (medical services during pregnancy, pre- and post-natal leave, etc.). However, this does not happen because, in the regulation for the execution of the 1896 law (July 1974), a distinction was made between domestic workers employed by businesses and those employed in private homes; the latter were specifically excluded. This exclusion is an illegality that affects more than one-quarter of the female urban EAP in the country. To rectify it requires not new legislation but the application of the provisions of the law of 1896 (see Duarte 1982b).

6. Note that this constitutes only a half-day, since the working day begins at 7:00 A.M.

7. The sample attempted to cover different strata (low, medium, high) of the *pequeña burguesía*. At this level, however, the only indicator was the neighborhood or residental zone.

References

Corten, André, and Isis Duarte. 1981. *Encuestas efectuadas en tres zonas francas industriales, República Dominicana*. Santo Domingo: Universidad Autónoma de Santo Domingo, Centro de Estudios de la Realidad Social Dominicana (CERESD).

———. 1983. "Procesos de proletarización de mujeres: Las trabajadoras de industrias de ensamblaje en la R.D." *Revista Archipélago* (Edición Caribennes, París) 1, no. 2.

Duarte, Isis. 1980. *Capitalismo y superpoblación en Santo Domingo: Mercado de trabajo rural y ejército de reserva urbana*. Santo Domingo: CODIA.

———. 1982a. "Las mujeres en la sociedad: Aspecto económico laboral." *Revista Ciencia y Sociedad* 7, no. 1:68–79.

———. 1982b. "La mujer en el mundo del la inseguridad social." *El Nuevo Diario*, Santo Domingo, 26 de agosto.

———. 1983. "Fuerza laboral urbana en Santo Domingo, 1980–1983." *Estudios Sociales* 16, no. 53:31–53.

Duarte, Isis, Estela Hernández, Aída Garden Bobea, and Francis Pou. 1976. "Condiciones sociales del servicio doméstico en la República Dominicana." *Realidad Contemporánea* 1, nos. 3–4:79–104.

Duarte, Isis, Pablo Tactuk, and Carmen Fortuna. 1983. "Encuesta de Trabajadoras de Hogar de la Ciudad de Santo Domingo," datos preliminares (July).

Larguía, Isabel, and John Dumoulin. 1976. *Hacia una ciencia de la liberación de la mujer*. Barcelona: Anagrama.

Pessar, Patricia R. 1982. "El significado del trabajo en la emigración dominicana." Duke University, Durham, N.C. Mimeo.

Ramíerez, Nelson. 1978. *Encuesta de migración a Santo Domingo y Santiago.* Santo Domingo: Consejo Nacional de Población y Familia (CONAPOFA), Informe General.

República Dominicana, Oficina Nacional de Estadística (ONE). 1955. *Censo de Población de 1950.* Santo Domingo: ONE.

——. 1966. *Cuarto Censo Nacional de Población de 1960.* Santo Domingo: ONE.

——. 1975. *Censo Nacional de Población de 1970.* Santo Domingo: ONE.

——. 1983. *Censo Nacional de 1981.* Santo Domingo: ONE.

República Dominicana, ONAPLAN. 1980. *Encuesta nacional de mano de obra.* Junio. Santo Domingo: Oficina Nacional de Planficación.

——. 1982. *Encuesta nacional urbana de mano de obra.* Junio. Santo Domingo: Oficina Nacional de Planficación.

——. 1983. *Encuesta de mano de obra de Santo Domingo.* Documento Misión de PREALC, abril. Santo Domingo: Oficina Nacional de Planficación.

11 Politics and Programs of Domestic Workers' Organizations in Mexico

MARY GOLDSMITH

> When industrial development of the country obliges us to go work in factories and offices, and attend to the house and the children and our appearance and social life, and etc., etc., etc., then we'll get down to the nitty-gritty. When the last maid disappears, the little cushion on which our conformity now rests, then will appear the first enraged rebel.
>
> *Rosario Castellanos (1982)*

Domestic service historically has served as a backdrop to Mexican society. Sometimes the subject of maternalistic journalism and, more frequently, of employers' gossip and popular humor, its existence is rarely assigned political significance. Nonetheless, the fact that a least 814,963 women[1] are household workers is significant for both feminist and labor movements.

In Mexico, domestic service continues to figure as one of the most important occupations for women. According to the 1980 census (República de México, Secretaría de Programación y Presupuesto 1984) approximately 13.3 percent of the female economically active population (EAP) nationwide were household workers, and within the Federal District, 13.0 percent. As indicated in Table 11-1, there seems to have been a considerable decline in the percentage of domestic workers since 1970.[2] However, a 1978 study conducted in metropolitan Mexico City concluded that 23.7 percent of all women workers were employed in domestic and cleaning services.[3] This suggests

This article summarizes some of the ideas in the author's dissertation, "Domestic Service and Dependent Capitalist Development: The Case of the Metropolitan Area of Mexico City," currently in preparation for the University of Connecticut, Department of Anthropology. Fieldwork and documentary research were carried out in several phases in 1977–83.

TABLE 11-1.

Household Workers in Female Work Force, Mexico

YEAR	FEMALE EAP	HOUSEHOLD WORKERS		WORKERS IN INSUFFICIENTLY DEFINED OCCUPATIONS	
		% of EAP	Number	% of EAP	Number
1970					
Nationwide	2,466,257	19.8	488,344	9.6	238,117
Federal District	711,741	24.1	171,822	4.1	129,050
1980					
Nationwide	6,141,278	13.3	814,963	22.9	1,409,541
Federal District	1,201,896	13.0	155,880	19.5	238,610

Sources: República de México, Secretaría de Industria y Comercio 1971, Table 27; República de México, Secretaría de Programación y Presupuesto 1984, Table 10.

that the results of the 1980 census are somewhat dubious. The demand for domestic workers seems to have continued, and household workers would not have had easy access to alternative employment. One could argue that many domestics within the 1980 census were captured in the "insufficiently defined occupations" section.

During the 1970s, it is clear, women were increasingly integrated into the labor force, as illustrated in Table 11-2. Rendón and Pedrero (1982) have attributed this to rising inflation, consumption patterns, and the opening of new and expansion of already existing labor markets.[4]

As in most Latin American countries, in Mexico the majority of workers in the domestic service sector are women who have migrated from rural areas. They have lower educational levels and ages than the majority of the other economically active women, and they earn less. In my own research I found that most live-ins earn somewhat less than half the general minimum wage, while those who live out receive nearly the daily minimum.[5] Wages vary somewhat according to the social characteristics of the neighborhood. Some subcategories, such as cooks, are also better paid. Generally, only one's lack—not possession—of experience is taken into account by an employer in hiring a

TABLE 11-2.
Integration of Women into Work Force, Mexico

YEAR	TOTAL FEMALE POPULATION (12 and older)	FEMALE EAP Number	%
1970			
Nationwide	15,071,713	2,466,257	16.4
Federal District	2,395,430	711,741	29.7
1980			
Nationwide	22,128,830	6,141,278	27.6
Federal District	3,274,577	1,202,896	36.7

Sources: República de México, Secretaría de Industria y Comercio 1971, Table 25; República de México, Secretaría de Programación y Presupuesto 1984, Tables 4, 10.

new worker. Employers frequently pay younger, more recent immigrants abysmal wages on the grounds that they are "in training" yet extensive years of service receive no reward on the grounds that these workers are no longer as productive. As an unemployed woman with emphysema put it: "While you're young and healthy, you're 'part of the family.' Later, nobody wants you" [M.S., approximately seventy years old, originally from the State of Mexico].

At present in Mexico there are various programs aimed at the domestic service sector. These range from schools that prepare women to be more docile, skilled domestic servants, to government legislation, to progressive organizations founded and controlled by domestic workers themselves. This chapter focuses on the Mexican legislation related to domestic workers, the social and economic obstacles that hinder their ability to organize, and three case studies of Mexican organizations that have affected domestic service. They are the Asociación Nacional de Trabajadores Domésticos (National Association of Domestic Workers), which has close ties to the government and reflects its philosophy; the Colectivo de Acción Solidaria con Empleadas Domésticas or CASED (Collective for Action in Solidarity with Domestic Employees), which is an outgrowth of the Mexican feminist movement; and the Hogar de Servidores Domésticos, (Domestic Workers' House), which began as a religious discussion group concerned with the living conditions of domestics.

Government Legislation and Policy

Much of Mexico's present domestic labor legislation dates from 1931. Additions were made in 1970 regarding domestic workers' labor obligations and conditions for the termination of labor contracts. Currently, Chapter 13 of the *Ley Federal de Trabajo* describes many of domestic workers' rights and obligations in such a way as to exclude them from the rights that other workers have; it supports the employers' viewpoint rather than that of the workers.

The legislation does not explicitly state whether domestics, like most other workers, are entitled to paid vacations and holidays, a weekly free day, maternity leave, and retirement pay. The limited rights granted to household workers are very ambiguously stated. The chapter stipulates not the length of the workday itself but only that the worker should have sufficient time to eat and to rest during the night. Similarly, the wording regarding salary is vague and therefore subject to a variety of interpretations. Some lawyers contend that the minimum wage for domestic workers is composed of one-third in-kind and two-thirds cash (Trueba Urbina and Trueba Barrera 1977, 151); others, that is is one-half in-kind and one-half cash (Cavazos Flores 1972, 388); and still others, that it is entirely a matter of personal agreement between employer and employee.

Other legal rights such as "comfortable room and board," respectful treatment, and an opportunity to study are also ill defined. The only clear statements are those obliging employers to pay severance benefits and medical and funeral expenses,[6] but enforcement is difficult. One finds that the majority of domestic workers are ignorant of their rights. In practice the employer, usually on the basis of family customs, personal experience, and present needs, decides which benefits a worker will receive.

In 1973 a special household workers social security program was instituted that covered sickness, maternity leave, work-related accidents, retirement, and day care for insured workers' children. The program was initiated with the abundance of demagoguery so characteristic of the Mexican State and fits nicely with the populist image projected by Luis Echeverría Alvarez's regime. In fact, however, the actual benefits accruing to household workers were minimal. The program's coverage was very limited; only 1,000–2,000 persons were enrolled.[7] Various factors contributed to the program's overall failure. There was a lack of planning and research; the program operated on a voluntary basis that left it to the employer to decide whether to enroll her worker or not; and enrollment was restricted to two sixty-day periods over the past decade. In 1981, the Instituto Mexicano de Seguro Social (Mexican Institute of Social Security) considered formulating a new, more flexible program, offering different types of coverage and a variety of premiums; the plan was abandoned in October 1984 on the alleged grounds that domestic workers' lack job stability (*Ovaciones* 1984).

Unionization has been another area of sporadic government concern. While only twenty-five workers are necessary to form a union, no domestic worker union now exists, and there is no record that any have registered during the past twenty-five years. In December 1980 the Confederación de Trabajadores y Campesinos, or CTC (Confederation of Workers and Peasants) of the State of Mexico publicly announced the creation of the Sindicato de Trabajadores Domésticos y Similares (Union of Domestic and Similar Workers) (*Uno Mas Uno* 1980), whose demands centered on the rights to a minimum wage, an eight-hour work day, and social security. Various incongruities in information plus government control of the labor movement led one to view this would-be union with some skepticism.[8] The union reported that it was going to request registration within the local Department of Labor, but it did not. A membership of 1,700 was claimed, but later there were only 250 participants. Moreover, the economic crisis of the early 1980s debilitated the incipient organization. Participants became discouraged as they faced increasing job competition with unemployed factory workers. Participation had always been erratic at best, and the group finally disbanded in early 1984.

Obstacles to Organizing

In addition to the various well-known difficulties that inhibit women's political and social activism—such as family opposition, a double workday, sexism of male counterparts, and lack of expertise and confidence—domestic workers are further limited by the peculiarities of their labor situation, which inhibits both the development of class consciousness and any political involvement.

Live-in workers, particularly, find not only their public but their private lives submerged within the private sphere of the lives of their employers, who unconsciously foment this intimacy in an intricate and subtle process.[9] The female employer sets the parameters to the relationship by speaking with *tú* or *usted* (the informal and formal "you"), and by inviting or not inviting the domestic to share the same table or the same food and dishes. The employee may resist her absorption into the life of her employers by insisting on eating in the kitchen or maintaining a certain reserve in her relations with the family. Some employees realize that an apparent closeness is often a means through which an employer controls the servant both physically and psychologically. One worker who confided personal problems to her employer found this confidence later used against her in a work-related issue. Her employer blackmailed her emotionally by arguing: "Given your temper, let's see who puts up with you elsewhere. You're always fighting with everybody" [R.S., nineteen, originally from the State of Mexico].

Another frequent ploy of the *patrona* is to adopt a maternalistic attitude, referring to an employee as another daughter. This relationship, permeated by power based on class and age, is demystified when the employer demands breakfast in bed from her "daughter." She may also encourage the worker to imitate her in personal appearance by giving her hand-me-down clothing; when the domestic worker initiates this mimicry on her own, however, wearing nail polish or pants, she may become the object of insults.

Similarly, an employee may at one time be applauded for assuming responsibility; at other times, if she makes a simple decision such as what to cook and serve to the household, she may be reprimanded for thinking herself "the *señora*." Any situation implying a relationship based on equality, or suggesting that the employer has been replaced in her role as mother, wife, and household authority, represents a threat to the mistress-servant relationship.

In some cases, the worker is aware of her oppression, but even so, she may internalize her employer's attitudes and values. For example, one worker who was earning 7,000 pesos a month (at the time, about $44 U.S.) by doing three jobs—primarily as household worker but occasionally as receptionist and packer in her employer's business—complained that she was tired of being exploited; her employer was demanding, and unappreciative of her efforts. Yet in another situation, this same domestic espoused a typical employer ideology in rationalizing the exploitation of others:

> I'm going to work as an intermediary between a garment factory and a bunch of women in the neighborhood where my

boyfriend lives. I'll keep half what the factory pays me and pay the other half to the women. . . . They can stitch up the clothes at home, and that way have the chance to make a little money. [L.B., twenty-one, originally from Hidalgo]

Similarly, a live-out worker bitterly accused employers: "They have their mansions and big cars because they don't pay us what they should. That's where they get their money from" [A.S., approximately forty, originally from San Luis Potosi]. Yet this same domestic dreamed of building a two-story home with a big garden in the back.

Language usage illustrates more subtle forms of identification. The domestic worker often refers to the house, work-related areas, and implements (kitchen, refrigerator, and so on) as "mine" and cares for them as if they were her own. The employer frequently reinforces this attitude by not permitting the worker to leave the house if no one else is at home, in order to ward off robberies.

The domestic worker may respond to her own lack of intimacy with the impeccable fulfillment of her job; this is evident in the frequent competition that exists between co-workers. It may assume various forms: informing on a sister worker's mistakes, negligence, morality, or even political involvement, or scolding new employees by virtue of greater seniority. Domestic workers with years of service in the same household are particularly critical of new employees: "I don't know what to do with A. The *señora* told me to keep an eye on her. But she's so clumsy, she broke an ashtray today" [M.T., nineteen, originally from Veracruz]. In another case the chambermaid told the new cook, as she grabbed a tortilla purchased that day: "Finish yesterday's tortillas. The fresh ones are for the *señores* and their children. What is left over is for us" [T.R. approximately fifty, originally from Michoacán].

Such competition usually works to the advantage of employers, but it can act to their detriment when conflicts result in frequent labor turnovers. This explains in part why some employers prefer hiring domestic workers who are related: although their relationship may not be conflict-free, its parameters have already been established.

Senior workers also may have fixed concepts regarding the "proper" fulfillment of their jobs. A domestic who was asked why she didn't leave the dishes for later, so that she could arrive on time for a catechism group, answered: "It wouldn't be right. It would look bad if one of the *señores* went into the kitchen for a glass of water and found a mess in the sink" [I.N., approximately sixty, originally from the state of Hidalgo].

Perhaps an extreme case of such absolute identity with one's work was that of a seventy-four-year-old woman who had worked in the same household for fifty-five years. As of 1982 she was receiving 5,500 pesos a month and did not have a day off. When another worker, recently retired, suggested that this woman also retire, she was dumbfounded. With few friends and family, all she had was her job.

The fact that the household worker is submerged within the employer's life implies the negation of her own existence. Wearing a uniform, which accentuates the home's elegance and cleanliness, and the discreet use of the radio and telephone minimize her presence. The worker responds to this situation with a variety of defense mechanisms. Her imitation of her employer implies a questioning of her own place in society as well as the belief that the only alternative would be for her to assume her employer's place. When a worker cleans less frequently or thoroughly than ordered, she is imposing her own standards. When she rips or "loses" her uniform or turns up the radio so that *música ranchera* blasts away, she is reaffirming the fact of her own existence.

Some forms of domination evident within the *patrona*-worker relationship are particularly humiliating: being required to use separate dishes and utensils, eat different foods, or serve the employer breakfast in bed; being denied phone access or the right to receive friends and family in the workplace; having to ask permission to leave the house for any reason. The employer often advises her worker to be careful about her associates, or does not allow her to attend school for fear that she will be exposed to new ideas and become more demanding. Clearly, such treatment reinforces the employee's isolation. As a result, domestic workers usually do not have close friendships; their main relationships are with their relatives or members of the household in which they work. All of this, of course, bears negative implications for their possibility of reflecting upon work conditions, the development of class consciousness, and the creation of labor organizations.

Several aspects of domestic service account for women's attitudes toward this occupation. First, domestic labor, as one aspect of reproduction, forms a crucial part of the underpinnings of society yet is not valued. The reasons for this situation have been discussed amply within the feminist housework debate and will not be analyzed in depth here.[10] However, it is clear that while the role of mother-housewife is greatly romanticized on an ideological level, its apparent importance is contradicted by reality. The ability to carry out housework is considered a secondary female sexual characteristic and, as such, is considered menial, unskilled labor. Most women, as housewives, carry it out as a "labor of love." Their wageless status explains in part why domestic employees are so badly paid. Given that the social recognition granted an activity is based upon the salary earned, housework is viewed as worthless.

In addition, in Mexico, where social divisions are so rigidly defined, there is symbolic meaning attached to domestic labor: any woman who does it, whether as housewife or maid, is implicitly a poorer member of society. In light of this situation, it is little wonder that most domestic workers do not identify with their jobs.

The attitudes of domestic workers also vary according to life stages. Initially, when a young woman migrates to the city, she regards domestic service essentially as a means of assisting her family or acquiring at least a primary education. She does not have a clear view of future aspirations such as marriage, a different job, or further studies.

When a household worker studies, she enters into contact with other domestic workers and acquires more self-assurance. This, ironically, results in her "rebellion" as a domestic worker, precisely because she is preparing herself for alternative employment. Yet as she becomes aware of her oppression, rather than attempting to organize and better her present working conditions, she focuses upon the future. In addition, since her main social relations are still with relatives, she is primarily tied to her household of origin; she identifies herself as a peasant more than as an urban working-class woman.

For women with children, particularly older workers, domestic service represents a permanent phenomenon. Usually, such a worker dreams of her children's future rather than her own. Not surprisingly, she does not want her daughter to repeat her life history and instead envisions for her a job in accounting or typing. Faced with fewer job alternatives, live-in workers with children feel particularly trapped.

Live-out workers are often more conscious of their oppression. They may combine and/or alternate domestic service with other activities such as construction, petty vending, sewing, and/or prostitution. As well as imposing a double workday, this further distracts these women from any possible identification as household workers and restricts their political participation.

The consequence of all these factors is that while other employees have historically have been able to organize and articulate their interests via the media and the state, domestic workers have been largely unable to do so.[11]

Domestic Workers' Organizations

Aside from the three case studies discussed here, two organizations that originated outside Mexico have influenced much of Latin American domestic worker initiatives: the Juventud Obrera Católica, or JOC (Young Catholic Workers), and Opus Dei. The JOC was founded in Europe in 1912 by Canon Joseph Cardijn, who first began to work with domestics and later with other sectors of the working class. Active in Mexico since 1957, the JOC currently operates in Mexico City and Guadalajara with domestic workers, factory workers, and unemployed youth in poor neighborhoods. Its short-term goals for domestics are the creation of an organization and center, the establishment of a legal group to defend the domestics' rights, and the promotion of legal reform to guarantee domestic employees the same rights as other workers.

Opus Dei, a lay group of the Catholic Church founded in Spain in 1928, claims a membership of over 60,000 in eight countries, with 8,000 in Mexico (Saunier 1976). This conservative organization, while promoting abstract concepts of love, justice, service, and self-sacrifice, also emphasizes that the means of attaining sainthood is through one's vocation and that one fulfills this vocation best by not striving "to occupy a different place from that in which he/she belongs" (Escrivá de Balaguer 1985, 278).

Besides regarding class differences as inevitable, Opus Dei pays special attention to gender differences and holds that women, via their "natural" attributes of tenderness, generosity, and piety, represent a positive force in family, society, and church. Domestic service is regarded as a pillar of society and as fulfilling to the worker because of the self-sacrifice and opportunity to serve God that it provides. Opus Dei views domestic service as a profession that requires training; in its schools for domestics its philosophy of organizational methods reflects Taylorism. One might suggest that its concern for the well-being of domestic workers is also motivated by an opportunity to provide better-trained, more docile servants for its members, its university domitories, and the hotels which sympathizers of this organization run.

The Asociación Nacional de Trabajadores Domésticos, while not officially affiliated, strongly sympathizes with the PRI (Partido Revolucionario Institional, or Institutionalized Revolutionary Party), which has controlled the Mexican government for over half a century. During elections, the association's offices are decorated with campaign propaganda, workers are encouraged to vote, and party officials participate in the annual festivities honoring Santa Zita, the patron saint of domestic workers.

The director of the association, Profesora Fernández de Lara, has held a variety of government positions over the years. During the 1930s she collaborated with the Department of Health in a program geared toward workers, and during the Adolfo Ruíz Cortines presidential administration she was secretary of the female section of the Confederación General de Trabajadores, or CGT (General Confederation of Workers). She regards her present activities with the association as a reflection of her long-standing concern with the situation of poor women. In 1944 she founded a social service group dedicated to domestic workers, which was given nonprofit status in 1956 when the present organization began to function.

While the association occasionally has sponsored sewing and literacy classes, its principal activity has been to function as a job placement service. As is the case with approximately twenty other employment agencies dedicated to domestic service within the Federal District, the association—after the employer pays a nonrefundable fee—supplies recommended personnel. During the first month, employers have the option of one replacement but none after that.

While the association boasts that this service is provided free to workers, it is worth observing that the law prohibits any employment agency from charging workers. The association will intercede on the worker's behalf in the event of any legal problem, but this appears to be motivated by self-interest, as the agency will not support a worker whom it has not placed. It is also interesting to note that the labor conditions specified within the association's regulations are inferior to those stipulated by law.

Each year the association receives media coverage when it holds a party for domestic workers on April 27, the feast day of Santa Zita. The overall spirit of the festivities is totally devoid of any political consciousness; rather, the virtues of Santa Zita—sweetness, self-denial, and resignation—are exalted.

The association's slogan, "Mutual support in favor of humble women," is rather confusing in practice, since domestic workers do not assume any responsibilities within the group and are treated maternalistically. The director claims 150,000 affiliated members; in fact, she is referring to the number of persons who have been placed through the employment service. Despite these large numbers the association has never made any serious attempt to create a labor union or to address such issues as working conditions, oppression, and exploitation—because of "opposition on the part of the employers, as well as the workers," according to the director. The workers are worried about being controlled—a fear well founded, given the association's history and that of government manipulation in the Mexican labor movement.

The Colectivo de Acción Solidaria con Empleadas Domésticas (CASED) emerged as part of the Mexican feminist movement of the late 1970s, during a period that was generally characterized by political growth and exuberance. In the Movimiento de Liberación de la Mujer or MLM (Women's Liberation Movement), a socialist feminist organization, two study groups were formed in 1979, one on methods of popular education and another on domestic labor. Toward the end of 1979 the two groups merged to carry out a project connected with domestic service. Although they had tremendous enthusiasm, there was little clarity regarding methods to achieve their goals.

Domestic service has long been a thorn in the side of Latin American feminism, since feminists themselves frequently employ maids. Middle-class feminists are forced to recognize that often they are able to participate politically only because a poorly paid household worker shoulders a large portion of their double day. This situation fosters a tense, power-ridden relationship that is the total antithesis of feminist sisterhood. Within feminist circles it has occasionally been acknowledged that domestic service soothes potential sources of conflict between middle-class couples, explaining at least in part the low level of gender consciousness of many employers.

In 1979 in Mexico, domestic service was the most important occupation numerically for women. Consequently, one could only imagine the latent political weight of this sector if domestics were organized. Conscious of these facts and inspired by the feminist housework debate, CASED decided to promote the economic and social importance of paid domestic labor.

The organization believed that the most feasible level on which to operate and to reach household workers would be the neighborhood.

Eventually, it hoped to establish a network of small, locally based groups of politically conscious domestics. Within these small groups, CASED set as its immediate tasks:

- promotion of mutual contact and support among household workers;
- encouragement of participants to assume leadership roles and to form similar groups in other areas of the city;
- creation of a forum for discussion, in which the participants would recognize that apparently personal problems are, in fact, socially based, and shared by other domestic workers;
- organization of literacy and elementary classes, as well as workshops, thus increasing the levels of skills and education;
- establishment of communication with other groups or organizations of household workers.

It was hoped that these activities would contribute to CASED's long-range goals, which included the drafting of legislative reforms that would better domestic labor conditions, and the creation of the bases for a broad organization of household workers (CASED 1981).

Given the characteristics and interests of most domestics, CASED thought the best way to reach them was to offer elementary classes within residential areas. A progressive priest in the area of Los Colibrís[12] offered the use of his parish facilities, and early in 1980 the collective began activities, initially attracting some thirty household workers. The sessions reflected a combined influence of Paulo Freire[13] and feminism. At first, discussion focused upon issues of migration and labor conditions but was later expanded to more explicitly gender-related issues such as sexuality and the division of labor.

Later the same year, CASED expanded its sphere of work to include part of another residential area, San Angel. What attracted CASED to the neighborhood was the presence of approximately twenty women who gathered daily in a local square, the Plaza San Jacinto, to await prospective employers. Relatively few of these accepted live-in jobs, preferring instead to hire out by the day as laundresses, ironers, and cleaning women. The basic structure of the San Angel sessions was the same as at Los Colibrís, although greater emphasis was placed on assertive training, labor rights, and alternative job skills.

Initially, the perspectives for political work with the live-out domestics seemed particularly encouraging, as they were far more conscious of their oppression—both as women and as workers—than the live-in maids. Most were unwed or abandoned mothers and often manifested a gut-level feminism. One woman commented:

> Ah, honey, love often hurts. . . . I was offered a job as a cook for over a hundred workers at a PEMEX plant. The pay was great! But knowing my husband, I didn't ask him for permission to go; rather I took control over my own life. And that's when things ended between us. [La Jarocha, laundress, approximately forty, originally from Veracruz]

Another woman, venting her bitterness, explained: "My husband was the classic *macho,* . . . a drunk, a womanizer, economically irresponsible" [J.D., domestic worker, house painter, and prostitute, approximately thirty, originally from San Luís Potosí].

Still other workers demonstrated considerable astuteness in negotiating with prospective *patronas.* An employer usually maintained that the housework in *her* home was easy and minimal. One intellectual even claimed that household chores were simply a matter of pushing buttons—on the blender, the washing machine, the vacuum cleaner—and therefore the household worker did not merit the salary demanded. The domestic responded sarcastically: "If it's so easy, do it yourself, and hold onto your money" [A.S., approximately forty, originally from San Luís Potosí].

Another employer demanded not only references but a visit to see where the worker lived, alleging that she was risking her property in employing someone she did not know. This feisty woman answered: "Well, what about your references? I risk my life working for someone I don't know. How do I know if your husband will treat me with respect? How do I know if you are going to pay me?" [H.R., approximately forty, originally from Michoacán].

The particular problems confronted by these women—frequent unemployment, lack of child-care facilities, a total absence of guarantees in their jobs, and sporadic government harassment—posed the need for concrete, immediate solutions. Drawing upon a similar organization's experience in Cuernavaca, CASED proposed the possibility of a domestic workers' center that would provide a meeting place, job placement services, temporary lodging, day care, and domestic-related as well as alternative job training.

At the Plaza San Jacinto the women competed aggressively for jobs, often underbidding one another or even resorting to physical violence. In light of this situation, CASED gave priority to the organization of the job placement service. This service initially operated within the plaza itself, but later was supported by the use of the telephone of the Centro de Mujeres (Women's Center). The results seemed promising: communication improved among the women as they shared experiences; bad employers and sexual abusers were identified and blacklisted; a fixed rate was established, thus diminishing competition. Several women demonstrated enthusiasm for a household workers' organization and even went so far as to distribute leaflets in shopping centers and construction sites advertising their services; others searched for places to rent where the group could locate permanently.

Nonetheless, various obstacles became evident. First, the composition of the group at the park fluctuated constantly as women found jobs and disappeared. Since they were often among those most interested in organizing, CASED promoters had the sensation of knitting a sweater that was continuously unraveling. Second, many of the workers blindly restricted themselves to exclusively economic demands. When a general salary increase was obtained, many immediately suggested seeking a further raise—a totally unrealistic proposition, since they would soon have bid themselves out of the job market. Third, a few women also worked intermittently as prostitutes, aggravating personal tensions and complicating the problems of the placement service. And finally, relatively few women participated actively in the incipient organization. For one thing, their "double day" presented a time constraint. For another, with few exceptions, most women were reluctant to assume responsibilities for the organization because they were accustomed to passively accepting services, jobs, charity, and so on. By 1982 no location for the center had been found, the work in San Jacinto seemed to stagnate, and CASED abandoned this phase of its activities.

In 1983 CASED found itself in crisis as it confronted difficulties on two not totally unrelated levels: first within the collective itself; second in the activities carried out with the domestic workers. At that point, the organization attempted to assess its work to date.

Within the collective there was political and personal heterogeneity that originally had been regarded as a source of richness. Over time, however, these differences had accentuated and created frictions. The differences were reflected in the collective's inability to establish common criteria for evaluation. There was consensus that most of the short-range goals had been achieved to some extent but that the long-range ones had not. However, there was no unity regarding the degree of success, potential organizing methods, or directions for future activities.

It was difficult to weigh contradictory events. Various domestic workers had participated in leftist political demonstrations, but later, at election time, they all voted for the PRI. While many of the domestic workers were aware of their conditions of oppression, they were hesitant to organize to change them. This worsened after the enraged, politically powerful employer of one of the participants brought on a period of government harassment of CASED. In addition, there was a lack of clarity regarding CASED's role *vis-à-vis* the domestic workers themselves. Initially, the collective had hoped to support and encourage domestic workers in organizing; however, these attempts were often characterized by maternalism, aggravated by the fact that most members were petit bourgeois. Participation in the collective gradually dwindled as these problems remained unresolved. Despite attempts to restructure the collective and to redefine methods and objectives, CASED has been unable to recover its initial momentum and, at this point, operates on a minimal basis.

Hogar de Servidores Domésticos, is perhaps the most encouraging organizational experience with domestic workers thus far in Mexico. This group operates in Cuernavaca, Morelos, a medium-sized city approximately fifty miles southwest of the Federal District. It is the only organization of its kind in the country and is planning tentatively to expand activities to Mexico City.

In 1977 four women who participated in a progressive religious discussion group and the newspaper *María Liberación del Pueblo* searched for a possible plan of action that would improve the living conditions of domestic workers. The women were motivated largely by their class and family background: they were all of working-class origin and often the daughters of household workers, if not domestics themselves.

Hogar de Servidores Domésticos, founded as an outcome of the discussion group, addressed the household workers' need for temporary lodging, day care, job placement, and workshops; and it was structured in such a way as to influence working conditions positively. The Hogar opposed live-in service because of the tendency for domestics to work long hours for lower pay, believing that live-outs were in a better position to demand an eight-hour day and minimum pay. Temporary room and board were available within the Hogar for recent immigrants and out-of-work domestics. Workers who used the day-care facilities it provided were required to pick up their children on time; if they failed to do so, they lost the privilege of day-care service. This requirement was imposed to reinforce the idea that domestics have an equal right to demand that their employers respect agreed-upon working conditions.

Through the years, the scope of activities has broadened. The Hogar now publishes a monthly bulletin, *Yaozihuatl: Mujer Guerrero*, which in Nahautl and Spanish respectively translates as "the Woman Warrior." This publication examines specific difficulties faced by household workers via the cartoon adventures of Canuta. The center sponsors workshops analyzing such issues as political parties and organizations, the United Nations Women's Decade, and domestic workers' rights. Every month there is a get-together, attended by an average of forty women, which includes discussions of a specific topic, a psychodynamic game, and a sociodrama. Domestic Workers' Day, April 27, is commemorated in a critical, combative spirit. In a leaflet advertising this event the members of the Hogar clarify their position: "We don't want gifts, not parties that only benefit big business. We want to be recognized as the workers that we are, with the same rights as other workers."

The original collective has added new members, but the core continues to be composed of working-class women.[14] Over the years, it has successfully confronted internal conflicts, frequently resulting from gossip and competition. Another difficulty has been a passive attitude on the part of many women who utilize the services. Serious efforts have been made to eliminate this, as well as the hierarchial relationship between the collective and the other workers. The group has attempted to share knowledge, experience, and—implicitly— power by training domestic workers to coordinate workshops and participate more actively in the organization.

Politically speaking, the Hogar is socialist-oriented but maintains its organic autonomy from leftist parties and other organizations. However, it has participated in coalitions with such groups and has shown support for strikes, grassroots movements, and similar political protests. This political stance has met with open hostility from the municipal authorities, who have attempted to undermine the organization with harassment and bribes.

Initially, the Hogar seemed to view the feminist movement with suspicion. This attitude was reflected in a criticism of legalized abortion, published by *María Liberación del Pueblo* (1980), a newspaper with close ideological ties to the Hogar. Later, however, the collective reevaluated this position and now supports abortion reform, as well as many other feminist demands. Because of class differences, however, the women of the Hogar continue to regard feminist sisterhood with some skepticism. As a Hogar leaflet stated: "Until domestic service ends, there will be no possibility of solidarity among women."

The group acknowledges that women are particularly oppressed in society but emphasizes that capitalists, rather than men, are the true beneficiaries of this situation. Still, it recognizes that husbands frequently are liabilities who do not share in economic responsibilities and who limit their wives' political participation. Within the collective, members have frequently been forced, because of their political involvement, to make personal decisions that have implicitly redefined their roles as women.

Currently, the Hogar's labor demands include an eight-hour workday and a minimum wage, a weekly free day, social security benefits, and paid vacations and holidays. The tactics required to achieve these goals have not yet been clearly defined, but the collective considers that the founding of a union would be an important step in their struggle.

The Future of Domestic Service

With regard to the immediate future of domestic service in Mexico, it is self-evident that female employment has been negatively affected by the economic crisis. Some unemployed women may be forced into domestic service for survival; in addition, working-class housewives may seek jobs as live-out cleaning women and laundresses as a means of supplementing the diminishing real value of incomes. Unable to resolve increasing urban problems, the state has attempted to deter migration to the cities; this could discourage at least some female migrants and consequently lead to a decline in the supply of live-in domestic workers. One can nonetheless foresee a rise in the overall supply of household workers, particularly live-out domestics. The consequent increase in competition would favor employers. Changes within the composition of this sector may act to the latter's detriment, however, since women who have had prior nondomestic work experience or who have participated in grassroots community and/or labor organizations will be less docile and more demanding than other household workers.

In addition, it may be hypothesized that there will be a growing dissatisfaction with deteriorating working conditions. Workloads have often expanded as the employing household, in order to extend its budget, cuts back on the number of domestic personnel employed. A decline in the employment of live-in personnel can be expected because of the increased costs of providing room and board, resulting in an increase of live-out personnel and/or greater housework participation by female family members. Although salaries have increased, they have not kept up with inflation, and the decline in middle-class income makes it unlikely that domestic labor demands for better salaries or an eight-hour working day can be met. Also, given recent state cutbacks in social expenditures, social security will probably not be extended to domestic workers.

The domestic workers will likely confront this situation in a variety of ways. Some may turn to conservative religious groups for support. Others may simply ignore the bad times. Or, as in the case of the Hogar of Servidores Domésticos de Cuernavaca, domestics may organize in order to formulate strategies; grassroots neighborhood organizations have blossomed politically, while leftist parties generally have stagnated. Patently, the political response to these events will depend largely upon the domestic workers themselves.

Notes

Acknowledgments: Partial financial support has been provided by a U.S. National Defense Foreign Language fellowship and the Interdisciplinary Women's Studies program, Colegio de México.

1. Based on raw data in the 1980 Census (República de México, Secretaría de Programación y Presupuesto 1984, Table 10). Nationwide, 814,963 of a total of 913,558 household workers are female. Totals for the Federal District reflect a similar proportion, with 155,880 females in a total of 173,365 domestics (República de México, Secretaría de Programación y Presupuesto 1979, Table 14).

2. In 1970, 19.5 percent of all women workers were engaged in domestic service, and within the Federal District, 24.1 percent (República de México, Secretaría de Industria y Comercio 1971).

3. Expressed in absolute terms, the study shows that 332,859 of a total of 1,402,300 women workers in the metropolitan area of Mexico City were domestics (República de México, Secretaría de Programación y Presupuesto 1979, Tables 4.2. and 4.3). This study, carried out only two years prior to the 1980 census, revealed almost twice as many domestics as the census registered

in Mexico City, Guadalajara, and Monterrey. The principal geographic units of analysis in the population census are the Federal District and the thirty-two states; additional tabulations may employ as their geographic units of analysis "the urban areas." Metropolitan Mexico City includes the Federal District and several municipalities of the State of Mexico. Methods for data collection vary considerably, even from one census to another, making comparisons difficult. Nonetheless, it is not likely that the inclusion of various municipalities of the State of Mexico in the 1978 study accounts for the large proportion of domestic workers, since the latter are not particularly concentrated in those areas.

4. Regional economic variations have conditioned female recruitment into the work force. Garment and electronic assembly plants located along the border and the construction industry and clerical services in Mexico City, Guadalajara, and Monterrey have employed growing numbers of women.

5. In 1983 the minimum daily wage was 455 pesos and the monthly wage, 13,653 pesos (160 Mexican pesos = $1.00 U.S.). At that time, in middle- and upper-class neighborhoods, most live-out household workers earned about 400 pesos for seven to nine hours of work, and live-in domestics received 7,000 to 7,500 pesos a month.

6. The 1917 Mexican Constitution states that domestic workers are entitled to the same rights as other workers (República de México, Secretaría de la Presidencia 1971, Article 123.A). The federal labor law of 1931 contradicts the Constitution on various issues. De la Cueva (1967), renowned labor lawyer, has attempted to reconcile these differences. Historically, Supreme Court debates on domestic servants, instead of defending the domestic workers' rights, have supported the notion that this sector is not entitled to the same rights as other workers (particularly the minimum wage, an eight-hour workday, and paid vacations). Specific rulings in legal cases involving domestic workers are presented in *Leyes sobre el trabajo* (1973).

7. This figure was arrived at on the basis of interviews with social security employees connected with this particular program (L.C., interviewed January 14, 1980, claimed an enrollment of 2,000; C.H., interviewed the same day, claimed 800). There are no published statistics on the enrollment of domestic workers in social security.

8. Numerous historians have attested to the role of the state and the official party, the P R I, in the Mexican labor movement, including Maldonado (1981) and Vizgunova (1980).

9. Memmi (1972) has discussed the master-servant relationship in depth, drawing analogies between it and other power relations; however, he does not question how the specificities of gender condition this relationship.

10. Many authors have summarized the highlights of this debate, among them Fee 1976; Himmelweit and Mohun 1977; Malos 1980; and Molyneux 1979.

11. There have been few antecedents to domestic workers' unions in Mexico. During the 1930s, a period characterized by intense political activity, at

least four such unions were registered officially with the Department of Labor. All existed exclusively on a local level: two in the Federal District, the Sindicato de Domésticos del Distrito Federal (Federal District Domestics' Union) and the Sindicato de Servicios Domésticos del Distrito Federal (Federal District Domestic Services Union); one in Guadalajara, the Unión Unica de Aseo Particular (Household Cleaning Service Union); and one in Támpico, the Sindicato de Domésticos y Trabajadores Similares (Domestic and Related Workers Union) (República de Mexico, Departamento de Trabajo 1934). Other unions may have existed, but did not request government recognition.

Historically, employers have had at their disposal a variety of means to protect their interests. For example, during the nineteenth century, the local governments of Mexico City, Puebla, and Guadalajara promulgated decrees controlling the freedom of movement of domestic servants (Gobernador del Distrito Federal 1866; Alcalde Municipal de Puebla 1866; Aldaña Rendón 1982). During the Porfirio Díaz administration, employers protested publicly in newspapers when they discovered that their servants had become outspoken and less submissive; the enraged employers demanded church intervention in convincing domestics to recognize "their place" and suggested, if all else failed, an employers' strike or the importation of more docile workers from Asia and Africa (Gónzalez Navarro 1957: 391–92). At that time, domestics could find alternative employment only in the tobacco and textile industries. Today, household workers continue to be the target of criticism and derision in the newspapers and on television, and "Domestic Workers' Day," April 27, often elicits sarcastic jokes in the media.

12. Los Colibrís is a fictitious name for the neighborhood where CASED carries out its present activities; it is used in an attempt to avoid further government and employer harassment.

13. Freire devised an educational methodology that critically examines texts within the framework of everyday life and politics, at the same time emphasizing the commonality of personal problems.

14. About 20 women are involved through the day-care center at any time. About 300 women apply to the placement service annually, and some 60 women were reached last year during consciousness-raising by the Hogar social worker in working-class neighborhoods (M.T., personal communication, July 15, 1986).

References

Alcalde Municipal de Puebla (General Luís Tapia). 1866. *Reglamento de criados domésticos* (23 de julio). Puebla: Imprenta del Gobierno del Hospicio.

Aldaña Rendón, Mario A. 1982. "La mujer jalisciense durante el Porfiriato." *Familia y Sociedad* 1 (marzo–mayo): 4–6.

Castellanos, Rosario. 1982. "La liberación de la mujer, aquí." In Castellanos, *El uso de la palabra*, pp. 63–67. Mexico, D.F.: Editores Mexicanos Unidos.

Cavazos Flores, Baltasar. 1972. *El derecho del trabajo en la teoría y en la práctica*. México, D.F.: Confederación Patronal de la República Mexicana.

Colectivo de Acción Solidaria con Empleadas Domésticas (CASED). 1981. "Proyecto de trabajo con empleadas de hogar." Unpublished manuscript.

De la Cueva, Mario. 1967. *Derecho mexicano del trabajo*, vol. 1. México, D.F.: Editorial Porrua.

Escrivá de Balaguer, Josemaría. 1985. *Camino*. México, D.S.: Editora de Revistas.

Fee, Terry. 1976. "Domestic Labor: An Analysis of Housework and Its Relation to the Production Process." *Review of Radical Political Economists* 8, no. 1:1–9.

Gobernador del Distrito Federal (Miguel M. de Azcarate). 1866. *Libreta de criado doméstico*. México: Imprenta Económica.

González Navarro, Moisés. 1957. "El Porfiriato: la vida social." In Daniel Cosio Villegas, ed., *Historia moderna de México*. Vol. 4. México, D.F.: Editorial Hérmes.

Himmelweit, Susan, and Simon Mohun. 1977. "Domestic Labor and Capital." *Cambridge Journal of Economics* 1, no. 1:15–31.

Leyes sobre el trabajo. 1973. Vols. 2–3. México, D.F.: Editorial Andrade.

Maldonado, Edelmiro. 1981. *Breve historia del movimiento obrero*. Culiacán, México: Universidad Autónoma de Sinoloa.

Malos, Ellen. 1980. "Introduction." In Malos, ed., *The Politics of Housework*, pp. 7–44. London: Allison & Busby.

María Liberación del Pueblo. 1980. Numeros 5–6 (mayo–junio).

Memmi, Albert. 1972. *El hombre dominado: Un estudio sobre la opresión*. Trans. María Luisa León. Madrid: Edicura.

Molyneaux, Maxine. 1979. "Beyond the Domestic Labour Debate." *New Left Review* 116 (July–August): 3–29.

Ovaciones. 1984. "Sirvientes, comerciantes y tianguistas no tendrán I.M.S.S." (October 28).

Rendón, Teresa, and Mercedes Pedrero. 1982. "El trabajo de la mujer en México en los setentas." In *Estudios sobre la mujer: Bases teóricas, metodológicas y evidencia empírica*, 1:437–56. Serie de Lecturas 3. México, D.F.: Secretaría de Programácion y Presupuesto, Departamento de Trabajo.

República de México, Departamento de Trabajo. 1934. *Directorio de asociaciones sindicales de la República Mexicana*. México, D.F.: Oficina de Informaciones Sociales.

República de México, Secretaría de Industria y Comercio. 1971. *IX censo gen-*

eral de población, 1970: Resúmen general abreviado. México, D.F.: Dirección General de Estadística.

República de México, Secretaría de la Presidencia. 1971. *Constitución política de los Estados Unidos Mexicanos* (1917). México, D.F.: Secretaría de la Presidencia.

República de México, Secretaría de Programación y Presupuesto. 1979. *Información básica sobre la estructura y características del empleo y el desempleo en las áreas metropolitanas de las ciudades de México, Guadalajara y Monterrey.* México, D.F.: Secretaría de Programación y Presupuesto.

———. 1984. *X censo general de población y vivienda, 1980: Resúmen general abreviado.* México, D.F.: Dirección General de Estadistica.

Saunier, Jean. 1976. *El Opus Dei.* México, D.F.: Ediciones Roca.

Trueba Urbina, Alberto, and Jorge Trueba Barrera. 1977. *Nueve ley federal del trabajo reformado: Comentarios, jurisprudencia y bibliografía pronotuario de a ley.* México, D.F.: Editorial Porrua.

Uno Mas Uno. 1980. "Quedó constituido el Sindicato de Trabajadores Domésticos del Estado de México" (December 8).

Vizgunova, I. 1980. *La situación de la clase obrera en México.* México, D.F.: Ediciones de Cultura Popular.

12 Feminists and Domestic Workers in Rio de Janeiro

HILDETE PEREIRA DE MELO

The purpose of this chapter is not to deal with the particulars of remunerated domestic service theoretically but to get to know the situation of domestic workers in Brazil through an analysis of census data and, at the same time, to study the situation in relation to the women's liberation movement in Rio de Janeiro. Thus, the objective is to determine the relations between a social-class category (remunerated domestic workers) and a gender-sex category (women).

It is extremely difficult to carry out an economic analysis of remunerated domestic work because economic indicators fail to reveal the ideological and cultural subtleties surrounding this question.[1] For this reason, census data cannot be used to define the situation regarding salaries, workday and productivity.

The occupational fields within the category "remunerated domestic work" are very heterogeneous. On the one hand, there are live-in domestic workers who reside in their place of employment and either receive a monthly salary or work in exchange for food and lodging. On the other hand, there are day workers who do not live on the premises; they either work for a single family and receive a weekly or monthly salary, or render their their services for several households and receive daily wages. Both categories may or may not work under a formal work contract (Almeida e Silva et al. 1979, 9–10).

Remunerated Domestic Service in Brazil

How many domestic workers are there? How much do they earn? Remunerated domestic work in Brazil, a country with huge social contradictions and forty million people living in absolute poverty, is the most important source of employment for women working outside

TABLE 12-1.
Workers in Remunerated Domestic Service Occupations
by Sex, Brazil, 1970 and 1980

	1970		1980		GROWTH RATE
SEX	Number	%	Number	%	(%)
Women	1,655,384	97.5	2,367,616	95.6	43.0
Men	41,658	2.5	108,907	4.4	161.4
Total	1,697,042	100.0	2,476,523	100.0	45.1

Source: Governo do Brasil, Fundação Instituto Brasileiro de Geografía e Estatística 1970; 1980a.

their homes. In 1980 more than two million women (19.9 percent of the female labor force) worked as domestics.

The period between 1970 and 1980 was highly significant for women in terms of their participation in the labor force. Female employment in the economy grew 92 percent, and remunerated domestic work grew 45.1 percent, indicating a slight decline in importance of this sector for women (see Table 12-1). This loss also can be seen when comparing the participation of domestic workers in the female labor force: 27 percent in 1970 versus 19.9 percent in 1980. Furthermore, Table 12-1 points to another fact: while female participation in the domestic worker category stayed proportionately very similar (97.5 percent in 1970; 95.6 percent in 1980), male participation, although small in numbers, showed a dramatic increase of 161.4 percent for the same period.[2]

Domestic work is still the primary occupation among Brazilian women, but it is shrinking. In this decade there has been a diversification in occupations among Brazilian women. According to the 1970 census, the main female occupations (domestic workers, peasants, primary school teachers, seamstresses, sales clerks, nursing assistants, office clerks, janitorial workers, and weavers) represented 80 percent of the economically active female population. In 1980, these were still the main occupations among Brazilian women, but their relative weight had gone down: they represented barely 64 percent of female employment.

This diversification can be seen even more readily by focusing on service occupations. In 1970 female workers in these jobs represented 35 percent of the economically active female population; in 1980, 30 percent. Occupations with increased share in the sector are lodging and food services (0.4 percent in 1970 and 0.8 percent in 1980), confirming the fact that "at higher levels [of development] some services have become commercialized outside the household" (Boserup 1970, 103).

Remunerated domestic work plays an important role in the incorporation of unskilled and uneducated women in the labor market. Migrants whom the advance of capitalist relations in the countryside forces into cities find in domestic work "the road to socialization in the city, shelter, food, home, and a family" (Garcia Castro 1982, 102). The abundance and low cost of these human resources have made it possible to incorporate middle- and upper-class women into the labor market without having to pressure society into providing social services such as day-care centers and full-time schooling, partially freeing women from child rearing. A hybrid work relation is established, a mixture of remuneration and servitude favorable to the reproductive process of the labor force in the economy.

Wages are the main indicator in analyzing the process of buying and selling labor power in the economy. We must take into account the fact that most domestic workers' salaries have a component paid in cash and another in kind, thus creating a gamut of possibilities ranging all the way to those who get no money at all. According to Saffioti (1984, 51):

> Although they receive a salary . . . this labor force behaves in a noncapitalist way in the midst of social formations dominated by a capitalist mode of production. Since they are organized in a noncapitalist way, domestic workers' activities take place inside a noncapitalist institution, the family, which nevertheless proves itself quite adequate to assist in the extended reproduction of capital.

Traditionally, domestic workers live and eat in their employers' households, thus increasing the category's real wages in relation to the rest of the workers, a fact acknowledged by domestic workers themselves. But they add that "we already pay for food and lodging by not having a work schedule" (*Brasil Mulher* 1979). Moreover, the quarters

TABLE 12-2.

Workers in Remunerated Domestic Service Occupations
by Income and Sex, Brazil, 1980

AVERAGE MONTHLY INCOME (in minimum salaries)	WOMEN		MEN		TOTAL	
	Number	%	Number	%	Number	%
From 0 to ¹/₄*	511,452	21.6	11,167	10.3	522,619	21.1
From ¹/₄ to ¹/₂	678,151	28.6	13,184	12.1	691,335	27.9
From ¹/₂ to 1	763,105	32.2	35,526	32.6	798,631	32.3
From 1 to 1¹/₂	275,529	11.6	30,283	27.8	305,812	12.3
From 1¹/₂ to 2	58,228	2.5	8,964	8.2	67,192	2.7
More than 2	81,151	3.5	9,783	9.0	90,934	3.7
Total	2,367,616	100.0	108,907	100.0	2,476,523	100.0

Source: Governo do Brasil, Fundação Instituto Brasileiro de Geografía e Estatística 1980a.
*Includes workers who receive no income or did not respond.

reserved for household workers are a sorry sight in present Brazilian apartment house architecture: a room of two or three square meters, without windows—just a small opening for ventilation—located next to the kitchen. As for food, the leadership of the Associação Profissional dos Empregados Domésticos (Domestic Workers Professional Association) of Rio de Janeiro says that in a period of crisis a differentiation in the quality of food eaten by employers and employees is taking place (although they acknowledge that the quality of food generally has worsened for everybody).

Remunerated domestic work is one of the worst paid of working-class occupations, even when taking in-kind payment into account. When compared to work in the construction sector—a male occupation equivalent to domestic work, carried out chiefly by men who are also generally migrants with little education—we find that 48 percent of construction workers, but 93.6 percent of domestic workers earn salaries less than 1.5 times the legal minimum (see Table 12-2).[3] Among female farm workers (the second largest occupation for Brazilian women), 40 percent are in the same income range, and another 44 percent do not receive any income; therefore, 84 percent of female farm workers earn no more than 1.5 times the legal minimum—still less than the percentage of domestic workers included in this income bracket.

The most dramatic fact is that 21.6 percent of the women employed in this sector earn only one-quarter or less of the minimum salary and 50.2 percent earn from nothing to one-half the minimum salary—in other words, one-half (1,189,603) of all the women employed in this category. By contrast, only 10.3 percent of male domestics earn one-quarter or less of the minimum salary, and only 22.4 percent earn one-half or less.

Domestic work is said to be a job requiring no qualifications for the persons doing it, whether women or men. However, such a comment is a distortion because domestic work is thought of as women's work. Even so, men who are employed as domestic workers are concentrated in two income brackets (from one-half to one, and from one to one-and-a-half times the minimum), totaling 65,809 persons or 60.4 percent, while women in the same two income brackets total 1,038,634 or only 43.8 percent.

There are also anomalies in salaries in relation to race. Census data do not differentiate between black and white in "remunerated domestic work," but for 1980 the data do give the global average monthly income of men and women by race. All blacks (including mulattoes) receive less income, but black women are victims of both racial and sexual discrimination: 68.5 percent of them earn only the minimum salary or less, as opposed to 43 percent of white women and 44 percent of black men (Valle Silva 1983, 61). If we visit the kitchens of the middle and upper classes, we will usually find only black and mulatto women as domestics. It can be concluded that in Brazil, blacks went from their slave quarters straight into remunerated domestic service. According to Gonzalez (1982, 98), when a black women "is not working as a domestic, we find her performing other low-paying jobs in supermarkets, schools, or hospitals, under the general term of 'janitor.' "

On the basis of the data in Table 12-3, we can conclude that in this occupation the work schedule for many exceeds the normal eight-hour workday or five-day work week: 79.5 percent of all domestics work forty or more hours per week; 42 percent work forty to forty-eight hours, and 37.5 percent work 49 hours or more—or 79.4 percent of the women and 84.9 percent of the men. These figures explain why the domestic workers' associations struggle to establish a working day for this sector. Further, how does one measure the working day for the live-in domestic, when she is available twenty-four hours and lives in her workplace?[4]

TABLE 12-3.
Workers in Remunerated Domestic Service Occupations
by Hours Worked and Sex, Brazil, 1980

	WOMEN		MEN		TOTAL	
HOURS PER WEEK	Number	%	Number	%	Number	%
Less than 30 (or no response)	235,301	9.9	8,717	8.0	244,018	9.9
30 to 39	253,546	10.7	7,771	7.1	261,317	10.6
40 to 48	993,887	42.0	47,759	43.9	1,041,646	42.0
49 and more	884,882	37.4	44,660	41.0	929,542	37.5
Total	2,367,616	100.0	108,907	100.0	2,476,523	100.0

Source: Governo do Brasil, Fundação Instituto Brasileiro de Geografía e Estatística 1980.

Economic Crisis and Domestic Work

Data showing how the economic crisis affects domestic work are available from the National Household Surveys (Governo do Brasil, Fundação Instituto Brasileiro de Geografía e Estatística 1979; 1981; 1983) but are grouped under a single item—service occupations—that does not permit the breakdown needed for exact analysis. Nevertheless, since remunerated domestic work is the *main* service occupation, these data, even when aggregated, are meaningful.

The Brazilian economic crisis reached its peak in the years 1981–83, and as we can see in Table 12-4, employment in the service sector for both men and women increased during the same period. It is significant that the increase was among self-employed workers (see Table 12-5). The resolution adopted by the fifth domestic workers' national convention, held in Olinda (State of Pernambuco) in February 1985, reports that three of every four domestic workers who paid to the social security system in 1981 were not doing so in 1984. The economic crisis greatly reduced the bargaining power of the working class to demand the enforcement of labor laws, thereby increasing employment in the informal sector.

This situation is acknowledged by the leaders of the Domestic

TABLE 12-4.
Service Workers as Percentage
of Total Employed Persons, by Sex,
Brazil, 1979, 1981, and 1983

	YEARS		
SEX	1979	1981	1983
Women	31.5	31.8	32.3
Men	7.8	7.8	8.4
Total	15.3	15.3	16.3

Source: Governo do Brasil, Fundação Instituto
Brasileiro de Geografía e Estatística, 1979;
1981; 1983.

Workers Professional Association, who point out that the economic
crisis has not had major repercussions in this sector; the demand for
domestic workers continues unaffected because the crisis forced middle-class women to look for jobs outside their homes to increase their
household income, and their employment requires the hiring of other

TABLE 12-5.
Service Workers by Employment Status
as Percentage of Total Persons Working
in that Status, Brazil, 1979 and 1983

	YEARS	
EMPLOYMENT STATUS	1979	1983
Service workers	15.3	16.3
Employees	15.4	15.3
Self-employed	21.9	24.4
Employers	14.9	13.6
Nonremunerated workers	3.2	4.1

Source: Governo do Brasil, Fundação Instituto
Brasileiro de Geografía e Estatística 1979; 1983.

women to do their work in the house. According to the newspaper
Folha de São Paulo (June 17, 1985),

> that's the case of Suzete, a geographer who has no time to
> keep her house or to cook; and Maria Josina, Suzete's 48-year-
> old domestic worker, who earns 30,000 *cruzeiros* per month[5]
> and is the mother of 11 children: "Close to where I live (the
> Jardim Bonfiglioli area in the city of São Paulo) I am not
> going to get a job commanding a higher salary," explains Mar-
> ia Josina. "Nowadays it is a luxury to have a domestic worker,
> but there is no other choice because we must work outside our
> homes," adds Roseli (an employer) who lives in Santana (an
> area in the city of São Paulo).

Live-Out Domestic Workers

In studying the number of domestic workers in Brazil, we cannot
leave out domestics who work by the day, even if we must resort to the
usual "no data available to draw a conclusion" line. It is assumed that
recently the number of domestic day workers has increased, but the
leadership of the Rio de Janeiro Domestic Workers' Association says
that the question of day workers was raised only after 1982 (personal
interview). The president of the association is herself a domestic day
worker. She notes that live-out domestics predominate in the Baixada
Fluminense neighborhoods (Rio de Janeiro): that is, in the periphery
of urban centers, where very poor women with children have no
other way of earning a living. Day workers have no signed employment books and none of the few benefits granted to live-in domestics by the social security system. However, this is a type of household help gaining adherents among some *patroas*, who claim that
having live-in domestics takes away from their own freedom. For the
middle class the use of day workers also saves the expense of the live-
in domestic's food and lodging.

The condition of day workers represents a more clear-cut form of
remunerated employment. It permits us to make explicit the issue of
capitalist relations, whereas the work relations of live-in domestic
workers are masked; food and lodging are seen as the employer's gift.
It is easier for day workers to set up a work schedule and to define
their relationship to their employers.

The States of Rio de Janeiro and São Paulo

How many domestic workers are there in Rio de Janeiro and São Paulo, the two largest industrial regions in the country? And how much do they earn? On the basis of census data, we can establish that 42 percent of Brazil's domestic workers are found in the two states: São Paulo has 27.4 percent; Rio de Janeiro, 14.6 percent. We need to emphasize the difference between these two states. Rio de Janeiro's importance is based on its metropolitan area; São Paulo is more populated, and its interior has a higher level of industrial development. These differences limit the comparison, but lacking special tables we fall back on global data.

Although there is a larger male participation in these two states than elsewhere (in Rio de Janeiro, male participation is almost twice the national mean), in general the national trend—that domestic work is a female sector—is maintained (Table 12-6).

Table 12-7 shows income distribution within domestic service. National trends are maintained except for some small improvement: in São Paulo 90.3 percent and in Rio de Janeiro 92 percent of those employed earn up to 1.5 times the minimum salary, a slight reduction from the national figure of 93.6 percent for the same income brackets. When we compare income brackets up to one-half the minimum salary, we find only 28.4 percent of women in Rio de Janeiro and São Paulo, while for Brazil as a whole 50.2 percent are in these

TABLE 12-6.
Workers in Remunerated Domestic Service Occupations by Sex, States of Rio de Janeiro and Sao Paulo, 1980

	RIO DE JANEIRO		SÃO PAULO	
SEX	Number	%	Number	%
Women	336,436	93.0	633,783	94.4
Men	25,404	7.0	37,509	5.6
Total	361,840	100.0	671,292	100.0

Source: Governo do Brasil, Fundação Instituto Brasileiro de Geografía e Estatística 1980b; 1980c.

TABLE 12-7.

Workers in Remunerated Domestic Service Occupations by Sex and Income, States of Rio de Janeiro and São Paulo, 1980

AVERAGE MONTHLY INCOME (in minimum salaries) AND SEX	RIO DE JANEIRO		SÃO PAULO	
	Number	%	Number	%
From 0 to ¼*				
Women	28,231	8.4	49,468	7.8
Men	1,503	5.9	1,102	2.9
Total	29,734	8.2	50,570	7.5
From ¼ to ½				
Women	65,271	19.4	132,290	20.9
Men	2,244	8.8	2,269	6.0
Total	67,515	18.7	134,559	20.1
From ½ to 1				
Women	141,363	42.0	262,800	41.5
Men	8,333	32.8	10,668	28.4
Total	149,696	41.4	273,468	40.7
From 1 to 1½				
Women	76,849	22.8	133,739	21.1
Men	9,111	35.9	13,942	37.2
Total	85,960	23.8	147,681	22.0
From 1½ to 2				
Women	14,892	4.4	35,358	5.6
Men	2,463	9.7	4,895	13.1
Total	17,355	4.8	40,253	6.0
More than 2				
Women	9,830	2.9	20,128	3.2
Men	1,750	6.9	4,633	12.4
Total	11,580	3.2	24,761	3.7

Source: Governo do Brasil, Fundação Instituto Brasileiro de Geografía e Estatística 1980b; 1980c.
*Includes workers who receive no income or did not respond.

low income groups. If we compare the income brackets between half and one-and-a-half times minimum salary, Rio de Janeiro and São Paulo share 63.4 percent of employed women, as opposed to 43.8 percent at the national level. Therefore, salaries are markedly better for women working in this sector in these two states. This improvement can be explained by the fact that the Rio de Janeiro/São Paulo axis is the most important industrial region in the country, which must stimulate female employment outside the home. The lack of adequate day-care centers, full-time schools, cafeterias, and laundry services increases the demand for domestic workers, which, together with the presence of other economic sectors, makes higher income levels possible.

Furthermore, great differences in income levels are noted when residential areas are distinguished according to class. In the city of Rio de Janeiro this becomes obvious in separating the neighborhoods of "the rich" (Southern Zone) from the periphery. In the Southern Zone, most domestic workers earn approximately the minimum salary and have their employment books signed; in the Northern Zone and the periphery of the city monthly income averages only one-half the minimum, and it varies according to the size of the household, the amount of work, and the work schedule. Conceição, a thirty-eight-year-old married domestic worker with one daughter, explains: "When I was working in Nova Iguaçú [in the periphery of the city of Rio] in 1982, I was making 20,000 *cruzeiros*. Then I left for the Southern Zone of the city to earn 60,000 *cruzeiros*."

In São Paulo the same thing is true. In upper- and middle-class neighborhoods such as Pacaembu, Morumbi, and Jardins, domestic workers have social security. According to Graça, who, three months after her arrival from the countryside, was working as a housekeeper, "I know how much I am worth; many people don't know it. I earn the minimum salary, and I know my rights and obligations" (*Folha de São Paulo*, June 7, 1984).

Table 12-8 shows that differences between the two states are not significant—thus confirming the national trend—though it is important to note that in the State of Rio de Janeiro 39 percent of women work forty-nine or more hours per week, and in the State of São Paulo 32.1 percent do, thus falling below the national mean (perhaps the high degree of industrial development in São Paulo creates a better situation for salaried employment opportunities). Even so, men and women who work in remunerated domestic service, almost 80 percent in the two states, said that they put in longer hours than other workers.

TABLE 12-8.
Workers in Remunerated Domestic Service Occupations by Hours
Worked and by Sex, States of Rio de Janeiro and São Paulo, 1980

HOURS PER WEEK	WOMEN		MEN		TOTAL	
	RJ	SP	RJ	SP	RJ	SP
Less than 30 (or no response)	35,583 (10.5%)	53,338 (8.4%)	1,826 (7.2%)	1,431 (3.8%)	37,409 (10.3%)	54,769 (8.2%)
30 to 39	34,050 (10.1%)	69,125 (10.9%)	1,886 (7.4%)	1,537 (4.1%)	35,936 (9.9%)	70,662 (10.5%)
40 to 48	135,764 (40.4%)	307,939 (48.6%)	11,235 (44.2%)	17,864 (47.6%)	146,999 (40.6%)	325,803 (48.5%)
49 and more	131,039 (39.0%)	203,381 (32.1%)	10,457 (41.2%)	16,677 (44.5%)	141,496 (39.1%)	220,058 (32.8%)

Source: Governo do Brasil, Fundação Instituto Brasileiro de Geografi é Estatística 1980b; 1980c.

Feminists and *Patroas:* Class Conditions Dividing Women

Actions of the international feminist movement have brought to the fore the problems of unpaid domestic work. Every single productive activity carried out by women at home—washing, cooking, cleaning, marketing, and child care—has been considered a woman's "natural" activity and thus not a subject for research by social scientists. Then feminists began to talk about the importance of these chores and their economic role in society. The feminist movement seeks to promote equality between the sexes and envisions a society in which the sexual division of labor would be abolished and men would dedicate part of their time to domestic chores on an equal basis with women, who could finally take part in political and social activities. The goals of the feminist movement—social recognition, liberation, and participation of women in every aspect of life—coincide with the priorities established by domestic worker associations concerning women's worth as human beings and workers.

However, there is on the part of the leadership of the Rio de Janeiro domestic workers' movement a degree of resentment toward the feminist movement.[6] Zica, president of the Domestic Workers' Association, comments, "I don't think that our and their struggles coincide"; "I don't quite understand their ideas," adds Odete, founder of the domestic workers' movement in Brazil (see Chapter 18). According to feminists:

> In Rio de Janeiro our group thought about researching remunerated domestic work. We got in touch with the Domestic Workers' Association and met with a leader who, after hearing about our plan to study salary structure in this sector, said that this was not a major problem, but that the acknowledgment that domestic service was a valuable job like any other in society was. We agreed that this was exactly the problem. There was no social recognition because domestic work was a woman's job. However, our ideas met with so little enthusiasm that we gave up on the study. [Interview with member, Woman and Work Group of the Center for Brazilian Women]

Feminists believe that the activities of the associations are motivated by class interests, not by the fact that domestic workers are women. The domestic workers' struggle for their rights conflicts with those of their employers, who are mostly women. The problems facing both as women are apparently the same, but because of class distinction, differences exist.

Two issues set domestic workers off from feminists. First, the struggle for survival conditions their lives. Securing their daily bread is their first priority. Therefore, education, health, family planning, abortion are problems designated as their own because they are part of daily life. According to Zica, these issues, which have less importance for middle- and upper-class women, become "a life and death situation, for instance, purchasing medicine for a sick child." Second, there is a different perception of work. According to a Domestic Workers' Association document for internal debate:

> Work is an economic necessity that dominates everything else, enslaves at times, and, because of its conditions, keeps us

from enjoying life, not only as women but also as human beings. We are forced to work even before we understand ourselves as girls or adolescents. Our need to work in order to survive destroys whatever other hopes we have.

Domestic workers perceive that for upper- and middle-class women, by contrast, work brings a kind of liberation, social recognition, individual assertion; moreover, most of the time it is an option, a free choice. In reality, work in a capitalist society cannot be understood as liberation, but it does allow participation in society. For women, this participation means to become visible, to be a person with civil rights. Remunerated domestic work is seen as a situation where some women discriminate against and enslave other women, but their views are contradictory. The internal document continues:

> Because the Association is made up totally of women, besides the contempt for domestic workers in society, we are victims of a more shocking disrespect: the scorn for, and exploitation of, our condition as women, a kind of discrimination and a social control at home, in male-female relationships, at work, and in society at large. It is even more painful when it happens in the very households where we work as domestics. The similarities between the goals of the feminist movement and our struggle are important, but they are not on our list of priorities.

For Brazilian feminists this is a delicate question.[7] On the one hand, remunerated domestic work is the most important labor market for poor women; on the other, Brazil does not have the infrastructure that would allow women of the upper, middle, and lower classes to free themselves from domestic chores. This lack can be explained by the traditional social inequality pervading Brazilian history, where slaves and, later, domestic workers were always available to take care of household duties for the ruling class.

Attempts at Forming Alliances

In Rio de Janeiro, the feminist movement has several times tried timidly to establish contact with the Domestic Workers' Association. One attempt, mentioned earlier, was on the part of the Woman and Work Group of the Center for Brazilian Women.

Another was on the part of the Organization Brasil-Mulher (Brazil Woman), which had branches in several Brazilian cities and published a feminist journal, with nationwide distribution, also called *Brasil Mulher*. This feminist group met for some time with the association in an attempt to write articles for the journal. The strain between these two groups was reflected in the resulting number of articles written: only two. The first, "Domésticas: Queremos ser vistas como trabalhadoras" (Domestics: We want to be seen as workers), published in August 1977, dealt with the main demands of the domestic workers' movement. The second, "As domésticas e a CLT" (Domestics and the Consolidation of Labor Laws), examined a failed proposal by the federal government to guarantee the minimum salary for domestic workers, although allowing employers to withhold up to 60 percent to defray food and lodging expenditures. Among the other issues of *Brasil Mulher* (which was published between October 1975 and September 1979) there is one more story about domestic workers, in Portugal, and a note about the third Domestic Workers' National Meeting in Belo Horizonte (State of Minas Gerais).

Another attempt was the pamphlet *Vidas Paralelas* (Parallel lives),[8] by Beti and Eliana (Elisabeth Magalhaes and Eliana Aguiar), which was in their words "a sincere attempt at outlining some ideas on the complex and unexplored topic of domestic workers." The authors were activists in the Rio de Janeiro feminist group Agora é Que São Elas" (Now it is their turn), which was active during 1981. Its goal was not reflection on their life experiences but theoretical discussions of the diverse feminist trends and women's strategies for liberation. All eleven members were women who had lived the feminist experience in Europe; upon returning to Brazil they were, according to Ligia, "appalled at the situation of slavery surrounding domestic workers" and began to ask how the feminist movement could live with it: In Ligia's words,

It was difficult for feminist women to accept another woman in their everyday lives who was their domestic worker, and at the same time, to understand that their own liberation as middle-class women did not take place because they found themselves in a conflict with their partners concerning the division of domestic chores or because of the way this type of work was socialized in society, but because they were replaced by another woman who did this work. [personal interview]

In *Vidas Paralelas* Beti and Eliana (1981, 3–4) state:

> Our relationship with domestic workers is, then, a class relation, between employer and employee. But it is also permeated by the specific oppression felt by women, common to us all. However, we got the domestic chores off our backs by paying another woman (who happens to be poorer than we) a salary which, unfortunately, is a pittance.
>
> The fact that the problem was explained at a social level—both from the employer's point of view, who does not have many alternatives in a country without full-time nurseries or schools funded by the state, and from the domestic worker's point of view, who has no means of survival other than this exploitative, unpleasant, and illegal work—must not be used as a hiding place where we can avoid our responsibility and refrain from taking necessary steps, both in terms of supporting and expanding the domestic workers' struggle and in terms of our everyday relationship with them.

Unlike *Brasil-Mulher*, which tried to fuse life experiences but in practice ended up dealing with this question within the framework established by the domestic workers' movement, the women in Agora é Que São Elas did not contact the Domestic Workers' Association to discuss the issue. They circulated *Vidas Paralelas*, as the product of their discussions on the topic, especially among militant feminists; however, difficulties in articulating their feminist consciousness and class condition silenced it.

Wanting to break the barriers to the understanding of these issues, I interviewed three Rio de Janeiro feminists to determine, through their experiences as *patroas*, the boundaries of their relations with domestic workers. Their participation in feminist groups or work on publications about the condition of women were the criteria for choosing them. The excerpts below are expressions of this difficult relationship.

My Domestic Worker Is My Other Self

According to thirty-nine-year-old Leila, who is married, a lawyer, and the mother of three children, "the domestic worker is a double, the other self one leaves at home doing those things that traditionally you, as a woman, should be doing. If she does not perform well, you feel guilty; family and husband complain because the food is not good or she didn't iron the clothes well. I felt it in my own flesh, this other self who freed me so that I could perform my other roles. At the beginning, I felt very guilty: guilt for having a domestic worker, guilt for exploiting another woman's work. But suddenly I began to question why I alone should be feeling guilty, as she is not working just for me but for everybody in my house. This type of guilt is felt by most feminist women who have domestic workers because it seems a contradiction to be a feminist and to employ a domestic worker. But if there is guilt, it should be shared by the entire family—husband, wife, and children—who are actually benefiting from somebody else's poorly paid work.

"In Brazil, upper- and middle-class people are raised as in the period when we had slavery. They do not know how to prepare their own meals or coffee, wash their clothes, or make the bed. On the contrary, since they have a domestic worker, they almost feel an urge to dirty more than they would if they had to clean up after themselves. On the one hand, people hate to clean what they soil, and on the other, Brazil does not offer other alternatives; therefore, if one has small children and both parents need to work, what to do?

"I remember a conversation with my husband. He said that college-educated women where he works did not have any sensitivity toward the issue of day-care centers. My thought is that they are not worried because they have domestic workers. For low-income women it is a very important topic, but for us middle-class women it is something you do not talk about. Why worry about day-care centers if you can afford to have a woman in the house? Everybody thinks this way. Suddenly, the question of day-care centers is a problem only for female factory workers who need a place to leave their children, not for middle-class or college-educated women who have to work. It is important to continue to demand day-care centers.

"As for me, I have had a domestic worker for many years, and I understand very clearly her role in my life, as a person who occupies my husband's place and mine. In order to cope with my guilt regarding domestic work, I do two things. First, I abide by the labor code, not only regarding specific domestic worker legislation but by giving her an extra one-month's pay, a paid thirty-day vacation, a work schedule with beginning and end, and free weekends.[9] All of us in the family had to start doing all kinds of things, for example, preparing

breakfast and serving supper. Everybody became aware of their capacity to do things they did not value.

"Second, your domestic worker lives in your home, shares your
privacy, and vice versa. It is a difficult relation. She is an outsider,
sometimes without a family. If she gets sick, you give her medicine,
you take her to a doctor because you are responsible for a person who
depends on you. It is a feudal relationship with mutual obligations.
She renders her services with the hope that you will look after her
when she is sick and old. It is a kind of paternalistic involvement; you
assume a responsibility, and she becomes your dependent.

"Such a relation from a certain perspective conceals the issue of the
employer, since the situation of the domestic worker is very ambiguous, somewhere between a paid job and slavery. It is not a clear-cut
employment situation. In a way, you must keep her because you live
all your life in a slave, not a capitalist, relation. It is a paternalistic
relation that blends work and affection and that creates in the reasoning of the ruling class the image of the domestic worker as a privi-
leged being among all other workers because she has a salary, lodging,
food, and clean clothes. This privilege is a function of this servi-
tude/work relation.

"However, in a society such as ours that is so individualistic and has
so little solidarity, it may be better not only that salaries mediate labor
relations but also that people relate to each other in a humane way,
unlike what happens in the brutal world of capitalism."

Remunerated Domestic Service
Lessens Family Conflicts

According to forty-year-old university professor Rosiska, who is married and has no children, "remunerated domestic service in Brazil is a
terrible thing; the pay in no way corresponds to the value of this work.
In other societies it is a highly paid job and even has a higher status. I
was a *patroa* twice, once in Brazil and another time in Europe. In Brazil I had a domestic who worked the whole day at my house, and her
monthly salary was the same amount I would pay a woman in Europe
who came twice a week for two hours of work.

"For me, remunerated domestic work has pernicious effects on the
family. The domestic worker is like a buffer between the husband and
wife who employ her, keeping the conflicted situation of who is to do
what domestic chores from exploding. It is this contradiction that is

the origin of the feminist movement in those countries where domestic workers have practically disappeared.

"Domestic work is a hard job. I know it is hard because I did that work by myself. It was only in my last years in Europe that I paid to have it done. By doing this work, I began to understand the difference in status between my husband and me. Outside the house we both worked in the same institution and got the same salary. At home I did not understand why I had to do domestic chores by myself. Eventually, we divided the chores, but from the tenor of our discussion I realized that domestic work reveals the nature of the relations between the sexes. The presence of a domestic worker eliminates those contradictions. By putting the work on another woman's back, women avoid confrontation with their husbands over these chores, which are part and parcel of life.

"There is another observation I would like to make about the effect of remunerated domestic work on one's personality. I always had a domestic worker before I left Brazil. When I faced the situation where I did not have a domestic worker, I began to ask, where did food come from? How do you buy it? How do you cook it? Food had been a 'God-given gift.' It appeared on the table by miracle. Till then I couldn't see the value of these chores. I could dirty things up or throw food out; everything was a 'God-given gift.' People who take care of themselves, feed themselves and wash their clothes, become aware of the situation. One is closer to reality than when somebody takes care of you. Having a domestic worker is a form of infantilization of the individual. The more you are able to know your needs and to know how to take care of those needs, the more you become an adult. Nowadays I have a day worker who comes for an average of two hours per day in my house, and I pay her the minimum salary plus social security."

Remunerated Domestic Service
Is the Worst Type of Work

According to thirty-one-year-old Ángela, who is a historian, is married, and has one child, "before I had my son it was different. I employed a day worker to do specific chores. It was very simple. She did just the things I employed her for, and then she would go home. It was a working day like any other. It was a professional relationship. I would sign her employment book. It is more complex when a household worker lives in, because she becomes part of our life and we become part of hers. The space between employee and employer is different when she spends twenty-four hours a day in your place. You exchange many things, including bad moments and other things that normally do not occur in work relations. Ever since my son was born I have been facing this problem or dilemma.

"Last week something happened that illustrates what I am talking about: somebody called my domestic worker to tell her that her thirteen-year-old daughter (she has five children, the youngest is seven or eight years old) had taken an overdose of tranquilizers; she had had an argument with her father, whom she hates. My domestic worker answered that she could not go until the next Sunday. I was absolutely astonished, horrified, and told her to go see her daughter right that minute.

"Suddenly, I began to question my actions, since I was behaving according to my own feelings. I believe she went to see her daughter because I told her to, because of the way I reacted. I was astonished at the way she dealt with her family. I reacted the way I would behave with a friend. I told her to go and asked if she needed money. I said I could lend it to her and that she could stay for as long as she wanted to. As for my son, I did all I could and took him to his day-care center. All my other commitments were put on the back burner.

"What happened created a big mess, the extent of which I cannot gauge because she is a woman as I am. But every minute in my life I am confused, invaded. I would like for her not to be here. On the other hand, I suppose she feels exactly the same way when I invade her space. There is some comfort in the fact that I am out all day, and that gives her more freedom. Remunerated domestic service is the worst possible type of work. And now I understand its isolation. Domestic workers do not have relationships other than those with domestic workers in neighboring households, which is not necessarily encouraged by mistresses.

"I believe domestic work should disappear. The problem is that in Brazil there is a huge army of women ready to do it, with almost no skills for any other type of work. The feminist movement has this goal: to do away with housework. But how can you do away with it without providing a solution to the problem? We feminists feel very uncomfortable about using another woman to play the role assigned by tradition to us. I put up with it because I live in Brazil today with an economic crisis and poverty, and there is this available human resource without the infrastructure to collectivize domestic chores. I have a son and cannot afford a babysitter in the evenings whom I would have to pay by the hour.

"During the day my son is in a day-care center, but I am a militant, and I have meetings to go to in the evenings and I don't know where to leave my son. This problem is hard to solve because I already pay minimum salary, social security, holidays, and an extra one-month salary. I have already taken my domestic worker to a meeting of the Domestic Workers' Association, but she was not interested."

Conclusions

I think it is a step forward for domestic workers to talk about their condition as a social class and as a driving force, but militant feminists state that in spite of class contradictions, there can be solidarity among women by the very fact that we are women, even if it is a solidarity in process.

Remunerated domestic work, the primary occupation among Brazilian women, is going through a period of contraction. The economic crisis might change this trend. Even if we take into account salary in kind, remunerated domestic work is one of the worst-paid occupational sectors for the working class, where 49 percent of those employed in this category earn one-half or less of the minimum salary. This category does not have a clear-cut working day because of its hybrid work relation, a mixture of paid job and slavery. No doubt industrial development helps to improve this work relation. The examples of Rio de Janeiro and, above all, São Paulo point in the direction of better salaries and a more clearly defined working day.

Notes

Acknowledgments: I want to thank Mary Garcia Castro and Anne-Marie Delaunay Maculan for their comments. However, they are not responsible for possible mistakes in this article. I also wish to thank my mother-in-law, Irene Araújo, and my son, Rodrigo Hérmes de Araújo, for their patience in transcribing the tapes.

1. According to Saffioti (1984, 47): "The activities of domestic workers in private homes are not organized according to capitalist forms; thus, they are

not capitalistic. Such workers are not directly dependent on capital but are paid from personal income. . . . Even if there is a work contract, verbal or written, domestic workers perform tasks whose 'product,' goods and services, is consumed directly by the employer family; thus, it does not circulate in the market for exchange and profit. There is no use of capital for this type of employment. Only personal income or money spent as income is used."

2. Britto da Motta (1984, 7) observes: "When men are employed in 'family households' in dependent capitalist societies, they are employed in small numbers. They are employed not as males, or preferential manpower, but as social misfits, in the same way as the masses of female domestic workers."

3. Since most domestic workers live and eat in their employers' households, salary in kind refers to food and lodging. The Brazilian government defines a base salary as the minimum amount a person must receive to live on. No Brazilian worker is supposed to receive less than the minimum salary. The fixing of this minimum salary is very important for the working class because their work contracts are based on it.

4. In 1972, Law No. 5859, regulated by Decree No. 71885, was approved, recognizing the profession of domestic worker and its rights: social security, employment book (see below), and paid vacation (Governo do Brasil, Ministerio do Trabalho 1972). But as Almeida e Silva et al. (1979, 38) note: "This law did not prescribe the length of the working day, and the amount of the minimum salary is left out. It does not guarantee either the right to a weekly day off or the payment of an 'extra one-month salary' " (see below). The employment book is a document showing the employment status of workers, their salaries, and the tasks they are to perform. Having their books signed by their employers allows domestic workers to enjoy what rights they have. The extra month's salary means that workers accrue a bonus, equal to one-twelfth of each month's wages, which they receive with their December salaries as extra pay.

5. In June 1984 $1.00 U.S. = 1,728 *cruzeiros*.

6. See Chapter 18 by the leaders of the Rio de Janeiro Domestic Workers Association in this book.

7. "The feminist movement in Brazil," says Rosika, a university professor, "ends up being an ambiguous idea, because of the generalized presence of domestic workers in the family."

8. See the reproduction of this newsletter in Chapter 22.

9. These are privileges that do not form part of the Brazilian legislation on waged domestic service.

References

Almeida e Silva, M. D'Ajuda, Lilibeth Cardoso, and Mary Garcia Castro. 1979. "As empregadas domésticas na região metropolitana do Rio de

Janeiro: uma análise atravez de dados de E N D E F." Governo do Brasil, Fundação Instituto Brasileiro de Geografía e Estatística (I B G E). Also in *Boletín Demográfico* 12, no. 1 (1981): 26–92.

Associação Profissional dos Empregados Domésticos. 1985a. Resolução do V Congresso Nacional.

Beti y Eliana. 1981. *Vidas paralelas.* Rio de Janeiro: Grupo "Agora e Que São Elas."

Boserup, Ester. 1970. *Woman's Role in Economic Development.* New York: St. Martin's Press.

Brasil-Mulher. 1979. "As domésticas e a C L T." 4 (Setembro): 16.

Britto da Motta, Alda. 1984. "Emprego doméstico masculino." Paper presented at the eighth annual meeting of the Associação Nacional de Pos-Graduação e Pesquisas em Ciências Sociais.

Folha de São Paulo. 1984. "Empregada doméstica é um luxo?: Um salário no orçamento familiar." 17 de junho.

Garcia Castro, Mary. 1982. "¿Qué se compra y qué se paga en el servicio doméstico?: El caso de Bogotá." In Magdalena Léon, ed., *La realidad colombiana,* vol. 1, *Debate sobre la mujer en América Latina y el Caribe,* pp. 92–122. Bogotá: Asociación Colombiana para el Estudio de la Población.

Gonzalez, Leila. 1982. "A mulher negra na sociedade brasileira." In Madel T. Luz, ed., *O lugar da mulher: Estudos sobre a condição feminina na sociedad atual.* Rio de Janeiro: Edições Graal.

Governo do Brasil, Ministerio do Trabalho. 1972. *Lei do Emprego Doméstico Num. 5859.* Brasilia: Ministerio do Trabalho.

Governo do Brasil, Fundação Instituto Brasileiro de Geografía e Estatística. 1970. *Censo Demográfico do Brasil de 1970.* Rio de Janeiro: I B G E.

——. 1979. *Pesquisa Nacional por Amostra de Domicílio do Brasil.* Rio de Janeiro: I B G E.

——. 1980a. *Censo Demográfico do Brasil de 1980.* Rio de Janeiro: I B G E.

——. 1980b. *Censo Demográfico do Estado do Rio de Janeiro de 1980.* Rio de Janeiro: I B G E.

——. 1980c. *Censo Demográfico do Estado do São Paulo de 1980.* Rio de Janeiro: I B G E.

——. 1981. *Pesquisa Nacional por Amostra de Domicílio do Brasil.* Rio de Janeiro: I B G E.

——. 1983. *Pesquisa Nacional por Amostra de Domicílio do Brasil.* Rio de Janeiro: I B G E.

Saffioti, Heleieth Iara Bongiovani. 1984. *Mulher brasileira: Opressão e subordinação.* Rio de Janeiro: Edições Achimé.

Valle Silva, Nelson. 1983. "Notas sobre o censo demográfico de 1980." Fundação Instituto Brasileiro de Geografía e Estatística, Mimeo.

PART IV
Organizations and the State

13 Organizations for Domestic Workers in Montevideo: Reinforcing Marginality?

SUZANA PRATES

Domestic service workers are an extremely fragmented sector of poor urban women, and they become aware of their work and social conditions only with difficulty. They need organizations that will extend their perspective beyond their individual participation in work and stimulate collective reflection toward consciousness of their rights as workers and as women.

The existence of an organization, however, does not in itself guarantee that *empleadas* in domestic service will engage in reflection and become more *conscientizado*.[1] Whether or not they do so depends on the ideological stance of the organization toward the condition of women in society and this category of workers in particular, as well as on the organization's goals and whether or not these are actually carried over into program activities. The actual support an organization provides will depend on whether in its action and its stimulus to reflection there is recognition that "differential access to economic and social resources, and consequently to power, exists within society not only between classes but also between men and women" (Moser and Young 1981, 61).

This chapter considers what role private (as opposed to state-run) nonprofit organizations in Montevideo play in relation to the problematic of domestic service workers in cases where domestics either make up the majority of the "beneficiary group" or are the "target group" of the organization. Of particular interest is whether or not these organizations stimulate collective reflection and thus help their beneficiaries to gain a sense of their social identity. Because the data base is drawn from case studies, the hypotheses do not constitute a general evaluation of women's support and advocacy organizations in Uruguay.

Macrosocial and economic conditions interact to define how wide is the margin wherein these women find it possible to organize and de-

271

fend their rights. Conditions of high competition in the labor force minimize the possibilities workers have to defend their rights, just as politically coercive conditions hinder their ability to organize.

The recent glut on the market of domestic servants in Montevideo means two things: wage levels for these workers have dropped, and what possibilities they did have of defending their labor rights have now been curtailed. Coupled with these is the fact that since 1973— when the parliament was dissolved and trade union activity outlawed—the labor force as a whole has been left without any protection.

There are two issues here, however: one is immediate success in obtaining demands and in the defense of labor rights; the other— very different—is the process of becoming aware that one actually *has* labor rights. Even though women's support organizations and domestic employees' associations may not be able currently to engage in the struggle to win their rights, they can make some headway in other areas. By helping *empleadas* to become collectively conscious, these organizations can contribute to the process whereby this dispersed sector of workers achieves a "group" identity.

The following section analyzes aspects of domestic service in Montevideo in terms of current structural, socioeconomic, and political conditions. The problematic of the group each outside organization seeks to support or unite provides the context for the study of the role of the organizations.

Economic Change, Social Cost, and Domestic Service

According to statistics supplied by the Comisión Económica para América Latina (1982) in 1970, 28 percent of the women in Uruguay over the age of twelve were part of the economically active population, while 43 percent were *dueñas de casa* (literally, "housewives"). Female economic participation in Montevideo grew at a steady rate throughout the decade of the 1970s. Between 1975 and 1976 there was a sharp rise in the growth curve: the index went up from 30.4 percent to 36.5 percent and in 1979 reached a high of 37.1 percent. This shift does not indicate that the percentage of housewives decreased but that the growth was fueled by women who were either married or in free unions (Laens 1985).

Coupled with the fact that more women engaged in wage work for more hours per week, the shift also suggests that the "double day" characterized the changing situation of women during this decade. In 1974–75, 69 percent of female wage workers worked more than 31 hours per week. In 1979 this proportion rose to 80 percent.

In fact, the occupations showing the most growth for the economically active female population during the period are those associated with employment alternatives of working-class women. These women do not have paid substitutes to perform the domestic work, nor can they replace the goods and services produced in the domestic sphere with those produced in the market. Moreover, relative to female wage workers in industrialized countries, they have limited access to labor-saving household appliances. The number of female factory workers and laborers increased between 1976 and 1979 in both absolute and relative terms. While relative participation of personal service workers decreased, their absolute numbers increased.

Unfortunately, published household surveys do not disaggregate "personal services." Nevertheless, it can be argued that participation in the domestic service sector is not only very high but has increased since the decade of the 1970s. This increase is directly related to the national economic and social crisis and to the deteriorating living standards of the working class. In 1963 domestic service accounted for 76.8 percent of the "personal services sector" in Montevideo; by 1975 it had increased to 82.2 percent (Taglioretti 1981).

The overall increase in poverty can be attributed to the political-economic model imposed on the country since 1973. Under this model the authoritarian state and the new monetarist orthodoxy were welded into a coherent entity. The new strategy implied more than simply readjusting the economy or enforcing temporary political control. It ushered in a new social philosophy and conception of society that drastically redefined the conditions under which the labor force was maintained and reproduced.

Despite the doctrinaire "liberalism" of the managers of the political economy, the state was characterized by an "absence/presence" dynamic: whether or not to intervene in the economy depended on what favored a concentrated redistribution of profits. Thus, the state allowed the market to fix prices but froze wages; it encouraged private enterprise and allowed it to organize but dismantled and outlawed labor unions; it cut back the social services budget but increased the defense and internal security budgets.

The social effects of this entire process were felt immediately. Real wages fell by 40 percent between 1971 and 1979, and by 55 percent in the manufacturing sector between 1970 and 1980 (PREALC 1982). The drop in real wages was not, however, the only factor in the erosion of the material bases of social reproduction of the labor force. The state cut the education and health budgets and transferred public housing credits to private enterprise, providing an incentive for high income housing construction. Social and pension payments were effectively frozen, and these suffered a drop greater than did real wages, putting the total tax burden on salaries and consumer goods.

What this meant was that interpretations of women's economic participation would center, in terms of supply, on the hypothesis of "family survival strategies" or, perhaps more accurately, resistance strategies (Laens 1985; Prates 1981; Prates and Taglioretti 1980). Under these conditions, women—just as they have done in other contexts and social circumstances—entered the work force by participating in cash-income-generating activities both inside and outside the household sphere (Milkman 1976).

If the "social crisis" of the wage sectors pushed women into the labor market during the 1970s, it did so at a time when demand for labor, particularly female labor, was high. During that period, when the country was experimenting with an export strategy of manufactured goods, many women entered the industrial work force (Prates 1983). Between 1976 and 1979 the most important relative and absolute female participation comprised factory workers and laborers, while the domestic service sector expanded at a lower rate.

By 1980 the manufacturing export strategy had begun to fail (Macadar 1982). The economy went into crisis, and between 1979 and 1983 the official unemployment rate almost trebled. This unemployment rate does not include the "discouraged workers," the majority of whom are women and young people from the upper-income sectors who retired from the labor market when the depression set in.

The rate of unemployment among women from the popular sectors, who had participated in large numbers in the export industries, was particularly high (Prates 1983). This had immediate repercussions on the supply of labor for domestic service: in one year—between 1981 and 1982—the number of applicants for domestic service positions in Montevideo doubled, from 11,565 to 23,256 (Uruguay, Ministerio de Trabajo y Seguridad Social 1982).

This was not accompanied by a growing demand for domestics; on the contrary, demand contracted because the economic crisis was beginning to affect the middle sectors, meaning that many middle-class women who were newly unemployed "disappeared" into the domestic realm as a way of absorbing the cost of their unemployment. As a result, there was a reduction in the effective number of openings for domestic employees. For example, Ministry of Labor and Social Security data indicate that in 1981, 68 percent of the applicants for wage work in domestic service did not find jobs. Although these data are not representative, they do indicate a possible invisible contingent of unemployed domestic workers (Uruguay, Ministerio de Trabajo y Seguridad Social 1982).

Notwithstanding, the wage level started to "flatten out." In 1981, 22.7 percent of domestic workers who had been placed through commercial agencies were earning salaries that were either on par with, or double the minimum wage. In 1982, only 6.6 percent earned between two and three times the minimum wage.[2] This situation suggests a special problematic for the domestic employee and for those women whose only source of employment is this type of occupation. It means that the role of the organizations that offer support, or a space for participation, becomes more crucial.

Support Organizations and Targeted Beneficiaries

In the circumstances described above, church-sponsored organizations took on special importance and sociopolitical potential. The extensive network of Catholic agencies, and the church's long history of social involvement in Latin America, meant that its social services were called upon to play a role—but a role which, with some exceptions, they were not fully equipped to carry out. For one thing, potential clients and beneficiaries of these services increased as the poverty index rose, putting growing pressure on existing institutional resources. For another, the objective of guiding the activity of these services and agencies was, for the most part, formulated in accordance with an "evaluative climate" (Mayntz 1967) that assumed charity to be the only socially legitimate goal they were entitled to pursue.

The following analysis seeks first to identify the relation between the objectives and the beneficiary group formulated by the leaders of the services and organizations under consideration, then to explore the extent to which these objectives are translated into real activities. This presupposes that the concrete activities carried out by the organizations do in fact "translate" an ideological conception that explicitly or implicitly determines how the directors of the organizations perceive the beneficiary or target group.

The information used here was gathered from studies of eight different centers of advocacy services. Seven of them are part of the "social work agenda" of the Catholic Church; the eighth, although its directors are associated with the church, is autonomous.

For the purposes of the analysis undertaken below, two primary aspects of these organizations are examined. In the first place, they are classified in terms of the target group of their activities, *empleadas* being one of the specific categories. Then the degree of complexity and diversification of their activities is analyzed, which for our purposes represents the expression of objectives expressed as goals. In accordance with these two aspects, the eight cases are distributed as shown in Figure 13-1.

A and B in Figure 13-1 are included as services or support centers for domestics because even though they do not define these workers as their target group, domestics are the beneficiaries of the services. In the A cell in particular, *empleadas* are greatly overrepresented. The fact that the four empirically distinct types of services all define their goals differently and have considerably diversified activities means that each one has to be analyzed separately.

		Target Group		
		POOR	POOR WOMEN	EMPLEADAS DOMÉSTICAS
Complexity of Activities	LOW	A Employment Agencies		C Training Center
	HIGH		B Advocacy Center	D Advocacy Center

FIGURE 13-1   Classification of Organizations by Target Group(s) and Degree of Complexity and Diversification of Activities

The Employment Agencies

Although the employment agencies[3] do not designate domestics as their target group, the majority of their clients are persons seeking to be placed in domestic service. The goals that determine the activities of the agencies are neither occupational nor sex-specific in terms of their clients. The leaders have defined these goals as follows: to help people who need work; to find employment for those most in need; to counsel people with problems; to provide other support services to poor families. These charitable, clearly *asistencialista* (welfare-oriented) formulations lump all the "clients" together in a diffuse social category that bears little resemblance to the actual beneficiary group:

• The majority of the clients are women who come to apply for domestic service work. Few clients specify that they want to work in supermarkets, hotels, stores, offices, and the like. The demand for domestic service began to decline in late 1981, at the same time as the supply of women for those services had increased significantly. Now the number of women who are looking for work for the first time has increased.

• Most of those who apply are women who will work in domestic service and clean, care for single people and children, do family laundry, and so on. Applicants come from low-income sectors both nearby and far away. Many women who come to apply for jobs are accompanied by their children.

• Most applicants looking for positions in domestic service are women over the age of forty.

The generic mode in which these organizations define their objectives as "aid" determines an organizational format that leaves no margin for the beneficiaries to engage in active participation. They are invited neither to define the objectives nor to determine the activities (the "wherefore") of the organization itself.

The purpose of the aid is to provide a service, which is concretized in one sole activity: engaging as an intermediary in the marketplace between the supply and the demand for labor power. The fact that the service is oriented in this particular way means that the domestic employees who benefit from it relate to each other as clients rather than as members. As Mayntz (1967, 175–76) observes, the participants "see the organization as a useful instrument that satisfies their personal needs without obligation; neither does it demand that they identify with its philosophy. . . . because it discourages active participation, this orientation strengthens the oligarchic tendencies in the organizations."

This "benefactor-client" orientation is clearly related to the more broadly defined agenda of the parent organization, the church. Because of its origin in the church, it is likely that the general framework that sustains the particular objective of the service is diluted, since it is externally determined, then translated by the leaders as a partial commitment—in this case to look for work for the poor and the needy.

The problem is that this partial and at the same time, diffuse way of concretizing wider goals is that they eventually either recede from view or are reduced to a simple welfare perspective. Thus clients are unable to become members capable of acting and influencing the activities of the organization through their participation and from their own perspective.

The scarce material and human resources at the disposal of these agencies and the fact that most of the staff is volunteer are further indications that such services, and consequently the work situation of the domestic employees, rank low in the list of priorities that constitutes the organized social service system. Clearly, the fact that resources are scarce is a limiting factor on the activities that these services are in a position to carry out, but their activities are limited in addition by the criteria the directors use to determine the agenda and allocate the resources. In other words, the activities reflect an ideological posture, one that clearly translates into one of two major options: either the beneficiaries of the service are able to see themselves as a group, as members of an organization that will enable them to define themselves as workers, or they will continue perceiving themselves as "poor individuals" who are dependent upon charity.

In terms of quantity, quality, and working conditions (volunteer or paid) of human resources, then, the registered employment agencies are in a particularly precarious situation: of the thirteen people involved, eleven have no qualifications whatsoever. Even of the two who are paid, only one is qualified. Clearly, the scarcity of resources assigned to the agencies implies that the volunteer leaders are strongly identified with the aims of the service and the parent organization. But this identification is frozen, to all intents and purposes, at the level of individual commitment; it consists in intermediation rather than projection toward even the minimal organizational requirements that the service must adopt if it is to fulfill its objectives.

First of all, none of the employment agencies uses a registry to record the data and situation of the women seeking work, which would make possible a follow-up of the beneficiaries. Only one of the agencies keeps records, and it does not process the data or prepare any sort of report that would permit an overall view of the problematic of women and domestic service. The records are maintained merely as "client files" so that staff can attend to individual problems as they come up.

It is clear that the attitude of the team in charge—a paid social worker and five volunteers—is not conducive to a collective process wherein the problematic would be evaluated with the beneficiaries of the service themselves, encouraging reflection on their social reality and situation as workers. Although the "top down" focus shows some effort to improve the quality of assistance provided, there is no thought that the "beneficiary" group itself should become "*conscientizado*" and define the activities of the service. *Conscientização* appears to be necessary, at least for those in charge, who do not belong to the beneficiary group.

Moreover, none of these agencies integrates into its activities such services as legal counseling on the labor rights of domestics. The fact that most domestics work in situations that flagrantly violate labor regulations is taken for granted. This is particularly true now that the supply of domestic service workers has undergone quantitative as well as qualitative changes. As we have seen, the supply increased as more women, probably less aware of their rights than those already employed, began to enter the work force for the first time. Their decision to join the work force, moreover, was complicated by anxiety, as statements of the directors of several of the employment agencies interviewed for this study illustrate:

> These days, about twenty-five or thirty women come in every day to look for work in domestic service. Many of them come back repeatedly to find out if there is anything to suit them. At the moment, the housing problem is driving many women into the workplace, mainly women with children.

> More mothers with children are looking for work now. Since employers prefer domestics without children, this lowers their chances of being hired.

> At first they ask for $2,000 N.[4] After a while, though, they'll settle for whatever they can get. The women who want jobs in domestic service work in order to eat and also because they

are lonely. For the most part, they see the salary as a way to escape from their personal situation, not as salvation for their families.

Training and Advocacy Centers

What the church-sponsored training and advocacy centers have in common is their target group: low-income women. The training center is especially oriented toward *empleadas.* Although the majority of the participants in the advocacy center are either currently employed—or expect soon to be hired—as domestics, the advocacy center itself defines its target group in terms that are at once more general and more specific: "women with families, women with children, and pregnant women between twenty-five and fifty years of age." The ıact that the woman's position as mother or wife is adopted as the criterion for advocacy clearly signals the existence of a "model" or a norm as to what is considered primary in women's lives. Women who join the center receive prizes that explicitly benefit the family. In 1984 one strategy to help support the family and boost and retain membership was to award a $50 N bonus in clothes and food.

This is consistent with the way the objectives of the advocacy are articulated: to form work groups with women in situations of extreme need and to help them find employment outside the home. This particular center did sponsor talks aimed at helping the beneficiaries become better informed, but there was no provision for evaluation of the way the topics were focused—in either their theoretical or their ideological premises—or of how the information was processed.

The work carried out by this center leads to doubts about whether it considers the problematic of poor women in terms of their situation as women who are also members of poor families, or whether such topics as "women," "the neighborhood," "children," and so on, consider women only as members of the family and as potential or current income earners for the family. In other words, is the focus on women's reality only as a subordinate problem derived from that of the family?

The evaluation by the directors of the center (five paid professionals) suggests that the participants do not achieve a sense of group identity:

> The women have trouble acting as a group, refusing to take any kind of leadership role themselves . . . [making] the group increasingly dependent upon those of us who run the

center. . . . At the moment we are having trouble attracting new clients, since the women we have approached dislike the idea of getting together as a group.

What such statements reveal is that despite the prizes women are refusing to accept "membership." This is probably related to the failure of the center to transform the recipients of its services into subjects and, at the same time, to come to terms with their problematic as women, not only as members of a family unit.

The training center, on the other hand, is geared almost exclusively toward *empleadas*. Unlike the advocacy center, its activities are not highly complex; its short-term, goal-oriented approach considers the domestic only in terms of her personal situation as an employee, not as a member of the labor force: "The [goal of] training domestics from the slums . . . is [to] improve their efficiency in the jobs they are able to secure. They are trained to use household appliances, answer the telephone, and perform other domestic chores for their employers."

Where the advocacy center is family-oriented, the training center is paternalistic and confined to assisting the *empleada* to improve her skills; it does not aspire to train her as a worker. The agenda of the training service does not include a course that would inform and increase the awareness of the domestics-in-training as to their labor rights and obligations. The purpose of the training course is to guarantee that the *empleada* perform efficiently for her future employers; it is not concerned with the development of the woman as a person. In neither one of the cases analyzed—even when there is a greater range of activities, even when the target group is either poor women or domestic employees—is there any social training that would enable these women to become conscious of their reality and contextualize their problematic from their own point of view and in terms of their own interests.

ANECAP: The *Empleada* as Subject or Object?

The Asociación Nacional de Empleadas de Casa Particular, or A N E C A P (National Association of Household Workers) is the most complex of the centers and services considered here. Moreover, as its name indicates, *empleadas* are its target group. One purpose of the project was to discover whether or not the domestics who are members of this institution are also subjects of the activities. This meant investigating its goals and current activities and its history.

ANECAP has undergone a series of changes since its founding (1964–67). These changes reflect the struggle between conceptions of it: as an "advocacy" service for domestic employees, and as a corporate body that is representative of its rank and file. A brief review of how the organization has changed will put us in a better position to interpret the current situation and determine the prognosis for the social participation of the domestic employees who are members.

History

Unlike the previous agencies analyzed, ANECAP was founded as a "grassroots" organization. This dynamic defined its subsequent development and set it apart from other domestic service advocacy centers.

ANECAP was founded by a group of domestics, almost all of whom had migrated from the rural areas to Montevideo and were active members of the Juventud Obrera Católica or JOC (Young Catholic Workers), which sponsored the organization. At first the *empleadas* themselves ran the association, although they had professional social services and legal advisors. Around 1967 they began to act as a professional association and joined the labor movement (even sharing office space with other unions).

At this point a split appeared between the "militants" and the "conservative Catholics." The association stagnated and began to fall apart, and the militants joined the Confederación Nacional de Trabajadores or CNT (National Confederation of Workers), while the conservative Catholics retained control of ANECAP. When the military government outlawed union activity in late 1973, the domestic employees group in the CNT was disbanded.

In 1971, ANECAP was reorganized under totally different conditions, which prevail to this day. Catholic institutions abroad began to finance it, and the *empleada* became the object, rather than the initiator, of the activities. A technical team (social workers, a lawyer, a psychologist, and a priest-coordinator) took control. The aim of the organization, newly reformulated, is to provide domestic *empleadas* with a full range of services. According to the professional team, the *empleadas* are to take the lead both within the organization and in their communities of origin. They are to be assisted in this by means of various activities and organized services recently placed under the control of different committees of empleadas.

Services and Activities

Empleadas' committees administer eight different services, which can be classified as either "mutual aid" or "welfare." The mutual aid subset includes a savings and loan association, a used clothing store whose profits help fund the organization's activities, and cultural dissemination by means of billboards, bulletins, publications, a library, subscriptions. These services benefit the individual members and the organization as a whole. The welfare services, on the other hand, benefit members and nonmembers alike: they provide shelter and a place to leave personal belongings, and are mostly used by *empleadas* arriving from rural areas.

At the same time, the organization maintains an artisan workshop and a lecture series. The workshop is coordinated by a paid professional whose goal is to "improve skills, develop perseverance, and awaken creativity" (personal interview). The lectures are based on topics the *empleadas* choose from a list compiled by the professional team to "broaden the horizons of the domestics and situate them in the world."[5]

Up to this point, the evidence suggests that the *empleadas* who join ANECAP are the target group of the activities, and that the manner in which these are directed and developed is both very complex and clearly contributes to the enrichment of the *empleada* as a person. It also suggests, however, that the *empleada*'s participation as a subject of the activities is very limited and delegated. The members do choose topics (from a list proposed by the professional team, however) and administer the welfare and mutual aid services, but there is no prospect of their participating in the decision-making process of the organization's social advocacy program.

Decision-Making

In addition to the professional team that took over the reins of ANECAP in 1971, there is another group within the organization called Grupo Madre Dinamizador or GMD (Dynamizing Mothers'

Group) with twenty members, older leaders of ANECAP and new *empleadas* who joined this group in 1982. According to one leader, the GMD "has been evaluated very positively because it acts to keep the larger organization from becoming too set in its ways." Despite its acknowledged tradition of leadership, however, only in 1983, according to another of its leaders, has the GMD "begun to collaborate in the planning and preparation of ANECAP's annual program; it also convened and presided over a membership assembly whose purpose was to evaluate the previous year's program and propose the new one."

Since it is this assembly that decides on the mutual aid and welfare services described above, the organization clearly appears to function democratically, at least at the level of consultation and debate. The GMD acts as the nexus between the professional team—which controls the resources of the institution—and the mass membership. Nevertheless, the GMD membership is not regulated by formal rules or established channels; neither is its participation at the decision-making level formally regulated. The GMD seems to be an ad hoc group whose spontaneous activity is taken for granted and tolerated by the professional team.

Rank among members is based on two clearly differentiated criteria: seniority, and power based on technical-economic control. On the one hand, the professional team has access to and manages the economic resources that flow in from abroad. The team decides which activities will be developed, and allocates the resources accordingly. Moreover, it determines what professional personnel to hire and what their policies should be, since the resources come from proposals that the team has written and presented to foundations. On the other hand, the criteria of seniority seems decisive in terms of authority because certain members have more power than others, even though there are no established access routes to the decision-making levels and the GMD members are not elected by an assembly.

The organization may once again be confronting the same kind of split as in 1967. One group of members has suggested that it is time for the association to form a labor union. For several reasons, however, the time was not deemed appropriate: politically, union activity is still experiencing difficulties in this country; by law, the unions cannot be financed from abroad, and ANECAP is unable to be self-sufficient; moreover, according to the professional team, "society does not think of domestic service in labor union terms."

It is important to bear in mind that it was the professional team and the GMD who decided "the time isn't right to unionize"; the decision was not processed at the assembly level or endorsed by the rank and file. The reasoning behind the decision not to unionize brings us back to the issue of the decision-making process, the different interests of the group, and how the problematic of the domestic service sector is focused.

A Temporary Balance

Clearly, under the aegis of ANECAP, domestic *empleadas* are finding an opportunity to pursue meaningful activities and participate in collaborative social activity. This contributes to their building up an identity as women and as workers, the clearest evidence being the desire to unionize. This suggests that the target group is seeking to convert itself into a participatory subject group, challenging the authority of the professionals. The professionals evidently did not take over the organization, which has no existence apart from the participation of the membership; they took over the effective social participation of the domestics themselves.

Underlying the team's judgment that it was inadvisable to unionize at present were not only its opposition to the unsupervised social participation of domestics but also the focus, ideology, and interests that define the professional team as a group—a group which, although identified with the problematic of the domestic *empleada*, does not live it and is therefore not part of that sector. To accept the difficulty that "society does not think of domestic service in terms of union activity" is tantamount to accepting the social reality as it is, not working toward what it should be from the standpoint of domestic *empleadas* themselves.

From the legal point of view, it seems there need not have been any contradiction between ANECAP's remaining an association while its members unionize as autonomous entities. The question is to what extent a competitive objective—one coordinated with other institutions in the union system—would undermine the base of social participation of the domestic *empleadas* in ANECAP and lead to policies, priorities, and strategies that would leave the present professional team behind. To what extent would the creature become autonomous, independent of the creator?

Final Reflections

In introducing this chapter I argued that a particular social group can build up its identity and achieve political visibility through collective reflection and the process of *conscientizaçao*. These would seem to be preconditions of the groups organization and the possibility of achieving its demands.

The problematic of the economic participation of women from the popular sectors derives from the fact that although they have high rates of participation, the returns are low and are confined to the private sphere of the household and immediate community. Most poor women enter the job market through the so-called informal sector, where they participate in fragmented activities and are "unprotected" in terms of labor rights. Because this is particularly true for the domestic employee, it is important that *empleadas* have access to spaces for social participation that encourage them to reflect collectively on their condition as women and as workers.

Given the heterogeneity of the services and organizations analyzed, no uniform recommendations can be applied. The nonspecific programmatic and group objectives of the employment agencies appear to perpetuate rather than modify the situation of precariousness and marginality that domestic *empleadas* face in the job market. The characteristics of the "casual worker" become the norm in a labor situation wherein women who apply for these services seek to save their personal situation or generate income for the family but are not given the opportunity to see themselves as workers in their own right.

The activities of the training and advocacy centers for domestic employees and women from the marginal sectors, although specifically targeting those two groups and in fact appearing to be the means for achieving the group objectives, tend to reduce the problematic of the *empleada* to a family problematic—just as the marginal woman is not perceived from her own viewpoint and her individual condition in family and society but primarily as existing for the family.

There is some possibility, however—at least for ANECAP—that *conscientizaçao* and the acquisition of group identity will have ramifications in the realm of political-union activity. The history of the organization, the fact that it was founded by the rank and file, and its earlier contact with the union domain (which the domestics entered as workers and not as "poor," "needy," or "marginal" women, meaning that they participated as peers)—all have some bearing on the present situation and on the emerging demands for unionization.

If the *empleadas* are to become unionized, it will be necessary to evaluate the extent to which their participation will be determined by the agenda of the union movement as a whole—which historically has been defined by its leaders, usually men—rather than by their particular problematic as women and as workers.

The preliminary balance of this exploratory analysis suggests that the process conducive to the achievement of a degree of group identity through support and advocacy organizations is undermined when this support is superimposed, verticalist, and welfare-oriented. In order to achieve this identity the domestic employee must be more than the target, the object, of the action; she must be the subject of the action. However, is it not at this point that the advocacy organization loses its reason for being?

To "educate" domestics or "change the way they behave" is one of the objectives of ANECAP. Is this possible, or even the appropriate response to the problematic of these workers? Does not the teacher also have to be taught? (Lukács 1960, 256)

Editors' Note

Suzana Prates: A Tribute: In the early months of 1988, as this book was going to press, Suzana Prates died in Montevideo. We thought it appropriate to reprint here a translation of the tribute sent to her friends by her colleagues of the Grupo de Estudios sobre la Condición de la Mujer en el Uruguay (GRECMU):

> Suzana has died. Her pain in living proved more powerful than she herself. She was very, very Brazilian, but settled in Uruguay where her personal search and her collective commitment led her to be a pioneer of GRECMU, of the women's movement, and of global feminism—a pacifist but a revolutionary of our decade.
>
> Her efforts—and what she accomplished—have given visibility and scholarly status to a matter that was forgotten here: we ourselves, the women. She created a space to push forward this goal that grew and was transformed through the joining together of efforts and alliances, of multiple initiatives, inside and outside GRECMU, to bring about "the utopia."

Our commitment—today as before—compels us to continue creating this "space," to which she gave herself and dedicated her last years. Because of all that she believed in, because we and many women share with her the collective search for ideas, explanations, solutions for a better life, our desire is that Suzana will continue to be with us not only in memory, but also in our actions.

Her Compañeras of GRECMU

Notes

Acknowledgments: I am indebted to Enrique Mazzei and Carina Perelli, who kindly provided me with the results of research conducted under their supervision (see Mazzei 1983) in the preparation of this chapter.

1. "*Conscientização*," a term first employed by Paulo Freire in his numerous studies on education, refers to the process by which persons, particularly the poor and oppressed, acquire the mentality that makes it possible for them to participate actively in their own education, development, betterment. More specifically, "the term refers to learning to perceive social, political, and economic contradictions, and to take action against the oppressive elements of reality" (Freire 1968, 19).

2. These wage levels of domestic service clearly are surprising in comparison with the rest of Latin America. Three elements in particular contribute to the high level of remuneration of registered domestic service. First, these salaries are paid to women placed through commercial employment agencies. Second, as demand and successful placements are effectively reduced, it seems reasonable to suppose that the wage levels correspond to demand by high income sectors for highly qualified domestic *empleadas*. Third, until recently, the supply of domestic service in Montevideo has been limited, and the wage level has traditionally been very high. This is related to the small rural population of the country on the one hand and, on the other, to the relatively high living standards—above all in the urban sector—guaranteed by the family wage and the liberal orientation of the state.

3. The employment services considered in this article constitute 50 percent of the total number of services of this type (Arzobispado de Montevideo 1981).

4. In 1983, at the time of the interviews, $1.00 U.S. = 43 New Pesos.

5. In these lectures, priority is given to the domestic as a woman and to all aspects of her life (work, individual, family). Among the topics studied are "Social Thought: The Answer to Our Needs?"; "What Is a Professional Association, Unionism?"; "The Problems and Aspirations of the Female Worker"; and "Single Motherhood."

References

Arzobispado de Montevideo. 1981. *Guía de la Iglesia Católica del Uruguay.* Montevideo: Arzobispado de Montevideo.

Comisión Económica para América Latina. 1982. *Cinco estudios sobre la situación de la mujer en América Latina.* Estudios e Informes No. 16. Santiago de Chile: CEPAL.

Freire, Paulo. 1968. *Pedagogy of the Oppressed.* Trans. by Myra Berman Ramos. New York: Herder and Herder.

Laens, Sylvia. 1985. *Cambio económico y trabajo femenino.* Montevideo: Grupo de Estudios sobre la Condición de la Mujer en el Uruguay, Centro de Información y Estudios de Uruguay (GRECMU-CIESU).

Lukács, Georg. 1960. *Histoire et conscience de classe.* Paris: Minuit.

Macadar, L. 1982. *Uruguay 1974–1980: ¿Un nuevo ensayo de reajuste económico?* Montevideo: CINVE, Editorial Banda Oriental.

Mayntz, Renate. 1967. *Sociología de la organización.* Madrid: Alianza Editorial.

Mazzei, Enrique. 1983. "Organizaciones no-estatales de apoyo a la mujer." Grupo de Estudios sobre la Condición de la Mujer en el Uruguay, Centro de Información y Estudios de Uruguay (GRECMU-CIESU), Montevideo.

Milkman, Ruth. 1976. "Women's Work and Economic Crisis: Some Lessons of the Great Depression." *Review of Radical Political Economists* 8, no. 1.

Moser, Caroline, and Kate Young. 1981. "Women of the Working Poor." *IDS Bulletin* 12, no. 3:50–62.

Prates, Suzana. 1981. "Women's Labour and Family Survival Strategies under the Stabilization Models in Latin America." Document prepared for the United Nations, Center for Social Development and Humanitarian Affairs (Vienna), Expert Group Meeting on Policies for Social Integration.

——. 1983. "Estratégia exportadora y la búsqueda de trabajo barato: Trabajo visible e invisible de la mujer en la industria del calzado en el Uruguay." Grupo de Estudios sobre la Condición de la Mujer en el Uruguay, Centro de Información y Estudios de Uruguay (GRECMU-CIESU), Montevideo.

Prates, Suzana, and Garciela Taglioretti. 1980. *Participación de la mujer en el mercado de trabajo uruguayo: Características básicas y evolución reciente.* Montevideo: Grupo de Estudios sobre la Condición de la Mujer en el Uruguay, Centro de Información y Estudios de Uruguay (GRECMU-CIESU).

PREALC (Programa Regional de Empleo para América Latina y El Caribe). 1982. *Mercado de trabajo en cífras.* Santiago de Chile: Oficina Internacional de Trabajo.

Taglioretti, Graciela. 1981. *La participación de la mujer en el mercado de trabajo.* Montevideo: Grupo de Estudios sobre la Condición de la Mujer en el

Uruguay, Centro de Información y Estudios de Uruguay (GRECMU-CIESU).

Uruguay, Dirección General de Estadísticas y Censos. 1968–79. Encuestas de Hogares.

———. 1963, 1975. Censos Nacionales de Población y Vivienda.

Uruguay, Ministerio de Trabajo y Seguridad Social. 1981. *Agencias privadas de colocación, enero-junio.* Montevideo: Dirección Nacional de Recursos Humanos.

———. 1982. *Agencias privadas de colocación, oferta, demanda y colocación, enero-junio.* Montevideo: Dirección Nacional de Recursos Humanos.

14 Household Workers in Peru: The Difficult Road to Organization

THEA SCHELLEKENS and ANJA VAN DER SCHOOT

In Peru many young girls from the Sierra (highlands) work as live-in domestics. They do not select this occupation voluntarily but are forced by circumstances to place themselves as household workers in the homes of families not their own. The JOC, or Young Catholic Workers, (Juventud Obrera Católica 1978, 1) estimates that some 200,000 women are employed as domestics in Lima. According to 1981 census data, they constitute 19 percent of the economically active female population in Peru.

From an early age, domestic workers have to face limited possibilities for survival and advancement. Opportunities for employment and education provide the most important motivation for these women to leave the Sierra and join the multitudes who migrate to the greater Lima area hoping for a better life. In the majority of cases, her family arranges in advance for a daughter's employment as a domestic worker in a Lima household. The most specific arrangement is a form of indenture (*enganche*, literally "entrapment") under which a domestic worker is totally dependent on her employers, to whom she is given over as an *ahijada* (goddaughter) by means of a signed contract that remains in effect until she comes of age.[1]

I was hardly with my parents at all. When I was five, my father went away. He left me with my mother, who had a lot to do and never had any spare time. One day, when I was barely six years old, my mother died.

After a while my brothers took off for the coast. I was left up in the air. I did not know what was happening, and almost by magic I fell into my grandmother's care. At first she was good to me, but then she changed. She gave me three hard chores: I had to take care of the animals, and cook and wash for my cousin. After a while my grandmother said, "You are going to go to Lima with some people who are going to love you very much and give you an education. You will only have to play with their daughter." I didn't say anything, although I didn't want to go anywhere. I was afraid they would beat me in the place they were going to take me. They took me to those people against my will. [María]

For the young, single, uneducated women from the Sierra, working as a domestic offers one of the few possibilities for earning money, usually a pittance, over and above receiving food and shelter. But to be a domestic is to work long hours for low pay. Early in the morning while the streets are still dark and empty, domestics can be seen sweeping the sidewalks and lining up at the bakery in order to serve their employers fresh bread for breakfast. Then there are the innumerable chores that last until well into the night: cleaning, washing, ironing, caring for children, shopping, cooking. They also have to work on Sundays, because domestic work is never-ending. A household worker is not free to schedule her daily chores, because she must follow her mistress's orders. Moreover, within the family she occupies a marginal position, which is manifested in many ways.

They would give us two rolls to eat with tea. After that I used to go to bed. Meanwhile, they were eating buttered toast, coffee with milk, steak, and on top of that, grapes, pears, apples, and peaches.

We had to take their breakfast up to the second floor. They ate it at a table. We ate it in the kitchen and only had tea with bread. While they had breakfast at seven in the morning, we couldn't do so until nearly ten, once some of the work was behind us. We had to cook separately for them. While they were eating good chicken soup, we would have a watery noodle broth with a spoonful of rice. [María]

To be a domestic worker is to live in a house belonging to people of another social class, to be humiliated in every way: as a woman, as a *cholita* (that is, a person of an indigenous race) and as a member of an inferior class.[2] Although there have been improvements over the years, the occupational category continues to show many characteristically servile tendencies.

In 1981 we lived in Lima for six months in order to study the problematic of household workers. Our study emphasized working conditions and the organization of domestic employees into household workers' unions. We obtained organized data from thirty-four domestic employees, fifteen of whom were unionized and nineteen non affiliated, the majority of them being "live-ins." We supplemented the report by reading and by informal conversation with domestic workers and others. With the data from our project we have prepared a thesis, but not wishing to limit ourselves to this goal, we are endeavoring to acquaint a wider audience with the situation of household workers.

Almost all the domestic workers surveyed described their situation as being very difficult. Nonetheless, only a small group, the unions in particular, are pursuing fundamental changes within this occupational sector and are debating its status—based on class, gender, and racial inequality—in the society.

The first domestic workers' unions were founded in the early 1970s. In the short term they demand improved legislation to obtain equal rights with other workers. Their long-term goal is "a new society with a new person," as one union leader put it: "a classless society where there are no domestic workers but where there are child-care centers, peoples' cafeterias, and work for all. A society in which women are an integral part of the productive process."

The Development of Household Workers' Unions

In order to understand the development of the household workers' unions, we have to consider the role of the Catholic Church. Religious institutions have, in fact, taken the initiative in offering training courses and providing assistance services. But because the Catholic Church has historically played an important role in the justification of class and sex distinctions, these efforts are characterized in general by their conservatism.

One example is the international organization Opus Dei, which organizes religious and cultural activities for domestic workers. In its Cenecape (*Centro no estatal de calificación profesional extraordinaria,* private center for special professional training) the aim is to train girls who have had five years of elementary schooling for positions as "professional" maids. "Flexibility for adapting to the circumstances of the particular family or business they serve" is demanded. When they offer their collaboration with love, they are told, they perform a great task in the Christian sense of life (Ho 1981, 69–71). During our visit to the Cenecape Alcabor, we frequently heard the words "resignation" and "adaptation." The director did not allow us to speak with the Cenecape girls, however. She told us that "their cultural level is very low, and they speak very little Spanish. Because of this they sometimes tell untruths."

The sisters of the Congregation of Mary Immaculate also run a school for country girls fourteen to eighteen years old. After some months in primary school, plus religious and domestic training, they are placed as household workers. The sisters have a limited control over the employers, who are obliged to comply with the law and give their domestic employees sufficient rest time to attend classes and participate in Sunday recreational activities. The position of domestic worker is considered a temporary one; according to the Mother Superior, "It is a means of earning a living while training for individual advancement."

In addition, various parishes organize recreational activities, sewing courses, preparatory meetings for baptisms and first communions. All these church-sponsored activities are designed to promote the welfare of the domestic workers and offer them some opportunities for recreation and improvement of their skills.

During the 1960s small opposition groups appeared within the church espousing "liberation theology" and opposing the church's role in perpetuating the status quo. One of these progressive religious groups was the Young Catholic Workers (JOC), which played an important part in the formation of the household workers' unions. To a certain extent, the JOC followed a line that emphasized "assistance"[3] to domestic workers in their individual development. In the climate of the 1970s, however, the work of the JOC changed.

The popular movement grew during the crisis years leading up to the 1968 coup, a trend that would continue after the coup. In order to attract support for its policies, the reformist military government allowed a certain amount of organizing to take place. The popular movement took advantage of this opening by founding new organizations and developing existing ones. During the Juan Velasco government, for example, 2,066 new unions were recognized (Sulmont 1980. 213). The issue was one of increasing politicization throughout the popular sectors. The government's efforts to regulate the movement were unsuccessful.

Influenced by these developments, the JOC from 1966 on intensified its work in developing class consciousness among young people, including young domestic employees. Simultaneously, a group of anarcho-syndicalist students, Tupac Armando Yupanqui, was organizing household workers in Lima. JOC domestic workers and members of other Christian groups participated in Tupac, putting pressure on the government to improve existing legislation affecting domestic service. For the JOC, one of the critical points of this effort was that Tupac was organizing the household workers to demand their rights but was not inserting them under the umbrella group of other mass organizations. As a result, when after two years Tupac could not withstand the outside pressures and internal problems, the JOC household workers and other domestics reinitiated the failed Tupac efforts to found a union (Rivera 1979, 4:44–45).

For a union to be recognized in a workplace, twenty or more workers—with the exception of the directors of the business—must be employed by the same boss. Since household workers cannot comply with this requirement, neither are they able to form a legally recognized union. Yet, as one JOC advisor pointed out, "this rule for the recognition of unions is arbitrarily applied. For example, barbers and newspaper vendors unions are recognized, although their members work independently. Also, the Cusco household workers union was officially recognized in 1972."

In a mutual agreement with the household workers in Lima, the Labor Ministry and the General Workers Confederation (CGTP) proposed alternative criteria for the recognition of unions: they were to be organized by district and to have at least two hundred members each. In 1973, a union leader recalled, "the various organizations of household workers began to coordinate in several Lima districts. We organized the political-union training for the members of our household workers' unions and a drive to strengthen the leadership cadres."

On December 24, 1973, five household workers' unions presented to the Minister of Labor a list of about 2,500 members and demanded that they be recognized. These organizations represented the districts of Surquillo, Miraflores, Pueblo Libre, Magdalena, Orrantia/San Isidro, and Santiago de Surco. They were not recognized (COSINTRAHOL 1979, Minutes).

In December 1975 a protest march aimed at obtaining union recognition was held in Surquillo. Some five hundred domestic workers took part. After this protest the household workers' unions underwent a crisis. The *patronas* (employers) wrote newspaper articles and visited the schools attended by household workers, reacting against the unions. Some domestics who joined in the march were dismissed, and others were warned not to have anything further to do with the unions. Moreover, some of the leaders left, for personal reasons. This resulted in the disbanding of some unions while others lost many of their members (Rivera 1979, 4:54). Also in 1975, the military government began its second term under Morales Bermúdez, and repression against all forms of social protest intensified.

In the midst of all these difficulties the household workers in Lima tried to regroup and in a short time had formed new unions: in 1975 the Breña union and in 1976 that of Jesús-María. Unions had also been formed in other cities, and contacts throughout Peru were coordinated. Two national congresses were held: the first in 1979 in Lima, the second in 1981 in Juliaca. During the first congress the household workers' unions presented a list of demands for better legislation for the sector. Despite the official name "household worker," the legal position of domestics in Peru is marginal, in comparison with female factory workers. This is evidenced in the lack of legislation related to the minimum wage, employment stability, working hours, vacations, compensation for time in service, and so on. The position of household workers is not established in labor legislation but by special decrees. Officially, they do not have the right to organize in unions (though we will continue to use that term here).

The household workers' unions demanded a minimum wage, an eight-hour day, job stability, one whole free day per week and national holidays off, one-month paid vacations, mandatory social security, indemnization for years in service, written work contracts, child labor regulations, the right to mandatory education, the abolition of commercial employment agencies, and recognition of their unions. To date, the government has not responded to these demands. The unions have tried on many occasions to explain their position at the Ministry of Labor but for the most part their representatives have been put off or even refused admittance.

By 1984 household workers' unions in all the Peruvian cities were having problems, for either political, economic, or personal reasons, but they continued to seek alternative ways of structuring themselves in order to strengthen their organizations and make better contact with the household workers at the base.

The Problems of Organizing

According to their own estimates, household workers' unions have 6,000 members in Peru; half of these are in Lima. This means that no more than 5 percent of all domestics in Peru are affiliated. Nevertheless, this small number represents an admirable effort, given the obstacles this sector must overcome. The very nature of their occupation hinders organizing efforts, and there are many problems inherent in enlarging the membership.

Isolation

The working conditions themselves constitute a considerable obstacle to organizing. Long workdays and residence in the homes of people belonging to another social class make for considerable isolation of the household workers. In these circumstances it is difficult to make contact with them. Domestics barely have time to make friends and keep in touch with their families.[4] "I started to feel sadder and more lonely because nobody loved me. I never had any friends and I felt humiliated" [Margarita].

They are also very isolated in the workplace itself. To work as a domestic is to spend long hours in a house where one meets few people and interpersonal relations are very limited. If it is possible to speak of a personal relationship with the *patrona*, it is not in terms of equality. Consequently, isolation not only means loneliness and the absence of social networks that could provide emotional or material support but also limits the possibility for development of class consciousness. The household workers do not live with people of their own class in the slums or shantytowns; they live with people of different classes and cultures. They are, above all, subjected to their employers' bourgeois ideology, which makes a heavy impression on them because they are young and very dependent on their employers. The result is that they hardly identify with each other at all and have even less solidarity with the popular movement. As one union leader put it: "There are still *compañeras* [sisters/comrades] who have not seen reality for what it is. Many don't know why we are exploited, why we are marginalized, why we are cheap labor. They are blindfolded by the system. This is the result of our isolation."

The Patronas

"The expectations of the domestic with regard to the *patrona*,"[5] says Figueroa (1975, n.p.),

> always refer to her desire to work for a pleasant person who is not rude or violent. The second desirable characteristic in a patrona is that she establish a paternalistic relationship with the domestic.
>
> It is interesting to note that it is not particularly important to the domestic that the *patrona* recognize her social rights, that she treat her as an equal. Thus, the *patrona* is seen from the standpoint of a dependent relationship and the need for her to closely resemble the image of the benevolent *ama* [lady of the house].

The *patrona*'s personality is often much more important then working conditions or salary, particularly for young domestic workers. The desire to establish a paternalistic relationship is easily understood. The majority of domestics were taken from their own families when they were very young and had to look for affection from other quarters. Because the domestic has few other contacts in her work environment, the *patrona* seems to be the most appropriate substitute. Many household workers even form considerable emotional bonds with the *patrona* and thus do not feel their situation to be an exploitative one. "In my present job, I am better treated; they even help me sweep and cook. The *patrona* is good because she does the chores with me. She lets me have Sundays free and gives me the same food as everyone else" [Rosa].

However, as the years go by and a domestic worker becomes more experienced and makes more contacts outside her job, dissatisfaction with her situation increases. She may then form another image of her employer, demand better working conditions, and become more independent of the *patrona*. This is very evident among the domestic workers affiliated with the unions. Said one member:

> I think my *patrona* is unjust, and unconscious of Peruvian reality. She does not see us as human beings of flesh and blood, who feel hunger and thirst. I don't like it when she doesn't recognize my rights, such as to vacation time, social security, recreation, study, rest, salary, and compensation. We know we have no alternative but to unite to change our working conditions. We would like the labor legislation pertaining to domestic workers changed.

Shame

Every day the *patrones* make the household worker feel that they consider her to be inferior, a *chola* servant. The great influence that her *patrones* exercise over the domestic can convince her that in fact she is worthless. She can even be ashamed of herself and her profession to the point that she will try to hide it. It is understandable, given her situation, that the household worker would not want to share her problems or join an organization based on her type of work. "When I met my boyfriend, I told him I worked in a store. Last Sunday I told him that I am a household worker, but he didn't mind. Great guy, huh?" [Lydia].

Household workers in Peru are little appreciated and relegated to a very inferior position. In our opinion, an important reason for this is that the work done by the domestic employee, housework, is not considered real work in the capitalist system. It appears as a task that is naturally performed by women, and not as the product of a long process of socialization. Moreover, household workers' low pay is justified by the classification of their work as unskilled.[6]

In fact, domestic work "degrades" all women, but middle- and upper-class women can partly exempt themselves from it precisely because of the existence of domestic workers. The women of these classes are responsible for running the household but don't do all the housework themselves. Moreover, as married women, they assume their husband's social position.

Added to these degrading elements is the fact that in Peru the profession of household worker is reserved almost exclusively for indigenous women. The majority of the *patrones* are *criollos* (Spanish persons born in the New World) and consider indigenous women to be inferior. It is precisely because of their dependence on these *patrones* that the household workers are ashamed of their origin and tend to adapt themselves to rather than oppose the norms and values of their employers. For example, many domestics start to dress like their *patronas,* making up their faces and cutting off their braids. But the clothes and the makeup do not change the household worker into a *limeña.* She is still a *chola,* and she continues to be discriminated against. "They tell us: why train ourselves, if we are *cholas* and will never amount to anything. We don't need to study to know how to sweep" [Bertha].

Household Work as a Temporary Occupation

Given poor working conditions, isolation, inferior social position, and feelings of shame, it is not surprising to anyone that the domestic employee wishes to leave her occupation as soon as possible. Because of their isolated position, it is also understandable that household workers—if they do think about changing their situation—seek individual solutions to their problems. The fact that they think of their jobs as temporary is not conducive to seeking structural changes by means of union organization. Instead, they try to choose another, more prestigious occupation. And the majority try to achieve this through education.[7]

However, they have few possibilities of joining the professions they covet. On the one hand, the job market is highly competitive, and their indigenous origin works against their being chosen for a position with public contact. On the other hand, the household worker who wants to be self-employed—for example, to start a sewing shop—is unable to save enough to start, given the low salary she earns. The reality is such that some household workers, having left their jobs, return to them when they are old; they work by the hour, or wash or sew for other people in their own homes (see Chaney 1985).

None of this means that going to school is superfluous. It is understood that reading, writing, and other skills are very useful; in addition, the educational system is one of the most important ways of making contact with other household workers. Together, they can discuss their problems and become more aware of their situation. Education can give them more confidence in themselves. Only contact with others can make them reflect on their own situation and give them a different perspective on their relationship with their *patrones,* who daily confront them with bourgeois ideology. In this way, education can play a very important role in breaking the isolation of household workers and stimulating their organization, even though they may initially have had no intention of organizing.

Unfamiliarity with Unions

Their isolation puts household workers out of the reach of unions, which can make contact only with those workers who have begun to break out of this isolation by attending classes or going out, perhaps to the Campo de Marte, a recreation area where many *domésticas* congregate on Sundays. Most domestic employees know little about unions; some who are aware of their existence know almost nothing about their activities and goals.

Every household workers' union sponsors various activities and distributes information aimed at promoting the organization of domestic employees. The members try to speak with the household workers about their situation and about their rights. They do this in schools and in parishes, trying to motivate them to participate in the union meetings. The majority of the domestic employees who have joined the unions have done so as a result of such personal contacts. Said one member:

> Before, I knew nothing. I thought that it would be this way for the rest of my life. The exploitation of household workers seemed normal to me. Now I know a lot about worker and peasant problems, the national situation, etc. We have to organize ourselves, but we do not have the time to devote to organizing, yet we have to organize household workers who know nothing of the reality within which they live.

In almost all cases both union members and prospective members are employed as live-in domestics and work long hours, which leaves them little free time to attend meetings.

Shortage of time is another reason household workers become intimidated by the prospect of participating in a union, even when they recognize the importance of becoming organized. In their little spare time they want to attend classes, participate in parish recreational activities, and enjoy themselves, as union leaders recognize:

> Yes, getting the household workers to meet together is a real problem. They have little time off, and on Sundays want to enjoy themselves after working hard all week. Many *compañeras* go to the movies or the dance halls which are the city attractions. We have to take this reality into account in relation to our activities. When we organize meetings we also need to have some relaxation time: singing, dancing and the music of the Sierra people.

And over and above the lack of time, the unions' scarce financial resources limit their outreach work.

Opposition

The attitude of *patronas* toward the unions has also limited their organizing capacity. The threat of dismissal and other reprisals makes the domestic employees afraid of becoming involved. "On many occasions the *patronas* spread lies about our unions, saying that we are all thieves, prostitutes and Communists so that their own employees will stay away," said a leader.

Not all workers are intimidated by these efforts, but few tell their *patrones* that they are union members. As one leader recalls:

> When I was eighteen years old, the Coordinator of Household Workers Unions of Greater Lima chose me as a delegate to the National Congress of the Confederación Campesina del Perú [Peruvian Peasants Confederation] which was held in the countryside, in Cusco. This opportunity resulted in my being forced to leave the job I had held for five years; in other words, I was practically fired. I had to travel immediately to Cusco to participate in the congress and always do whatever possible to comply with the union base, do what my class entrusted me with. It was either my class or my job. It was a very hard struggle, but I decided to leave my job. This was the reason for my dismissal after five years, with no right to compensation for the time I had been in service, nor for vacation time.

It is especially difficult for union members who live in to escape the social control of the *patrones*. "I have to lie to them because they won't let me go to meetings," said one. And another: "I was dismissed from my former job because I distributed flyers and posters and demanded my rights. I have suffered a great deal. My *patrones* have scolded me many times. I have cried a lot. The worst time was when they threatened they would go to the police."

The knowledge that they can be dismissed is a serious obstacle to the willingness of domestic employees to rise up against injustice. The *patrones* consider household workers' unions a threat to their interests. The existence of a cheap labor force frees the upper and middle classes from domestic work; they do not need to make costly collective provisions and can use their savings in other ways.

By not recognizing household workers' unions and their demands for improved labor legislation, the government perpetuates the *patrones*' interests. This deficient legislation has to be considered in relation to the form in which domestic work is organized. A capitalist society benefits when women do domestic work in the private sphere in a practically gratuitous arrangement. At the same time, the importance of this work is minimized when it is considered a private and not a public affair. Domestic employees, who work in private homes, are regarded as (inferior) members of the family rather than as female wage laborers. This is why the government takes so little interest in the issue and why the *patrones* have so much freedom to determine working conditions for their domestic employees. These women are very dependent upon the good will of their *patrones*.

Lack of Support

Household workers unions claim that until recently they have received no significant support either from the political parties of the left or from other unions and federations. These organizations pay little attention to the problematic of household workers, union leaders assert, because their tasks are carried out in the private sphere:

> The parties still do not adopt the problematic of the household workers as their concern. They are only interested in our leaders because of their clear thinking and in the members because of their support. But they still do not have specific programs for our sector because domestics are not inte-

grated into the productive system in the same way as peasants and workers. Recently we have been seeing some moving closer, but it is not very clear.

Concrete support from the feminist movement is also beginning only very slowly: "There is talk of solidarity among women, but feminists are middle class. They work and they need domestics in their own homes."

There are no indications that feminists, who for their own liberation depend on having other women work for them in their homes, are coming to feel this contradiction as a problem (see Vargas 1981). As the presence of employees in domestic work continues to belong to the private sphere, men can continue to exempt themselves from this work, thus reinforcing their *machista* attitude. Real liberation is possible only in a society in which domestic work is organized in another way, without being reserved exclusively for the female sex.

Conclusion

To work as a domestic employee in Peru is to have a very hard life. To confront its problems through union organizations presents still further difficulties. The servile conditions of this occupation—living in, unlimited work hours, a dependent and unequal relationship with the *patrones*—cause many problems, not just for the employee as an individual but also for the organization of this sector.

Since 1973 some household workers have organized in the Greater Lima area and other Peruvian cities, but these unions still have few members.

Above all, the isolated living situation of household workers is a serious problem. The characteristically dependent and paternalistic relationship between household workers and their *patrones* influences the domestics to adapt to the norms and values of another social class. The discriminatory treatment of domestic workers by the *patrones* makes the former feel inferior to the point of being ashamed of their occupation, and wanting to leave it as soon as possible.

This situation does not motivate them to organize into unions. Even workers who have become organized find it difficult to attract new members. Not only do the working conditions themselves hinder the class consciousness and organization of household workers, but unions also meet opposition from the government and *patrones*. Despite this, household workers unions persevere, even in a time when the popular movement as a whole is experiencing a great many difficulties. They have developed a very persistent and aware leadership cadre which, though it has problems reaching the base, continues to seek new ways to strengthen household workers' organizations.

Notes

Acknowledgment: We would like to thank the household workers who, in their scarce spare time, were willing to discuss this article with us.

1. People in Lima, above all in the middle class, go to the countryside to sign up girls as household workers for themselves or their acquaintances. They offer the girl's parents a small amount of money, a donkey, or a ewe in exchange for their daughter. Parents give up their children because they barely have the means to educate them and hope that they will fare better in Lima.

2. *Cholo(a)* is a term designating a person who has left his/her community of origin but has not yet integrated him/herself into the national culture and modern society—in simplest terms, one who has done no more than leave off Indian dress; in the city, he/she is hired for the lowest jobs and is classified as indigenous. In Peru the term often is used perjoratively to describe a person who lacks culture and refinement, though it can also be a term of affection for a person of darker complexion—but only among intimates, such as university students. A *mestizo(a)* is a person of mixed blood (Indian and Spanish) who has taken on a Spanish lifestyle.

3. *Asistencialismo,* welfare mentality, conveys the idea of doing things *for* people instead of guaranteeing and increasing their autonomy.

4. In contrast to female wage laborers who work together in a business or factory and have daily contact among themselves, household workers for the most part live and work scattered throughout the city, isolated from one another. Long distances and little free time also prevent frequent visits with their parents, most of whom live in the country. Nor is it always possible to write, since many household workers and their parents are illiterate and mail service uncertain.

5. We consider the relationship with women employers because it is with the women, who are responsible for running the household, that the domestic workers have the most contact. Sexual abuse can make the relationship with the man of the house humiliating for the household workers. We do not go into this issue here.

6. The aspects of domestic work related to maternity (the birth, care, and

upbringing of children) offer women the greatest prestige. In our opinion, this explains why nurses (nannies) have the highest rank in the household workers' hierarchy; even in the sixteenth century, wet-nurses received the highest salaries (Burkett 1978, 111). Household workers who do the "dirty work" have the lowest prestige.

7. The majority of household workers have received little education at home. However, since 1973 a form of late afternoon primary education for adults, "Basic Workers' Education," has been made available, and many domestics take advantage of it.

References

Burkett, Elinor C. 1978. "Indian Women in White Society: The Case of 16th Century Peru." In Asunción Lavrin, ed., *Latin American Women: Historical Perspectives*, pp. 101–28. Westport, Conn.: Greenwood Press.

Chaney, Elsa M. 1985. "'Se necesita Muchacha': Household Workers in Lima, Peru." Paper presented at the annual meeting of the American Anthropological Association, Symposium on Domestic Workers.

COSINTRAHOL. 1979. "Actas." Lima: Coordinadora de los Sindicatos de las Trabajadoras del Hogar de Lima Metropolitana.

Figueroa Galup, Blanca. 1975. "Diagnóstico del rol ocupacional y de la educación formal de la mujer: Domésticas." Instituto Nacional de Investigación y Desarrollo de la Educación "Augusto Salazar Bondy," Lima. Mimeo.

Ho, Y. 1981. "Auxiliar de hospedaje y del hogar: Una profesión de gran demanda." *Documenta* 9:69–71, 79–80.

JOC (Juventud Obrera Católica). 1978. "Informe 'Trabajadoras del Hogar,' Perú." Paper prepared for the Encuentro Latinoamericano, Colombia.

Rivera, Olga. 1979. "Situación de la trabajadora del hogar en Lima Metropolitana." Tareas para el Trabajo Social. Mimeo.

Sulmont, Denis. 1980. *El movimiento obrero peruano, 1890–1980*. 2d ed. Lima: TAREA.

Vargas, Virginia. 1981. *El Diario*, September 28.

15 Housework for Pay in Chile: Not Just Another Job

THELMA GÁLVEZ and ROSALBA TODARO

The aim of this chapter is to analyze the nature of salaried household labor and its effect on workers and their organizations. The research is based on our observation of the working conditions of female domestics in Chile, and the quotations derive from the interviews and workshops we conducted.

Our investigation began with a fundamental question: Why are the majority of domestic workers not organized? The purpose of our study was to assist organizations of household workers in improving their situation. We began with the premise that the relations of production in salaried household work determine to a great extent the behavior and the consciousness of household workers and, in turn, of their organizations.

An Overview

Household work is not chosen, nor is it a vocation. People become domestics simply because they need to survive and receive an income. For most lower-class Chilean women, household work is the first job they take, hoping to improve their chances of obtaining a better job, forming a family, or just having a stroke of luck.

In Chile domestic service employs the largest number of women; it is not just another job that many women take once in their working life. In 1980, 96.2 percent of a total of 248,000 domestics were female, and they represented 23.3 percent of the female work force.[1]

A version of this article appeared in Rosalba Todaro and Thelma Gálvez, *Trabajo doméstico remunerado: Conceptos, hechos, datos*. Santiago de Chile: Centro de Estudios de la Mujer, 1987. Used with permission of the authors and publisher.

Almost half of the household workers were found in Santiago, the capital. Most were young, rural migrants.

Since the 1970s the two extremely opposed forms of government that existed in Chile have had different social points of view and have affected the economy through very different activities. The Popular Unity Government (1970–73) increased per capita income in its first year, maintained a constant growth of jobs, and reduced unemployment to 4 percent. Under the military government, economic activity fell off in 1975 but then recovered, although the years of "recovery" were characterized by high unemployment, accompanied by some growth in the production of goods and services and the concentration of wealth. Starting in 1981 there was a greater downturn and crisis.

During the 1970s, the economically active female population grew more than the male, and the participation of women over twelve years of age in the work force increased from 23 percent in 1970 to 29.3 percent in 1980. These statistics obscure behavioral differences related to income levels; it should be taken into account that "the participation of women of low income brackets tends to increase in times of high unemployment and significantly decreases in real income levels" (Rosales 1979).

In the previous decade (1960–70) the number of women employed in private homes decreased, and that trend continued until 1974. In the recovery period of the military government, the percentage of the work force employed as domestics was stable, but since 1981 it has declined.

Economic fluctuations also influence the composition of the domestic work force between live-in (*puertas adentro*) and daily (*puertas afuera*) workers. Since the 1960s, day work has tended to increase in relative terms. In Santiago, 39.7 percent of household workers in 1980 were day workers. During the past two years this percentage has fallen by 5.1 percent, while the number of live-in workers has fallen by 11.8 percent.

As a group, household workers are younger than the rest of the economically active female population. In 1980, 28.9 percent of the female work force was younger than twenty-five years, compared to 39.6 percent of the domestic servant population as a whole and 50.3 percent for live-ins.

Statistically, women who enter domestic service at a very young age are more likely to find that their jobs will be temporary. Between 1960 and 1970, domestic employment was down by 9.8 percent, and women domestics between the ages of fifteen and nineteen numbered

48,387. Ten years later the domestic worker population between twenty-five and twenty-nine numbered only 22,017; apparently 55 percent had retired from the profession. Between 1970 and 1980, when there was a 40 percent increase in employment, 27 percent of the household workers aged fifteen to nineteen left household employment.

The level of formal education attained also influences domestics' tenure in household service. Often they identify their reasons for staying on the job as poverty, economic need, and lack of preparation for other kinds of work. In 1980, domestics had an average of only 5.2 years of formal education, while the female work force as a whole had 7.2 years. Since 1960, the educational level has increased for both household workers and the female work force as a whole, making job mobility more possible. Those who stay in domestic service tend to have fewer years of study. This is true for both live-in and day workers.

In 1980, among household workers aged twenty to twenty-nine, there was an increase of those with more than ten years of formal education, 16.5 percent for those aged twenty to twenty-four and 19 percent for those aged twenty-five to twenty-nine. Most probably, these women entered the occupation with these years of formal education already completed. Since the preparation necessary to become a domestic worker did not change, the increase in educational level must reflect the deterioration in available jobs. This is a warning to the many domestics who believe that education is the road to a better occupation.

Chile has had household workers' unions since 1926, but the principal problems these organizations have faced are low membership and lack of influence. Members have always been few even though the potential influence is high because no other occupation employs as many women as domestic service. Although these labor organizations have survived, the situation is even worse today because of the unfavorable government attitude toward workers in general.

The household workers' unions have functioned under different names and forms, and the history of the different organizations is intertwined. Today, the two principal unions are the Asociación Nacional de Empleadas de Casa Particular or ANECAP (National Association of Household Workers) and the Sindicato Interempresas de Trabajadoras de Casa Particular or SINTRACAP (National Union of Household Workers).

ANECAP has its own leadership and is supported by the Catholic

Church. The union provides services to household workers for their religious needs, personal and professional information, basic education, housing, and placement. Currently, it has 3,000 members and thirteen centers throughout the country; each year it services the needs of around 10,000 household workers.

SINTRACAP is concerned with the defense of workers' rights and the professional training of its members and leadership. Although SINTRACAP has fewer resources than ANECAP, at the end of 1973 it had a total of 2,500 members in seventeen regional unions. Because of official government policies, this number has been reduced to six regional unions with 330 members. The unions sponsor savings, credit, and home construction cooperatives. Until 1987, the SINTRACAP unions were joined together in the Comisión Nacional de Sindicatos be Trabajadoras de Casa Particular or CONSTRACAP (National Coordinating Commission of Unions of Household Workers), the embyro of a federation of unions. Recently, the CONSTRACAP has ceased to function, and whether the attempt to federate will continue remains unclear.

The Nature of Salaried Housework

The most remarkable characteristic of housework in general is that it is assigned to women as part of their "natural" role. In Chile in 1981, 2,090,100 women (49 percent of the women older than twelve years) who declared "housework" as their main occupation were considered inactive in the labor force. This confirms that "housework" is viewed as a role, not an occupation.

Housework can be defined as an individual work process that takes place isolated within a home, organized by the delegation of certain activities to one or more persons, usually the women of the house. The boundaries of housework vary according to time, place, social class, and other cultural determinants; always, however, it provides free time and leisure for those who are "served and attended." This can cause a conflict of interests within the family.

In housework, there is usually neither cooperation nor division of labor; since it is commonly assigned to only one worker in the household, there is no need to coordinate the tasks and efforts of different workers. And although there are a few ordered sequences and timetables related to the routines and tastes of the family, there is a degree of freedom because the "products" are many and their production can be combined. Housework is a simultaneous execution of distinct tasks that are frequently interrupted to carry one forward while the other tasks wait. As Clementina stated: "I left the diapers and went upstairs to make the beds; while the soup was cooking, I tidied up the living room."

The way housework is organized gives it a craftlike nature, no matter who does it or the types of social relations under which it is performed. Even though modern technology—electrical appliances, cleaning products, prepared foods—may be employed, housework results in a nonstandardized product.

Taking into account the social conditions of paid live-in domestic workers in private homes, we see that housework is differentiated from other types of salaried jobs in the following ways:

- The domestic worker's salary is a consumer expense to whoever employs her. She produces a service that does not belong to her, nor is it sold to a third party; it is consumed by her employer—the very people who direct her work.
- The domestic worker sacrifices her chance for a private life by selling almost all of her time.
- She is paid partly in money and partly in goods.
- Her workplace is the home of others, where a family not her own lives and consumes and with whom she cohabits in a socially inferior status.
- In most cases she is the only salaried employee in the house who does domestic work; therefore, she works isolated from others in her field of work.

Something new is added to this craftlike process of production when the condition of being a live-in worker is examined in detail. Management of the work process itself is not necessary because there is neither cooperation nor division of labor, but it becomes necessary because of the social relations and individual standards of housework.

Generally, it is the woman of the house, the *ama de casa*, who is the boss and who would be the one to perform the work if the maid were not present. Usually, the mistress relates to the market as a consumer: she buys another woman's time, consuming it according to her needs. In this transaction the mistress does not create capital; she creates value as the one responsible for the household work. She does this as the direct manager responsible for the work of the paid employee, and if the household tasks are not done to the family's satisfaction, the mistress receives the complaints.

Since the activities in housework are less precise than in industry, the rhythm with which they are carried out may vary, and the intensity and quality of work are difficult to measure. Furthermore, work that produces a service is not evaluated according to objective criteria but depends on the tastes and needs of those who receive the end product.

The whole work process is controlled by the *patrona,* who not only has final power to approve or reject the product but can also monitor, change, or interrupt the work process. The mistress, therefore, not only contributes to the product but reaffirms her managerial role. If the worker increases her efficiency and fulfills her tasks in less time, it is possible that she will have new tasks thrust upon her in order to appropriate this "extra" time.

Another source of conflict between management and domestics is related to materials—soap, foodstuffs, fuel oil, and so on—because it is difficult to establish standards of use. For example, the proportions in which food are combined are less defined than the proportions that are used in producing an industrial product, and waste is harder to measure than in industry, though in both cases it can be controlled.

A good part of housework involves cleaning and maintaining the domestic infrastructure. That is why the standards are less absolute. The use of alien artefacts—equipment not found in the worker's home—and the relative freedom with which the worker can use them may create, in practice, conflicts of interest between the employer and the salaried worker.

We conclude that in live-in salaried housework there exists a contradiction between the craftlike work process and the management of that process. This is manifested in the contradictory interests of the two women, the salaried worker and the *patrona,* who are dedicated to the common task of service to the family. Also, since there is no clear distinction for the worker between work time and her own time, this manifest contradiction is expressed in the work and in most other everyday aspects of both worker's and mistress's lives.

The contradiction between the craftlike process and housework management is essential to the modality of live-in housework. The following elements are present in this contradictory relation and characterize it as servile:

• the availability of the worker's time without the limits of a schedule;

• the nature of her tasks as part of the feminine role, which includes elements of sacrifice and abnegation;

• The production of services to be consumed by her employers without mediation of the market;

• The coexistence of two lifestyles in the same "space" that is the place of living for one, and the place of living *and* work for the other.

In live-out work, a fixed schedule has a greater chance of being respected, but the hours are still long, and the pay is lower than in any other trade. Other costs are time spent traveling to and from work, the expense of meals, and the maintenance of a home.

Emotionally and personally, day work represents a great advance over the live-in situation, despite the disadvantages, because the day worker has a private life clearly separated from that of her employers. Even so, the work is done within a private home, is perceived as having little social value, and is viewed as a nonprofessional occupation governed by the immediate desires of the employers. The service produced is still consumed by employers who are the absolute owners of the contracted day's work. Therefore, the work relation continues to be servile in nature. Domestic work will begin to lose its servile characteristic only when it becomes work contracted for defined services, not while it constitutes the consumption of someone else's time and labor.

There is no clear consciousness among domestic workers that their *patronas* feel any dependency on them or feel insecure about the possibility of having to change maids, especially in a family with small children.

Consequences for the Household Worker

Since housework is considered an extension of the feminine role, the person who does it for pay models herself on the housewife, whom the servant to a great extent replaces. Therefore, housework does not have the benefit of schedules. The houseworker can be interrupted when she rests; holidays can be her hardest workdays because either visitors are invited or special meals are cooked; and she does not have the right to rest on Sundays, as do other workers.

The well-being and comfort of the family are the principal objectives of housework, and existing legislation confirms this attitude. A forty-eight-hour week, the rule for other workers, is not applied to live-in domestics. Instead, the domestic worker's schedule is based on what the legislation explicitly calls "the nature of her work". There is no legal limit to the workday; since the law only establishes a minimum of ten hours rest, the workday can be as long as fourteen hours. The employer can terminate the contract without explanation by giving a thirty-day notice or corresponding salary. If the worker becomes ill with a contagious disease, however, her contract can be terminated immediately without notice or indemnification. Obligatory maternity leave can be easily evaded in the case of houseworkers.[2]

This identity between life and work determines times of activity and rest. With respect to time, certain rigidities in the schedule provide a rhythm and the possibility of planning work: "The children go to school at eight; I clean the bedrooms after everyone gets up; lunch is served at one," and so on. But the maid's rest can be interrupted at any moment: to respond to a call, answer the phone or the door, or serve coffee; because her employer unexpectedly goes out or because a child returns sick from school. Such interruptions can invade even the worker's room, which she does not consider her own. She can identify as free time only the hours spent outside the employers' residence. As she does not have her own home, she sometimes rents a room for her free days or aspires to buy a house, even if she thinks she will continue to work as a live-in maid.

In addition to "proper" workplaces such as the kitchen and the laundry, housework must also be done in the rest of the house. And since a maid works where the family lives, the work itself is frequently considered a nuisance. To work where people live requires more than doing a good job. The domestic also must avoid annoying those who live there. "I can't stand the vacuum cleaner's noise, the cold from the open windows, the dust that has been kicked up, the smell of food when I am not hungry"—these attitudes determine the organization of the work and its evaluation. Even if the product is well regarded ("the house is clean; the food is tasty"), the work process itself can be bothersome.

Working as a live-in maid also has consequences for the worker's relations with the outside world. Many of the domestic's needs are satisfied without going to the market as a consumer. She does not pay rent, electricity, or gas; she does not buy her own food; often her work clothes are provided. Her salary is usually sent to her family, put in savings, or used for personal consumption other than basic subsistence. The monetary part of her salary has less importance for and influence on her standard of living than in the case of other salaried workers.

Since part of the salary is paid in kind, differences between jobs may be determined more by the customs of the house than by salary. The family has the opportunity for manipulation and savings in that it can use the maid's room for storage, control or deny the use of hot water, lower the food quality and quantity, provide no food when the family goes out. These measures are much more subtle than lowering cash wages and are harder to complain about.

For live-out workers, whose payment in goods is limited to some meals, the monetary salary has greater relative importance. The worker is responsible for her lodging, food, and transportation. This puts her in daily contact with the market, and she is directly affected by changes in the economic situation, such as inflation, layoffs, and shortages.

The isolation of live-ins has important consequences for the material reality and the consciousness of the workers. Existing legislation is not very protective of the domestics' interests, but even those interests protected by law are difficult to control in a work situation that has no witnesses. When a conflict arises, it is the word of the *patrona* against the word of the maid—persons in very unequal power situations. Live-in maids do not feel that they have the right to complain, nor do they believe—given Chile's high unemployment rate—that they will benefit from their complaints. The argument "I am already accustomed to this job" is heard often and has greater weight than in any other sort of work. Unequal as the worker's position may be in the home, a change of job is faced only after the relationship between family and worker deteriorates, and abuse passes tolerable limits. Houseworkers also experience a kind of fatalism about the possibility of improving their work conditions in a new job.

The prestige of the maid depends on the social prestige of the employer. More money goes to those who have had experience in "good" homes; who have knowledge of their work, good bearing, and good manners; and who know their "place." Demand for these workers is divided by social sectors, stratifying the supply. The employment agencies in Santiago reflect the clientele they serve in location, appearance, the domestics whose services they offer, the *patronas* who patronize them, and the salaries these *patronas* are willing to pay. The habits and options of domestic workers are strongly conditioned by employers, whose way of life becomes a model for their ambitions.

This influence arises not only because workers and employers live together but also because the patrona sees it as her responsibility "to teach and correct" the worker so that she will respond to the needs of the family.

The day worker has a life in which she can relate to people of a similar station, and she has a greater opportunity to be in direct contact with the public realm. But she too comes under the ideological influence and lifestyle of the employing family and tends to imitate behavior, at the same time noting the contrast between her budget and that of her employer's household.

Employers prefer to limit contact among household workers and their membership in labor unions because exchange of information about work conditions can raise the domestic's level of consciousness.

> I talked in the garden with the nextdoor maid, until they found about it, and they prohibited me from doing so again.
>
> She says to me "I do not know who you are running around with that you return so argumentative."
>
> If I told them that I went to a labor union meeting, they would instantly fire me.

This isolation of the live-in domestic makes it difficult for her to understand what is happening in the public realm; hence, workers' concerns are generally centered on personal or domestic matters. Information they receive reflects the employers' point of view. Events in the larger society do not appear relevant to their lives or seem to have any effect on them. Domestic workers believe that change occurs through luck and not through their own efforts.

The servile elements found in the domestic's work relation clearly delineate the limited value housework has in the eyes of society and the low esteem for the live-in maid as a person. Rules of behavior surround not only the work as such but also the living arrangements in the house: the maid must go as unnoticed as possible; she must not give her opinions; she must obey; she must be ready when she is needed and vanish when she is not. Visitors should be made aware that she is a member of the service staff, not of the family. When she goes out, her status must be reflected in the way she dresses: she must make a good appearance but not look so chic that she is mistaken for family.

Domestic workers' low level of education appears to have an important role in their "internalization of inferiority." Maids claim they have "fallen" into domestic work because they lack education, but the claim appears to be more myth than reality. The reasons they work as live-in domestics are the slack demand in other lines of work requiring little training and the need for a place to live. Increase in the educational level of live-in domestics has not led to other types of employment.

Consequences for Organization

The domestic has a fatalistic view about her ability to change her living and work situation. The only improvement she can imagine is a change in profession. Consequently, domestics do not believe that joining a labor union will improve their real circumstances. Their poor self-esteem is reflected in their labor organizations. Their unions are not valued at the same level as other unions—even though their *sindicatos* are modeled on the labor organization of other trades—and the particular needs of household workers are ignored in both trade unions and political organizations.

The need is to link the private to the public—a slow, difficult process—rather than to attempt an escape from private concerns to a more valued public realm. Such a dichotomy can produce divisions between a leadership more concerned and knowledgeable about national problems, and workers who sense that their organizations are removed from their specific needs.

The emotional loneliness of domestics and their material insecurity often makes them demand support and services from their labor organizations rather than vindication of workers' rights. Workers need a place to go to on their days off, a home when they are unemployed, leisure activities, self-improvement courses, and savings, credit, and home-buying cooperatives. Often the leadership must take a maternal role. Since the greatest ambition of live-in maids is to change their profession, their labor organizations respond to this aspiration in the courses and activities they offer.

The domestic worker, out of fear, usually hides from her *patrones* that she belongs to a labor union. This makes it very difficult for organizations to defend the rights of domestic workers, except in extreme cases where the work relation is broken. In Chile, domestic unions have a very low membership and an even lower percentage of active participants because of the domestic workers' restricted and irregular free time. The activities of their unions are less important to household workers than the activities of their *patrones.*

Live-out domestics have even less time for union activities. They have a "double day" in the care of their own families and the maintenance of their own homes. Moreover, day workers feel less need of going to the labor union than live-ins because its support role is to some degree supplied by their families.

Despite all this, active participation in a labor union clearly changes the self-esteem of domestic workers. From their viewpoint, the *patrones'* dislike of labor union activity is largely justified: there are definite changes in behavior as the worker become less submissive and more knowledgeable about her labor rights.

Some Proposals

The following proposals are related to two principal issues: the possibility of short-term gains and middle-term alternatives within the system as we progress toward a more just and equal society, and the search for ways of working within labor organizations that would lead to strong unions by changing the fatalistic behavior and submissiveness of household workers.

Some minimal changes are necessary to begin eliminating elements of servitude. The first would be to change the relationship between a worker who produces a service and a *patrona* (or family group) who buys her time. It is in the interest of the *patrona* to have the maid available at all times, but the servile characteristics can be minimized and the work conditions improved by: the establishment of normal working hours with absolute respect of free time and how that time is spent; a clear definition of the tasks that are expected of the worker so that she is not always on call simply to serve and attend in general; a distinction between work activities and personal activities, including the right to use freely the facilities allotted to her and the freedom to relate to others: friends, boyfriends, organizations. Such norms can be established only through massive and concerted action taken by workers and coordinated by their organizations.

Theoretically, the work modality of live-out domestics allows some of these conditions, at least those that have to do with the use of free time and space. But as we have seen, the treatment of the day worker is nearly identical to that of the live-in. The *patrona*/employee dichotomy still persists even when the maid is a salaried person working in the house for a limited time.

Two alternatives can be identified: the domestic worker might sell specific services, instead of time, to different clients; or she might sell her time to a business enterprise that provides domestic services to homes. This enterprise could be a capitalistic venture or a cooperative one. The business needs to be headed by someone with whom the salaried domestic worker has a work relation, not a service one, and who becomes the intermediary between the client and the domestic. Further, sharing this relationship with other workers would improve the chances that legislation governing domestic service will be observed.[3]

With these changes the work may or may not lose its craftlike quality, but the trend will be toward a work regime with cooperation and/or division of labor. If the work process is organized in this way, workers will be under pressure to raise productivity. Management will appear necessary and have its proper functions, both in the work process and in relationships to clients, coordination, the provision of appliances, the establishment and enforcement of regulations. The servile relation will disappear and the intensity of work increase.

But neither the short-term goals nor the proposed strategies can be consolidated unless some changes occur in the labor organizations, among the domestic workers themselves, in society, and, more specifically, in the organization of housework in general. This change in society would mean that all family members would take on more of the tasks related to their own consumption in order to diminish the domestic work burden. This burden would be distributed among the different members of the family rather than falling only on the women of the household. The end of discrimination against women within the home and the socialization of housework would allow for a change in the work relations of salaried domestic workers.

Labor organizations need to increase and diversify group work and to overcome the separation between the personal and the social. This implies the ability to evaluate everyday situations in terms of the problems of the profession and to discover the causes of personal plights (instead of seeing them merely as individual cases determined by fate), thus motivating domestic workers to action.

Group work confronts the most obvious problem of the isolation the live-in domestic faces in her work and life. Group work provides the chance to trade and discuss experiences and an interval when the right to think for oneself is valued, as is the right of dissent. Such discussion allows everyday personal problems to be related to the problems of the profession as a whole and uncovers the causes that determine personal situations.

Group work is an important step in developing self-esteem, since it permits the development and testing of analytic capabilities, the capacity for speaking out, and overcoming the fear of self-expression. It is necessary to put special emphasis on group work dynamics in order to stimulate the critical and creative capacities of the participants. This can be done by setting aside any relation of authority that evokes submissive attitudes similar to those that household workers assume in their daily lives and that annul creative capacity.

These orientations are suggested by the analysis carried out in this chapter. They can be used as a basis on which to continue the necessary search for concrete and practical ways of improving the situation of live-in domestic workers.

Notes

Acknowledgments: These reflections were made during a study financed by the Inter-American Foundation.

1. These statistical data and those that follow are taken from the Population Censuses of 1960 and 1970, the National Employment Survey of 1980 and special tabulations of that poll.

2. Annual vacation time is 15 workdays per year. If the domestic has worked over 10 years in the same household, a day is added for each year over 10. A mimimum wage is not established by law. If the household worker has been in the same home for more than one year, in the case she becomes ill, her job must be kept open for her for 30 days. The household worker has the right to maternity leave of 6 weeks before giving birth and 12 weeks after birth. But because a worker can be fired at any moment, even during pregnancy, in many cases maternity leave cannot be utilized.

Other current legislation relevant to household workers in Chile provides for one day off a week (twenty-four hours), which can be divided into two half-days if the worker so desires (the day is determined by agreement between the parties; Sunday is not an obligatory day off, nor are holidays); and obligatory social security that provides a retirement pension, medical assistance, a pension for disability or sickness, and a family stipend. Payments equal 27.6 percent of the worker's salary, 24.8 percent from the worker's paycheck and 2.8 percent paid by the employer.

3. *Editors' note:* Such an enterprise, Servicios Quillay, exists today, employing eighteen members of the S I N T R A C A P Metropolitana of Santiago. While still providing specialized services to households (e.g., rug-cleaning),

the business has lately been seeking contracts to clean small offices of international organization affiliates and voluntary groups that abound in Santiago. Once the business is in the black, the organizers intend to use profits to fund services to the union membership.

Reference

Rosales, Osvaldo. 1979. "La mujer chilena en la fuerza de trabajo: Participación, empleo y desempleo (1957–1977)." Thesis, Universidad de Chile.

16 Domestic Labor and Domestic Service in Colombia

MAGDALENA LEÓN

This chapter describes and analyzes the series of activities making up the project called "Actions to Transform Socio-Labor Conditions of Domestic Service in Colombia," in the context of the relation between domestic labor and domestic service. It also considers the social context of the *empleada's* labor relation and, in conclusion, the problems faced and the lessons learned. Work on the project began in Bogotá in March 1981, and some of the activities were extended to the cities of Medellín, Cali, Barranquilla, and Bucaramanga in 1984.[1] The project is sponsored by the Asociación Colombiana para el Estudio de la Población, or ACEP.

The Social Context of the Domestic *Empleada's* Labor Relation

The labor relation of domestic service which the project seeks to understand and transform extends beyond a strictly labor-legal context.[2] A domestic *empleada's* work is not only an external relation—a market activity wherein labor is bought and sold—but a "way of life." It is the relation between domestic labor and domestic service that allows us to transcend casting the problem strictly in terms of employment.

Domestic labor has been culturally assigned to the woman as her fundamental role and defines her socially as *ama de casa* (mistress of the house), mother, or wife. Directed toward family consumption activities, domestic labor basically implies provision of a personal ser-

---

This chapter was presented at the Third World Forum on Women, Law, and Development, at the NGO Forum, UN Conference on Women, Nairobi, in July 1985. It also appears in Margaret Schuler, ed., *Empowerment and the Law: Strategies of Third World Women* (Washington, D.C.: OEF International, 1986). Used with permission of the author and publisher.

vice, and women have internalized the ideology of "service to others" as a natural condition of their social role. An *ama de casa's* work for her family, performed as a service and without a wage, is not considered work: hence the concurrent social devaluation placing the woman who performs it in a subordinate position in the power relations within family, community, and social spheres.[3]

Domestic labor becomes *wage labor* when the *ama de casa* delegates part of her responsibilities to another woman who, within the very same ideology of service to others, seeks payment for performing the same work of reproducing the labor force, but for the *ama de casa's* family and in the other woman's house. In Colombia, women who do this work are either live-in or live-out *empleadas:* either living in the home of the *patrones* or living elsewhere and working during the day only and maybe having more than one *patrona.*

Wage labor performed by paid domestic workers is subject to the same social stigma as domestic labor carried out by the *ama de casa.* Their devalued social role, derived from an ideology considering their service to others as natural, involves the *patrona* and her *empleada* in a relation of identity. Because domestic service is supplied by women from the popular sectors, and set up as a vertical-asymmetric power relation with the employers, the social devaluation is augmented, and contradictions are generated between women of different social classes. The labor relation between *patronas* and *empleadas* is clouded, therefore, with effects both of the class contradictions and the gender identification established between the women. On the one hand it is possible to speak of women's social subordination, and on the other, of class exploitation.[4]

The labor relation becomes a way of life for the *empleada* in several ways. Setting the salary does not follow strictly economic considerations; factors such as those the *empleada* calls "good treatment" interact in the development of the relation.[5] The relation established on the job is a combination of the work with emotional and personal aspects; the *empleada's* workplace is also her living place, but she is confined to a physical space different from that of the family, rendering explicit the class difference. Because the live-in *empleada's* social and sexual relationships are restricted, her entire life is a function of the labor relation, which in itself carries a sense of round-the-clock availability—a phenomenon arising from the lack of legal regulation of work hours.

Furthermore, when the workplace is also home and place of consumption, it is impossible for the relation to be an impersonal one. The *empleada* who has just left her family of origin is in a situation of cultural and emotional dislocation and transfers her attachments to those who live in her substitute "home." As long as it does not cross the class lines that define the relation, the attachment is permitted; it becomes part of the *empleada*'s psyche within the differences. As a result, she internalizes a sense of inferiority and is unable to develop the class consciousness that would otherwise allow her to perceive the contradictions in the relation.

Labor relations, wherein class antagonisms are more obvious, become entangled with and obscure the mutual identity of *empleada* and *patrona* with regard to their acceptance of women's assignment to domestic labor. This mutual identity is experienced as an affective relation on the personal level that is limited by the asymmetric power relation defining each woman's class position. Given these central ideas, the question arises, what strategies could be implemented that would allow these relations to change?

Two points must first be clarified. We reject the ideological position that considers domestic service essential. Those who hold to this position assert that paid personal services are needed to reproduce the labor force in the home, and they propose providing training courses to improve the social position of the *gremio* (occupational group). This approach leaves untouched both the assignment of the domestic sphere to the woman—that is, the sexual division of labor—and the labor relations wherein the *empleada* provides the service.[6] Neither does it take into account the government's obligations with regard to the cost of reproducing the labor force. In a society characterized by social inequalities, this process will generate similarly imbalanced private responses as long as it is left to each family's private resources.[7]

Another thesis suggests that domestic service will be phased out as the society develops and modernizes. This would mean that sufficient female employment must eventually be generated to absorb the large numbers of women who currently use domestic service as a work strategy. Since the large numbers of women who engage in domestic service are, in themselves, evidence of how important it is for reproduction of the labor force, this hypothesis is not the most accurate for developing societies.[8]

Proof for the "phasing out" hypothesis has yet to be produced either for Latin American society in general or for the Colombian case in particular.[9] While conventional statistics show that live-in domestic service is declining, these data can be explained by two factors. In the first place, live-in domestic service is statistically underestimated, both because it is confused with unremunerated family labor and because child labor is omitted; second, live-out domestic service, a recent and increasingly common phenomenon, is excluded.[10] The sector is undergoing internal structural transformation, changing from the live-in to the live-out mode, not being phased out or tending to decrease. At the end of the last decade, 37 percent of the female labor force worked as domestic servants (live-in and live-out) in the five largest Colombian cities (Rey de Marulanda 1981).

If domestic service is to be phased out, the socio-occupational structure of the country will have to undergo further structural changes. Underemployment and a job shortage for unskilled women coexist with the absence of collective services to replace personal services. Besides, the sexual division of domestic labor and its accompanying power relations are far from disappearing (Garcia Castro 1982).

Who are the domestic workers?[11] Migrants from rural areas, with peasant and/or agricultural-proletarian family origins, concentrated in young age groups, predominate in this sector. Some withdraw from the labor market at the beginning of their reproductive cycle to set up their own households and/or to raise their children. Others reenter the work force upon completing these life cycles, and the majority of these swell the ranks of the live-out *empleadas*.

A high proportion are single, and among these the group of unmarried mothers is very important. Single motherhood is associated with a young age group and the fact that live-in *empleadas* cannot both work and sustain a marriage or stable union. Many women who work as live-in *empleadas* have been abandoned by their husbands or partners.

The majority of women who work in domestic service have very little education; many are illiterate or have not completed primary school. This is particularly true of the older women. Those who are able to upgrade their education—even if they can do so only with difficulty—can find a different type of occupation.

The question of how to conduct an action project led to a search for strategies which,

(1) since the majority of the *empleadas* live and work under discriminatory conditions, would allow us to develop programs directed to-

ward transforming the labor relations of domestic service and organizing the occupational group to defend its legal rights;

(2) since the gender ideology binding both *empleadas* and *patronas* to domestic labor is so deep-rooted, would allow us to develop programs that promote a process of *conscientização* leading to personal autonomy-identity (empowerment).

Thus we saw the need to undertake two complementary actions: one to stimulate gender awareness among *empleadas* and *patronas;* the other, class consciousness among the *empleadas.* Gender awareness endeavors to demythify why women are assigned domestic labor; class consciousness allows *empleadas* to identify with each other, perceive the contradictions inherent in the class relation, and create an organized movement.

Actions are classified as follows: direct actions with *empleadas* and *patronas,* and "multiplying" or outreach actions (see Figure 16-1). The first include (1) *apoyo laboral* (labor support), or provision of resources and support through the process wherein *empleadas* learn of their labor rights, as well as the various phases of class and gender identification and of organizing (see below); (2) support for the *empleadas'* identity-autonomy (empowerment) process; and (3) socio-labor reflection with *patronas.* The second phase involves (1) attending to and encouraging the organizing process of the *empleadas;* (2) exposing and seeking to change the subordination-exploitation structure of the *patrona-empleada* relation at an ideological level; (3) fostering the legal profession's correct interpretation and application of the law; and (4) promoting changes at the government level to benefit the occupational group.

The aim of labor support to the *empleada*—one of the direct actions—is twofold: to awaken class consciousness, and to provide assistance in arriving at gender identity. These activities are mutually reinforcing and channel the rank and file toward the organization phase. Outreach support offered the already organized sectors of the occupational group aims to strengthen their organization.

Direct actions with *patronas* endeavor to instill both gender awareness and a sense of class obligation: that is, their obligation to *empleadas* in the work relation. Outreach actions seek to affect the ideology of servitude that society in general and the professional legal community in particular hold toward the domestic service sector, and finally, to promote change at the government level.

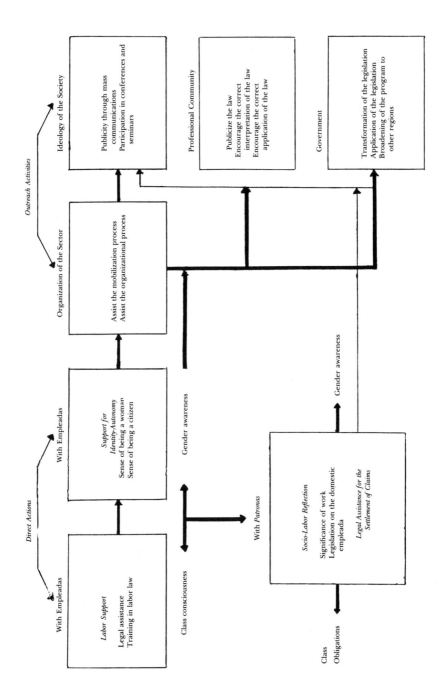

FIGURE 16-1 Direct and Indirect Actions

Direct Actions

Direct actions are those in which the participants are *empleadas* or *patronas* with whom we have personal contact. Two of the direct actions target *empleadas* and one, *patronas*. During the phase of labor support for *empleadas*, the existing labor laws are presented, and groups discuss how to better understand, enforce, and challenge them. The *empleada's* sense of autonomy-identity (empowerment) is explored and developed in the context of her situation both as a woman and as a citizen. Connections between these two levels—that is, daily personal problems and work problems—are stressed with a view to penetrating the hidden determinants of both the personal and collective situations with a view to organization.

Having considered the individual labor relation, the project then moves to the collective nature of the *empleada-patrona* problem; in other words, the project is able to awaken class consciousness by collectivizing individual claims and exposing the contradictions in the labor relation not as conflicts between individuals but as functions of class positions. We also encourage women to reflect on their roles as individuals and members of the social community, the object being to initiate processes of personal identity and autonomy in the women's management of relationships. We hope that the mutual reinforcement between identity as a person and as a social being, combined with the as yet embryonic discovery of class contradictions, will encourage the domestic service sector to become mobilized and therefore visible and organized.

Patronas are offered courses whose purpose is to demythologize the ideological values underlying their social assignment of domestic labor; in this context, they are presented with the labor legislation that contains their contractual obligations toward their domestic workers. The direct actions are explained in more detail below.

Labor Support for the Empleada

The principal goal of this action is to enable *empleadas*, both individually and collectively, to use law as a tool to improve working and living conditions. Legal aid is made available, and *empleadas* are instructed in their labor rights and contractual obligations.

Legal Aid. Labor support for individual cases goes through four phases: settlement of fringe benefits, legal counsel during negotiations, legal counsel during settlement, and judicial processes.

Legal aid is used as a means to an end, or starting point, as can be seen in Figure 16-1. Although it is primarily associated with material recovery, its long-term goal is to facilitate the *empleada*'s improved training, awareness, and eventual incorporation into the union.

Given that they have never been aware of or protected by their legal rights, *empleadas* feel the need for legal counsel. They have developed a fatalistic outlook wherein change is considered a matter of luck rather than the result of specific actions. So long as there was no legal support for their demands, the word of the *patrona* was the only one having any validity. Disclosure of the existence of legislation and the fact that its compliance can be assured by means of legal assistance fills a gap in legal practice.

Laws governing domestic employment were promulgated more than twenty-five years ago, when the live-in mode was the most common form of domestic service. Live-out domestic service is a more recent trend, and the fact that labor laws do not make explicit reference to it does not mean, as some *patrones* and legal professionals assert, that it is not covered.

Owing to the absence of a separate chapter on the subject in the Substantive Labor Code, the legislation is dispersed and applied through extension of general legal principles. For these reasons, it has been necessary to hold discussions about how the law applies to the live-in empleada and how it may be extended to the domestic worker who lives out,[12] as well as effectively translated into mathematical formulations taking legal rights, especially benefits, into account.

Analysis of the laws permits focus on various general points:

First, they were written from the viewpoint that the *empleada* was part of the family and that the family was not a unit of production. Although neither supposition is operative in the real world, both serve to establish a discriminatory legal order.

Second, in some aspects discussed below, the laws are restrictive and do not confer the same rights on *empleadas* as on ordinary workers.

Third, the legislation has gaps. Colombian law is positive and extremely formal. The way lawyers are trained itself eliminates a universal overview of law: if no exact legislation governing the case can be found, the tendency is not to recognize the existence of the right. This being the case with the live-out *empleada*, extensive recourse to analogy and general legal principles is required.

Fourth, because the law's content is limited, it lacks social justice in some respects; for instance, it makes no provision for health care, does not regulate the work hours of live-in *empleadas,* and calculates fringe benefits solely on the basis of cash wages, disregarding in-kind salary.[13]

For the purposes of our project, an information booklet summarizing existing law is distributed to the *patronas,* and the *empleadas* receive pamphlets that have been prepared using a particular didactic method. The information booklet is sent to the *patrona* along with all the *empleada's* work-related demands as a way of substantiating her claim; it is also made available to *patronas* in the courses offered them. *Patronas* are encouraged to solicit further information or services on their own initiative, and information on the project is published in newspapers and magazines.

The fact that legal advice is available to *empleadas* is spread through the mass media—radio, print press, and television; via personal contacts with *empleadas* at continuing education and recreation centers; and through trade unions, women's organizations, and employment agencies.

The benefits settlement service is offered to the *empleada* who has terminated her employment contract or intends to do so. Severance pay, paid vacation, and accrued interest on severance pay are all calculated. This includes unpaid wages, compensation for unjust termination of a contract by the *patrona,* dismissal during pregnancy, or unilateral dismissal of the *empleada* for a just cause. Because of work schedules, the service has to be offered on Sunday afternoons to large numbers of people; for this reason, a special team of *liquidadores,* or adjusters, was trained in a systematized methodology to assist *empleadas* in calculating their accrued benefits.[14]

By October 1985, 7,330 adjustments had been completed in Bogotá, and 1,898 in Medellín, Cali, Barranquilla, and Bucaramanga by September 1985. Underlying the mass-based provision of the service was the idea that "one swallow doesn't make a summer," since high levels of participation are necessary to achieve the desired impact. This is possible when the methodology is systematized and work is undertaken with motivation and commitment.[15]

If, after the settlement calculations are made, the claim is rejected either partially or totally by the *patrona,*[16] legal counsel with the direct assistance of attorneys is begun. The first phase of the counseling involves making an appointment with the *patrona* and seeking, by means of a personal interview, not to polarize the relation. Direct contact, considering the educational value of presenting the content of the law and the social context of the relationship, has proved to be the most useful way to reach a positive solution. During 1984 and up to October 1985, 4,172 legal consultations had been held (not to be understood as the number of persons attended).[17]

Legal consultations involve working directly with the *patrona* and *empleada* through written notices, personal interviews, telephone contacts, and hearings. The *empleada* is helped to understand the claim she is making, an understanding strengthened by a course offered on labor relations. The *patrona*, who is generally taken aback by the claim and in some cases sends a legal representative to refute it, is presented with the information that the law is on the books and that she is obliged to comply with it.

When *empleada* and *patrona* cannot negotiate a settlement, the case goes to the National Labor Office, which, as a nonjudicial administrative body, can enforce no sanction other than a fine—which bureaucratic inefficiency prevents it from levying. In fact, no real redress is available, and the only recourse is to initiate a court case. During the hearing the program's lawyer assists the *empleada* to seek a settlement. Most cases have, in fact, been successfully resolved at the negotiation stage.

All cases that go through the benefits claim process and legal aid phases are subjected to follow-up procedures employing specialized methods. So far as resolving cases within a short time is concerned, and encouraging *empleadas* who have become interested in the continuing programs at ACEP to attend more regularly, the results have been positive. The judicial process, the most recent phase of the project, is carried out only in prioritized cases with a view to developing jurisprudence.

Throughout this phase, *empleadas* participate as contacts with *patronas;* they personally deliver correspondence and, in the follow-up work, regularly visit the program in order to work out their claim. The service aims to transcend a dependency mentality by emphasizing that the *empleada* should be responsible for her individual problematic and apply it to the wider group.

Labor Law Education. As a first step in the process of education and *conscientizaçao,* *empleadas* are offered workshops in labor law. The objective is to interest them in learning the relevant law so that they can understand and conduct their individual cases. Courses are given once a month on Sunday afternoons for eight months. While attendance has fluctuated, the dropout rate has fallen. The sessions are held in places where domestic workers congregate for special activities: centers for single mothers from the popular sectors, adoption agencies, employment agencies, or training schools.

The methodology is participatory and aims to develop topics from the viewpoint of participants. The facilitator-teacher encourages dialogue and, from the comments that are forthcoming, draws together the various experiences to highlight how the law applies to each topic. The methodology also seeks to convey the complex content of the law in simple form to people whose educational level is very low. To do this, teaching aids are employed, based on the qualitative information developed from the legal consultations between *empleadas* and *patronas*. Converting information gathered during the judicial activities into teaching material is one way to return their experiences to the participants.[18]

The labor law course covers seven topics: work contract, probationary period, hours, salary, paid time off (Sundays and national holidays, vacations, and family crises), benefits (severance pay and compensation for on-the-job injury, sickness, pregnancy, abortion, and uniforms), and termination of contract.

The guiding theme of each section represents the central point to be emphasized or clarified. For example, the work contract section must clarify the validity of the verbal contract from which the relation's legal implications are derived. The depth to which the material can be gone into at each session depends on how much the participants are able to understand.

The workshops, apart from providing the *empleadas* with information, are occasions where they can meet and build solidarity; above all, where they can "socialize" the problematic. Realizing that their situation as domestic workers is not simply a personal one but is common to a larger group participating in an unequal power relation with the *patronas* makes a strong impression on the *empleadas*. Three group activities (two of which were public) convened by ACEP and the trade union were mass actions that gave *empleadas* an opportunity to air their grievances and signaled a shift toward group consciousness (see the outreach section below).

The Development of Autonomy-Identity (Empowerment)

The Workshops related to autonomy-identity complements what *empleadas* have learned about their labor rights in the law workshop, as well as the breakthroughs they have made in terms of their individual and collective consciousness. By focusing on how the *empleada* experiences subordination as a woman, this workshop aims to demythify patriarchal ideology. It reveals how subordinate relations—which operate in the *empleada's* role as daughter, wife, mother, or housewife in her family of origin—are transferred to the substitute "home" of the employer family and hinder the development of class consciousness. Workshops on two central themes, the *empleada* as woman and as citizen, provide support for growth of autonomy-identity.

The workshop's subject matter is developed along broad lines, according to the group's interest; the motivator-guide, who previously gave talks and conferences, becomes a facilitator. Groups are small (from six to twelve people), and courses are spread over a period of four or five Sunday afternoon sessions. Like the legal courses, these workshops are offered where *empleadas* generally congregate.

Methodology is participative and permits the *empleada* to grow in the identity process, both as a woman and as a social being active to some extent in the public world. The participants' commitment to, interest in, and understanding of the workshop is derived from their own personal experiences. The workshop sets up a dynamic, flexible, and unthreatening working method wherein each person may express her point of view and, by comparing it with those of others, gain new attitudes and perspectives on her life. The workshops emphasize personal experience and, by specifying a central topic, allow emotional aspects to contextualize the facts.

It is important to stress that participants do not come from a single community, but because of the nature of their work—which in itself is isolating—live apart. Workshops attempt to break through the isolation and silence; they provide an opportunity to consider alternatives that extend beyond the private situation, as well as the necessary security and motivation to unite and organize—both as workers and as women—and thus precipitate social change.

Workshop on Identity as a Woman. This workshop, by extracting the culturally defined aspects of domestic roles and sexuality, and exploring strategies to challenge them, encourages individual and group reflection on the elements that constitute gender identity. This approach centers on the *empleadas'* personal experiences of confrontation or denial, plus information presented by the facilitator.

Discussion of subjects such as the human body take a holistic approach and explore a perspective on the sexual relation that is broader than the genital; groups cover reproduction in terms of the different stages common to all women and the relation between fecundity, pregnancy, and birth during the fertile period. The workshop's objective is to differentiate women's sexuality, discussions of which generally focus exclusively on the reproductive process. While the workshop agenda includes a technical session on family planning and contraceptive methods for both partners, it also touches on such concepts as the importance of bearing children who are wanted, and sexual relations for the woman's sexual pleasure rather than simply as a reproductive function.

The topic "women and work" helps participants understand notions of femininity and masculinity, how women are subordinated, domestic labor, and the relation with domestic service.

Civic Identity Workshop. To enable the *empleada* to better perceive her social roles as woman, worker, and citizen, participants in a third workshop describe, analyze, and compare their individual situations. The general purpose is to show *empleadas* that they have a place in social life and to help them understand their problematic. The workshop stimulates participants to interrelate, while positing organization and group action as strategies to overcome the domestic service sector's problematic.

Other discussions center on employment and unemployment, rural-urban migration and its causes, the problems derived from the educational and training opportunities, and public services available to female domestic workers in the city. To elucidate the various kinds of violence that women—in particular, those in domestic service—are subject to in the city, participants talk about situations in which they feel insecure and afraid. In other sessions they review health problems and the sources of care they have access to and, finally, discuss how they participate in city life.

The woman and civic identity workshops facilitate the initial reflection essential to a process of identity. Each workshop has four or five sessions, too short a time to expect profound changes to occur, but we believe they provide a starting point for individual and/or group responses to the *empleada*'s problematic.

Socio-Labor Reflection for Patronas

The aim of these courses, which deal with the social and labor aspects of domestic service, is twofold: to stimulate the *amas de casa* to an understanding of the concept of gender, and to clarify their contractual obligations as an employer class in relation to the domestic service sector. The social aspect considers the concept of domestic service, the theories proposing its disappearance or decline, and the sociodemographic conditions of the sector in terms of current modes and tasks performed.

At this point, courses encourage *patronas* to think about the relation between the domestic labor they perform themselves and the paid service provided by the *empleada,* about how society values these activities and assigns women to "serve others," and about women's social role and their conditioning and subordination in family and community power relations.

The labor legislation governing contracts with *empleadas* is introduced in this context, and the relation is extracted from the paternalistic framework that considers *empleadas* "members of the family" and, as such, without workers' rights.

Organizations coordinating work with women set up the *patronas'* courses: volunteer groups, women's associations, training centers, social work faculties, female government employees' clubs (teachers, community workers, and so on), businesses employing predominantly female personnel, and *amas de casa* interested in coordinating private groups for these activities.

Motivating *patronas* to participate has not been easy, given the class consciousness that prevents them from facing labor obligations toward their subordinates, and their own oppressed identity as women that prevents them from reflecting on their social role.[19] Nevertheless, twenty-three sessions with a total of 633 participants were given in the first part of 1985.

Should an *ama de casa* solicit it and be clearly willing to comply with her labor obligations, the legal aid service will supply information and a settlement service. As the program broadens its base, requests for this service increase, and more people become aware of the legislation.

Outreach Actions

Outreach includes activities planned with representatives of the domestic service sector, efforts to reach society at large, discussions with legal professionals, and, finally, actions for policy change.

Domestic Service Representatives

Work with representatives of the sector has a twofold objective. First, it serves as a bridge between rank and file and leadership; second, it supports the organized sector of the occupational group as a whole. Class and gender awareness instilled in the rank and file through earlier direct actions provide the foundation for the mobilizing and unionizing phases. ACEP has not itself attempted to create an organization but refers program participants showing interest in collective action to the Sindícato Nacional de Trabajadores del Servicio Domestico or SINTRASEDOM (National Union of Household Workers).[20] Union representatives and program participants collaborate; the former, for instance, provide information about the union and its activities (assemblies, courses, and the like) to participants in the labor course and workshops.

In an effort to mobilize the rank and file, ACEP has also organized larger meetings, such as the May 1, 1985, event held to celebrate May Day and call for enforcement of the health provisions found in the labor legislation. Another public meeting was held on August 25 to demand that *empleadas* be enrolled in social security programs and that the law stipulating rest and pay on Sundays and national holidays be enforced. Five hundred *empleadas* attended the meeting, determined to air their grievances in public. Another rally was staged in October 1985 to call for enforcement of social security laws. This event had a dual purpose: to apply pressure to improve material conditions, and to strengthen the union.

The research team provides support for the organized sector of the occupational group by working directly with the union. One great difficulty is coordinating schedules. The union members, like almost all *empleadas,* cannot always count on having Sunday free for their training, outreach, and union activities. The various ACEP direct action programs for the rank and file also take place on Sunday afternoons, meaning that the professional team is deluged with work. Matching up schedules in order to keep activities going is quite a juggling act, especially when a certain amount of continuity is needed, and when workshops and meetings demand several hours at a time.

The team provides support for the union's different events and trains leaders on the substance of the labor law and methods used to settle claims.[21] Preparation of teaching material has also been coordinated. The booklet for the labor law course prepared by ACEP was discussed with SINTRASEDOM members before its joint publication. Likewise, proposals to reform the Substantive Labor Code were considered at meetings held with the union before being submitted to the Ministry of Labor. Project representatives have made international contacts for the union at different events, and our bibliographical resources are at its disposal or donated as reference material for the SINTRASEDOM documentation center.

Underlying our support or accompaniment of the organizational process is a determination not to reproduce the asymmetric power relations between *patronas* and *empleadas* in the relation between the ACEP professional team and the union members. For this reason, "assistance" that tends to replace the sector's autonomy is avoided as much as possible. The project functions as a bridge between the rank and file and the leadership; the union, however, will accept those *empleadas* and organized groups wishing to become members and direct them to more complex collective action.

Changing Social Ideology

This phase focuses on making the labor legislation known to the general public, clarifying the relation that allows society to devalue domestic labor, and highlighting the veneer of servitude that persists in domestic service relations.

Articles, interviews, and denunciations have appeared consistently in the print press and on radio and television. Participating radio programs are most often community or news programs dealing with women's interests. The legal consultation program that was widely broadcast for three months is particularly worth mentioning. In three weekly radio spots, the project's three lawyers presented "typical cases" derived from experience and, using these as examples, explained the legislation applying to the *patronas*. The program continued until the station canceled the contract; the support it provided to the *empleadas* was considered counterproductive for the radio audience (*amas de casa* and middle- and upper-income sectors).

To enable the program to reach a larger audience, the labor legislation has been outlined in pamphlets—distributed mainly to *patronas*—and published in popular magazines. By presenting the gains and limitations of the project at national and international seminars and conferences, the research team has reached the professional community, agencies working for change, and groups engaged in research-action projects.

Legal Professionals

Serious problems of interpretation arise both from the scattered and ambiguous condition of existing law and the fact that, in comparison with other workers, the domestic *empleada*'s rights are limited. This legal problem is further aggravated by the male and female professional communities' deeply rooted patriarchal ideology, which devalues the work performed by the domestic service sector.

The specifics of the law as it relates to household workers are not taught in law schools or in individual labor law courses; the program's legal work has demonstrated that both practicing lawyers and students are unaware of the law's content and, worse still, of how to make the law operative at a quantitative level. Thus we have shown the unconcern and "mental laziness" preventing the legal profession from grasping the different results of distinct mathematical applications. Given that the consequences of an erroneous interpretation are damaging at a material level, we have stressed this particular aspect; although it is of a speculative nature, it is crucial to redress. Debate with legal professionals has been encouraged with a view to resolving these problems and enforcing the rights conferred by the law. Dispute about whether or not a body of law even exists has, to a large extent, been overcome; that fact constitutes one of the most important victories of the program.

By analyzing the essential elements of the work contract—provision of personal service, a wage, and continued dependence or subordination—lawyers have acknowledged the legal rights of the live-out *empleada*. Dispute arose on the "continued dependence" point, and sophisticated arguments adducing that the contract is occasional—continued dependence or subordination not being an element when the work is not full time—were presented. However, by demonstrating that the particular working day of the live-out *empleada* meets the criterion of being usual or customary, and that continued dependence or subordination refers to the *patrona*'s ability to direct the work and give orders about the way it is to be done during those hours, the project defeated this argument, more soundly so upon observation that Colombian law contemplates the coexistence of contracts and benefits.

Although the live-out *empleada*'s contractual rights are not yet the focus of legal discussion, how to make her benefits operative remains a serious technical problem. The *sui generis* nature of her contract implies that a different, proportionally derived formula should apply as a matter of mathematical logic.[22]

Actions at the Government Level

There is no government activity whatsoever designated to respond to the *empleadas*' labor demands. Consequently, we designed a series of actions to change the legislation, correct its interpretation, and encourage further legislative activity.

Actions to Change Legislation. Changing legislation may seem next to impossible, given both the political structure of the government and the interests represented by those who manage the state apparatus. We did, however, try to take advantage of one favorable opportunity that came our way. When a female Deputy Minister of Labor in 1983–84 shared and defended the interests of working women,[23] we began to survey the most important points of the labor legislation in need of reform. The basic goal, reflecting the demands being made by the domestic service sector itself, was to achieve equal rights with other workers. Its practical legal experience enabled the ACEP professional team to specify those points needing reform, which were then discussed with SINTRASEDOM.[24] Unfortunately, this project languished in the subsequent absence of governmental interest.

Actions to Interpret and Enforce Existing Legislation. Three basic actions have been developed in this area. First, because the work inspector's interpretation of the law plays a fundamental role, we have stressed both ideological and theoretical work with the officials in the Ministry of Labor, which is the administrative tribunal where worker-employer conflicts are heard. Their high turnover rate, however, requires us continually to start over. We must emphasize that legal interpretation does not hinge simply on points of law; patriarchal ideology, which devalues domestic service work, also comes into play.

Second, during 1985 the project campaigned to enroll *empleadas* in social security programs. Because there are no sanctions to enforce the existing law and because the enrollment procedures are very confusing, few *empleadas* are affiliated. The battle for enrollment is being waged at both individual and collective levels, and the goal is to publicize broad-based demands by taking to the streets. Officials at the Social Security Institute say that their doors are always open for any *patrona* or *empleada* wishing to apply, but in practice the law is "obeyed but not enforced." Generally, *empleadas* and *patronas* are both unaware that the law contains provisions for social security rights, and the procedures and bureaucratic state structure make application very difficult. Basic information about the necessary procedures and potential benefits is contained in a leaflet prepared by the research team and distributed in the *patronas'* courses, during the legal consultations, and to participating *empleadas*. The greatest obstacles to enrollment are the perception that the law is non-binding and that no sanctions are applied in the event of non-compliance. Other factors hindering enrollment are the labor instability of a part of the domestic service sector and, finally, the fact that there are no regulations governing enrollment of the live-out *empleada* having one or more contracts.

Although the social security services provided are inefficient and inadequate, and are not the magic answer to the health problems of the occupational group, the problems of old age and invalidism are so severe that social security can be of great assistance. Domestic service is contracted very selectively, and an older woman who is beginning to have health problems and is less productive has no alternative employment. The mental disorders that develop as living conditions deteriorate during old age are totally unprovided for.

Third, we have sought to gain access to the government by increasing the legal aid actions within its administrative structure. Response to these initiatives has not been encouraging, and we believe that for the foreseeable future the government will continue to fail in its social responsibility to enforce the laws.

Problems Encountered and Lessons Learned

The task of devising multilayered strategies that considered both class and gender issues and took into account gaps and ambiguities in existing law was extremely problematic, but it taught us a great deal.

Problems

Major problems we have encountered involve the *empleada's* personal situation, the "patronal" ideology, and difficulties derived from the labor relation.

The Worker's Personal Situation. Some *empleadas*—because of their isolation, sense of the transitoriness of their work, shaky faith in individual and union actions, scarce free time, and the feeling of being subordinate to the *patrona* as a result of having internalized a sense inferiority—do not initiate labor claims at all; others simply drop out of the process along the way; still others do not see training in specific rights as promising anything substantial. Those problems have gradually been resolving themselves, for the most part in Bogotá, where the activities are more developed. The high enrollment for the labor law workshop shows that *empleadas* who participated in the groups went on to become outreach workers. Recognizing the labor relation in each contract as one that is neither isolated nor unique is a particularly difficult step for an *empleada* to take, since it means shifting from an individual to a group consciousness. While this process is crucial in mobilizing for an organizing campaign, it is a very gradual one.

Another problem is the frustration that surfaces as members of a traditionally subordinated sector, having just come to understand that they have certain rights, find that they must wait for long periods before they can enjoy them. If an *empleada* whose personality structure tends to be aggressive can manage to overcome her sense of internalized inferiority, deep levels of frustration-aggression may be awakened. Equally, when the *empleada* begins to feel a sense of autonomy-identity (empowerment) and manages to question her subordination in personal and family relations, the clash between the identity achieved and the precarious socioeconomic situation she seems trapped in may cause her to feel powerless to manage her life. The live-out *empleada* experiences this phenomenon more acutely, since although she may be able to separate her workday from her life as a whole, she must overcome numerous housing, health, and recreational problems.

So long as there is a labor market for domestic service workers, changes in class and gender consciousness must be incorporated into a larger scheme for structural change. The alternative is to alleviate only individual situations and create slightly more pleasant living conditions for a few. It is crucial, therefore, to encourage *empleadas* to become organized.

The "Patronal" Ideology. The *ama de casa* who does not recognize her own level of subordination feels aggrieved by a project that defends *empleadas*. Some, afraid of having claims initiated against them, argue that publicizing the legislation and working for its enforcement will raise unemployment rates, because "they would rather do things themselves than employ people with so many demands."

But the unemployment problem is not a function of peoples' attitudes. In a crisis situation like the present one, demand for domestic service—especially among the middle classes—tends to decline. Employment opportunities for males also tend to decline, and the increased cost of living among the popular sectors drives women to go out and look for jobs, flooding the domestic service market. Facing the alternative of absolute poverty, women will offer their labor almost unconditionally and not demand their legal rights—especially if they are unaware of them and/or there are no tribunals to see that the law is enforced. In these circumstances, it is difficult to establish that the drive to enforce the law exacerbates unemployment.

Other variables, such as rates of female employment, also influence the demand structure. As long as the sexual division of domestic labor prevails and the state fails to provide support for the work of reproduction, middle-class women—who are entering the labor force in large numbers and therefore confront a double day—will employ paid domestic labor within the legal requirements. Skilled workers, trained *empleadas* who inspire high levels of confidence, will be more in demand. In the atmosphere of insecurity characterizing Colombian society today, upper-class families even hire *empleadas* to "house-sit."

Alternatively, once the patronal ideology is infused with reflection on their own subordination, complex attitudes and responses are released in the *amas de casa*. These range from political considerations implying new lifestyles to concern for social justice issues; from fear of being outside the law to hiding behind classist ideology and refusing any concession or change, however insignificant.

Why the Labor Relation is Unclear. Because confusion surrounds the domestic service labor relation, difficulties arise when the attempt is made to enforce the law. Confusion arises because the relation is usually derived from a verbal contract; because it is affective and personal, since services are provided in a family environment; and because fallacious arguments—such as considering the *empleada* to be a "member of the family," within moral law—are adduced. This is why severance pay is usually calculated on an annual basis and is neither retroactive nor cumulative; why interest is not paid regularly; why full vacation time is either denied or demanded by an *empleada* who may not yet have earned it; and, finally, why she may be dismissed while pregnant. The problems are aggravated during the *empleada*'s probationary period, since in disputes involving verbal contracts the tribunal must weigh the *patrona*'s word against the *empleada*'s, creating bitterness on both sides.

Lessons Learned

In addition to those already discussed above, the following categories of lessons learned have broad application.

Legal Recognition and Assistance. The effort to have *empleadas*' rights legally recognized has been generally successful, and the work is being consolidated among legal professionals. *Patronas* are less receptive; rather than countering the legal arguments, they revert to emotional or paternalistic tactics, which we try to confront by defining the class and gender contradictions inherent in the relation.

The legal aid work has focused fundamentally on assuring *empleadas* their basic fringe benefits: severance pay, interest on severance pay, vacations, maternity leave, compensation for unjust dismissal. Other patronal obligations, such as providing medical attention during illness or double pay for holiday work, are more difficult to enforce; they are used to persuade and reinforce the claim during the negotiation phase, since even though such discussion does not affect the amount of the settlement, it opens the way for recognition of basic obligations and for a different mentality that directly confronts unjust and widely practiced customs. Legal assistance thus constitutes a "point of departure." Provided to the *empleadas* as an integral part of all the other actions, not as an act of charity, it represents a tool for change that extends beyond simply alleviating the work situation.

Organization and Wider Change. Although domestic servants live isolated from one another and work in alienating jobs that reinforce their social anonymity, if systematic methodologies that respond to their needs are established, and allow them to mobilize for further action, important work can be done. Such work satisfies individual material demands and, by reshaping gender and class consciousness, motivates the sector to organize.

The actions described above are strategies to demythify the situation in which domestic *empleadas*—a significant group of women from the popular classes—are subordinated and exploited, and to stimulate collective activities that will lead to organization. At the same time, we work with the *ama de casa* in her double role: as the *patrona* who represents the opposite pole in the labor relation, she is urged to comply with her contractual obligations; as a woman subject to the social subordination imposed on her by the assignment of domestic labor, she is stimulated to develop gender awareness.

It is extremely complex work to design actions that lead to a sense of the inherent class contradictions in the *empleada*'s labor relation, while instilling gender awareness in both the *empleada* and the *ama de casa*. When such actions are successful, however, each is able to translate her new-found awareness into a search for wider change that will eventually dismantle classist and patriarchal social structures.

Notes

Acknowledgment: The author wishes to thank the team of the Asociación Colombiana para el Estudio de la Población (ACEP)—in particular, Angela Melendro—for their comments on this work. The project team comprised a director, general secretary, two full-time lawyers, a full-time social science professional, and a team of adjusters who worked on Sunday afternoons. In all the cities but Bogotá a lawyer and a team of adjusters worked together.

1. In this way we covered the five largest cities that, in 1983, represented 51 percent of the urban population. In Medellín and Cali the project covered the labor support activities discussed in the document, and in Barranquilla and Bucaramanga we began support work for the autonomy, identity, and organization processes. The project has been financed during limited periods by the Inter-American and Ford Foundations. Its continuation will depend on outside funding, since its actions do not easily attract national support, and its self-financing conflicts with the limited resources of those employed in domestic service.

2. Labor relations refer to the work contract, working conditions, hours, paid vacations and days off, salary, and fringe benefits as well as compensation for on-the-job injuries, illness, maternity or abortion leave, provision of uniform or work shoes, and severance pay.

3. There is ongoing debate about domestic labor. One expression of its devaluation is that the *ama de casa* is considered inactive in the recent statistics and, as such, is excluded from the economically active population. See Wainerman and Recchini de Lattes 1981; León 1985.

4. Exploitation is a more complex phenomenon than a simple polarization between dominated and dominating classes. Within each class there is a series of subsectors, requiring more detailed analysis, that reflect a more accurate structuring of social differences. This aspect is particularly important in studying the relation of the domestic *empleada* and the *patrona*, as it involves contracts between very different social sectors.

5. Garcia Castro (1982) suggests that elements determining wages for other workers, such as hours, productivity, the particular family's needs for reproduction, etc., are adjusted differently in the case of domestic workers.

6. This alternative has been adopted in Colombia by religious groups and orchestrated by women of the upper class who, within the ethic of servitude, wish to improve the skills of the domestic labor force for the reproduction of their own families, thus lightening—not challenging—their own socially assigned responsibilities. Although we consider it essential that *empleadas* be trained, we would not confine this simply to household tasks but would extend it to a campaign to overcome high rates of illiteracy and low educational levels. We believe that training must be given within the framework of the labor relation, rather than as a separate activity.

7. The relation between the state and the reproduction of the labor force is a central analytical point in the debate on the social meaning of domestic service; it is not dealt with here.

8. Garcia Castro (1982) expresses this relation as follows: "Domestic service is a throwback to precapitalist relations of work, convenient to the process of reproduction of the labor force in the present state of the economies of underdeveloped capitalist countries. Despite its being an activity not directly creating value, it is socially necessary because it daily contributes to reproducing the labor force."

9. Domestic *empleadas* are called the "fourth world" of development, in the same sense that for Latin American and Caribbean society this group represents more than one-quarter of the urban female labor force.

10. In the 1951 census the percentage of women in live-in domestic service among the economically active female population was 43 percent; for 1973 it dropped to 24 percent (see Garcia Castro et al. 1981).

11. This sketchy profile of the profession is based on information in cases registered by the ACEP project. Garcia Castro et al. (1981) take into account the available census data of household questionnaires and other types of information on the sector. See also her article in this volume.

12. To define the general framework of the law was the aim of a bibliographic study and preparation of monographs (see Vallejo 1982). For the first time, the regulations governing the labor of the domestic *empleada* were subjected to systematic legal analysis and presented as a summary to the professional community.

13. Briefly, the rights conferred by the law may be described as follows: (1) probation period: fifteen calendar days, both for the live-in and live-out *doméstica;* (2) hours: the live-in *empleada's* hours are unlimited, but the live-out *empleada* may work a maximum of eight hours; (3) rest and pay on Sundays (this applies only to the live-in *empleada* and the live-out who works six days a week for the same employer): Sunday work can be done if double pay or compensatory time is given; (4) paid vacation and national holidays: apply to all empleadas; (5) paid annual vacations: the live-in *empleada* and the live-out

who works six days for the same employer are entitled to fifteen full days (those who work fewer days are entitled to adjusted vacation time in proportion to days worked in each household); (6) salary: the *empleada* is entitled to the legal minimum wage; (7) severance pay (a benefit accrued from the time the contract is entered into, and payable upon termination in accordance with the salary earned and time worked): the *empleada* is entitled to fifteen days' wages for each year worked (other workers receive thirty days' pay), and the live-out *empleada*'s severance pay is calculated proportionately; (8) interest on severance pay: if not paid on time, interest on wages, accumulated from the previous December 31, is automatically doubled; (9) illness: medical and pharmaceutical attention must be provided by the *patrones;* (10) work-related injury: whatever first aid is required for an injury must be given; (11) maternity leave: a paid leave of eight weeks around the time of birth (if the *empleada* is dismissed, three and a half months' salary must be paid in compensation, over and above the paid leave).

14. The schedule is arranged on Sundays because it is the only time available to the *empleadas* (when the legislated paid Sunday holiday is given). The team of adjusters is made up of both male and female university students of various disciplines (accounting, law, medicine, social sciences). Domestic *empleadas* with more education, or former *empleadas* who have since taken up other occupations, also participate.

15. A questionnaire is used to gather basic socio-demographic data on the domestic and permit simplified mathematical calculations of the claims. The questionnaire is precoded so that it may be systematized for future analysis. Its current version has benefited from our experience of the direct work with the *empleadas*. To be able to reach large numbers is one challenge of research/action projects, which have been criticized as being directed only at small numbers of people. Our project seeks to provide a response, but analysis of this point is not an object of this chapter.

16. A courteous letter is sent explaining that the adjustment is based on information supplied by the *empleada*. The letter asks the *patrona* to contact the ACEP office if she has any questions or comments about the matter. The *empleada* is responsible for delivering the letter.

17. To maintain statistical records of the ways services are provided, forms have been designed for all the legal aid activities. This system allows for monthly self-evaluation of the work by the team, and for coordination of program development in the different cities.

18. Three types of teaching aids have been developed: (1) bulletin boards that illustrate different themes with attractive images or illustrations that assist understanding and permit a greater degree of concentration; (2) primers containing words, diagrams, and special illustrations covering the principal sections into which the law is divided; (3) games of various kinds—e.g., one has been designed to test whether the participants have understood the course content.

19. Response to a general notice was practically nil. Flyers posted in public places (churches and supermarkets), or delivered door to door, and notices placed in the newspapers inviting *patronas* to the course were insufficient to displace the dominant patronal and paternalistic ideology as expressed by one *patrona:* "It is better not to know the law, so we don't have to obey it."

20. SINTRASEDOM was formed in 1978 by workers having ties to religious organizations that promoted the founding of cooperatives. After a long struggle, during which it was denied legal standing, the right to organize as a labor union was granted in January 1985. See Chapter 19, on SINTRASEDOM, in this volume.

21. Three labor law courses have been run for the union. The first one began in February 1985, and is scheduled for two hours every Sunday. First, the legislation is reviewed, and then members of the group are trained as adjustment workers, so they may offer this service within the union and thus provide more incentive for others to join. The course is intentionally gradual and time-intensive to ensure effective training.

22. Domestic workers are entitled to severance pay calculated at fifteen days of salary for each year of work. This amount is arrived at through a complicated mathematical formula, involving multiplying the final month's salary by the total years worked, then reducing the results by one-half, since the domestic worker receives only fifteen days' severance pay, while other workers get one month's pay for each year worked. Errors are often committed in calculating the amount due, particularly in the case of day workers; the formula is often applied incorrectly not only to the time period worked but to the salary paid, resulting in a lowering of the amount of severance pay the domestic worker should receive.

23. Dr. Helena Paéz de Tavera, Deputy Minister of Labor, has participated in the civic-social struggles of Colombian women; she made defense of the working woman her particular area of concern while in office.

24. The main points of the reform were to clarify what is understood by "domestic service worker," making explicit recognition of the external (day work) and internal (live-in) modes; to establish a limited working day for the live-in *empleada;* to stipulate mandatory rest and pay on Sundays and national holidays, as well as enrollment in social security; to increase the *empleadas'* rights in case of accident as well as both work- and non-work-related illness; to recognize their equal right with other workers to unemployment benefits (thirty days per year); and to calculate benefits on the basis not only of cash but of in-kind wages.

References

Garcia Castro, Mary. 1982. "¿Qué se compra y qué se paga en el servicio doméstico? El caso de Bogotá." In Magdalena León, ed., *La realidad co-*

lombiana, vol. 1, *Debate sobre la mujer en América Latina y el Caribe,* pp. 92–122. Bogotá: Asociación Colombiana para el Estudio de la Población.

Garcia Castro, Mary, Bertha Quintero, and Gladys Jimeno. 1981. "Empleo doméstico, sector informal, migración y movilidad ocupacional en áreas urbanas en Colombia." Programa Naciones Unidas, Proyecto Oficina Internacional de Trabajo sobre Migraciones Laborales, Bogotá. Final report, mimeo.

León, Magdalena. 1985. "The Program for Domestic Servants in Colombia/El Programa de Servicio Doméstico de Colombia." Paper presented at the Twelfth Congress of the Latin American Studies Association.

Rey de Marulanda, Nohra. 1981. "El trabajo de la mujer." Centro de Estudios sobre Desarrollo Económica, Universidad de los Andes, Bogotá.

———. 1985. "Discusión metodológica y conceptual acerca de la medición del trabajo de la mujer en América Latina." In Elssy Ramos, ed., *La medición del trabajo femenino en América Latina: Problemas teóricos y metodológicos,* pp. 205–22. Bogotá: Plaza y Janés.

Vallejo, Nancy. 1982. "Situación socio-jurídica del servicio doméstico en Colombia." Tesis, Facultad de Derecho, Universidad de los Andes, Bogotá.

Wainerman, Catalina, and Zulma Recchini de Lattes. 1981. *El trabajo femenino en el banquillo de los acusados: La medición censal en América Latina.* México, D.F.: El Consejo de Población y Terra Nova.

17 Sharpening the Class Struggle: The Education of Domestic Workers in Cuba

ELENA GIL IZQUIERDO

As in every real revolution, that of the Cuban people inherited from capitalism many nefarious things, including discrimination against women because of sex, race, and social origin.

Not only for ethical reasons but also because women are an important and powerful factor in building a new society, from the start the Cuban Revolution tried to unite the great feminine mass, giving this effort priority as one of its most urgent tasks. The different progressive women's groups that had participated in the struggle before the victory of the revolution merged into one organization. This necessary unification created the Federación de Mujeres Cubanas or FMC (Federation of Cuban Women) as we know it today, with its more than two million members. The primary and permanent task of the FMC is to educate women so that they arrive at a mature understanding of how, why, and for what purpose they should become active participants in the new society. In the context of this specific task the supreme leader of the revolution, Commander-in-Chief Fidel Castro, singled out two urgent objectives: the education of female "domestics," and the education of peasant women.

The Domestics

Domestics constituted a large segment of the female population, mainly in the cities and larger towns. At that time it was calculated that there were about 50,000 domestics in Havana alone and a few less in the rest of the country. This social group was made up almost entirely of women of very humble origin: peasants who had migrated to the city from the countryside looking for work, and women from the poor suburbs of the city—usually with very large families—who were struggling to survive. They were an easy prey for iniquitous exploitation by the country's upper and middle classes.

Domestics were dependent on a miserable salary that they knew they could lose at any moment, given the ease with which they could be replaced because of the existing high unemployment rate. They were subject to the daily influence of the environment and mentality of the bourgeoisie; they were isolated in the homes of their masters, lacking any contact with the struggle of the working class, without the possibility that this class could defend them. Domestics were not allowed to organize in labor unions, nor could they participate in the political struggle by voting (beca·ise their vote was co-opted and used freely by their masters). They could not better their lot in other ways because they could be instantly fired. In these circumstances, as simple spectators and victims of a situation that would end with revolutionary victory, the revolution caught them unaware.

As we said before, the education plan came out of the concern of Compañero Fidel and the Revolutionary Government to incorporate massively and in an active manner the most humble levels of our population. Among these, because of their characteristics, women in domestic service and peasant women represented the most backward sectors, the ones most subordinated to the ideological influence of the bourgeoisie. That is why Compañero Fidel decided that together with the literacy campaign, special schools had to be established for domestics and peasant women, with the double objective of raising their cultural level and, at the same time, freeing them of the influence of the bourgeoisie. This would be accomplished through the study of the social realities that had determined their servitude and of the ideological principles of our revolution, which opened before them the road to a new life.

The School for Teachers

The first step that had to be taken was the preparation of teachers suitable to fulfill this task. These teachers had to be capable of instructing but above all of educating, forming, and maturing the consciousness of those women burdened by a heavy weight of prejudices against the revolution.

The forge for this new type of instructor was the Conrado Benítez School for Women Instructors, a new model school created by the revolution. Six hundred girls came to the school, selected from among thousands of volunteers who had already taught in the mountains and whose early preparation had been in the roughest and most distant places of our countryside.

It was a new kind of school because for the first time it implemented the study-work regimen that later became a central point of our curriculum. Not only did the students prepare themselves to graduate as primary school teachers and revolutionary instructors, but simultaneously they had to organize, direct, and teach in night schools for domestics. Experienced teachers guided their preparation and advised on all aspects of this ambitious plan for the advancement of the domestics. The students would attend class in the morning, study individually or collectively in the afternoon, and in the evening go to their respective schools as either principals or teachers.

The Schools for Domestics

The night schools for domestics in Havana began functioning in April 1961, scarcely two months after the School for Women Instructors opened. During the rest of the year the night schools increased in number and enrollment until in December there were sixty schools with an enrollment of 20,000 students.

Before opening each school, the Federation of Cuban Women and the Party carried out a brief period of agitation and propaganda in the suburb where the new teaching center would function. They convoked meetings in the parks in which the revolutionary instructors would participate, and they distributed leaflets from house to house and in food stores where domestics, buying daily supplies for the homes where they worked, constituted the majority of the customers.

This is how the domestics learned that in the schools they would be trained for another kind of work with a better salary, and without the shame and taunts that accompanied the work they were then doing. The response to these efforts of the FMC and the Party was a massive turnout and the enthusiastic participation of thousands of women, who filled the schools to overflowing.

The schools for domestics used buildings occupied by primary schools in the daytime, and each was named for a woman who had a notable role in the liberation of peoples, beginning with the martyrs of our country's wars of independence. This decision was made in order to honor heroic women who in all times and in every nation have offered their lives for freedom; it also served to begin making domestics aware of a world as yet unknown to them: that of struggle, of humanity's tireless fight for a better society.

The study program of the schools was based on assignments corresponding to the primary grades, but it also included a daily forty-five-minute period of revolutionary instruction conducted by the director—not to provide theoretical knowledge of Marxism but simply to explain to the students the tangible problems the revolution was facing daily. In the houses where they had worked they heard innumerable malicious accounts of the purposes and the work of the revolution. Some of them were even influenced by these opinions and could in turn influence the rest of their families, who were also poor. For this reason the objective of this revolutionary instruction was to claim these women and their families for the revolution and to keep them from becoming confused by the counterrevolution, widening in this way the support base of the revolution and, at the same time, preparing domestics for work that was not demeaning.

The revolutionary instruction they received every night permitted these women to participate in street discussions with the solid and clear arguments they had learned in school. This was a valuable help during certain events that occurred in those times, as when a false decree was circulated and there was a rumor that the revolution was going to take away parents' rights. The servants, enlightened in the schools, confronted that rumor with great energy and decisiveness.

At that time many curious things happened. The first right that servants demanded in some homes was that they be permitted to leave at a certain hour to go to school (since they lived in the houses of the people they served, the family was accustomed to the servant's being always on call and absent only on her day off). When domestics began to leave at the same hour every day, the first clash between the subjugated women and the bourgeoisie took place, the first quickening of the class struggle of which they were not even yet aware but in which they were already an active force.

In each school, as rapidly as possible, a delegation of the Federation of Cuban Women was organized. This small nucleus, already integrated by the most decisive and enthusiastic women, encouraged the others to advance on the road of learning. On Fridays the delegations collaborated with the school administration, preparing modest artistic events in which the women themselves would participate, even providing ideas for the little plays they put on. Occasionally in these functions a brief statement was included concerning a burning political question of the day, but political teaching was present in the very design of the theatrical presentations—which reflected facts from their lives in the homes of their masters—and also in the lyrics of the revolutionary songs they sang.

The Revolutionary Government again demonstrated its concern for them and for their school attendance by assigning a modest monthly stipend of five pesos for the cost of transportation. They received this stipend in a check (just like the ones their masters used!) that could be cashed at the bank. It is surprising how this detail made them feel more confident. In order not to lose this aid, they would take care to achieve the minimal class attendance required for receiving the check.

In this way, step by step, we fulfilled the objective of claiming them for the revolution. The other objective, preparing them for dignified work, was approached by organizing a boarding school to train these women in different specialties; it succeeded in accommodating more than 1,700 students in each of its courses.

The School of Specialization for Domestics began to function eight months after the opening of the night schools. It was installed in the lecture halls of the Catholic University of Villanueva, used before only by the children of the richest families. The students lived in various mansions nearby, where some of them had worked during the prerevolutionary stage. Their concern and care in maintaining the furniture and valuable decorations left behind by the owners as an inheritance for the revolution was admirable. Later, the school was transferred to the National Hotel (the best in the city until the Hilton chain was introduced into the country's economy), where it took over two floors of the hotel and used all its services, including the attendance of the hotel staff in the dining room.

The students would enter the School of Specialization after finishing sixth grade in night school; since they had to leave their jobs to do so, they were assigned a stipend of thirty pesos a month so that they could continue to meet the needs of their families. They were taught in groups a variety of courses: shorthand, typing, accounting, management of telephone exchanges, preparation for specific bank jobs. Some received training as teachers of the people, pedagogical auxiliaries, and sports instructors.

The Graduates

One of the first experiences of the graduates' incorporation into new jobs was in the Institute of Urban Reform. Since its staff was not large enough to handle the plans that had to be implemented, a number of young women were chosen from the school to be specially prepared to work in the new system of collecting payment for the use of housing.

Bank employees had always been part of the aristocratic sector of the labor movement, a sector that did not feel linked to the common destiny of workers. When the exodus of professionals began, provoked by imperialism to weaken the revolution, their domestic servants were trained to take over their jobs.

In the case of the banks and the urban reform office, there are some nice anecdotes to relate. One day, after the young women had started to take over some jobs, including that of cashier, a former mistress who went to the bank to cash a check found herself at the window of her ex-servant. That encounter made an impact: a humiliation that wounded her in the deepest part of her being, her sense of class. Rarely had the past so clearly confronted the present.

These new job experiences were successful for the former domestics, and they were not the only ones. When an institution such as the Ministry of Internal Commerce needed a number of graduates for a certain kind of work, it would notify the School of Specialization, and a group would be trained in the appropriate courses with the help of technicians from whatever institution required them.

In the first class, 1,068 young women were graduated in office work. Of these 865 went to fill vacancies in branches of the National Bank of Cuba; four who were exceptional in shorthand joined the stenography staff of the Revolutionary Government; the remaining 199 took jobs as auxiliary office workers in other state offices. In the following years, although enrollment fell off as the "domestic" sector of the economy diminished, the contribution of the School of Specialization for Domestics included 208 shorthand/typists, 50 accounting auxiliaries, 191 telephone operators, 24 sports auxiliaries, 30 pedagogical auxiliaries, and 65 teachers for people in the mountainous regions.

The School of Specialization functioned for almost five years. During this time the Ministry of Education created various kinds of technical schools, and other state organisms established their own training schools. Thereafter, the School for Specialization was no longer necessary because the ex-domestics, once they finished their elementary education, could choose the specialization they preferred and take night courses while they worked during the day at their new jobs.

The night schools for domestics functioned for seven years, during which they were extended to the more important towns in the interior of the country: as some of the Conrado Benítez revolutionary instructors were graduated and returned to their homes in distant provinces, the Federation of Cuban Women and the Party became interested in organizing schools in other towns similar to those in Havana. Gradually, thirty schools were opened, drawing approximately 10,000 students living in twenty-six cities or large towns. All the night schools for domestics in the interior were named "Fé del Valle" as a tribute to a person who throughout her life had been a consistent revolutionary and who had been martyred in a contemptible act of sabotage by the hate and desperation of the counterrevolutionaries. The greatest boom in schools for domestics took place between 1962 and 1965, when thirty schools were fully functional in the interior and sixty in Havana.

A characteristic of this type of school, based on the experience of the School of Revolutionary Instructors, was their collective administrative "councils" made up not only of principals, assistants, and teachers but also of student delegates from each classroom. This participation of representatives chosen by the students made for close ties among the professors, the administration, and the student body. The students felt it a privilege to be able to express their judgments and take to the council the point of view of their groups with respect to the schools themselves, their methods, or whatever doubt or difficulty might come up in relation to the development of the revolution.

The student delegate became not only the representative of her *compañeras* but also the advisor of her group concerning the problems she had presented in the council. At the same time, in each classroom a group of students learned how to organize assemblies for purposes of criticism and self-criticism. Sometimes it was a marvel to experience the logic, common sense, and revolutionary spirit that kept on growing among the students through taking part in these meetings.

Throughout 1964 and 1965, enrollment began to diminish. As the number of graduates grew, especially in Havana, the schools began to close; in 1965–66 only thirty-seven were left. In the interior of the country, however. where the possibility of transferring to other courses was limited, the thirty schools were maintained without any change.

These years provided the revolution with a valuable harvest through its plans for the betterment of women. Today, former domestics are to be found doing all kinds of work in all parts of society as well as in higher education. One of the achievements was to instill in them a desire for knowledge, a desire to reach higher goals. It is not an exaggeration to say that they constituted one of the first "small brooks" forming the great river of the feminine mass that today is being incorporated to build a new society in our country.

Editors' Note

Elena Gil Izquierdo—An Appreciation: As we began our editing work, we requested from the Federation of Cuban Women information on the schools for domestic workers, and we carried on a cordial correspondence with Elena Gil Izquierdo, who never revealed that she herself was the moving spirit behind these schools. Elena Gil Izquierdo died in April 1985, and we would like to share the following biographical notes supplied, at our request, by the FMC.

Elena Gil Izquierdo was born in Mexico on September 5, 1906, the daughter of a Mexican mother and a Cuban father in a middle-class family. In 1909 the family established itself definitively in Cuba. In 1924 Elena began work at the Cuban Telephone Company, where she joined the revolutionary groups and made her first contacts with the Popular Socialist Party.

Elena worked to organize women and to encourage them to fight for their rights. She joined the National Union of Women and participated in the Third Feminine Congress celebrated in 1939. As a consequence of this struggle in solidarity with other workers, she was forced to retire in 1949. Joining the Association of Retired Telephone Workers, she held the leadership of this group until 1956, when she was removed by government decree because of being a Communist.

With the triumph of the revolution, Elena joined in the preparatory activites of the Cuban delegation to the Latin American Congress of Women, held in Santiago de Chile in 1960. After the founding of the Federation of Cuban Women, she worked in the national office as a member of the bureau and of the national secretariat.

When the Revolutionary Government took over the magazine *Vanidades* (Vanities), Elena was assigned the responsibility of administrative assistant to the editors of *Mujeres* (Women), the publication that came out of the revolution.

In 1961, she became the director of the Ana Betancourt schools for peasant women, one of the most appealing activities that the FMC carried out in its early years. A militant in the Communist Party of Cuba, she was a member of its central committee for fifteen years. In 1976, she led the Movement for Peace and Sovereignty of the People, a labor that she carried out with the responsibility and tenacity that characterized all her activities until 1982, when she retired because of serious health problems.

"Elena Gil, active, responsible, efficient worker and concerned mother, conscientious revolutionary who fulfilled her duties until the last moment of her life."

Vilma Espin, speaking at the memorial service, April 27, 1985

PART V

In Their Own Words:
Testimonies of Workers

18 Domestic Workers in Rio de Janeiro: Their Struggle to Organize

ANAZIR MARIA DE OLIVEIRA ("ZICA") and ODETE MARIA DA CONCEIÇÃO
with Hildete Pereira de Melo

In writing this history of the struggles of domestic workers in Rio de Janeiro, Hildete Pereira de Melo used the text of the Rio de Janeiro Domestic Workers' Professional Association titled "We Do Not Have the Same Rights as the Working Class as a Whole" (1983a), as well as interviews with the leaders of the association, who thus are co-authors of this report. Zica is president of the association; Odete founded the domestic workers' movement in Brazil. What follows is essentially theirs.

Domestic workers are migrants. They come from the countryside, hoping to improve their lot. They are young girls who get jobs as domestic workers in big cities. "Life was hard. That's why I left. . . . Nobody came because they chose to. I didn't have a choice; I came out of necessity" (NOVA 1982, 12).

The domestic worker leaves her family, which is waiting for her to come back, and moves into the household of another family not her own. "You live in a house that has everything, that you clean, and you don't have access to. . . . the only thing you have some access to is your own room . . . but you can't bring people into your room. There are households that don't even let you bring in a friend" (NOVA 1982, 16).

The domestic worker faces a series of problems. She wants to have the right to an education to improve her lot, but she is unable to get it because she has no rights. She belongs to the family she works for. She has no work schedule, nothing at all. She is very oppressed. While she is still a girl, she gets a job in a household, and she dedicates herself to the care of this family. "I found out why nobody in that household wanted me to study. Because they couldn't do without me. And they were afraid that if I studied, I would leave" (NOVA 1982, 14).

In 1960, faced with a reality that did not change over time, a group of domestic workers became aware of their situation of helplessness and exploitation. They decided that it was necessary to join forces to change their lives. The domestic workers who took part in Ação Católica (Catholic Action), a group from Juventude Operária Católica or JOC (Young Catholic Workers) were the ones who decided to unite and to form an association after seeing (according to Odete) that "whenever domestic workers got together with other workers, everybody argued and we were left behind. We began to meet only with domestics to find a way to get an association started."

Through JOC activities, this movement spread to other Brazilian cities; later, in Rio de Janeiro and São Paulo, work groups got started to form domestic workers' associations.

In December 1961 sixty domestic workers met to form the Associaçao Profissional dos Empregados Domésticos do Rio de Janeiro (Domestic Workers' Professional Association). They made a public declaration denouncing the situation of helplessness and insecurity in which they lived. Acording to Odete, "We are human beings and have dignity." It was the first public demonstration of courage on the part of domestic workers. Each one talked about her hardships and the activities the association should support to protect her workmates. It was a very difficult undertaking because, at that time, domestic workers were unaware of their situation, and it was hard to bring women together to take part in anything. Female domestics were not used to collaborating with others and demanding what was due them.

There was a desire to form an association, but no meeting place was available. It was very difficult to meet. Many times meetings were held on a bench in the *praça*, on the beach, in the parish church. Through the church in Rio de Janeiro we got a small room. It was great because we had a place to keep our literature and the first membership cards and to draw up the statutes. We began the struggle to demand a law that would recognize our rights as workers. With a concerted effort on our part, we began to study our problems, to fight together for our education and for our rights at work, to help each other, and to have an organization that would speak on our behalf to employers and authorities.

In 1963 we managed to hold the first meeting that brought together domestic workers from all over the State of Rio de Janeiro. We studied several legislative bills. For the first time many demands were made: a fixed work schedule, a weekly day off, a fair salary, and a work contract. In 1967 the association with the help of the church managed to rent a house, the first headquarters of the association, where it was possible to carry out other projects: meetings, conventions, services, and courses of study. In 1968 we held the second state meeting and the First Domestic Workers' National Convention in São Paulo. One hundred domestic workers from the States of Maranhão, Paraíba, Pernambuco, Bahia, Minas Gerais, Rio de Janeiro, Rio Grande do Sul, and São Paulo were present. It was a great step forward. For four days we discussed our situation in relation to the authorities. We demanded a fair labor law and social security.

Finally, in 1972, the Brazilian parliament approved Law No. 5859 (Governo do Brasil 1972), which covered some of our demands: the use of employment books,[1] vacations, and social security. Not much, but a beginning! The struggle to organize domestic workers nationally went on, and in April 1974 the second Domestic Workers' National Convention was held in Rio de Janeiro. The five associations in Brazil (São Paulo, Rio de Janerio, Belo Horizonte, Juiz de Fora, and Piracicaba) took part in the national convention; in addition, groups of domestic workers came from several other cities. In spite of some dissenting opinions, the objectives of the five associations were the same:

- the human, social and professional development of domestic workers;
- the organization and formation of class consciousness;
- the rendering of services;
- the association as the representative organization of domestic workers in the expression of their needs and hopes and in the defense of their rights and demands.

The second convention, nevertheless, concluded that the biggest problems facing domestic workers in the entire country, were low salaries and the lack of work schedules. According to Zica:

Domestic workers feel devalued, humiliated, and want to leave their profession because they cannot find the stimulus to stay and better themselves. The situation of domestic workers can be changed only through their own initiative, beginning with their becoming aware of their reality and their value as human beings and as workers.

Regarding domestic work legislation, the convention concluded that it was not complete: Law No. 5859 did not cover all the benefits other workers are entitled to by law.

In 1978, at the third Domestic Workers' National Convention, held in Belo Horizonte, a labor law identical to that of other workers was demanded again, and the desire that domestic workers would have their associations all over the country was stressed. In January 1981 the fourth Domestic Workers' National Convention, held in Porto Alegre, brought together eighty-two delegates from eight associations from the cities of Recife (State of Pernambuco); Patos (State of Paraíba); Belo Horizonte, Uberaba, and Monte Carmelo (State of Minas Gerais); São Paulo, Campinas, Piracicaba, Araçatuba and Fernandópolis (State of São Paulo); Rio de Janeiro (State of Rio de Janeiro); Curitiba (State of Paraná); Florianópolis (State of Santa Catarina); and Porto Alegre, Pelotas, and Erexim (State of Rio Grande do Sul).

At this convention it was concluded that domestic workers are not valued as human beings or professionals. They work all day long, do not have a weekly day off, and receive salaries below the minimum wage. According to Odete: "There are domestic workers who have been working in households for seventeen years, and the *patroas* don't pay their social security. They don't pay, period." Building contractors do not follow the construction code regarding the size and ventilation requirements for rooms for live-in domestics in apartment buildings. Domestic workers enjoy only minimum work protection; therefore, we demand an eight-hour working day, a minimum wage, a paid day off per week, family salary, termination notice in advance, a retirement fund, one-month extra pay, maternity benefits, accident insurance, and the upgrading of domestic worker legislation to match that of rural workers regarding holidays. We insist on the recognition of the professional category of "domestic worker" so that we can form unions.

The struggle to guarantee the rights of the domestic worker is difficult. Zica tells the case of a typical worker:

She's been working for twenty years for the same family. Her employment book was signed in 1973 by her employers for the first time. Her employer hasn't been paying social security for two years. Because of that she lost her rights, and she is now fifty-eight years old and almost ready to retire. Another case was that of a girl brought up in a household from fifteen years of age. She never received any wages, but she did everything in the house. It was not until 1978 that her employment book was signed. And what about the period between 1963 and 1977? And what about the wages she is not receiving?

It is difficult to get domestic workers to bring their complaints to trial. They are afraid. Some do come to the association for help, and we study their cases and set dates to go to court, but often they do not show up when they are supposed to. Those who do go to court lose their jobs. Even their participation in our conventions is sufficient reason to lose their jobs. A young woman from Paraíba was fired upon returning from our convention in Porto Alegre. She is still without a job because nobody wants to hire her. According to Zica: "One of the difficulties the association has with these young women is their way of doing things because of their fear to create problems for their *patroas*. In addition, they work in isolation."

It is very hard to go into a family household. In a factory, for instance, fifty or a hundred people work together; the domestic worker is by herself and under the influence of her *patroa*. The domestic worker brings up the *patroa*'s child. If she makes the slightest mistake, she is fired on the spot, because it is very easy to get another domestic worker. The live-out domestic worker faces a different position because she is in the same situation as the working class: getting up very early in the morning, transportation problems, and cost of living. On the other hand, the live-in domestic worker goes shopping with her employer's money and goes home only on her days off.

The day worker knows that her home is somewhere else and that her family lives there. It is a good idea for the domestic to get out of her employer's house. Every domestic should be aware that she must have her own place. The employer's house is her place of work; she also needs to have a place to live. Domestics need to have their own places in order to feel their hardships as poor working persons. It is necessary for them to get out of their employers' houses and to assume their poverty.

The convention also denounced the exploitative aspects of the work performed by girls who, starting at seven or eight years of age, come from the countryside to big cities in order to get a job in a family house:

> I began working at age nine as a babysitter for two children. I worked and studied until I was eleven. Afterward I went to work for a family with three children. [Zica's words]
> I began to work early. I was ten years old when I arrived here and began to work in Caxias [county in the state of Rio de Janeiro] looking after a child. At age fourteen I came to this house, and I have been working here for the last forty years. [Odete's words]

Nowadays, all these associations celebrate April 27 as Domestic Workers' Day.[2] For the first time, on this day in 1983, they demonstrated in a public square in Rio de Janeiro, demanding that

> (1) domestic workers be respected as human beings and workers by the families for which they work and by society at large;
> (2) domestic work legislation be expanded immediately to include the rights granted to other professional categories;
> (3) our associations be recognized as class organizations so that we can join in the common struggle for the liberation of workers. [Associação Profissional dos Empregados Domésticos do Rio de Janeiro 1983b]

The association's struggle is the class struggle of domestic workers. We view the association as the domestic workers' union, where we are involved in the defense of our rights, carrying the banner of our emancipation in society. The association's leadership thinks of it as a workers' organization, not a female organization, so much so that our name is written *Empregados Domésticos*. [*Translator's note: Both male and female domestic workers are included when the masculine plural form is used.*] We once had a male association member who later vanished. "In our struggle we never think about asserting ourselves as women, but as workers" (internal document of the Domestic Workers' Professional Association).

However, this contradiction usually appears when we talk about the number of female members—800. According to Zica:

Among the working class it is hard to recruit members. Something I find interesting is the difficulty in dealing with women. When we formed our group in Vila Aliança, we wanted to do something, but we didn't quite know how to go about it. Getting a meeting place wasn't difficult; we got advice and encouragement from a priest. However, getting people to come to the meetings was very hard because most were day workers and they had only weekends to be with their own children . . . because, in addition to being domestic workers, they are also women. This creates obligations to husband and children. If they don't realize that they must fight for their rights, they'll never have them.

Thus, in October 1983 at the Rio de Janeiro–Espírito Santo Regional Meeting of Domestic Workers, the need to overcome many difficulties was acknowledged. Why? (1) Because we are women; (2) because domestic work is not valued (men say we do nothing); and (3) because we live in isolation. We need to get together and discover new things about our reality and value, and, more than ever, we need to find new ways to join forces in our struggle.

Nowadays there are associations in fourteen cities in Brazil (Rio de Janeiro, São Paulo, Piracicaba, Campinas, Brasília, Recife, Porto Alegre, Pelotas, Passo Fundo, Curitiba, Florianópolis, Belo Horizonte, Uberaba, and Juiz de Fora).[3] The work of these associations is important. They provide help and shelter, hold social and cultural meetings, publish newsletters, and, in São Paulo, offer training for other professions and run an employment agency for domestic workers. We understand that our associations can grow only with our efforts to secure the individual and professional recognition we deserve as domestics in society.

Until 1981 the association's participation in activities with the union movement was kept at a minimum, but after that year it increased. We took part in the organization of the First Working Class National Convention (Congresso Nacional da Classe Trabalhadora or CONCLAT) by sending four delegates. We sent eight delegates to the second convention and seventeen to the latest Working Class State Meeting (Encontro Estadual da Classe Trabalhadora or ENCLAT). Right now we have one of our members in the National Coordinating Committee for the United Workers Central Union (Central Única dos Trabalhadores or CUT).

The organization of domestic workers continues, and in January

1985 the fifth Domestic Workers' National Convention was held in Olinda (State of Pernambuco) with the participation of 126 delegates from the States of Ceará, Rio Grande do Norte, Paraíba, Pernambuco, Alagoas, Bahia, Minas Gerais, Espírito Santo, Rio de Janeiro, São Paulo, Paraná, Santa Catarina, Rio Grande do Sul, and the Federal District. The Rio de Janeiro Association with thirty-four delegates and the São Paulo Association sent the two largest delegations.

At the convention, it was concluded that inhuman and unfair working conditions, denounced in previous conventions, persisted in spite of the fact that domestic workers form the largest category of working women in Brazil and that we represent a very important force in the economic, social, and cultural life of our country. (Imagine what would happen to our country if we, the domestic workers, were to strike!) In view of our real value and importance to our society, we called upon our associates not to feel ashamed of being *compañeras* and to assert themselves as women, professionals, and members of the working class. We resolved to continue organizing ourselves in neighborhoods and cities, to expand grassroots activities to groups, to form and to get official status for our associations. Only if we are organized as class associations can we offer our associates the conditions they hope to achieve for their defense and recognition, and render services leading to a greater awareness. We agree that we must work toward a free, independent, and strong Domestic Workers' Union in the future. We call upon all workers' unions to view us as an integral part of the working class. The convention approved a bill expanding domestic worker legislation, to be used by the Brazilian parliament as a guideline:

1. Minimum wage, subject only to social security withholdings, given the specific conditions of domestic work.
2. The need to guarantee school attendance for minor domestic workers, and light work that poses no health hazards and does not prevent their physical and psychological development.
3. A thirty-day vacation, on equal terms with other workers.
4. An eight-hour working day, with the possibility of overtime at 20 percent over the hourly pay rate. Overtime for one day can be exchanged for a shorter work schedule another day if it does not exceed forty-eight hours a week.
5. A weekly day off as well as religious and official holidays.
6. One month's extra pay.
7. A twelve-week maternity leave with pay funded by the Social

Security Administration (Instituto Nacional de Previdencia Social, INPS). Employers will pay 0.3 percent more to the Social Security Administration to help defray this benefit.

8. The right to register the Domestic Workers' Association with the Regional Labor Councils and the right to have counsel in individual or collective disputes before a labor court. [Associaçao Profissional do Empregados Domésticos 1968–85]

Enough of suffering and oppression, a legacy from the time of slavery. We demand fairness in the recognition of our profession, which must be on an equal footing with that of other workers.

Notes

1. The employment book is a document showing the employment status of workers, their salaries, and the tasks they are to perform in their jobs. Anyone holding an urban job (in the industrial, trade, or service sectors) on a permanent basis and receiving a salary is protected by the Consolidation of Labor Laws (CLT) legislation, which does not, however, cover domestic workers. The rights of *domésticas* are guaranteed by separate legislation (Law No. 5859/72, Decree No. 71885/73 [Governo do Brasil 1972; 1973], and Law No. 6887/80). Therefore, domestic workers have only the following rights: remuneration for their services, twenty days of vacation, and social security benefits and services (provided they pay for them). Having their employment books signed by their employers allows domestic workers to enjoy these rights.

2. The Domestic Workers' Professional Association established April 27 as the holiday for domestic workers. The Catholic Church celebrates Saint Zita, a domestic worker, on that day.

3. *Editors' Note:* As this book goes to press (Spring 1988), the associations have increased to thirty-three in twenty-two cities.

References

Associação Profissional dos Empregados Domésticos do Rio de Janeiro. 1968–85. Resoluçaos do I, II, III, IV y V Congressos Nacionales das Empregados Domésticos, Brasil. Rio de Janeiro.

———. 1983a. "Não temos os dereitos a classe trabalhadora tem como um todo." In *Mulheres en Movimento,* Proyecto Mulher, Instituto de Ação Cultural (IDAC). Rio de Janeiro: Editora Marco Zero.

———. 1983b. "Comemoração do dia da empregada doméstica, carta a las autoridades, 27 de abril." Rio de Janeiro.

NOVA—Pesquisa, Assessoramento e Evaliação em Educaçao. 1982. "Só a gente que vive é que sabe: Depoimento de uma doméstica." *Cadernos de Educação Popular* 4:9–78.

19 The History of Our Struggle

SINTRASEDOM (National Union of Household Workers, Colombia)

In 1977 a group of household workers met in the streets and parks of Bogotá. The outcome is that we decided to issue a proclamation that would reveal the problems that concern us and our need to organize. We were invited by two sociologists to participate in the Congress of working women that took place November 4–5 of 1977, where we explained in a paper some of our problems:

- The fact that there is no minimum wage for working as a household employee. The exploitation of minors who are not paid because it is thought that young girls do not have the necessary capacity or the knowledge to work at a job.
- The fact that many of our companions become old with their health ruined; they are oppressed, working in one or more homes, with no compensation, pension, social security and without legal protection.
- The fact that young girls are brought from the countryside to be kept as slaves; they are paid with secondhand clothes or low salaries, and they are mistreated. The *patrones* take advantage of them.
- The fact that many household workers can neither read nor write; they are not given time to study, nor to go out, and that is why few can prepare themselves for the future.

Because of all these problems, the idea was born of forming a union to bring us together in our common defense, and that is how on July 18, 1978, the first General Assembly took place with the presence of twenty-six members. In this assembly we agreed to compose the documents to send to the Ministry of Labor. The juridical status of the organization—a necessary first step to unionization—was not conceded at first because the identity number was missing from the petition, and it was returned to us according to resolution 03275 of August 30, 1978. The second assembly took place on April 11, 1979, with thirty-one members present. Again, we sent the documentation to obtain juridical status.[1] Again, it was denied with the excuse that family residences were not businesses motivated by profit.

On November 2, 1979, for the third time documents were presented to the Ministry of Labor and Social Security; by then we had forty-eight members. Again, the petition was denied for the same reason as above. Faced with such government injustice, we presented a demand to the Council of State on January 16, 1981. The Council of State also denied our request, arguing that the president of our organization did not have a professional degree in labor law. In 1982 the papers were returned to us by the Council of State. Finally, the union was legally recognized on January 10, 1985 (resolution 0012).

In 1982, planning began for the First National Meeting of Domestic Service Workers, which took place in December 1983. This was a very signigicant event for us in which more than eighty persons participated. (Elsewhere in this paper there are detailed comments on the meeting.)

Activities since 1974

Some of the founders of SINTRASEDOM belonged to a savings and credit cooperative for domestic workers connected to a religious center that provided services to train domestics. It was managed by ladies who were not themselves domestic workers. Why should we have a union?

> Because, as for me, I learned that I ought to defend my rights on my own, I really did not need the union, but what happens? . . . there are many girls who do not know how to look out for themselves, they do not know how to speak up. At that time, I had thought a lot about that, since I had connections with other organizations, at least in school. There the household worker is helped a lot, but not to defend her rights. We also had a cooperative, but what happens? . . . The cooperative helps you economically when a calamity strikes, but it does not help you to speak up for your rights.

That is why there is a need to form a union. Because we have a school where more or less we can progress in our studies, a cooperative which can help us with our savings—a bit, a lot, some—then they can give us credit through our savings, but the juridical part is not provided by the cooperative, nor the school, but a union, on the contrary, seems to me the ideal organization for these things. [From an interview with one of the founders][2]

We had been meeting periodically on Sunday for courses on union matters, labor law, and to show movies. In 1980, elementary school courses were given, oriented by volunteers from the Instituto Sindical (Union Institute) María Cano, ISMAC. In 1981, Capacitación Popular (Training for the People) provided elementary school courses and courses on union work. We have carried out field trips and organized seminars for training the managing directorate of the union. In 1983, courses in cloth painting, leather work, tailoring, sewing, and human relations were offered. Why does the union have courses in literacy? "In order to be better trained and acquire more understanding, whether the domestics want to continue with their present work or change occupations" [interview with a SINTRASEDOM leader].[3]

Since May 4, 1983, the union has had an office that attends to the different needs of its members. On October 25 we were interviewed on television; as a result of that interview, there was a need to create an employment agency, which opened on October 26, 1983. Union members, other organizations, and private persons have participated in these activities, and that has helped us carry many of them out.

Despite our efforts, in 1980 less than 5 percent of domestic employees in Bogotá were members of SINTRASEDOM.[4] We have encountered many obstacles in maintaining the union:

• Pressures brought about by the *patrones* against the union.
• Lack of economic resources. Other groups that serve the needs of domestic workers (such as juridical counseling, courses, etc.) receive loans from international organizations or they are financed by the church. As for us, we have had to basically count on ourselves and on the help of researchers and other local organizations. Only for the meeting did we receive some external help.
• The isolation that characterizes domestic work makes it difficult for domestic workers to meet with their companions and to become aware of their situation.

• The difficulties in gaining the attention of domestic workers for national campaigns, such as the one we have begun for the purpose of informing them on how to enroll in the Social Security Institute (see Appendix A).

SINTRASEDOM'S Heroic
First President

Pastora Jiménez, our first president, was the victim of the oppression of her employers. When her *patrones* found out that she belonged to the directing council of the union, they started making life impossible for her, demanding that she resign from the union and never return there. To which she answered, "They had no right to force me to resign, because that was something only my *compañeras* had a right to do."

They put on these pressures because Pastora was an intelligent and responsible officer who confronted those who attacked us. She was attacked so often that on May 8, 1979, she decided to take her own life rather than betray the organization. She was miraculously saved, but her health was broken, and she could not return to the organization. Nor were we permitted to visit her or call her by telephone. The same thing happened to María Carmen and other colleagues who were humiliated and fired. They had to go from job to job because of persecution, and labor and social injustice.

The First National Meeting

The objectives, organization, and conclusions of the First National Meeting of Domestic Service Workers are described in what follows. The reason we met was, and continues to be, the difficult situation that we domestic workers encounter: workdays of 12, 16, or 18 hours; salaries very much lower than the legal minimum salary recognized by the government; lack of social benefits; discriminatory labor legislation; lack of respect; authoritarian and humiliating treatment and violation of the right to privacy.

Because of all these factors a group of companions organized in SINTRASEDOM met every Sunday to think about and analyze the innumerable problems of the sector. The situation is very similar for the workers of the rest of the country, and we already had had the opportunity of visiting the groups that are in the process of organizing in different cities (such as Cali, Barranquilla, Bucaramanga, Fusagasugá), and that is how we have established permanent communication and correspondence. Because of all of this we decided to hold the First National Meeting of Domestic Workers in Bogotá in December 1983.

In order to organize an event so important for us, we set for ourselves a number of tasks that were fulfilled little by little with a lot of hard work. The meeting itself was organized by domestic workers from different parts of the country (such as Cali, Barranquilla, Bucaramanga, Bogotá) and a special guest: a colleague from the sister country of Peru, Adelinda Díaz.

The development of the congress was guided by the following work methodology; it was an active affair more than an expository one, and it had a fixed agenda.

Sector Problems

- Treatment by the *patrones*
- Payment in cash or goods
- Free time, vacations
- Studies
- Work contracts
- Social security
- Work schedule
- Half-yearly bonus
- Termination notice, settlement of back pay, indemnifications

The groups analyzed these problems in the following way: as a rule the *patrones* treat their employees poorly; the domestic servant may not be respected sexually; she is accused of stealing objects lost by the *patrona;* there is a lack of communication with the *patrones;* and there is discrimination during leisure hours. Domestics are not allowed to study. It is common for the domestic to be lent to family members. For many, domestic tasks are not really considered work. Work contracts are not written up but rather are verbally agreed to, leaving the domestic servant without protection.

There are no established hours for the workday; when the *patrones* arrive, we have to get up. Generally, days off are conditioned; we have neither a regular nor a continuous rest period. Free days are given to us every two weeks or every month; very few get off every Sunday. Most domestic servants do not have vacations, or if we get them, we are not paid.

We have no benefits, not even health benefits, because we do not have social security. The salary is paid according to the economic circumstances of the hiring family; taking into account the family status, it is established in the following ways: upper class, 4,000 to 6,000 (Colombian pesos); middle class, 1,000 to 3,500 (Colombian pesos). Taking into account that part is given in goods, especially used objects, these salaries are low.

Work hours: the workday can be 12, 16, and 18 hours long, with no extra pay. If a domestic works well, she gets more work.

Notices and settlements: domestic service has been considered a nonproductive activity; therefore the labor code for domestics is known only in exceptional cases. The worker is given no protection and is abused and fired without just cause.

Experiences in Organizing

To these questions

- How did the work of the group begin?
- How did each member come into the group?
- In the last few months what has been done in the group or in the organization?
- What difficulties are encountered in the work of organization?

the groups responded in the following way:

- The workers in other sectors have a lack of awareness of our problems.
- The values of domestic workers are acquired from radio, television, religion, and the *patrones* themselves.
- Among the members of the union there is individualism, racism, sectarianism, and personal interest.

• There also is the intervention of political sectors and parties under the guise of fulfilling union objectives, but which actually have nothing to do with those objectives and which bring with them problems and divisions for the group.

• There is also repression by state organizations and the *patrones:* threats, aggressive actions, and psychological pressure.

Labor Legislation

• Work contract
• Trial period
• Work day
• Extra hours
• Social benefits
• Social security
• Sick leave; maternity leave; time off for accidents and invalidism; old age pension and death benefits
  • A regimen for those who have children and live with them
  • Minimum salary
  • Child labor
  • Professionalization or training
  • The socialization of some services that ease the work of the domestic servant

The groups had the following opinion about these topics: in general, most of them said they knew nothing about the small amount of labor legislation on the books. They were made aware of the conditions of household workers, which were the most unjust conditions of all. Since this was the special point of this program and was the most deeply felt of all the issues, it was considered first.

Conclusions of the Meeting

In the second day, work was carried out on the conclusions, which were the result of the meetings of the different groups. It was agreed that there was a need to strengthen the organization by obtaining the participation of workers who lived in working-class districts and who worked by the day, and also the participation of live-in workers, using for this purpose the communications media: talks, conferences, pamphlets, *chapolas,* movies that relate to our shared social problem.

It was also decided to:

• Distribute propaganda in places were workers meet, such as stores, supermarkets, schools where they are trained, parks where they spend their leisure time on Sundays or holidays. To take advantage of the political moment, since workers can now discuss their own and union-related problems and, especially, the problems of the domestic worker.

• Search for closer ties with other entities—popular and worker organizations—that can strengthen the union.

• Find more appropriate hours for meetings with workers and continue with the program of women's formation in general.

• Teach members of the union the objectives, duties, and rights they have in the organization.

• Write documents concerning such topics as the problems of domestic servants in Colombia and in other Latin American countries.

• Edit a national and international journal and establish a mechanism of communication with different national and international groups.

• Develop a legislative proposal that will provide the form in law for a Substantive Code of the Domestic Worker, taking into account that we should be treated as humans like any other workers, and that should include the following:

Trial period. both live-in domestics and those who live out should have a month-long trial period in their jobs.

Workday. domestics should work no more than ten hours a day, including two hours for meals.

Study. domestics should have the right to study, outside of work hours.

Salary. the minimum salary should be respected, but providing for increases for years on the job. For live-out domestics, the proposal is to increase daily pay on a percentage basis in order to include pay for Sundays in the six days of the week. To pay up to one-third of the salary in goods; if the domestic has a baby, one-half the salary can be paid in goods, but no more than half. In this case, the employer maintains the baby; otherwise only one-third of the minimum salary can be paid in goods.

Extra Hours. after ten hours of a normal workday, overtime work must be paid with an add-on charge of 35 percent if it is during the day and 75 percent if it is during the night. Work on holidays or Sundays is to have a 100 percent overtime charge; at the same time the normal pay rate for those days, as established by the contract, is respected.

Contract. to establish clearly in the contract the rights and the duties of the employees and the *patrones,* including the form of treatment and mutual respect.

These are other rights in the program of struggle of SIN-TRASEDOM:

• To find out through Family Compensation Service how to obtain collective insurance for union members.
• To petition the Colombian Institute of Family Welfare to obtain child-care service for the children of domestics, and to take the necessary steps to create a child-care center in the union.
• To start a specialized training center for employees, for example, in the care of children, sick people, nutrition, etc.
• To create a cooperative for domestic servants.
• To take into account the proposal that came out of the meeting that took place in October of 1983 in Mexico City of organizing a meeting of domestic servants at a Latin American level where a document will be elaborated to present to the International Labor Office in defense of domestic service.

(For an evaluation of the importance of having such an organization as SINTRASEDOM, see Appendix B.)

SINTRASEDOM Today

Today SINTRASEDOM has 180 members. Consider this recent testimony by Compañera Lucila Morales, secretary of the organization:

"It was in 1979 that I learned of the group of domestic workers SINTRASEDOM. On May 1, as I was going to participate in a workers' march to which I had been invited, I met this group. After this I did not return. But one day the treasurer called me to participate in a meeting, and from then on I became fully integrated with the group.

"We kept on meeting every Sunday, and a meeting place was lent to us. Some times we met in the parks because we did not have a fixed place to meet. We rented an office together with another organization; from May 1979 until May 1980 we were open to the public one afternoon a week. We did not continue to do this because we did not have money. That same year we obtained lecture halls in the Autonomous University, and from then on we dedicated ourselves to a recruitment campaign, inviting our companions to become members; we also taught reading and writing.

"As part of the campaign, we did a program in the National Park. During this time we also fought for our legal standing that had been three times denied to us. But we have continued to struggle for this objective, and we invite all our companions in domestic service to support us, and the same for all our companions in union organizations, given that in Colombia there is a great number of domestic servants."

Next follows a personal history narrated by one of our *compañeras*. It could be our own history of S I N T R A S E D O M:

"I was born on the ninth of October, of a year without a number. My parents did not love me, I was rejected when I was born because they wanted a boy. Neither my mother nor my brothers wanted me. My mother would go to town and leave me with my brothers, who would take care of me until she returned. My brothers did not want to see me; they would break things and say I had done it, blaming me for everything. My mother then would punish me, even though it was all a lie. I would wait for my mother in the street, but she would always elude me.

"When I was eighteen, my father died, and life became more complicated because my brothers threw me out, and I came to Bogotá. My mother said I should leave home because she did not want to see me again. Because of this loneliness I fell in love, and a child was born, but his father abandoned me without giving me any help. The *patrona* also threw me out, and I became a squatter where I live now.

"I worked in many family homes where I was ill-treated; I got tired and left, looking for another way of making a living. I continued working as a domestic during the day, but since I was born a long time ago, in that year without a number . . . no one wants me because of my age. My son is fifteen years old, he married but does not help me. In fact, he does not acknowledge me.

"My problem is that they want to take me from where I live, a shed. The government wants to throw us out because we are in a residential sector of the city. That is why I am going to be without a roof over my head, without family or *patrones*. I came to S I N T R A S E D O M because on the radio I learned that this union existed. It is now my consolation because I have found friends here, companions and collaboration."

Notes

1. At that time, the union's legal counsel was the Instituto Sindical María Cano (ISMAC).
2. Excerpt from an interview with a union leader of SINTRASEDOM in Garcia Castro et al. (1981).
3. Excerpt from an interview with a union leader of SINTRASEDOM in Garcia Castro et al. (1981).
4. "In 1980, about 20 percent of the female work force in the seven most important Colombian cities were concentrated in paid domestic service jobs. In Bogotá, the percentage was near 17.4, that is, 108,182 persons occupied this kind of job; of these, 98.9 percent were women" (Garcia Castro et al. 1981).

Appendix A

Report Prepared for the Asociación Colombiana para el Estudio de la Población (ACEP) Program "Actions to Transform the Social and Work Conditions of Domestic Service in Colombia" Bogotá, D.E.

Membership of Employees of Domestic Service in the Institute of Social Security (ISS) in Bogotá

Every worker who is a member of the ISS has the right to the following benefits: (1) sickness (general and specialized medicine, surgery, laboratory exams, dental care and drugs); (2) maternity; (3) accident; (4) incapacity; (5) old age; (6) death.

In Bogotá, the domestic service worker can become a member of the ISS, assuring herself the benefits described above and freeing the *patrón* of the obligation of providing medical care and pharmaceutical remedies in case of sickness, first aid in case of accident, and the payment of leave for maternity or abortion that is ordered by law.

Procedures

1. *Obtaining the number of the Patrón:* Every *patrona* must have a number in the *patrones* register. In window 8 of calle 19 No. 14-31, first floor, you can ask for the form (original and two copies) that must be filled out, to which must be attached a photocopy of the *patrone's* identity number, which is then brought to window 1, 2, 3, or 4 of the same office. In fifteen days the ISS will reply, assigning a number in the *patrones'* register.

2. *Register of Workers:* Once the number of patronal inscription has been obtained, the form "Report of the registration of workers" is requested at window 8 of that same office. This form is filled out with information about the worker, a photocopy of the worker's identity papers is attached, and it is handed in window 1, 2, 3, or 4 of that same office.

3. *Workers leaving an employment:* In case the worker quits, the *patrona* must request the form for withdrawing (original and two copies) and register the fact immediately; if this is not done, the quota payments will continue until the ISS is notified that the worker is no longer employed there.

4. *Pay:* Every month the ISS will send a receipt to the address registered by the *patrona*. With the authorization of the ISS payment office (first floor of that same building) you can pay at the bank where you have your account, and there you will receive, every two months, the cards certifying the employee's membership. With payment authorization, you must pay at the Treasury of ISS between 8:00 A.M. and 4:00 P.M.

5. *Quotas:* The *patrona* must pay the total value of the receipt of the ISS. In order to do this, the *patrona* will discount from the monthly salary of the worker a sum equivalent to one-third of the quota, and the *patrona* will pay the other two-thirds. The *patrona* can pay the whole sum if it is agreed. *Example:* If the monthly quota assigned by ISS is $1,271.40 the worker must pay $423.80 Colombian pesos and the patrona $847.60 pesos. *Note:* The ISS determines its payments by the number of weeks that the month has (four or five).

6. *Services:* Once the membership form has been presented, the worker remains affiliated and can receive services according to the following schedule:

Immediately: medical care in case of accident.

4 weeks: medical care (general or specialized attention).

12 weeks: has the right not only to medical care but also incapacitation pay provided by the ISS.

300 weeks: can be paid an invalid's pension.

500 weeks: can be paid an old-age pension.

7. *Places where benefits are available:* Services will be provided in the following local centers: North, South, Central or West.

FOR ALL TRANSACTIONS, IT IS IMPORTANT TO PUT DOWN ACCURATELY THE NUMBERS OR THE CODES ASSIGNED BY ISS.

Bogotá, D.E., March 20, 1985.

Appendix B

Mary Garcia Castro

The importance of having an organization like SINTRASEDOM in Colombia also can be evaluated if the kind of work other organizations have done in the past and are doing now in relation to domestic employees is taken into account. In 1981, when we researched domestic service, the situation was the following: most live-in domestic servants received training courses in organizations of lay religious orders such as the Opus Dei. These household workers are between fifteen and twenty years old, recently arrived from the countryside, and many of them are taken by their *patrones* to the training centers. The implicit aim of these lay-religious training centers is maintaining domestic service; therefore, the ideological outlook of the domestic worker is manipulated by spiritualizing the status of servility.

An excerpt from an interview with a director of a training center of a lay-religious nature corroborates this opinion:

> This center is connected to others at the national level. . . . It was created in 1965. Today it has 180 students, and since

1975 it has been trying to provide them with the degree of home auxiliaries. This has been getting very good results. On the other hand, the center emphasizes the dignity of this type of work; this is an important aspect from the point of view of the center's ideological foundations.

The content of the courses that are given in these training centers that have been at work in Bogotá and Medellín for twenty-six years clearly illustrates the philosophy of these institutions. Their clear aim is the support of domestic service, as a service. One of these courses, professional morality, is a two-year course that meets half an hour once a week, for a total of forty hours. In the "general objective of the program" of that course we read that the goals are

> to develop the principles of general morality in the family helpers for their personal lives and for their mission in homes. To provide a sense of eternity to the work, so that they will not be dependent for their satisfaction on the material basis of their pay at the end of the month. To orient the conscience securely, so it will not be abandoned to whim and improvisation.

SINTRASEDOM also has a training program that is guided by the principles of providing elements of a formal education, as well as knowledge about labor legislation and labor advances that promote job mobility, an orientation that differs from that of the lay-religious training centers (Garcia Castro 1982, 109).

At that time another organization coordinated by persons who were not domestics was working in this field, promoting the consciousness-raising of household workers in relation to their condition as exploited persons. This was the Juventud Obrera Católica or JOC (Young Catholic Workers), which represents another interpretation of Catholicism. Today, from the same perspective as the JOC, the Independent Church of the People collaborates in an auxiliary fashion with the union of Cali. Without attempting to take over the union from above, the Church of the People is providing day-care centers for the children of domestics of Cali. Also from a perspective that differs from that of Opus Dei, the Asociación Colombiana para el Estudio de la Población or ACEP (Colombian Association for the Study of Population) works more at the level of juridical counseling with domestic workers, by reporting problems of the sector and by organizing meetings even with the *patronas* (see León in this volume).

References

Garcia Castro, Mary. 1982. "¿Qué se compra y qué se paga en el servicio doméstico?: El caso de Bogotá." In Magdalena León, ed., *La realidad colombiana*, vol. 1, *Debate sobre la mujer en América Latina y el Caribe*, pp. 92–122. Bogotá: Asociación Colombiana para el Estudio de la Población.

Garcia Castro, Mary, Bertha Quintero, and Gladys Jimeno. 1981. "Empleo doméstico, sector informal, migración y movilidad ocupacional en áreas urbanas en Colombia." Programa Naciones Unidas, Proyecto Ofincina Internacional del Trabajo sobre Migraciones Laborales, Bogotá. Final report, mimeo.

20 The Autobiography of a Fighter (Peru)

ADELINDA DÍAZ URIARTE

I was born on the eighth of March 1948 in the province of Chota, department of Cajamarca, which is to the north of Lima, the capital of Peru. I am the eldest of five children. My mother carried me only seven months because of the severe conditions of her life and work.

My mother would tell that I was very small and sickly when born, and nobody thought I would live very long. Her friends made fun of her because she had such a small baby, and she was ashamed. My mother wanted God to take me because she did not know what would become of me. At first, she fed me only liquid milk in drenched cotton, as I could not hold onto her breasts.

I was born out in the countryside; they say my grandmother was the midwife. A neighbor who was a friend of my mother had lost her baby, and she breastfed me until I was a year and a half. My parents are also from the same province of Chota in Cajamarca; my father's name is Herminio Díaz Bustamante, and my mother's name is Hermilia Uriarte Nuñez. She was a seamstress who worked at home and could neither read nor write.

My father is a peasant and also a bricklayer. He is eighty years old and the eldest of five children. When a child he worked a lot in the fields and suffered very much as a consequence. He was engaged to my mother after he was widowed; his first wife died, leaving five very young children. Three of them also died; the last two lived. My mother also brought a child to the marriage: my sister, her first daughter. My sister's father deceived my mother and left her. From my father's first marriage only one son survives: my elder brother. We love each other very much.

When I was six, my parents put me in school near home. Most of the students were male; there were only three or four women. The thinking was that only men had the right to schooling, and women were made for the home. I was the best student; the boys would hit me, but the teachers took care of us. At that age I did not work; I helped my mother with the household chores.

At this stage my parents were very strict with us. My father always had to have the last word, and we could not answer back, not even a word, because he would hit us. What he said, we had to do. He would tell us that he also had been brought up in that way. My mother, instead, was the opposite: she would neither shout at us nor hit us.

My mother died when I was eight years old, and for me my childhood ended. I quit school in the second grade. I am moved every time I recall what my mother said to me before she died. These were her words: if she would get better I would be the first she would buy a dress for, but if not, I would have to take care of my little brothers and sisters. My older half-brother had gone, so five of us were left; I was the eldest; my sister who followed me was six years old, the third was five, the fourth three years old, and the fifth a seven-months-old baby. My half-sister, from my father's first marriage, was fifteen years old, but she lived with my uncles.

It was then that I inherited the responsibilities of an adult: I had to take care of my little brothers and sisters, especially the littlest. We suffered a lot, because father was rarely home. He worked in the city every day as a bricklayer and constructor of homes. He would leave at seven in the morning, returning at five or six in the afternoon, or sometimes at night. He would shop so we could prepare our food, but on many occasions we did not have time to prepare it because we also had to take care of the animals: sheep, pigs, three cows, chickens, and even the vegetable garden.

My father would leave chores for us to do. To cook we also had to find firewood and sometimes it rained, which made it difficult to find. I remember once the five of us got sick (it seems that we all got food poisoning); we all had a high fever and were vomiting throughout the day. My father returned at six in the afternoon, and when he saw all of us sick in bed, he went back to the city to buy medicine. I had to wash, cook, take care of my brothers and sisters, and also look after the animals.

Six months after my mother died, my little brother died. He was about to have his sixth birthday. It was very painful because he was an intelligent child. I do not want to remember those sorrowful moments because I cannot hold back my tears when recollecting them. Three months later my eldest sister, from my father's first marriage, died. She had married, and a month later got sick. My father spent a lot of money in the attempt to cure her, selling more plots of land as he had during my mother's sickness. But the doctors were no good; my sister continued to get worse and died. This death was the third blow my father received. My little brother who was four years old was also sick, and two days after we buried my sister he died. Four had already died in nine months. My father got sick; he neither ate nor slept. We cried day and night.

My mother presented herself to me in a vision; I saw her sitting in the middle of the house. I called my father so that he could talk to her, but she was no longer there. I do not know what happened to me. I did not cease to think of her for a single moment; I was going crazy. To forget our anxiety we left our home for a year; they told us if we stayed, we would all die. This is how we came to rent a house far from the city. We were cured, but for our cure our father had to sell more plots of land because he had no more money. Later he took us to Chiclayo, where there were medicine and doctors.

The Anxieties and Work of Childhood

I do not recall having sexual anxieties and curiosity until I was twelve, perhaps because I was so busy taking care of my brothers and sisters and always thinking of my mother. The tragedies that had befallen us weighed more on me than on the others, but even at this level of my life my father's strictness was ever present. I did not think of sex as something normal as every young person would. Out in the country children start working at a very young age. We were not like the children of moneyed people who have almost everything and do nothing. The first thing to which country children awaken is sexual curiosity. But we did not have friends. I don't know why. We had only our brothers and sisters and our parents.

I learned how to weave when I was nine; I made knapsacks, blankets, bedspreads to sell them to small traders. Country people use these pieces of woven goods to carry things on their backs. Weaving is the first professional craft of every peasant woman. In this way I bought my clothes because my father had spent a lot trying to save the lives of my dead brothers and sister and did not have enough money. What he got from his work went for our food.

Three years after my mother died, my father wanted to marry a widow. He said we were very young, and he would get a person who would take care of us. But I had been told stepmothers were bad; I did not agree to the marriage, and I let my father know that if he married I would take my brothers and sisters and leave because she would make us suffer too much. For the first time I stood up to my father, sure about what I was saying. That is why my father did not have any more engagements. And now when we go to see him, he tells us that he did not have anyone else because of us, and then we abandoned him.

At fourteen I began to menstruate. It was a hard experience because no one explained it to me. I had heard about it, but the reality scared me. I menstruated for eight days, and I was ashamed of telling my father, because most country people never explain anything to their children—they are very reserved. My father asked me what hurt because he saw me so pale; I did not tell him anything. I went to a neighbor and asked her why was I bleeding so much. She told me that the first time was like that, and that I should not be scared.

At that age I enjoyed going to mass, to processions, and any other religious services; every Sunday I would go to catechism at a high school run by nuns because they told me that nuns were pure, perfect, and sincere persons; they were daughters of Jesus Christ. I liked them very much, and I wanted to be a nun because they do not sin. When I was ten, I was a traditional believer.

Adolescence

Our neighbor had three children. The eldest was a boy and he was my age. We trusted and liked them, and they played with my little brothers and sisters. One day that boy said he was in love with me. I do not know how to explain the immense emotion I felt at that moment; I do not know whether it was fear or happiness or sadness. This was the first time a boy had talked of love to me. So, because of nervousness, I said nothing. I was confused. I had never imagined he would tell me something of this sort, because we treated each other like brother and sister. From that moment on my ideas changed, and for the first time I began to discover tenderness toward him. He was in fourth grade.

But after he had spoken to me of his love, he stopped coming over so often. He seemed ashamed of his words. But when we were together, he would ask me what I thought of what he had said. My answer was no, but inside I began liking him very much. When he would not come, I would miss him, and when he was nearby, I rejected him. This went on for a year. Then one day when we were alone, he hugged me and tried to kiss me, but I did not let him. I rejected him, and he went away sad and cried. And he told me that I did not love him, but he would not lose hope and would continue to insist. I liked him more and more. No one even imagined that he had spoken to me.

When I was about to be fourteen, another boy fell in love with me, but I did not like him. He would tell everyone he was in love with me and that whatever happened, he would marry me. My father scolded me because he thought I was in love with this boy. My father became even more strict with respect to my chores, and he shouted at me. I was even angrier at that boy and hit him so that he would not come after me. He even spoke with my father, saying he wanted to marry me, but my father did not accept him.

Out in the country our parents, because of their lack of education, did not explain anything to us about couples and making men friends. They feared the girls could be seduced, and our relatives and friends would look at us in a bad light. When a boy and his parents would come before our parents, if they liked the boy and knew his family, they would accept him. In the Sierra you don't always choose your partner. Many times you are married without really knowing the man; he is imposed on you by your parents when you are very young. When the couple wants to marry but the parents disagree, they can run away: the boy takes the girl in the night to his home, or to some other place, and the girl's parents demand a marriage to save the family honor.

I continued seeing the first boy, but he and his parents went to live in Chiclayo. He promised to return in January of the following year. But then a misfortune occurred: they stole all my things and took the animals from the house. In desperation I traveled to Lima, and when I arrived in January of 1965, the boy was in Chiclayo. We wrote weekly to one another, and the farther away he was, the more I loved him. We were like that for twelve years. Here in Lima I had no other boyfriends because I only thought about him, and I respected him; I thought if I had a friend who loved me, I would be betraying him. I thought about him in a good way: not in making fun of him or tricking him. I never thought he would have a change of heart; I believed we would marry and make a home, and we would be happy with our children. When he wrote, I suffered very much. I helped him with money so that he could finish his studies and begin his career; I bought him books, paper, and other school materials—everything he asked. And I would send it to him from Lima.

In those days I earned 900 *soles*, which I used to help the boy and my father. Nothing was left for me. I thought he was going to finish his studies and marry me. But time passed, and his letters changed. They were colder; often they rejected the love I expressed in mine. This continued until he wrote to say he wanted to have sexual relations with me because only in that way could he be sure that I loved him and was not betraying him with another in Lima. He asked that I answer immediately so that he would travel to Lima just for this purpose, or that I go to Chiclayo and he would take me to a hotel.

This was a very hard blow for me. I did not believe he was asking out of love, and I reacted badly, thinking he neither loved nor respected me. I answered I would never give in to him before marrying, and that both of our families would know about it. Immediately he responded, asking me to forgive him and saying he had written while drunk. We continued to write until I decided to go to Chiclayo to confront him on why he was treating me in this way. That is how I discovered he had a six-year-old daughter. For me everything seemed to end there. But I loved him so much I told him I would accept him with his daughter—but first we had to marry. He did not live with the mother of his daughter; she was an older woman, and he said that he had gone with her only because she helped him with his studies. He finished these studies and became a mathematics teacher.

Again he insisted, in a much harsher manner, that I give in to him. But I decided to finish it off and went to Chiclayo with all his letters. I told him we could stay friends. I returned to Lima and for three months all I did was cry. After a time I overcame it, the greatest heartbreak of my life; of course it had been sown in my memory.

Since that time I have shied away from getting involved with men, even though I had quite a few opportunities. I dedicated myself to work for the union of household workers. I thought men were all alike, but I have overcome this, yet I have not had boyfriends again. Now I am older, and I believe if a sincere person were to offer himself, maybe I would accept him, but I am not desperate. Not only married women have a life; so do women who give their lives to the service of the community. Of course, to be frank, I feel lonely sometimes, even more so when there are controversies in the organization or problems at work, economic problems, sickness, but I overcome these feelings because I believe that life is constructed according to the situations we face.

My Arrival in Lima

I came to Lima the week after my house was robbed. I was friendly with the nuns who taught in a school near my town. They belonged to the Congregation of the Immaculate of the Sacred Heart. When I told them I wanted to leave home, the director of the school suggested I accompany her to Lima; she was planning to travel there in those days. She told me she would take me as her own daughter and put me in school; I would lack nothing. She told me about other girls she had taken to Lima. I did not know that this was the standard line told to all the girls who are brought here; I was happy; I wanted to go to Lima.

At the same time I felt very sorry about leaving my father and brothers and sisters. When I told my father that I was going to Lima with the nuns, he began to cry and told me not to go: "If you go, I will be left alone." But I was headstrong and let my father know if he didn't let me go, I would escape.

He went to talk to the nuns and asked them to sign a paper that would prove that they were responsible for me. In Lima the nun's father was waiting for me to take me to his house in Miraflores. When I arrived at the man's house, I was very much afraid. I did not eat that whole day, and every day I became more and more anxious because I missed my brothers and sisters and father. I cried for two months, not in front of the *patrones* but in my room. I always cry when I am worried. But I confide my problems and sufferings to nobody, and when I am with other people I hide my feelings.

In my first job in Lima I suffered a lot because it was very hard; I worked more there than in my own home. They would order me about all day. Nothing the nuns had told me was true. The second day there the *patrones* told me what I would have to do: cook, take care of a ninety-eight-year-old grandmother, clean the first floor, sweep the garage and the garden. The house had three floors, and my *compañera* cleaned the second and third floor, and I hand-washed everybody's clothes. The kitchen was very big; it had two refrigerators, two stoves, and three sinks. During my first days the *patrona* helped me in order to teach me the customs and the kinds of foods they liked, but as I am a quick learner, she soon stopped helping me.

I had to get up at five in the morning to make breakfast and take it to the *señorita* in bed, because at seven she went to work at the policeman's hospital. I cooked for fourteen people everyday. I could not even rest on Sundays because they always had visitors. At least they allowed me to go to school. I studied from three to six in the afternoon. On many occasions I went to school without eating lunch, and on returning I had to cook dinner because they ate at seven in the evening. I would finish all my work about eleven or twelve at night. This meant that I slept just five hours a day and did not have enough time to do both my work and study. When I had exams, I would greet the dawn studying on the terrace. Despite this, I got good grades and was the best student of my class until I finished grade school, but the teaching was not very good.

I was a victim of racial discrimination and unequal treatment in relation to my *compañera*. She had been brought in a year before me, and she was white and agreeable. The *patrones* would take her on outings. They never took me anywhere during the three years I worked there. My *compañera* told me they would not take me because the *señorita* said I was ugly, and she was ashamed of me before her friends. During this period I was already participating in the Juventud Obrera Católica (Young Catholic Workers), and the discrimination did not bother me. I got good grades in school, and I had to show these grades to the *señorita* because she had to sign the report card. She made my *compañera* envious of me, saying to her: "Well, Manuelita, you can get the best of Adelinda because you are such a beautiful girl. We love you very much, it cannot be that you will fail a grade." Manuelita did not like to study; she was very playful, but she must have liked me because I never argued with her. The *patrones* did not often allow me to see television, and if on occasion they gave me permission, I had to sit on the stairs next to the dog. My *compañera* would sit next to them on an old chair. That is why I did not like to look at television, and I studied in the little free time I had. We would have lunch after all the family had eaten. They never let me leave the house through the front door; I always left through the garage.

After I was two years with this family, relatives visited me from Chota. My father had suggested they see me. When they came, I was quite ashamed because my appearance was terribly neglected compared to what it had been in the village. Even though they were my family, the *patrones* did not ask them in; they received them out on the street. I felt very bad in having nothing to offer them, not even a place to attend them.

As they saw me thinner than I had been and poorly dressed, my relatives were amazed and asked why I was in that state. I began crying; I could not hold back, even though I tried. The nuns always reported back to the village that I was well. I told my relatives I was not that well and asked them not to tell my father. When the *señorita* asked who they were, I said they had come on behalf of my father. She told them not to worry: "The girl is all right; she is studying and needs nothing."

Anyway, my father sent a letter to an aunt who lived in Lima and asked her to see me. My cousins came, but the *señorita* told them to leave, saying I did not have any relatives in Lima: "Her father has told us that no one may visit her, so leave and do not return. The girl is with papers her father gave us." Afterward the *señorita* locked me in a room and shouted at me, "How did they know your address? Those men cannot be from your family; they must be your lovers."

After a month my aunt came to see me, and again they attended her out on the street. They told her she could see me every two or three months but not every week, because it would take too much of my time. My aunt asked that they give permission for me to go to her home. The *señorita* said no way, "because there are men in your house who are perverts." I wanted to go with my aunt; I was left very sad because the *patrones* bossed me around and I could not go. The only good thing about that house was that they sent me to school.

Something new came up when my *compañera* fell in love with a boy who worked in the construction of a building owned by the same family. He would come every day to work, and my *compañera* fell in love with him. That was why the *señorita*'s attitude toward her changed completely. They fired the boy, but Manuelita always saw him when she went to school. What the *señorita* did was to send her back to her mother, saying that her mother had sent for her. The poor girl was tricked. She did not take anything with her, thinking she would be gone just fifteen days. She did not take even a thousand *soles*, having worked there for three years. Nor did she take even the clothes they had given her; she only took what she wore. And she never returned. She dropped out of school. The *señorita* did not like us to have girlfriends, much less boyfriends.

How and When I Began Being Conscious

I arrived in Lima in January of 1965, and in April of the same year I entered a parochial school in Miraflores, Our Lady of Fatima, that was about eight blocks from where I worked. That same month, a small dark girl arrived at the school, Victoria Reyes. She told us she came from the Young Catholic Workers movement. She told us that house-workers should band together to help one another see our common problems and, if we wanted, she would come once a week to talk about forming a group of the JOC. The director of the school had given her permission to do this because it was a Christian group. The meetings were held every Thursday for half an hour. I remember the first meeting. We were fifty girls, and Victoria spoke of many things that we were not told about in school: how to share, how to help one another, not to be selfish. She spoke to us of who Jesus Christ was. But little by little the number of participants became smaller until only five girls were left, and later only three. This dwindling down took a long time.

When Victoria saw we were interested in continuing, she invited us to meet other groups of the JOC. There were talks, masses, and an advisor called Father Carlos Alvarez Calderón. I was understanding more and more. We would tell one another of our problems at work, of how much our work was worth, and of our dignity as persons and workers. Afterward, two more *compañeras* joined us, and we were five. An advisor named Mercedes Fus took over, and our *compañera* Victoria no longer came.

We became used to Mercedes because she was a good person. I found in her all the warmth that I lacked at work, and later they told me I would be responsible for that group. But all this was unknown to my *patrones;* had they known about it, they would have thrown me out. But I had to go out on Sundays to coordinate with the other groups of the JOC, and I could not manage it because the *patrones* did not let me leave the house.

A year went by that way. But I was very anxious to go out on Sunday because I wanted to know more about the movement. After two years I dared to ask the *señorita* permission to go out with a lady who taught religion at school, and she answered that she herself would go talk to that lady in order to find out where she would be taking me. That is how Vicky went to talk to the *señorita,* and since they thought she was a nun, they called Vicky "Sister Victoria." For the first time I had permission to go out, from three to six in the afternoon. The *patrones* went to pick me up because they wanted to know what it was about. I felt as though freed, happy to talk with my friends about something good. In my work they allowed me free time only for Sunday Mass.

But it happened once that I arrived late because it was the birthday of a *compañera*. It was 7:30 in the evening when I arrived home. They did not let me go out again. I then started to think about leaving and how to tell them. I did not want to stay any longer at that job because of all I had suffered. But I will admit they never hit me—many girls who are in my situation are physically abused.

Another event of my life was the attempt at a sexual assault that I suffered. This happens to most household workers. Every night I had to wait in the kitchen until 12:00 or 12:30 for the son of the *patrona*, who was thirty-eight and a bachelor, to serve him his dinner. If I would go to my room, he would come upstairs to knock at my door so I would come down to serve him. The night he tried to abuse me I was in the kitchen. He arrived at midnight and told me he had fallen in love with me. I felt chills and fear. I had heard of these things in the JOC, and I told him he was responsible for me. I was firm with him and got up to light the stove.

From his chair he looked maliciously at me, and while I was serving him his food, he stood up and came near me, putting his hand on my neck, trying to kiss me. I reacted by throwing the soup in his face, and most of it fell on his chest. He told me that if I would not do it peacefully, he would get his way by force. Everyone was sleeping. I told him I would shout and run out on the street; I said it would be known by his sisters—the nuns—and all his family. Since he realized that members of his family were being awakened by the racket, he let me go. At that moment I wanted to tell his mother, but he would not let me. He locked the door and said to me: "Idiot *chola*, if you go to my mother who is sick and something happens to her, it will be your fault." I went to my room and cried all night. I did not sleep. I thought of my father, my brothers and sisters, and my mother.

In the morning I went down to make breakfast. The *patrona* asked me why I was crying, and I told her the truth. She scolded him, standing up for me and telling him that if his sisters knew about it they would not think well of him. In order to defend himself, he denied he had done anything, but I intervened saying that was because I had fought him off. From then on he treated me badly. All this happened when they sent my *compañera* away to her home, and since they did not let me go out, I did not have anyone to tell my troubles to. I lost contact with the group of the JOC. I was treated worse every day, and I decided to leave, but I did not know where to go.

I sent my father a letter, and he answered that I was eighteen and could decide for myself. This gave me greater confidence to make my decision. I had only skirts and two very worn sweaters, one sheet, one blanket, also worn, and my school supplies. I bought a suitcase that cost 150 *soles*. Everything was ready, and I told the *señorita* that I wanted to leave. She shouted at me that I could not go because she had papers that my father had signed. I did not know where my aunt's house was, but by coincidence she came to visit me. I went down to the garage with my suitcase and told everyone I was leaving. The *señorita* stopped me and started to look into my suitcase, messing everything up. She told me to leave the sheet. The *señorita* said I was ungrateful because she had put me in school; she had bought me supplies; she had brought me from the Sierra to save me from ignorance, and that in another place they would treat me worse. I started to cry, thinking that perhaps she was right.

I went with my aunt to Comas, at Kilometer 18. In her house there was neither electricity nor water. There was only one bus line. I was there eight days. I could not get accustomed, and I wanted to see my school friends. But I could not go to them because they were far away, and I did not know how to go. I once tried to go, but I lost my way because I had no experience in traveling by myself. It was ten at night, and I decided to stay with a school friend, but the doors were closed and I had to sleep in the garden under a tree until dawn.

My school friend took me to her room without telling her *patrona*. She secretly gave me food. I wanted to find work, but they asked for recommendations and other documents. I was with my friend for two days; I went to school with her, and I met my other *compañeras*. They went to tell Victoria that I had left my work and was being put up by friends. Victoria recommended a job where they were going to pay me 800 *soles*, which made me very happy because it seemed like a lot of money compared to what I had been making (200 soles, when they paid me). The *patrona* was good to me, and I got on well with the children.

Trade Union Work

I now worked in a large house, but the *patrona* was not very demanding. I was paid regularly and could help my father with money, and they let me have Sundays as my day off. I also got permission to go to my meditation group, and I threw myself with even greater energy into the JOC. There I was given responsibility for the community group we had with Victoria, and there I rapidly became socially conscious. We were advised by Father Alejandro Cussiánovich. In 1974 I was appointed national leader of the JOC at the level of household workers. The JOC worked with laborers, and in the *barrios* principally with household workers. The other advisor was Sister Emilia Tarrico, a Bolivian; she later returned to her country to help form the Bolivian Houseworkers Union.

I owe a lot to these persons because they taught much about our reality. They led me and other *compañeras* to take the step toward organizing household workers in unions. As part of a church movement, they were not allowed to get involved in the defense of workers' rights, but the union could, because we ourselves were the ones who led it.

Every time my *compañeras* would tell me their problems, I would recall all I had suffered and become very indignant. This strengthened me in my decision to continue organizing. To organize the unions, we coordinated existing groups of household workers in parishes; in 1970 we united the groups of Surquillo and Miraflores, Pueblo Libre, Magdalena, Santiago de Surco, and San Isidro. We would meet with eight *compañeras,* and later more came to us. We worked on everything related to union organization and union structure, and we decided to work by districts, forming a union coordinating committee of household workers for metropolitan Lima in order to establish our federation. We met every Saturday. At dawn we would still be arguing and listening to lectures. The *patrona* gave me permission to go out. She knew I belonged to the movement. I never missed a meeting. At each meeting we had greater hopes that our organizational plans would become reality.

With all this effort, the unions started up in 1973.[1] On December 24 the papers were taken to the Ministry of Labor. I was elected treasurer of the Union of Surquillo and Miraflores, and *compañera* Victoria Reyes became general secretary of the Coordination of Metropolitan Lima. The secretary-general of my union resigned six months after taking office because she had fallen in love (the boy later abandoned her, leaving her with two kids). I took her position.

We had weekly assemblies. I was going to high school. Every Sunday forty to fifty household workers would come; sometimes even eighty. Surquillo and Miraflores were upper-class residential areas.

Every Saturday we would bring together persons from all the districts in order to evaluate our work. I studied, but I was more interested in union work than in my studies. When the teachers were late, I would talk to my schoolmates about our problems and our rights, and I would slip out to other classrooms and speak to them about these things. I had pamphlets and gave them out without the principal noticing. After school I would never leave alone; a number of school friends would accompany me. I would ask them how they were treated at work, how much there were paid, and then I would invite them to union meetings.

I had two responsibilities: on the one hand I was obligated to the JOC; on the other I had my union duties. We saw that we had to expand the union work to the provinces, and this was done starting from groups in Chimbote, Pucallpa, Ica, Chiclayo, Cusco, and Arequipa.

Representing Peruvian household workers, in 1975 I traveled to the world meeting of the JOC together with two *compañeras* who represented laborers and *barrio* workers. It was a good experience. I became aware that not only in my country were we hungry, exploited, and in misery but this was happening throughout the Third World. I began acquiring a greater international perspective: first we went to Caracas to a fifteen-day continental meeting, and then we went to Austria for the month-long world meeting. It was a very important experience; we could exchange personal ideas with *compañeras* in different lines of work. We were from different countries, but there were not many houseworkers (only one other one: a small dark woman from Singapore). I returned with a greater interest in going forward.

After two years I gave up my responsibility to the JOC and began working more at the union level. The unions weakened a little. After an evaluation we decided to branch out: union leaders went out to other areas of Lima where organizations had not been set up. I went to the district of La Victoria, and Vicky Reyes took over the union of Surquillo and Miraflores. I started working in La Victoria through the night schools, which gave me a place to teach religion in the classroom.

This is how I brought together many *compañeras* and gave union training to two hundred more household workers. In this task *compañeras* who worked in the Monterrey stores (five-and-ten variety stores) also helped. They supported us because they had their own union. In the new district we recruited leaders who strengthened the coordinating committee. We would meet every Sunday from 8.00 A.M.

until nightfall. In the afternoon I had other groups in the area. We met in parks because the priest, after he heard we were talking of unionizing, prohibited us from meeting in the parish.

To be frank, I was no longer so concerned about my boyfriend because I was so busy with my union responsibilities. When a letter from him arrived, I wished that he would also work in organizing teachers. I thought we would be happy if we shared the same ideas. But when he came and I told him what I was doing in Lima, he disagreed. He had different ideas, totally opposed to mine. He thought of succeeding individually, of being a professional, that each one should look out for himself. I never told him anything again about what I did, but I had hopes he would change—but it did not happen that way. His ideas remained the same, and this helped me forget. Of course the memories remain.

In school I made myself known, and many of my *compañeras* confided their problems to me. I did not finish high school with very high grades, since I skipped class because of union and community meetings. But I never failed a subject. Sometimes in written exams I would earn a low grade, but in the oral I would recover the lost ground because I would look in my notebooks searching for the content of the readings. My *compañeras* would sometimes question me as to how I could get such good grades, skipping class so often. What happened is that they would repeat the lessons by rote without taking in the meaning of what they read.

In 1975 there was a meeting of household workers in which seven hundred *compañeras* participated. This made me very happy; I thought our efforts and sacrifices had not been made in vain, and it gave me courage to continue. That same year we managed to convoke a meeting in the city of Juliaca with delegations from different unions. I and another *compañera* were chosen to go. It was decided to expand the union organization to other departments.[2]

In 1976 the first meeting of household workers at a national level took place in Cusco. I was elected to participate with *compañera* Victoria Reyes. The National Union Committee of Household Workers was formed, and I was elected secretary. In 1978 our first regional congress of metropolitan Lima met. For me, union organizing was a real challenge. I admit I did not pay much attention to my personal life and had little time to think about my future. It seemed as though I had bartered my life for the organization of the union. *Compañera* Vicky withdrew, and since I belonged to the organizational side, I had to take on all organizational duties. That is when I started relating to other unions and telling about ours. I always had an interest in learning more, but not just about unions. I was looking for a political orientation, so I started to reflect deeply on certain questions: Why were we household workers? What were the causes of this? Why was there so much poverty in our country? I became interested in the problems of other sectors of the working class, of peasants and street sellers and others.

At this stage I had some good experiences and also bad ones. Political organizations were not interested in our work. They thought we were a waste of time; they seemed to believe there was no way out for us. But I always criticized them, telling them: If you are fighters, you must show it in practical terms, and you must fight for those who are in need; it is not enough simply to declare that one is in the vanguard of the proletariat. I never let myself be manipulated, nor did I accept anything without first analyzing it. I perceived that there was no way for us in these political bodies, and I withdrew. But this does not mean I rejected these organizations. We support according to our means everything they do to help the people. We keep our autonomy, yet we always participate in public events, congresses, meetings, and so on.

The first National Congress of Household Workers met in Lima in 1979, and I had more responsibilities and so did my *compañera* Victoria. The congress was a success; our national platform was approved, and so was a petition to the government of Fernando Belaúnde. The latter was presented on the fifth of August. To hand in the petition we organized a march with four hundred household workers. But the government ignored us. So we broadcast it over the radio, and the petition became known. The second Regional Congress of Metropolitan Lima met in 1981. At that time progress was evaluated, and so was the work of each leader. I was elected secretary-general of the Coordinadora de los Sindicatos de las Trabajadoras del Hogar de Lima Metropolitana or COSINTRAHOL (Coordination of Household Workers' Unions of Metropolitan Lima), and I still have that job.

I must say that the life of a union leader is hard because we must give up many personal things. Since I started union work, I have not held a stable job. In order to find time for my work I have changed many jobs for the sake of the organization. On many occasions I have not been able to eat because of a lack of money (I started working on a live-out basis in order to have more time).

The second National Congress of Household workers took place in

Juliaca in 1981, where we elaborated the preliminary plan of Lima that was presented to parliament later that same year (in December) in a march that was brutally repressed by the police. In that congress, I was elected secretary-general at the national level, so my responsibilities grew. I am aware that I have not been able to fulfill them adequately because of lack of resources to travel.

In September of 1983 I went to Mexico for a small meeting of household workers. I was invited by Dr. Elsa Chaney. This seemed to me very important because I met there household workers from other Latin American countries who were also struggling to get ahead. I had the chance of meeting another worker from Chile, called Aída Moreno, and after the Mexican meeting she traveled back to Lima to spend four days with us. We always write. That year, I went to Bogotá, Colombia, to the first National Household Workers' Congress of that country, where we agreed to hold a Latin American congress of household workers and to establish an association of national organizations.[3]

Perspectives

I am resolved to continue my union work until such time as my *compañeras* dedicate themselves with greater earnestness to the fight for unionization and become more responsible. We are seeing what resources we can provide our colleagues: for example, an employment agency, development courses at every level, and other services according to our possibilities. My whole family is far away, but I believe that the *compañeras* near me are also part of my family because we share everything and help one another with our problems. I like to share the little I have. Rarely am I annoyed. And I am not resentful if offended.

Today my economic situation is what it has always been. I do not have a steady job; I live by working here and there. It is very difficult to make ends meet, given the economic crisis we are facing in Peru; what people earn is not enough. I have had experience at other jobs. I have worked in an optical shop where there also was severe exploitation. I was paid a commission based on what I sold. Before that, I worked in a tailoring shop and was fired because I wanted to form a union committee—I and four other *compañeras* were accused of stealing three rolls of material for uniforms. I also worked in a factory that produced garlic, where I was paid ten cents for filling a dozen little bags—sometimes it was not even enough for lunch.

Another experience of the struggle was when I was put in prison for defending a household worker. What happened was that the *compañera* was beaten and thrown out on the street, and when I went to see her, they also wanted to hit me. But I acted just like the *patrona,* and they denounced me, saying that I hit the *patrona*—but even then I did not stop saying to her what I felt. I was so angry that I even shouted at the police, and that is when they took me to jail. It was December 24, 1977, and I had a bitter Christmas.

Also when I finished high school I wanted to be well prepared to enter the university. But I could not enter because I did not have the money, and at the same time I was dedicating myself even more to the organization of household workers.

Notes

1. Although the *sindicatos* of household workers in Lima are not recognized as unions under the law, they will be called unions here.

2. Among the subdivisions into which Peru is divided, a department is equivalent to a state; a province is roughly equivalent to a county.

3. *Editors' note:* This has since been accomplished; in March 1988, forty representatives of household worker organizations in eleven countries met in Bogotá and founded the Confederación Latinoamericana y del Caribe de Trabajadoras del Hogar (Confederation of Household Workers of Latin America and the Caribbean).

21 History of the Household Workers' Movement in Chile, 1926–1983

AÍDA MORENO VALENZUELA

On beginning to write this brief historical resume, we ask ourselves about our own origins as a class and as a particular sector of workers. Going back in time, we find Chile—like almost the whole of Latin America—invaded by the Spanish who, in payment for their services to the King of Spain, received along with great landholdings a group of aborigines, called by them *encomendados* (literally, "recommended ones"), who became the property of the landowners. From having been a free people with their own culture, these aborigines became a conglomerate of servants in the style of the Middle Ages, with the added difficulty that the Spanish believed "these strange beings do not possess souls"; they were regarded as a new specimen within the animal kingdom.

From the mixture of Spanish and aborigines emerged the Chilean race, and the poor of the New World continued to carry out the same work as their ancestors, though now recognized as persons and as workers under the name of *inquilinos*. The dependence of the *inquilino* on the landowner is maintained to this day. The daughters of the peasants go to serve in the house of the *patrón*, first in the house on the country estate and then in the city house. Their work consists of cleaning, child care, cooking, and day work. Single and married mothers nurse the children of the *patrones*. Young male peasants carry out the work of houseboys, grooms, gardeners, and, when they are adults, overseers of other servants.

In the beginning with the parents' permission, and later on, domestic service became the only alternative for young women that permitted them to help their often very large families. The only work that the rural areas offered was the annual harvest—and this is true even today—for which young women received very low pay. In this way the migration of young women began, first to nearby towns and then to the cities and finally to the capital. At the beginning, this phenomenon was confined to the central zone of the country, but later the daughters of the Mapuche in the south and the Diaguitas of the north were incorporated into domestic work.

The characteristics of this work sector are dependence on the *patrones* and a traditional religiosity, one that maintains the forms and ideas transmitted by missionaries who were brought to the country estates by the *patrones*. These influences mean that, in general, household workers identify with the Catholic Church, along traditional lines. Their faith is based on a popular or pious religious orientation.

But it was not the church that helped household workers to organize in that era. Their organization came about rather through the political and social events that shaped the country's history. It was the advance of workers' organizations that brought about, in 1917, the founding of the Federación Obrera Chilena or FOCH (Chilean Workers' Federation), which, through its never-ending struggle, accomplished in 1924 the promulgation of the Código de Trabajo (Labor Code). This code regulated the work rights and the different types of organization of the various work sectors in the society. Almost at the same time, the Department of Obligatory Social Security was created to attend to matters related to workers' retirement and health insurance.

This fervor of the working class also reached the sector of household workers, who on January 1, 1926, founded the Sindicato Profesional de Empleados de Casa Particular de Ambos Sexos (Professional Trade Union of Men and Women Household Workers). As time went on, other organizations were created and disappeared: the Society of Domestic Employees of Santa Marta, the Religious of Domestic Service, the Feminine Union of Domestic Employees, the Daughters of Mary, and so on.

Of the groups mentioned, it was the union organization that endured—with a series of ups and downs—over time. This first union lasted about twenty years, gaining active participation in everything that had to do with organizing the workers. First it was affiliated with the FOCH, and when that entity was transformed into the Central de Trabajadores de Chile or CTCH (Workers Central of Chile), the domestic workers' union became an active part of it.

The domestic workers' sector also formed unions in Osorno, Curicó, and Viña del Mar, which collaborated through correspondence and visits of the leaders from Santiago. There also was contact with sister organizations of Argentina. Of the many activities that these unions carried out, we can highlight the following examples.

Promotion

- notification of meetings in the newspapers;
- participation in beauty contests of working-class women, sponsored by the magazine *Sucesos;*
- distribution of flyers in sectors where there were large numbers of household workers;
- letters to leftist members of parliament, asking that they promote the participation of their own domestic employees.

Social

- activities in the Casa del Pueblo—union meetings, cultural and recreational events, benefits for the organizations;
- low-cost vacations in the Campi union's site at Algarrabo.

Solidarity

- participation on commissions of the FOCH and CTCH;
- solidarity with workers on strike—printers, miners, hairdressers, hotel workers, etc.

Reform

- a bill proposed to the Cámara de Diputados (House of Deputies) to form an unemployment office with the 2 percent withholding from paychecks of workers;
- an interview with the president of the Republic to make known the preoccupations and problems of the domestic workers' sector— Casa de la Empleada (Domestic Workers House), permission to study, better treatment, obligatory unionization of the sector, etc.

Education

- primary level courses for illiterate members;
- courses in home economics;
- talks with movies, forums on health.

During the first stage this union was directed by men, but little by little the women began taking over the leadership responsibilities until finally only women were in charge. Meetings of the leadership group and of the members went on all the time.

In 1945 the people elected a government that said it was with them, but not long afterward it showed its real face and began to persecute all the workers who had a clear political and social consciousness and a serious commitment to their class. Many were sent to Pisagua, actually a prison without bars, and others had to flee the country. These events forced the domestic workers' union to dissolve.

During these same years, the Catholic Church began to evolve and form specialized movements, among them the Juventud Obrera Católica or JOC (Young Catholic Workers), in which young people had a broad social participation because they were in fact workers committed to their church and to their class. This movement spread all over the country, supported by priests who understood the problematic of the worker. Some of these priests are the most progressive bishops today.

On July 11, 1947, the second union of household workers was founded, and this one had a different orientation from that of the first. The new effort was pushed forward by women of Catholic Action, who had already supported the organization of parish centers in which household workers participated. They got together to meditate on religious themes and to learn different kinds of handiwork. These centers were created especially for young women from the provinces who had no training for their work and who found themselves alone in the city, far from their families.

These were the persons who made up the Sindicato Profesional No. 2 de Empleadas Domésticas de Santiago (Second Professional Union of Domestic Employees of Santiago), in which only women could participate. It had a religious orientation, and Cardinal José María Caro designated as chaplain the Rev. Bernardino Piñera, today Archbishop of La Serena. After a year and a half they succeeded in renting a house that was converted into the first Hogar de la Empleada (Domestic Workers' House), inaugurated by Cardinal Caro in the presence of various priests, women of Catholic Action, militants of the JOC, and household workers.

In 1949 the JOC of Domestic Employees began, under the guidance of don Bernardino and two JOC worker militants. In 1950 the Hogar mentioned above was inaugurated, after a long fund-raising campaign that was the start of the Federación de Empleadas (Household Employees' Federation), whose objectives were education, service, and religious formation. In this period the domestic workers' movement separated into two groups: the union wing and the federation. The Federación de Empleadas started a savings and loan cooperative, housing cooperatives, the Instituto Luisa Cardijn, and the magazine *Surge* (Arise). In 1964, the Federación de Empleadas became the Asociación Nacional de Empleadas de Casa Particular or ANECAP (National Association of Household Workers) with legal status; this organization carried on the objectives of the federation and also set about uniting all the domestic worker groups that the JOC had been promoting all over the country.

The union continued on its own road with very few possibilities of growth. Few domestics were recruited to the organization, and for about fifteen years the union barely survived—and then only through the efforts and commitment of some domestics who had a high level of social consciousness and understood the importance of maintaining a union organization.

After 1967 this union began to link up with other sectors inspired by Christian principles—with the Asociación Sindical Chilena or ASICH (Chilean Union Association); afterward with the Federación Gremial Chilena or FEGRECH (Chilean Union Federation), more independent that the former; and in 1970 with the Central Unica de Trabajadores or CUT (Sole Workers Council)—and began a new surge of growth and active participation with other sectors, joining in protest marches to demand worker rights, drawing up a legislative initiative that set forth the essential demands of the sector, and demonstrating when the bill was debated in the Cámara de Diputados.

In 1972 the first congress of leaders in the domestic worker sector took place, with the groups that ANECAP had been promoting throughout the country, to study the legislative bill and to lay the groundwork for the founding of the Sindicato Interempresas de Empleadas de Casa Particular (National Union of Household Workers). This initiative was realized in January of 1973, and the event was celebrated with a formal ceremony in one of the *salas* (meeting rooms) of the Diego Portales building,[1] with the participation of three hundred household workers, the Minister of Labor, and leaders of CUT. The SINTRACAP was made up of nineteen unions.

The Sindicato succeeded in obtaining an office for the organization in the Diego Portales building; low-cost vacations in the peoples' beach houses for the household worker and her family; an agreement for discount buying in the stores of the Linea Blanca del Area Social (stoves, refrigerators, and radios); a child-care center where household workers could leave their children during the day. President

Compañero Salvador Allende attended the inauguration, and Moay de Toha, wife of a minister of state, worked with the *sindicatos* in bringing about the event.

The Sindicato approached the Corporación de Vivienda (Housing Authority) about one of the greatest hopes of the sector: that the *corporación* would construct special buildings in a decent neighborhood for those domestics who worked by the day. This initiative was very well received; the reply was that it would be studied, and when there was something concrete to report, another meeting would be called.

In Santiago at that time, three more unions at the community level had gotten underway. This growth was due, in great part, to the fact that ANECAP released some of its members so that they could become active in these unions. The work of ANECAP was very important at this stage. There was such unity that persons freed to work for the domestic sector in the Hogar de la Empleada were elected by turn from a slate proposed by the four unions of Santiago and an additional *empleada* proposed by ANECAP. Of these five candidates, four would be elected. Today nothing of all this exists; ANECAP alone has assumed the responsibility, and the unions have no say at all in the *hogares* that remain.

The effervescence in which the Chilean people lived in that epoch was also experienced by the domestic workers' sector. Every day more and more household workers came to join the unions, and this allowed them to free up one leader for half a day. Others arranged to work shorter days in washing and ironing so that they would be able to devote some hours daily to union organizing.

One of the deficiencies, of which we are aware today, was that the union organizations did not train their members. They did not strengthen or elevate their level of consciousness and their commitment to their sector, their class, and, especially, to the importance of being organized. Because of these errors, after the military coup of 1973 everything fell apart, and almost nothing remained. The members dropped out of the organization, and for a year the leaders had to scurry around looking for some place to function; the landlord, out of fear, asked them to leave the office they had rented.

In spite of these difficulties a commission was constituted with the aim of coordinating those unions that had survived after the coup. This commission was made up of one delegate from each union in Santiago: Las Condes, Providencia, Nuñoa, La Reina, and Santiago, plus a delegate of ANECAP. The country was divided into three regions, North, Central, and South, and the commission succeeded in maintaining a constant contact with all the unions, supporting them and motivating the leaders. It managed to put out a bulletin that also fulfilled the aim of keeping the unions united. Very soon, however, this effort disappeared, along with the three community-level unions of Santiago.

In 1976, by decree of the Minister of Justice, ANECAP had to comply with a series of requirements in order to justify its existence, and from that date it began to recruit members. In time, ANECAP started to put up real competition with the unions, diverting them from their proper goals as set forth in their statutes. On the other hand, a series of legal decrees began to be issued with which the unions had to comply. To begin with, they had to ask permission to hold a meeting of their members, and for this they had to go through a series of negotiations. That fact alone—of having to ask permission—frightened many of the members, and almost all of the household worker unions began disbanding, with the exception of ours.

Other strategies were sought, and we began to participate in the courses for household workers offered by the Fundación José Cardijn. From this experience arose the notion of creating feminine departments in all of the union organizations. This objective was worked out with Teresa Carvajal, representing the pensioners, who had been active in unions in their working years; Georgina Aceituno, representing textile workers; and the household workers' unions, represented by Aída Moreno.

One of the first efforts was the celebration of International Women's Day. In 1976 permission was sought by the pensioners, and in 1977 our union assumed that responsibility. That last celebration was the most massive public act that took place during the present dictatorship, giving it the name of the "Gran Caupolicanazo" (literally, "big blowout in the Caupolicán," a downtown theater of Santiago). It was the leaders of our organization that had taken the responsibility with the authorities to carry out this demonstration. Never again has any kind of event for this day been authorized; on the contrary, any manifestation whatever, however insignificant, has been crudely repressed.

In 1978 the government again invaded the union headquarters of the federations of construction, textiles, mines, metallurgy, and peasants. Our few items of office furniture were finally returned after a series of negotiations, but without an office in which to function, we had to take up the offer of ANECAP to give us a small room in their central headquarters. All of this meant that our organization was going backward. On the one hand, the members' fear of belonging to an organization that is strongly repressed by the present authorities and, on the other hand, the cessation of work with other worker organizations dampened the recently acquired dynamism. Finally, for older members, to go back again to ANECAP was in a certain sense to lose autonomy.

The reactivation went very slowly for the Santiago household workers union, but with the help of our ex-chaplain, Bishop Piñera, we were able to free one leader for a half-day, and together with a social worker, a plan of work was drawn up that included the reconstitution of the provincial unions and the training of leaders. We have followed this line of work actively since July 1979, and the fruit of these efforts was the creation of the Comisión Nacional de Sindicatos de Trabajadoras de Casa Particular or CONSTRACAP (National Coordinating Commission of Unions of Household Workers), in which are represented unions of Concepción, La Serena, Santiago, Talca, and Temuco.[2]

This Comisión Nacional fulfills the role that earlier was carried out by the Federación, since it is not possible yet to develop union activity, because of the very exacting new labor regulations that govern the number of members. Only two of our seven unions fulfill the requirements. For this reason, it is the Comisión that coordinates and decides the yearly plan of work and evaluates the work that has been carried out. Given the distances and the lack of financial resources, the Comisión meets only twice yearly. In order to make the Comisión more responsive, an executive committee has been elected, consisting of three leaders and an advisor. This committee meets monthly in order to carry out the dispositions of the Comisión Nacional.

The tasks carried out to date by the executive, with authorization of the Comisión Nacional, have been the following:

• Three national workshops, lasting seven days, have been attended by the leaders and members who demonstrate leadership potential. The objective of these national workshops has been training in labor themes.

• Two national workshops, lasting three days, had the same objective; the most recent had as its objective the training of new members from the different unions. The content of the training program was developed by the leaders of the executive committee.

• In the unions of Santiago, Talca, Concepción, and La Serena at least four workshops lasting one day each have taken place, supported by the executive committee.

• Each union holds a monthly meeting of members, with the exception of the Curicó and Temuco unions, which have had a series of difficulties in maintaining their organizations.

• The executive committee has designed a statute in conformity with the new legal regulations; developed formation materials on work rights, social legislation, work contracts, and union organization; published a bulletin, titled *Caminando* ("On Our Way"); distributed documents interpreting the different regulations that affect or benefit the household worker; sent an expert representative to the Ministry of Labor.[3]

This series of activities may appear positive, but given our situation before the installation of the dictatorship, we believe that we are very far from where we would have been under a democratic regime. The years of dictatorship have been almost fatal for the working class, especially for their union organizations. We must recognize, indeed, that in spite of the efforts of the authorities to damage the reputation of our unions, stigmatizing us as political when we speak out for minimal rights, they have not been entirely successful: many union organizations in our country have managed to stand firm, including our own. With many difficulties in terms of growth and finances, we have succeeded in staying alive, and this, in our country, is to be successful.

In our sector, the greatest success has been that we have gone forward in raising the level of consciousness, in order that household workers will value themselves as persons; in order that they will understand that along with having duties they have inalienable rights, and that as workers and citizens they have a responsibility to intervene in the destiny of their country. We have not grown very much in numbers, but we do believe that the quality of our members is very much higher than the level of 1973.

Notes

1. The Diego Portales building in downtown Santiago houses many government offices.

2. In addition, there are two other regional unions in Viña del Mar and Curicó. Members of the ANECAP include groups in Antofagasta, Concep-

ción, Coyahique, Curicó, La Serena, Osorno, Puerto Montt, Santiago, Talca, Temuco, Valdivia, and Viña del Mar. ANECAP does not belong to CONSTRACAP, but some activities are carried out in common between the SINTRACAP unions and the ANECAP groups.

3. *Editors' Note:* In recent months, the work of the CONSTRACAP has been suspended because of internal disagreements, and the future of attempts at federation remains unclear.

22 In Their Own Words and Pictures

compiled by MARY GARCIA CASTRO

This poster, put out by the Professional Association of Domestic Workers, Rio de Janeiro, in 1983, declares, "Domestics in Struggle—Marching together, we will discover our value; we will conquer our liberty."

1

POR QUE UMA ASSOCIAÇÃO DE EMPREGADAS DOMÉSTICAS?

Faz 3 meses que LUIZA trabalha, e ainda não recebeu salário.
MARIA tem 15 anos, nunca estudou, trabalha até 9 horas da noite, sem tempo de estudar.
JOSEFA ficou doente, grave, não tem Carteira de Trabalho nem INPS. JOANA foi despedida, de repente, sem família, não tem para onde ir. ANTÔNIA vai trabalhar e volta todo dia para Nova Iguaçu, sofre cada minuto pensando nos filhos que deixou sozinhos, em casa, até chegar à noite.

Quanta gente conhecemos nessas situações?
Por isso fundamos a Associação.

- Porque sozinho ninguém pode viver nesta cidade do Rio de Janeiro, onde há tanto egoísmo e tanta injustiça.
- Porque, unidas, temos mais coragem de enfrentar as dificuldades e valorizar a nossa vida e o nosso trabalho.
- Porque todas unidas, podemos nos ajudar umas às outras, prestar serviços mútuos, desenvolver a solidariedade.
- Porque só uma associação, organizada por nós, pode acabar com a injustiça de ficarmos fora das leis do trabalho e conquistar leis justas na defesa dos nossos direitos.
- Porque a Associação é a nossa voz, e representa os empregados domésticos junto às autoridades e aos empregadores.
- Porque estamos dentro da classe trabalhadora, lutando juntos, para transformar este mundo de miséria e injustiça num mundo de mais igualdade e fraternidade.

This pamphlet tells why the Professional Association of Domestic Workers, Rio, was formed: "because together, we will have more courage to confront our difficulties and to place value on our lives and work." The second panel gives a brief outline of the association's program in Brazil. [Associação Profissional dos Empregados Domésticos, Rio de Janeiro, 1981]

2

O QUE VOCÊ ENCONTRA

NA ASSOCIAÇÃO

A FORÇA DA UNIÃO
a luta pelo respeito à nossa dignidade de pessoas humanas e trabalhadoras, a luta pela justiça, pela ampliação da lei do empregado doméstico: férias, descanso semanal, horário de trabalho, 13º salário, etc.

UMA CASA-SEDE
onde nos reunimos para estudar e debater nossos problemas e nossas reivindicações.

SERVIÇO JURÍDICO
uma advogada para defender nossos direitos no trabalho diante dos empregadores e da sociedade.

ORIENTAÇÃO PREVIDENCIÁRIA E SOCIAL
o esclarecimento sobre a previdência social, apoio na assistência médica, orientação nas dificuldades.

HOSPEDAGEM
em caso de doença, necessidade de repouso, férias, desemprego.

RECREAÇÃO
o aproveitamento do tempo livre, passeios, festas e jogos.

420

This and the next two panels reproduce the resolutions passed by the fifth National Congress of Domestic Workers of Brazil, held in Pernambuco in 1985 (see Chapter 18).

V° Congresso Nacional das Empregadas Domésticas do Brasil
24-27 de Janeiro de 1985 - Olinda (PE)

CONCLUSÕES DO V° CONGRESSO NACIONAL DAS EMPREGADAS DOMESTICAS

Introdução:
> Nós, I26 Empregadas Domesticas, delegadas do V° Congresso Nacional de nossa categoria, no Recife,

Constatamos:
> que somos a categoria mais numerosa de mulheres que trabalham no Brasil (I/4 da mão de obra feminina, quase 3 milhões de Empregadas Domesticas no país).

Constatamos:
> que há um crescimento significativo no número de Empregadas Domesticas (acentuado pelo desemprego nas outras categorias).

Constatamos:
> que representamos então uma força importantíssima na vida econômico-social-cultural do Brasil (é só pensar o que seria do país se todas nós domesticas, parássemos de trabalhar ao mesmo tempo).

Constatamos:
> que apesar de todo esse valor e importância, não somos reconhecidas como profissionais; continuam as desumanas e injustas condições de trabalho, denunciadas nos quatro congressos anteriores:
> - a) Salário injusto.
> - b) Jornada de trabalho excessiva.
> - c) Falta de descanço semanal.
> - d) Recusa de férias anuais para a grande maioria.
> - e) Impossibilidade de estudar, para um número elevado de domésticas.
> - f) Exigência de dormir no emprego, impossibilitando a convivência normal com a família e o próprio meio.

Constatamos ainda:
> que costumamos ouvir dizer que a Empregada Doméstica faz parte da família onde trabalha, mas continua o desprezo e a discriminação. A maioria não é tratada como pessoa humana, mas sim como objeto. São alguns sinais dessas discriminações: quarto de empregada, elevador de serviço, comida, apelidos humilhantes, etc. .

Todas essas condições de trabalho e de vida trazem como consequência um sentimento de solidão e revolta embutida e, por isso, na nossa profissão existem muitos casos de doenças nervosas.

Somos profissionais, mas costatamos que a Sociedade não nos reconhece. A própria Lei Trabalhista (CLT) nos discrimina: não temos nem todos os direitos dos outros trabalhadores e os poucos direitos que temos são negados à grande maioria.

1

Queremos ressaltar com maior força a nossa situação em rela.ão
à Previdência Social. As nossas dificuldades são tantas e o. direitos tão poucos que o número de empregadas domésticas que podem continuar a contribuir para o INPS diminuiu assustadora en-
te, conforme dados oficiais (quase um milhão de contribuin es
a menos); de cada 4 empregadas domésticas que pagavam em I.8I,
3 não estão mais pagando em 1984.

A quase totalidade de nossa categoria é de mulheres e por isso,
sofremos também toda a discriminação da mulher na nossa Sociedade machista. A mulher é sempre vista como inferior e com menos capacidade.
Sabemos que ainda há entre nós muitas companheiras que não se
aceitam como domésticas. Somos profissionais e por isso, trba--
lhadoras e somos parte da Classe Trabalhadora, classe que, no
nosso Sistema não tem vez nem voz.

Verificamos:
que, infelizmente, muitos companheiros de outras categorias não
nos reconhecem como trabalhadores. Várias companheiras part_ci-
pam de outros grupos o movimentos, como Sindicatos, Movimen o
Negro, Associação de Bairro, Pastoral Operária, etc. Vários sindicatos já, convidam a Empregada Doméstica a participar de c.
bates, de lutas (inclusive greves).

Isso se deu, especilmente, a partir da criação da CUT (Cen ral
Unica de Trabalhadores) da qual são membros Empregadas Don ésti-
cas de várias Associações do País.

O Congresso revelou também que temos uma relação especial com os ra-
balhadores do campo, vendo que se não houvesse tanta miséri no
campo, haveria menos mulheres procurando trabalho nas grand s
cidades e que a maioria das Empregadas Domésticas veio do c mpo
e tem aí suas raízes.

DIANTE DISTO ESTE CONGRESSO FAZ UM APELO ÀS COMPANHEIRAS:

a) Já que temos tanto valor e tanta importância na Sociedade, ninguém se envergonha de ser Empregada Doméstica e cada uma as uma
como mulher ,como piofissional, e como membro da Classe Trat lha-
dora.

b) Apelamos a todas as companheiras para continuarmos com cora em
que já começamos, isto é, nós organizarmos em grupos por ba rros
ou cidades, ampliar os grupos num trabalho de base, criar e fi-
cializar associações, fazer intercâmbio entre as cidades.
Sómente unidas em Associações de Classe poderemos oferecer è s
companheiras as condições que elas esperam para sua defcsa, para sua valorização e para uma prestação de serviços que cons ci-
êntize.

c) Decidimos que devemos trabalhar para chegar amanhã, a um Sin i-
cato de Domésticos, livre, autônomo e forte.

d) O Congresso insiste para que todas as Associações participem a-
tivamente de todas as lutas dos outros trabalhadores no campo e
na cidade.

e) Lançamos um apelo a todos os Sindicatos de Trabalhadores a que nos consideram como parte integrante da Classe Trabalhadora,com o nosso enorme peso econômico, com nossa força de mulher, para participar a título de igualdade, da mesma luta, e que dêem toda a sua força ás reivindicações específicas da nossa categoria. Esta reivindicações especificas estão contidas no projeto de Lei aprovado neste Congresso e que vamos encaminhar ao Congresso Nacional.
Para sermos fiéis às nossas origens rurais, sofrendo as consequências da migração, além destas reivindicações, solidarizamo-nos com o trabalho rural, afirmando a necessidade urgente de uma legítima Reforma Agrária, promovida pelo próprio trabalhador do campo.

Finalizamos, dirigindo o nosso protesto às autoridades constituídas e à sociedade em geral. Não podem mais ser ignorados os valores e o peso economico e social que tem a nossa categoria.
Somos milhões de Empregadas Domésticas.
Basta de sofrimento e de esmagamento que vem da escravatura. Exigimos Justiça pelo reconhecimento da nossa profissão, que nos coloque em pé de igualdade com os outros trabalhadores.

Olinda, 27 de Janeiro de 1985.

This front page and the next two pages are from *Vidas Paralelas,* published by the feminist group Agora e que são elas ("Now they shall arise"), Rio de Janeiro, 1981. Some of the questions the *patrona* agonizes over: "What proportion of the family budget does the salary of my *empleada* represent?" "What do I know of the affective and sexual life of my *empleada?*" "How long a workday does my *empleada* have?"

424

Vidas Paralelas

A MULHER NEGADA

Vamos falar daquela figura oculta, confinada na cozinha, escondida dos nossos olhos para o bem de nossas consciências; daquela figura ignora da, que está ao serviço pessoal de outras pessoas, no espaço impessoal de uma casa que não é sua para cumprir as extenuantes, invisíveis e desvalorizadas tarefas domésticas.

Na casa de sua patroa, isolada de sua família, sem poder receber seus amigos, com sua vida afetiva negada, sem lugar para namorar e trepar, vivendo uma miséria sexual impensável para nós, onde está o direito ao prazer da empregada doméstica? Queremos que seu corpo lhe pertença com os horários a que está submetida na maioria das casas onde trabalha?

Tudo nos leva a ver cada história de empregada como uma história separada, porque nos é difícil falar daquilo que não tem limites definidos. Isoladas, desinformadas sobre quem vive o mesmo dia a dia, elas tem mais dificuldade de lutar contra a sociedade que as explora e oprime e contra aqueles que fazem esta exploração concreta e presente : os patrões.

SERVIÇO OU SERVIDÃO ?

Nós feministas queremos mudar a vida, as relações entre as pessoas a forma de fazer política, desde agora. Chega de esperar pelo advento brilhante da era de aquarius ou do socialismo.

Somos contra todas as formas de exploração e opressão. Somos solidárias às lutas dos trabalhadores.

Parece fácil quando se trata, por exemplo, de ser solidária com a luta dos operários do ABC contra seus salários de fome. Ficamos indignadas quando um patrão alega "não poder" dar um aumento. Mas para nublar tão límpido céu surge logo uma contradição no horizonte.

Quando as patroas somos nós, o que acontece?

" A empregada doméstica é uma mulher e uma mulher é uma escrava. E a empregadora, é escrava ou patroa? " (Femmes toutes mains, G. Fraisse, Ed. Seuil, Paris).

Você poderia falar tranquilamente do salário que você paga para sua empregada?

426

LA NANA

Quién es la nana? ¿Cómo la ven los niños? ¿Cómo se expresan los niños sobre la mujer con la cual comparten muchas horas de sus vidas?

En un cuarto básico de un colegio particular mixto pedimos a 24 niños y niñas entre 9 y 10 años una composición sobre la "nana". De esas composiciones surge una imagen: cariñosa, generosa, mandona, hace todo el trabajo del hogar. Es gorda (o no lo es) y se llama casi siempre "mi nana", y a veces Gladys, Rita o Eliana. Impone la obligación de comer, bañarse y hacer las tareas.

Para la gran mayoría de los niños se trata de "mi nana", sin nombre. Sólo seis indicaron su nombre, entre ellos Jacques que dijo "se llama Felicinda, pero ella dice que se llama Pitti porque parece que no le gusta su nombre".

Casi todos la definieron como amorosa, cariñosa, juega conmigo, tiene una paciencia incalculable. El afecto cotidiano se traduce en que (Soledad) "cuando toca la bocina la liebre ella me abre la puerta" o (Pablo) "juega conmigo cuando estoy enfermo". También (Gonzalo) "me invita a su pieza para ver su álbum de fotos, su gato que ella hizo y muchas otras cosas".

Todos coinciden en que cocina muy bien y los postres y queques le salen muy ricos. Para Soledad "hace la mayor parte del trabajo en la casa" y para Valérie "en mi casa ella hace todo, pero cuando no entiende algo mi mamá le ayuda".

El trabajo de la casa y el hecho de estar continuamente en ella otorgan a la nana un elemento de estabilidad. En algunos niños esto se hizo muy notorio, como en el caso de Laurita que escribió: "siempre cuando vuelvo del colegio le cuento todo lo que pasó y ella también me cuenta cómo era su colegio y las amigas que tenía".

Antonio fue más extremo aún: "sin ella nuestra casa sería triste, sucia y desgraciada" (I).

La figura materna no aparece en las composiciones. Sólo dos o tres alusiones a la madre, a la cual la nana (Silvia) "le hace caso a todo lo que dice".

Salvo una excepción, todas las nanas son muy cariñosas e importantes, para los niños. Como dice Claudio, "una vez casi lloro porque ella estaba muy enferma".

La excepción es Angela: "me gustaría a veces que viniera menos días, a veces se enoja con mi hermana porque se cayó una gota de agua al suelo, o se cae la goma etc. Es demasiado acusete y mandona, no le gusta que comamos el postre como a las 5, 4 ó 6 de la tarde".

En algunas de las expresiones de los niños se refleja lo que han escuchado en sus hogares. Por ejemplo, Marcela: "me gusta mi nana cuando está humilde"; o Gonzalo: "nosotros la tomamos en cuenta como alguien de la familia".

A los niños se les pidió que agregaran un dibujo a las composiciones. Algunos de ellos la dibujaron colgando ropa lavada, al lado de la cocina, pasando una aspiradora. Otros, simplemente de pie, figuras grandes o muy pequeñitas, sólo en azul, o llenas de colores.

Los niños expresan de este modo cómo perciben a la nana, esa mujer tan importante en sus vidas, que los cuida y quiere "sin descanso, sin horarios, sin desear". Nana = amor y esfuerzo (Cecilia).

Isabel Undurraga

1

Pages from the bulletin on *domésticas*, published by the Center for Women's Studies, Santiago, Chile. The theme here is the *nana*, or nursemaid, who has special responsibilities for childcare. In the second panel, children write their opinions: the *nana* "is very nice, she likes to play with us, and she cooks what we enjoy."

2

This publication, detailing a survey of sixty domestic workers carried out by their own organization (Hogar de Servidores Domésticos of Cuernavaca, Mexico), reports that in some cases domestics are now getting a little better treatment because of the organization's demands—"not very pleasing to the *patrones* or the government."

LAS TRABAJADORAS DOMESTICAS
Y EL DECENIO DE LA MUJER
(1985)

P R E S E N T A C I O N

La CASA HOGAR DE TRABAJADORAS DOMESTICAS se creó en 1979,-- con el objetivo de apoyar a las trabajadoras de este sector en - la lucha para obtener mejores condiciones de trabajo. Sin embar- go el gobernador del Estado nos ha llamado a reuniones para rega ñarnos porque estamos alborotando a las"sirvientas'.' Esto demues- tra como el gobierno lejos de hacer esfuerzos por mejorar la si- tuación de las mujeres, se molesta porque nos organicemos para - defender nuestros derechos .

La Casa Hogar conciente de la explotación de este sector,-- realizó un Estudio Socioeconómico y Cultural a 60 trabajadoras,- cuyos resultados se han manejado en esta publicación. También -- hizo una   evaluación del Decenio de la Mujer junto con las tra bajadoras domésticas que asisten a ésta, para descubrir que lo-- gros se dieron en favor de ellas; por lo que partes de esta pu-- blicación .presentan las opiniones que dieron sobre los puntos -- que se trabajaron durante 10 años para promover el avance de la-- mujer, siendo estos: TRABAJO, SALUD, EDUCACION, EQUIDAD, DESARROLLO Y PAZ.

Se han logrado algunos cambios que no son beneficios gratis-de los patrones o del gobierno, sino que se han conseguido por -- las exigencias de algunas compañeras que están concientes de sus-problemas en el trabajo; pero que desgraciadamente son muy pocas.

"Sí, para mí si ha cambiado un poco la situación, ahora las -señoras me tratan mejor y antes no, antes casi todas las ---trabajadoras eran de planta y no habían de entrada por salida; pero ahora ya se puede uno ir a su casa y no trabajar --tanto como antes, que era toditito el día. Yo pienso que es-porque en algunas colonias nos han dado orientación, enton--ces la gente está más despierta y ya no se deja uno como --antes".

                              Hermelinda.

These items are from the Cuernavaca union's publication, "Big Woman." The first tells about a "combative" march on International Workers' Day, past the governor, who "smiled derisively" but this did not prevent the domestics from continuing to shout for their rights. The second relates the firing of several domestic workers for demanding their weekly paid day off. ["Zohuatl Zintli—Mujer Grande," Hogar de Servidores Domésticos, Cuernavaca, México 1983]

ZOHUATL ZINTLI
mujer grande

BOLETIN DE LAS TRABAJADORAS DOMESTICAS
AÑO 2 No. 16, SALE CADA MES
1 DE MAYO DE 1983.   **$1.00**

1° DE MAYO MUY COMBATIVO

Las Trabajadoras Domésticas de Cuernavaca nos unimos con diferentes organizaciones populares y partidos politicos a la marcha del 1° de Mayo para protestar y exigir nuestros derechos.

Por primera vez nosotras desfilamos unidas a la columna del CCL acompañadas de nuestros hijos, con el puño muy en alto y con nuestras pancartas de protesta siempre gritando consignas.

El Gobernador nos vió pasar con una sonrisa de burla, pero sin temor alguno seguimos gritando.

Este día nos dimos cuenta que ya no somos unas cuantas las inconformes con esta situación sino que miles y miles —— aquí y en todas partes estamos unidos en la Lucha de todo el Pueblo.

A partir de éste día nosotras las domésticas acordamos —— estar en contacto con las diferentes organizaciones para seguir en pie de lucha.

Estamos seguras que unidas lograremos el triunfo.

27 DE ABRIL NO RECONOCIDO

El pasado mes de Abril fueron despedidas injustificadamente varias trabajadoras domésticas, por pedir su día libre y pagado. Esto no admitieron las patronas porque no es un día reconocido comercialmente con mucha publicidad.

El equipo de la Casa Hogar unido con un grupo de trabajadoras domésticas, queremos que el 27 de Abril sea de Lucha laboral para que nos sean reconocidos los derechos —— que como clase trabajadora nos corresponden y que no sea utilizada por el comercialismo ni por la CTM para fines políticos.

Se festejó el día con un pequeño Acto Socio-Cultural, al que asistieron las pocas domésticas que lograron hacer valer su día.

Among organizations that support domestic workers in their efforts to organize and to secure their rights is the Asociación Colombiana para el Estudio de la Población (Colombian Association for the Study of Population), which published a booklet on workers' rights and legislation in 1985. The work of ACEP's "Program to Transform the Social-Work Conditions of Domestic Service in Colombia" is detailed in Chapter 16.

The sign in panel 1 says: "Just like any other worker, I have rights and duties."

1

Las mujeres del servicio doméstico son la mayoría de las trabajadoras en las ciudades del país y las leyes que regulan su trabajo existen desde hace 30 años.

Estas leyes establecen derechos y obligaciones para patronas y empleadas, pero como no se conocen, no se cumplen.

Es importante, para las empleadas domésticas, conocer los derechos que tienen y cumplir las obligaciones que les corresponden y de esta manera ser fuertes para exigir que no se atropellen los beneficios que la ley les ha otorgado.

Además las leyes son injustas en varios puntos: por ejemplo no hay horario para las internas, y la cesantía es menor que la de otros trabajadores y solo se paga sobre el salario en dinero, no hay primas y los reglamentos para el seguro social aun no existen.

Por lo tanto, mientras este trabajo exista y ocupe a tantas mujeres, es necesario conocer la ley que hay para hacerla cumplir y poder con la ayuda de la organización, luchar por su cambio cuando esta no es justa.

2

432

Panels 1 to 4 are from a pamphlet put out with the collaboration of the Juventud Obrera Católica, and used by the Sindicato Nacional de Trabadoras de Servicio Doméstico (SINTRASEDOM) in Bogotá, and the Hogar de Servidores Domésticos (Domestic Servants' House) in Cuernavaca. The prospective *patrona* is showing the new *empleada* around the house, telling her that there is not very much work—and that she will be treated like "a daughter of the family," then proceeding to detail a long list of heavy and exacting tasks.

Esta es la historia de BLANCA ...
Cuántas Blancas somos en Colombia ?

This pamphlet, depicting the history of "Blanca," a domestic worker ("How many Blancas are we in Colombia?"), is used to raise the consciousness of the members of SINTRASEDOM, Bogotá. The pamphlet was put together by the Women's Circle and published by the Servicio Colombiano de Comunicación Social (Colombian Service of Social Communication). [Serie *Mujer y Sociedad*, No. 1, Bogotá, 1985]

1

Servir

Qué es?

AMAR

El objeto fabricado, la Obra terminada
están destinados a prestar un Servicio.
El trabajo es un don a la sociedad, y a
través de él todos sirven.

Servir es Amar

Cuando nosotras, al Colaborar con una
familia, SERVIMOS, haciendo nuestro trabajo a veces monótono, y lo hacemos con
ánimo, y con interés, no estamos demos-
trando AMOR ?

Nuestro Trabajo es Amar

Santa Teresita del Niño Jesús, nos dice
que al final de la vida, Dios nos juzga
ra por el AMOR!

Y el Evangelio(Mat.XXV,34-40),nos dice
que SERVIR es cumplir las Obras de Mise
ricordia. De modo que cuando preparamos
la comida,cuando damos el jugo o la Co-
ca Cola a los niños, o cuando arregla-
mos la ropa. O cuando enseñamos a otra,
recibiremos el Premio por SERVIR!

These two panels are from the official organ of the San José Center of Promotion, Help, and Orientation for Household Workers, Bogotá (1980). Here the *domésticas* are told "to serve is to love and to perform the works of mercy." The message is conformity and resignation to a life of sacrifice, "serving God" in the family for which one works.

2

Oración a Nuestra Señora del Trabajo del Hogar

Haznos semejantes a Tí, María Madre de Jesús.

En Nazareth, Tu has repetido nuestros diarios gestos con paciencia y amabilidad.

Inspíranos ahora tus pensamientos,
sugiérenos tus palabras,
ayúdanos a imitar tus virtudes.

Nosotros queremos cumplir bien nuestro trabajo.

Enséñanos Tú, a santificarlo sonriendo cada día a las cosas a las personas, a las cruces.

Llena la soledad del corazón, serena nuestras melancolías.

Tu recuerdo nos preserve de todo mal,
nos dé fuerza para saber callar bondad para saber comprender.

Bendice, oh Vírgen, nuestros lejanos y queridos,
padres y hermanos.

Da a las familias donde trabajamos, la paz.

Dadnos a nosotros y a ellas lo que falta para la alegría de cada día.

Haz que todos puedan verte a Tí en nosotras.
Y haznos fácil el servir a Dios en ellos.

Esta estampa y oración, fueron el recuerdo de la Audiencia especial, concedida por S.S. el Papa Juan Pablo II a las Colaboradoras familiares Italianas y extranjeras, el 29 de Abril de 1979, con ocasión de la apertura del Congreso Nacional de API COLF. (Asociación Profesional Italiana de Colaboradoras Familiares.)
Cuando el Santo Padre pronunció el discurso que todas hemos estudiado.

8 DE MARZO: DIA INTERNACIONAL DE
LA MUJER

Participamos en el desfile organizado
por todas las mujeres que tienen organizaciones, comités, sindicatos o
grupos femeninos.
Participaron mujeres de todos los es-
tratos sociales. Hubo comparsas, dis-
frazes, danzas, conjuntos musicales.
Se lanzaron consignas alusivas al
trabajo de la mujer.
Se pidió al Gobierno protección para los hijos de las trabajadoras.
Se pidió que fuera relegada la JUBI-
LACION a los 60 años para las mujeres.
TAMBIEN la abolición de la doble jornada para las mujeres, el salario
mínimo.
Se pidió protección y seguridad social para el servicio doméstico.
Pudimos sacar nuestra pancarta....
y nos sentimos muy felices poder
participar con todas las luchas de
las mujeres colombianas.
El desfile fué nutrido, concurrido y
muy bien organizado; era la expre-
sión de todas nosotras, MUJERES,
identificadas con los mismos problemas, ya que nos toca atender todo
oficio del hogar, la crianza de
los niños y el trabajo remunerado;
la que el otro no se reconoce, ni
se valora, ni por los companeros,
ni por la sociedad.

These pages, from the bulletin "Let Us Join Together" (June 1985), of SINTRASEDOM, Bogotá, tell about the participation of domestic workers in the march celebrating International Women's Day and outlines "our solution, our struggle, our future."

$ 20   0001

PERIODICO INFORMATIVO
No. 0001

BOGOTA D.E. MARZO/ABRIL, 1985

DIRECTORA: Carmenza Bohorquez

SUB-DIRECTORA: Ma. Perpetua Delgado

REDACTORAS.   Josefina Caro

Fidelina Urrego

Margarita Cajicā

Margarita Gōmez

Teresa Moreno

DIAGRAMACION: Yenny del C. Hurtado
PROGRAMADO Y EDITADO POR el grupo
de periodismo de SINTRASEDOM
COLABORADORAS: Emma Girón Pino

Para el grupo de Periodismo de S I N T R A S E D O M es un orgullo presentar el primer número de su Periódico, que lo hemos llamado LLEGUEMOS, A UNA META A UN PROPOSITO A S I N T R A S E D O M . . .

Allí está nuestra solución, nuestra lucha, nuestra futuro.

Este periódico estará en circulación cada 2 meses con información de la organización. . . .

Páginas sociales. . . .

Recetas de cocina. . . Sopas de letras y algunas otras cositas . . .

ESPERENOS! SERA UNA GRATA SOPRESA!

Asamblea General

REFLEXIONEMOS

Cuál es la situación del servicio doméstico..? ? ?

Cuáles son nuestros prinicpales problemas? Cuál nuestra posible soluсión?

Le esperamos a la primera asamblea constitucional de 1985.
Se elegirá nueva junta directiva que regira los destinos del gremio.

Y nuestros derechos reconocidos por el gobierno? T O D A S estas cosas que nos aquejan, y cada día nos hacen más fuertes para luchar por una CAUSA JUSTA.

Poster announcing the first National Encounter of Domestic Workers in Bogotá, sponsored by the Sindicato Nacional de Trabajadores de Servicio Doméstico (SINTRASEDOM): "We don't beg favors—we demand our rights."

Pages from the bulletin "We Shall Overcome," published by the coordinating body of domestic worker associations in Lima. In panel 1 the text declares: "No more firings. We household workers are capable of uniting and organizing to overcome these abuses."

1

2

3

The six panels are from various bulletins of the Household Workers' Union of Cusco. Panel 1 shows the "two faces" of the *patrona*, speaking sweet words but denying the worker her rights; and panel 2, the way the *patrona* wants to appear to her maid: preponderant, while "the rich see us as insignificant." In panel 3, the union meets.

2

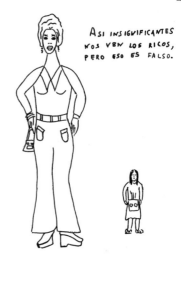

ASI INSIGNIFICANTES NOS VEN LOS RICOS, PERO ESO ES FALSO.

1

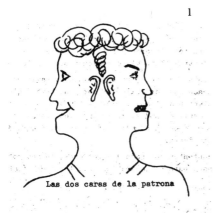

Las dos caras de la patrona

3

¡Abajo las patronas!

Pido la palabra

¡Estamos fregadas!

¡Los ricos nos explotan!

¡Abajo la injusticia!

¡Esto ya no se puede aguantar!

¿Hasta cuando, compañeras?

¡UNIDAS VENCEREMOS!

¡COMPAÑERAS! ¡LUCHEMOS POR NUESTROS DERECHOS!

In panel 4, we see the maid addressed as *chola* (an insulting term) by the son and not being called to account by his mother because he is a *niño fino* (aristocrat). Panel 5 compares rich and poor *patronas* and asks why the poor also exploit their domestic help. Panel 6 reminds domestic workers that some of them work in laundries, child-care centers, restaurants, and this enables them to attend to many families at the same time.
["Llallisunchis—Venceremos" Sindicato de Trabajadoras del Hogar, Cusco, Peru, 1973 and 1977]

5

4

444

These pages, from a Juventud Obrera Católica publication, outline the situation of domestic workers, showing (panel 1) their dispersion in the workplace as well as in their living arrangements and (panel 2) their remote relation to the production process—paid from what remains (surplus value) from the costs of production and the salaries of production workers. [Alejandro Cussiánovich, *Llamados de ser libres (empleadas de hogar)* (Lima: Centro de Estudios y Publicaciones, 1974)]

1

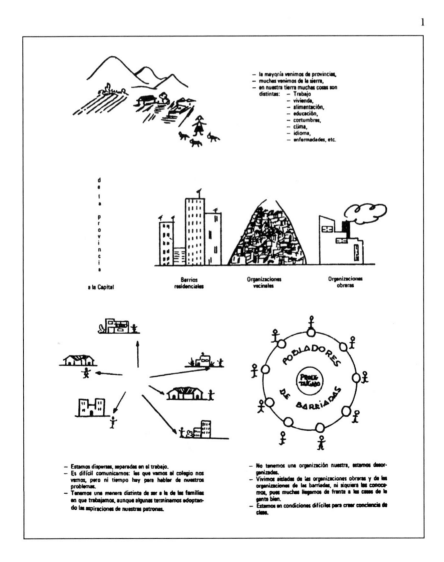

2

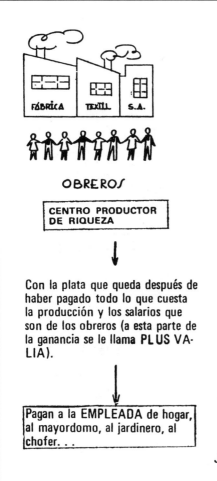

FÁBRICA TEXTIL S.A.

OBREROS

CENTRO PRODUCTOR DE RIQUEZA

Con la plata que queda después de haber pagado todo lo que cuesta la producción y los salarios que son de los obreros (a esta parte de la ganancia se le llama PLUS VA-LIA).

Pagan a la EMPLEADA de hogar, al mayordomo, al jardinero, al chofer. . .

MEDIOS DE PRODUCCION

DUEÑO DE

CASA PROPIA

Jardinero Empleada Chofer

This pamphlet first shows (panel 1) a *campesino* (peasant) giving his daughter, Eulogia, to the *patrón,* and the *patrona* telling her that she cannot go to school; then follows panel 2 comparing the rights of other workers to those of domestics. The final panel, not shown here, outlines the principal problems of the domestic service sector but informs readers that in various cities, domestics are organizing. [Comisión de Justicia Social, Prelatura de Chimbote, Peru 1980]

1

2

CONFORME A LA LEY PERUANA, ESTOS SON NUESTROS DERECHOS,

Al terminar este folleto, es importante subrayar que:

EN LA MAYORIA DE LOS CASOS,
NI SE CUMPLEN ESTOS DERE-
CHOS MINIMOS DE LA TRABA-
JADORA.

EN EL CASO DE LA TRABAJA-
DORA DEL HOGAR, SUS DERE-
CHOS SON MUCHO MAS LIMITA-
DOS, Y MUCHO MENOS CLAROS
QUE LOS DERECHOS DE LA MAYORIA DE LOS TRABAJADORES.

- JORNADA DE 8 HORAS.
- 30 DIAS DE VACACIONES ANUALES.

- JORNADA DE 16 HORAS.
- 15 DIAS DE VACACIONES ANUALES.

DERECHOS DE LOS TRABA-
JADORES

DERECHOS DE LA TRABA-
JADORA DEL HOGAR

Bibliography

Domestic Service in Cross-Cultural Perspective: A Computerized Data Base

MARGO L. SMITH

One of the most prominent features of the study of domestic service is its fragmentation. It has not been a field characterized by a cohesive group of activists and scholars who know each other well and whose interests and work are known to each other. Instead, it has been characterized by individuals who are primarily involved with domestic service in one geographic location. Only recently have efforts been made to bridge the gaps among these individuals in different countries.

The project presented here is intended primarily to assist the study of domestic service as a new field of research in search of an identity. It is also the direct outcome of the multidisciplinary panel on domestic service in Latin America which took place at the 1983 Latin American Studies Association meeting in Mexico City. There it became obvious to me that adequate collaboration among committed researchers and activists was not taking place, if only because those interested in domestic service did not know who the others were and were not in contact with one another. They published in diverse journals and other outlets, and presented papers in a variety of different conferences which reflected more the disciplinary home of the scholar/author than the topic of study. Consequently, to facilitate communication within this diverse group, I volunteered my then new Kaypro II portable computer to develop three computerized data bases, two of which have now been developed from customized data records set up using Perfect Filer software.[1]

1. The data base most requested by researchers so far includes the names and addresses of those who focus on the study of domestic service as a new field. It also includes each person's country of interest and disciplinary background. It currently lists forty-six members, thirty of whom are Latin Americans or Latin Americanists. It is kept up to date and provided to any interested person on request but is not duplicated here, primarily because the speed with which it can become

dated (as soon as someone moves or changes jobs) is not suited to a volume of lasting value.

2. The second data base, a bibliography of materials about domestic service around the world, provides complete bibliographic citations[2] and can be sorted according to author, title, disciplinary speciality of the author(s), subject matter of the particular citation, location (country) on which it focuses, time period presented, medium (book, article, unpublished paper, thesis, film, and so on), and whether or not the compiler has the author's current address and a copy of the item cited. Thus, one could readily identify all anthropological theses dealing with domestic service in Mexico, for example. Only the bibliographic citations are reproduced here. A few items are listed more once if they appeared more than once, on the grounds that a user may have access to one source but not to others.

3. A third data base, planned but not yet implemented, will consist of one- or two-paragraph noncritical summaries of the content of each item in the bibliography.

The literature on domestic service, particularly "how to do it" materials and fictional works in which servants are major characters, has a very long history, dating back to at least the eighteenth century. Only within the past twenty years, however, have scholarly literature and government reports on domestic service become dramatically more numerous. It is this recent period, since about 1965, that is emphasized in the accompanying bibliography. (Items that became available since March 1987 are not included.) This material, particularly in its Latin American coverage, primarily addresses domestic service in the contemporary period. For other world areas, especially western European countries and the United States, references are included to domestic service in the eighteenth to the early twentieth century.

The sources listed here are primarily scholarly literature and official reports prepared for government agencies; they include dissertations and theses, published books and articles, and unpublished papers presented at scholarly conferences. However, some popular material has also been included. Far more people have encountered domestic service through the popular *telenovela* of approximately 1969–71, *Simplemente María*, shown in many Latin American countries, and through the British television series *Upstairs Downstairs* and the commercial film *El Norte* (Nava and Thomas) than will ever see *The Double Day* (Solberg-Ladd) or *The Lady of Pacaembu: A Portrait of Brazil* (Moreira and Leal). Of the films about domestic service or particular servants that I have found, only *The Double Day*,[3] *El Norte*,[4] and *The Lady of Pacaembu*[5] deal with Latin America.

The bibliography also lists some biographical, autobiographical, and oral history accounts of domestic servants (which seem to be particularly rare for Latin America), and a few reprints of "classics" in the field (see Salmon 1897; Spofford 1881), none of which deals with Latin America. Only a few "how to do it" materials are included (Bowen 1970; Gordon 1974; South Africa, Non-European Affairs Department 1971)—again, none for Latin America—and the occasional work of fiction (Dawes 1974; de Lisser 1914) so that the user may be aware that a body of material from this perspective exists (the vast collection of fiction in which domestic servants are portrayed could easily be the topic of another bibliography).

This bibliography excludes specific *fotonovelas* (Flora 1985) which are abundant in Latin America; the numerous pamphlets and leaflets directed at servants themselves, which are abundant in Latin America but would be particularly difficult to locate; references to *yanaconaje* and other pre-Hispanic patterns now considered a form of domestic service; and references to domestic service in the context of slavery.

The scope of this bibliography is global, but every attempt has been made to locate the relevant material on Latin America and the Caribbean, although it is likely that some sources have been missed.[6] Material from other regions is included so that Latin American and Latin Americanist users might take advantage of comparative resources, different theoretical perspectives, and different formats of presentation successfully utilized in other parts of the world. For example, the treatment of domestic service in western Europe and the United States by historians (Fairchilds, Hecht, Lasser, McBride, Maza, Porter) is far more extensive than that for Latin America (Graham, Turković). Likewise, only one biography, autobiography, or oral history of a Latin American domestic worker was located (Díaz Uriarte), although they are somewhat more common for other parts of the globe (Brooks, Buechler, Cullwick, Grosvenor, Harrison, Hunt, Keckley, Parkinson, Pruitt). In addition, examining domestic service from racial or ethnic perspectives is more common in other parts of the world (Dill, Glenn, Hamada, Preston-Whyte, Rollins, Romero) than in Latin America (Turković).

Within Latin America and the Caribbean, it appears that domestic service has received the most attention in Peru, Brazil, Mexico, and Colombia. As prominent as domestic service has been as an occupation of women throughout the region for a long period of time, not all Latin American and Caribbean countries are represented in the bibliography. Some of this uneven coverage likely reflects the limits of the compiler's access to information, as well as lack of interest in domestic service in some countries.

The disciplinary backgrounds of the authors are diverse. Globally, domestic service has received attention from anthropologists, educators, attorneys, social workers, political scientists, historians, sociologists, psychologists, literary specialists, and folklorists. For Latin America the field is dominated by sociologists and anthropologists; in other parts of the world, by historians (grossly underrepresented in Latin America), followed by sociologists and anthropologists. This multidisciplinary nature of the interest in domestic service is positive in the sense that research enriched by the application of different methodological approaches and different disciplinary traditions can result in a more comprehensive view of the topic as a whole. However, it does not necessarily result in increased interchange among the researchers from the different disciplines. For example, probably few, if any, anthroplolgists attended the panels on domestic service presented at the fourth and sixth annual Berkshire Conferences on the History of Women. Likewise, probably few, if any, historians attended the panels on domestic service which took place in the mid-1970s and in 1985 at two of the annual meetings of the American Anthropological Association. The 1982 conference in Lima on Andean women and the 1983 Latin American Studies Association meeting were particularly refreshing because they did bring together scholars from different disciplinary backgrounds who share research interests in domestic service.

As another means of sharing information on domestic service, publication is also quite fragmented. There is no single journal with a reputation for publishing articles on this topic in Latin America, although political economy and social history journals have published several articles on domestic service in other parts of the world. Neither is there a publisher with a reputation for producing books on Latin American servants, although St. Martin's Press and Temple University Press have published several books on domestic service in various parts of the world.

Likewise, the theoretical perspectives of the authors have been diverse. The contexts represented here include activism, feminism, ethnography, economic development, race relations, biography, Marxism, employment, and child development. Authors have investigated domestic service as it is related to consciousness-raising, legal rights, industrialization, migration of Caribbeans to the mainland, labor force participation, urbanization, child labor, social class dynamics, group identity, children's socialization, social benefits, the informal labor sector, unionization, family education, rural-urban migration, values, marginality, exploitation of people, ethnic and/or racial dynamics, and the political economy. In Latin America, domestic service is most often also defined within the context of a "social problem."

Prior to the appearance of this volume, most authors, with the notable exception of Hansen, have ignored or de-emphasized the nature of domestic service in geographical locations other than their own, to stress instead materials that support their particular theoretical position. Chaplin and Vázquez have done comparative research on domestic service in several countries, including Latin American ones, although the former has not yet published any extensive comparative analysis on his research in Peru, England, and Spain.

Two authors used an innovative methodology in their research on domestic service: Bunster and Chaney relied heavily on photographs to elicit responses from the Peruvian servants they interviewed.

The overwhelming majority of the research on domestic service has been done about women (with the exceptions of Hansen's work in Zambia and Britto de Motta's in Brazil) by women, a trend particularly notable for Latin America and the Caribbean.

The approximately 425 items listed here will provide the user with a comprehensive understanding of domestic service around the world, and particularly in Latin America. They will expose the user to the wide variety of disciplinary and theoretical approaches to domestic service. Finally, they will facilitate communication and collaboration among committed researchers and activists by directing them to others who share similar interests and perspectives.

Notes

Acknowledgments: The compiler dedicates this project to the memory of her maternal grandmother, Irma Alida Hebben Van der Schaegh, who worked as a domestic in Chicago for a few years after her migration to that city from her birthplace in West Flanders, Belgium. I am grateful to the Committee on Organized Research and the University Library at Northeastern Illinois University, which provided financial support and access to computerized data bases to aid in the realization of this project.

456   Bibliography

1. Perfect Filer is a trademark of Perfect Software, Inc., Berkeley, California.
2. Some of these citations do not meet the specifications of professional librarians, in whose "secret codes" I am not skilled. I have not examined all the items personally, and more than a few require the use of unusual citation style.
3. Includes a segment on Argentine domestics as urban workers.
4. A Central American refugee finds work as a domestic in the U.S.
5. Portrait of a Brazilian woman who had worked as a domestic in her earlier life.
6. I would appreciate being informed of these omissions so that the computerized data base can be made as up-to-date and comprehensive as possible. Please write me c/o 508 Marengo, Forest Park, Illinois 60130.

Bibliography

Addams, Jane. 1896. "A Belated Industry." *American Journal of Sociology* 1, no. 5:536–50.

Aliaga Garate, Dora Nelida. 1970. "El servicio doméstico y su régimen jurídico." Tesis, Pontificia Universidad Católica del Perú, Lima.

Almeida e Silva, María D'Ajuda, Lilibeth Cardoso and Mary Garcia Castro. 1979. "As empregadas domésticas na região metropolitana do Rio de Janeiro: Uma análise atravez de dados de ENDEF." Governo do Brasil, Fundação Instituto Brasileiro de Geografía e Estatística (IBGE). Also in *Boletín Demográfico* 12, no. 1 (1981): 26–92.

Alonso, Pablo, María Rosa Larráin, and Roberto Saldías. 1975. *Realidad de las empleadas domésticas en Chile.* Santiago: Universidad Católica de Chile, Escuela de Derecho.

———. 1978. "La empleada de casa particular: Algunos antecedentes." In Paz Covarrúbias and Rolando Franco, eds., *Chile: Mujer y sociedad,* pp. 399–422. Santiago de Chile: UNICEF.

Anderson, C. Arnold, and Mary Jean Bowman. 1953. "The Vanishing Servant and the Contemporary Status System of the American South." *American Journal of Sociology* 60, no. 2:215–30.

Araujo Camacho, Hilda. 1977. "Posibilidad de conscientización de la trabajadora del hogar por la educación básica laboral." Paper presented at the Seminario de Investigaciones Sociales acerca de la Mujer, Lima.

Ariès, Philippe. 1962. *Centuries of Childhood: A Social History of Family Life.* New York: Vintage Books.

———. 1980. "Le service domestique: permanence et variations." *Dix-Septième Siècle* 32, no. 4: 415–420.

Armstrong, M. Joycelyn. 1985. "Female Domestic Servants in Industrializing

Malaysia." Paper presented at the annual meeting of the American An-
thropological Association, Symposium on Domestic Workers.
Ary Farias, Zaíra. 1979. "Mão de obra feminina nos serviços de consumo indi-
vidual—um estudo de empregadas domésticas em Fortaleza." Photo-
copy.
———. 1983. *Domesticidade: "Cautiveiro" feminino?* Rio de Janeiro: Achiamé and
Centro da Mulher Brasileira.
Aubert, Vilhelm. 1956. "The Housemaid—An Occupational Role in Crisis."
Acta Sociológica 1, no. 3:149–58. Reprinted in Richard D. Schwartz and
Jerome H. Skolnick, eds., *Society and the Legal Order: Cases and Materials
in the Sociology of Law.* New York: Basic Books, 1970.
Balderson, Eileen, with Douglas Goodlad. 1982. *Backstairs Life in an English
Country House.* Newton Abbot, Eng., and North Pomfert, Vt.: David &
Charles.
Base, E. D. 1979. *Empregadas domésticas, mulheres en luta, Lisboa, Col.* Lisboa:
Movimento Operario.
Berch, Bettina. 1984. " 'The Sphinx in the Household': A New Look at the
History of Household Workers." *Review of Radical Political Economists* 16,
no. 1:105–20.
Berkowitz [Luton], Susan. 1978. "Women Servants in Southern Italy: Chang-
ing Patterns of Honor and Economic Constraint." In *Female Servants and
Economic Development,* pp. 30–50. Michigan Occasional Papers in Wom-
en's Studies No. 1. Ann Arbor: University of Michigan.
Black, Clementina, ed. 1915. *Married Women's Work: Report of an Enquiry Under-
taken by the Women's Industrial Council.* London: G. Bell; rpt. New York:
Garland, 1980.
Bled, Y. 1965. "La condition des Domestiques Antillaises à Montréal." Mas-
ter's thesis, University of Montreal.
Bogotá, Alcaldía Mayor de. 1980. *Estudio socioeconómico laboral de los empleados
a domicilio en el servicio de empleo del distrito.* Bogotá: Departamento Ad-
ministrativo de Bienestar Social, División de Desarrollo Comunitario.
Boone, Gladys. n.d. "Household Employment: Lynchburg [Virginia] Study,
1936–1937." Amey E. Watson Papers, Cornell University, Ithaca, N.Y.
Boserup, Ester. 1970. *Woman's Role in Economic Development.* New York: St.
Martin's Press; London: Allen & Unwin.
Bossard, James Herbert Siward. 1966. "Domestic Servants and Child Devel-
opment." In Bossard, *The Sociology of Child Development,* chap. 12. 4th ed.
New York: Harper & Row.
Bossen, Laurel Herbenar. 1984. *The Redivision of Labor: Women and Economic
Choice in Four Guatemalan Communities.* Albany: State University of New
York Press.
Bowen, Uvelia S. A. 1970. *What Is a Day's Work? A Personnel Practices Guide for
Household Employees and Employers.* Philadelphia: HEART.
Branca, Patricia. 1975. *Silent Sisterhood: Middle-Class Women in the Victorian*

Home. Pittsburgh: Carnegie-Mellon University Press; London: Croom Helm.

Bravo Espinoza, J. F. A. 1975. "El proceso de adaptación al medio urbano: El caso de las empleadas domésticas en Lima Metropolitana." Tesis, Facultad de Ciencias Sociales, Universidad Nacional Mayor de San Marcos, Lima.

Breen, Richard. 1983. "Farm Servanthood in Ireland, 1900–1940." *The Economic History Review* 36, no. 1:87–102.

Britto de Motta, Alda. 1977. "Visão de mundo da empregada doméstica: Um estudo de caso." Diss. de Pós-graduação em Ciências Humanas, Universidade Federal da Bahia, Salvador.

———. 1981. "Emprego doméstico no capitalismo, o caso de Salvador." Paper presented at the fifth annual meeting of the Associação Nacional de Pos-Graduação e Pesquisas em Ciências Sociais.

———. 1984. "Emprego doméstico masculino." Paper presented at the eighth annual meeting of the Associação Nacional de Pos-Graduação e Pesquisas em Ciências Sociais.

Brooks, Sara. 1986. *You May Plow Here: The Narrative of Sara Brooks.* Thordis Simonsen, ed. New York: Norton.

Broom, Leonard, and J. H. Smith. 1963. "Bridging Occupations." *British Journal of Sociology* 14:321–34.

Brown, Jean Collier. 1940. *Household Workers.* Chicago: Science Research Associates. Occasional Monograph No. 14.

Buechler, Hans, and Judith-Maria Buechler. 1985. *Carmen: The Autobiography of a Spanish Galician Peasant Woman.* Cambridge, Mass.: Schenkman.

Bunster, Ximena. 1977. "Talking Pictures: Field Method and Visual Mode." *Signs* 3, no. 1:278–93.

Bunster, Ximena, and Elsa M. Chaney. 1985. *Sellers & Servants: Working Women in Lima, Peru.* New York: Praeger Special Studies.

Burkett, Elinor C. 1975. "Early Colonial Peru: The Urban Female Experience." Ph.D. diss., University of Pittsburgh.

———. 1978. "Indian Women and White Society: The Case of Sixteenth-Century Peru." In Asunción Lavrin, ed., *Latin American Women: Historical Perspectives,* pp. 101–28. Westport, Conn.: Greenwood Press.

Butler, C. Violet. 1916. *Domestic Service.* London: G. Bell; rpt. New York: Garland, 1981.

Byron, William James. 1969. "The Applicability of the Job Bank Concept to the Washington, D.C. Market for Domestic Day Workers." Thesis, University of Maryland, College Park.

Cadernos de CEAS. 1975. *Empregadas Domésticas.* Salvador: CEAS, março/abril.

Callahan, Helen C. 1977–78. "Upstairs-Downstairs in Chicago, 1870–1907: The Glessner Household." *Chicago History* 6, no. 1:195–209.

Calmy, Christophe. 1978. "Les Domestiques." *Histoire* 7:83–85.

Cárdenas de Matos, Moraima. 1944. "El servicio doméstico particular." Tesis, Escuela de Servico Social del Perú, Lima.

——. 1945. "Encuesta realizada en 100 familias de empleadas en servicio doméstico particular." *Servicio Social* 3, no. 3:133–35.

Caro Velazco, Elena. 1982. "La problemática del menor trabajador doméstico en el Cuzco." Tesis, Universidad Nacional Mayor de San Marcos, Lima.

Carter, I. 1976. "Class and Culture among Farm Servants in the North-East, 1840–1914." In A. A. MacLaren, ed., *Social Class in Scotland: Past and Present*, pp. 105–27. Edinburgh: J. Donald.

Castro, Mercedes. 1972. "La nueva situación de las empleadas de casas particulares." RIKCHAY 2, no. 3: 36–38.

Catalán, F. 1977. "Con las trabajadoras del hogar." *Pastoral Andina* 21 (marzo).

Chaney, Elsa M. 1976. "Women at the 'Marginal' Pole of the Economy: Domestics in Lima." Paper presented at the Wellesley Conference on Women in Development.

——. 1977. "Agripina: Servicio doméstico y sus implicaciones en el desarrollo." Paper presented at the Primer Simposio Méxicano/Centroamericano de Investigación sobre la Mujer.

——. 1985. "'Se Necesita Muchacha': Household Workers in Lima, Peru." Paper presented at the annual meeting of the American Anthropological Association, Symposium on Domestic Workers.

——. 1985. Sellers & Servants: Working Women in Lima (see Bunster).

Chaplin, David. 1964. "Domestic Service and the Negro." In Arthur B. Shostak and William Gomberg, eds., *Blue-Collar World: Studies of the American Worker*, pp. 527–36. Englewood Cliffs, N.J.: Prentice Hall.

——. 1967. *The Peruvian Industrial Labor Force.* Princeton, N.J.: Princeton University Press.

——. 1969. "Domestic Service and the Rationalization of Household Economy: An Outline for a Contemporary Study." Paper presented at the annual meeting of the American Sociological Association. University of Wisconsin, Madison, Department of Sociology. Mimeo, 1968.

——. 1969. "Private Household Employment in the United States: An Exploratory Project." Washington, D.C.: U.S. Department of Labor, Manpower Administration. Mimeo.

——. 1970. "Domestic Service as a Family Activity and as an Occupation during Industrialization." Paper presented at a meeting of the International Sociological Association.

——. 1974. "Upward Mobility for Private Household Workers." Paper prepared for the Workshop on Research Needed to Improve the Employment and Employability of Women, U.S. Department of Labor.

——. 1978. "Domestic Service and Industrialization." In Richard Thomasson, ed., *Comparative Studies in Sociology,* pp. 92–127. Greenwich, Conn.: Jai Press.

Chernow, Ron. 1976. "All in a Day's Work." *Mother Jones* 1:11–16.

Chimbote [Perú], Comisión de Justicia Social de la Prelatura. 1980. "Las tra-
    bajadoras del hogar también tenemos derechos." Serié Derechos Labo-
    rales, Instituto de Promoción e Educación Popular, Chimbote.
Christensen, Ethlyn. 1971. "Restructuring the Occupation." *Issues in Industrial
    Society* 2, no. 1:47–53.
Círculo de Estudios de la Mujer. 1981. *Boletín* No. 7 (special issue on domestic
    service), Santiago de Chile, diciembre.
Clarke, Duncan G. 1974. *Domestic Workers in Rhodesia: The Economics of Masters
    and Servants.* Givelo, Rhodesia: Mambo Press.
Clark-Lewis, Elizabeth. 1983. "From 'Servant' to 'Dayworker': A Study of Se-
    lected Household Service Workers in Washington, D.C., 1900–1926."
    Ph.D. diss., University of Maryland, College Park.
———. 1984. "Black Household Workers in the District of Columbia, 1900–
    1940: History through Women's Voices." Paper presented at the sixth
    Berkshire Conference on the History of Women.
———. 1985. "'This Work Had a' End': The Transition from Live-in to Day
    Work." In *Southern Women: The Intersection of Race, Class, and Gender.* Cen-
    ter for Research on Women, Working Paper No. 2. Memphis, Tenn.:
    Memphis State University.
Clegg, Brenda Faye. 1983. "Black Female Domestics during the Great De-
    pression in New York City, 1930–1940." Ph.D. diss., University of Mich-
    igan, Ann Arbor.
Cock, Jacklyn. 1980. *Maids and Madams: A Study in the Politics of Exploitation.*
    Johannesburg: Ravan Press; videorecording, New York: Filmakers Li-
    brary, 1985.
———. 1981. "Disposable Nannies: Domestic Servants in the Political Economy
    of South Africa." *Review of African Political Economy* no. 21:63–83.
Colen, Shellee. 1985. "'Doing Domestic' and Seeking Respect: West Indian
    Domestic Workers in New York City." Paper presented at the annual
    meeting of the American Anthropological Association, Symposium on
    Domestic Workers.
———. 1986. "'With Respect and Feelings': Voices of West Indian Child Care
    and Domestic Workers in New York." In Johnetta Cole, ed., *All American
    Women: Lines That Divide, Ties That Bind,* pp. 46–70. New York: Free
    Press.
Coles, Robert. 1971. "I Am a Maid, and What Do I Know?" *Atlantic* 228, no.
    2:64–68.
Coley, Soraya Moore. 1981. "'And Still I Rise:' An Exploratory Study of Con-
    temporary Black Household Workers." Ph.D. diss., Bryn Mawr College,
    Philadelphia.
Compton-Burnett, I. [Ivy]. 1947. *Manservant and Maidservant.* London: David
    & Charles; rpt. Oxford and New York: Oxford University Press, 1983.
Cooke, Merritt. 1985. "Domestic Workers and the Organization of Nisyang

Ethnic Identity." Paper presented at the annual meeting of the American Anthropological Association, Symposium on Domestic Workers.

Coser, Lewis A. 1973. "Servants: The Obsolescence of an Occupational Role." *Social Forces* 52, no. 1:31–40.

Cullwick, Hannah. 1984. *The Diaries of Hannah Cullwick, Victorian Maidservant.* Ed. and with an Introduction by Liz Stanley. London: Virago Press; New Brunswick, N.J.: Rutgers University Press.

Cunnington, Phillis. 1974. *Costume of Household Servants from the Middle Ages to 1900.* London: A & C Black; New York: Barnes & Noble, 1975.

Cussiánovich, Alejandro. 1974. *Llamados de ser libres (empleadas de hogar).* Lima: Centro de Estudios y Publicaciones.

Dahl-Jørgensen, Carla. 1983. "Role Distance and Group Identity: A Study of Identity Management among Domestic Servants in Puebla, Mexico." M.A. thesis, University of Trondheim, Norway.

———. 1985. "Housemaids and '*Patrones*': An Interactional Analysis of Their Identity Management / Sirvientes y patrones: Un estudio macrosociológico del manejo de identidad." Paper prepared for the twelfth Congress of the Latin American Studies Association.

———. 1986. "Domestic Servants and Work Identity: A Case from Puebla, Mexico." In Bjorn B. Erring, ed., *Orientations and Expectations: Social Anthropology and the Trondheim Connection, 1975–1985.* Trondheim: Tapir.

Davidoff, Leonore. 1973. "Above and Below Stairs." *New Society* 24, no. 551:181–83.

———. 1973. "Mastered for Life: Servant, Wife, and Mother in Victorian and Edwardian Britain." Paper presented at the Anglo-American Conference of Comparative Labor History, Rutgers University.

———. 1973. "Domestic Service and the Working-Class Life Cycle." *Bulletin of the Society for the Study of Labour History* 26:10–12.

———. 1973. *The Best Circles: Society, Etiquette, and the Season.* London: Croom Helm.

———. 1974. "Mastered for Life: Servant and Wife in Victorian and Edwardian England." *Journal of Social History* 7, no. 4:406–28; 446–59.

———. 1978. "Sex and Class in Victorian England: The Case of the Munby Diaries." Paper presented at the fourth Berkshire Conference on the History of Women.

———. 1983. "Class and Gender in Victorian England." In Judith L. Newton, Mary P. Ryan, and Judith R. Walkowitz, eds., *Sex and Class in Women's History*, pp. 16–71. London: Routledge & Kegan Paul.

Davidoff, Leonore, and Ruth Hawthorn. 1976. *A Day in the Life of a Victorian Domestic Servant.* London: Allen & Unwin.

Dawes, Frank. 1974. *Not in Front of the Servants: A True Portrait of English Upstairs/Downstairs Life.* New York: Taplinger.

De Barbieri, M. Teresita. 1975. "La condición de la mujer en América Latina:

Su participación social; antecedentes y situación actual." In Comisión
Económica para América Latina (CEPAL), ed., *Mujeres en América Lati-
na: Aportes para una discusión,* pp. 46–87. México, D.F.: Fondo de
Cultura Económica.

———. 1977. "Trabajo doméstico: Una interpretación teórica." Paper presented at the Primer Simposio Méxicano-Centroamericano de Investigación
sobre la Mujer.

———. 1977. "Notas para el estudio del trabajo de las mujeres: El problema del
trabajo doméstico." *Demografía y Economía* 12, no. 1:129–37.

———. n.d. "Trabajo doméstico—trabajo remunerado: Hipótesis para el estudio del trabajo de las mujeres en los sectores medios." Paper presented at the Reunión Nacional sobre la Investigación Demográfica en México, Universidad Nacional Autónoma de México.

———. 1980–81. "Las sirvientas no pueden decir mucho" *FEM* 4, no. 16:31–
36.

De Lisser, H. G. 1914. *Jane's Career: A Story of Jamaica.* Published as serial in
Jamaica Gleaner; rpt. London: Heinemann, 1972.

DeVita, Cara, Jeffrey Kleinman, and Lillian Jemenez. 1982. *What Could You
Do with a Nickel?* New York: New Times Television. Film.

Díaz Uriarte, Adelinda. 1983. "Asociación de trabajadoras del hogar de Lima,
Perú." Paper presented at the Pequeño Encuentro sobre el Servicio Doméstico en América Latina, Mexico City.

Dill, Bonnie Thornton. 1979. "Across the Boundaries of Race and Class: An
Exploration of the Relationship between Work and Family among Black
Female Domestic Servants." Ph.D. diss., New York University.

———. 1979. "Black Women in Private Household Work: A Study of Race, Sex
Roles and Social Change." Paper presented at the Southwestern Sociological Association meeting.

———. 1980. "The Means To Put My Children Through: Childrearing Goals
and Strategies among Black Female Domestic Servants." In La Frances
Rodgers-Rose, ed., *The Black Woman: Current Research and Theory.* Beverly Hills, Calif.: Sage.

Drury, Elizabeth. 1982. *The Butler's Pantry Book.* New York: St. Martin's Press.

Duarte, Isis, Estela Hernández, Aída Garden Bobea, and Francis Pou. 1976.
"Condiciones sociales del servicio doméstico en la República Dominicana." *Realidad Contemporánea* 1, nos. 3–4:79–104.

———. 1983. "Condiciones de vida, ideológica y socialización de los niños de las
trabajadoras de hogar en Santo Domingo, R.D." Paper presented at the
meeting of the Latin American Studies Association.

Dubofsky, Melvyn. 1980. "Neither Upstairs, nor Downstairs: Domestic Service in Middle-Class American Homes." *Reviews in American History* 8,
no. 1:86–91.

Dudden, Faye. 1981. "From Help to Domestics: American Servants, 1800–
1880." Ph.D. diss., University of Rochester, New York.

———. 1983. *Serving Women: Household Service in Nineteenth-Century America.* Middletown, Conn.: Wesleyan University Press.

———. 1984. "Why Not Domestic Service? The Twentieth Century." Paper presented at the sixth Berkshire Conference on the History of Women.

Dworaczek, Marian. 1981. *Domestic Workers: A Bibliography.* Monticello, Ill.: Vance Bibliographies.

Eaton, Isabel. 1899. "Report on Domestic Service." In W. E. B. Du Bois, ed., *The Philadelphia Negro*, pp. 427–520. Philadelphia: Ginn; rpt. New York: Schocken Books, 1967.

Ebery, Mark, and Brian Preston. 1976. *Domestic Service in Late Victorian and Edwardian England, 1871–1914.* Reading Geographical Papers No. 42. Reading, Eng.: University of Reading, Department of Geography.

Eltzroth, Marjorie. 1973. "Vocational Counseling for Ghetto Women with Prostitution and Domestic Service Backgrounds." *Vocational Guidance Quarterly* 22, no. 1:32–38.

Ely Santo dos Santos, E. de. n.d. *As domésticas: Um estudo interdisciplinar de realidade social, política, econômica e jurídica.* Porto Alegre, Brazil: Editora de Universidade.

Engelsing, Rolf. 1968. "Dientsbotenlektüre im 18 and 19 Jahrhundert in Deutschland." *International Review of Social History* 13, no. 3:384–429.

———. 1974. "Das Vermögen der Dienstboten in Deutschland Zwischen dem 17. un 20. Jahrhundert." *Jahrbuch des Institute für Deutsche Geschichte* 3:227–56.

Fairchilds, Cissie. 1979. "Masters and Servants in 18th Century Toulouse." *Journal of Social History* 12, no. 3:368–93.

———. 1984. *Domestic Enemies: Servants and Their Masters in Old Regime France.* Baltimore, Md.: Johns Hopkins University Press.

FEM. 1980–81. [Special Issue on Domestic Service] 4, no. 16 (México, D.F.).

Fernández Cazalis, Concepción. 1980/81. "La criada y la señora, dos servidumbres." *FEM* 4, no. 16:61–64.

Figueroa Galup, Blanca. 1974. *La trabajadora doméstica (Lima, Perú).* Lima: Asociación Perú-Mujer.

———. 1975. "Diagnóstico del rol ocupacional y de la educación formal de la mujer: Domésticas. Parte primero: Rol ocupacional." Instituto Nacional de Investigación y Desarrollo de la Educación "Augusto Salazar Bondy," Lima. Mimeo.

———. 1976. "La trabajadora doméstica en el Perú: El caso de Lima." *Boletín Documental sobre la Mujer de CIDHAL.* Also published in *América Latina: La situación de las trabajadoras domésticas.* Lima: Docet CELADEC No. 3, 1978.

———. 1977. "La doméstica en Lima metropolitana: Influencia del nivel económico de la familia patronal sobre su resocialización, condiciones de trabajo y aspiraciones futuras." Paper presented at the Seminario de Investigaciones Sociales acerca de la Mujer, Lima.

Flor Cuneo, Miguel de la. 1966. *Beneficios sociales de los trabajadores domésticos.* Lima: Escuela Sindical Autónoma de Lima.

Flora, Cornelia Butler. 1985. "Photonovel: Introduction" and "Maids in the Mexican Photonovel." *Studies in Latin American Popular Culture* 4:63–66, 84–94.

Flores Guerrero, Theresa. 1961. "Reglamentación y problemas que confronta del servicio doméstico en el Perú." Tesis, Escuela de Servicio Social del Perú, Lima.

Fox, Grace. 1940. "Women Domestic Workers in Washington, D.C., 1940." *Monthly Labor Review* 54:338–45.

Franklin, Jill. 1975. "Troops of Servants: Labour and Planning in the Country House, 1840–1914." *Victorian Studies* 19 (December):211–39.

Gaitskell, Deborah, Judy Kimble, Moira Maconachie, Elaine Unterhalter. 1983. "Class, Race and Gender: Domestic Workers in South Africa." *Review of African Politial Economy* nos. 27–28:86–108.

Gálvez, Thelma, and Rosalba Todaro. 1984. *Trabajadoras de casa particular.* Santiago, Chile: Círculo de Estudios de la Mujer, Proyecto Trabajadoras de Casa Particular.

———. 1985. *Yo trabajo así . . . en casa particular.* Santiago: Centro de Estudios de la Mujer.

Gangotena G., Margarita. 1974. "La influencia del servicio doméstico en la estructura del sistema familiar y en el desarrollo de la identidad del niño y del adolescente. . . ." Paper presented at the International Congress of Americanists.

Garcia Castro, Mary. 1979. "Migración laboral femenina." Programa de las Naciones Unidas, Proyecto Oficina Internacional del Trabajo sobre Migraciones Laborales, Bogotá. Mimeo.

———. 1982. "¿Qué se compra y qué se paga en el servicio doméstico?: El caso de Bogotá." In Magdalena León, ed., *La realidad colombiana,* vol. 1, *Debate sobre la mujer en América Latina y el Caribe,* pp. 92–122. Bogotá: Asociación Colombiana para el Estudio de la Población.

Garcia Castro, Mary, Bertha Quintero, and Gladys Jimeno. 1981. "Empleo doméstico, sector informal, migración y movilidad ocupacional en áreas urbanas en Colombia." Programa Naciones Unidas, Proyecto Oficina Internacional de Trabajo sobre Migraciones Laborales, Bogotá. Final report, mimeo.

Garduño A., M. 1979. "Las condiciones de trabajo de las mujeres ocupadas en el servicio doméstico en el distrito federal." Tesis, Universidad Nacional Autónoma de México, Facultad de Ciencias Politicas y Sociales.

Gavíria Villar, Alvaro. 1974. *El servicio doméstico: Un gremio en extinción.* Bogotá: Editorial Controversia.

Genet, Jean. 1962. *The Maids and Deathwatch.* New York: Grove Press.

Giffin, Karen. 1980. "A mulher na reprodução da força de trabalho: Serviço doméstico pago como estratégia familiar de sobreviencia." Paper presented to the 32d Congresso de la Sociedade Brasileira para o Progresso da Ciência, Rio de Janeiro. Photocopy.

Gillis, John R. 1979. "Servants, Sexual Relations, and the Risks of Illegitimacy in London, 1801–1900." *Feminist Studies* 5, no. 1:142–73.

———. 1983. "Servants, Sexual Relations, and the Risks of Illegitimacy in London, 1801–1900." In Judith L. Newton, Mary P. Ryan, and Judith R. Walkowitz, eds., *Sex and Class in Women's History,* pp. 114–45. London: Routledge & Kegan Paul.

Glenn, Evelyn Nakano. 1980. "The Dialectics of Wage Work: Japanese-American Women and Domestic Service, 1905–1940." *Feminist Studies* 6, no. 3:432–71.

———. 1981. "Occupational Ghettoization: Japanese-American Women and Domestic Service, 1905–1970." *Ethnicity* 8, no. 4:352–86.

———. 1986. *Issei, Nisei, War Bride: Three Generations of Japanese American Women in Domestic Service.* Philadelphia: Temple University Press.

———. 1987. "Women, Labor Migration and Household Work: Japanese-American Women in the Pre-War Period." In Christine Bose and Glenna Spitze, eds., *Ingredients for Women's Employment Policy,* pp. 93–113. Ithaca: State University of New York Press.

Gogna, Mónica L. 1981. *El servicio doméstico en Buenos Aires: Características de empleo y relación laboral.* Buenos Aires: Centro de Estudios e Investigaciones Laborales (CEIL).

Goisa Chambilla, Dora Gladys. 1968. "Situación socio-laboral de la empleada doméstica emigrada de provincias y aporte de la educadora familiar a la solución de los problemas encontrados." Tesis, Pontificia Universidad Católica del Perú, Lima.

———. 1978. "Empregada doméstica, a beira da vida?" *Revista Familia Crista,* fevereiro.

Goldman, Gary. 1980. "Yes, Ma'am." Videorecording. New York: Filmakers Library.

Goldsmith, Mary. 1980–81. "Trabajo doméstico asalariado y desarrollo capitalista." *FEM* 4, no. 16:10–20.

———. 1982. "Relaciones de poder y condiciones de trabajo de las empleadas domésticas." *Revista de Estudios sobre la Juventud In Telpochtli, In Ichpuchtli* 2, no. 5:13–24.

———. 1984. "La salud entre las trabajadoras domésticas." *FEM* 8, no. 35:8–9.

Gonzáles Nieves, O. 1980. *Breve estudio crítico de la legislación sobre los trabajadores del hogar y sus derechos sociales.* Chimbote: Instituto de Promoción y Educación Popular.

González, Léila, and Carlos Hasenbalg. 1982. *Lugar de negro.* Lima: Editora Marco Zero.

Gordon, Sue. 1974. *Domestic Workers: A Handbook for Housewives.* 3d ed. Johannesburg: South Africa Institute of Race Relations.

Graham, Sandra Lauderdale. 1982. "Protection and Obedience: The Paternalist World of Female Domestic Servants, Rio de Janeiro, 1860–1910." Ph.D. diss., University of Texas at Austin.

——. 1983. "Servants and PATROES: Domestic Life in Rio de Janeiro in the 1870s." Paper presented at the meeting of the American Historical Association.

Grau, Ilda Elena. 1980. "Las empleadas domésticas en la ciudad de México: Una análisis de las trayectorias de vida, los valores y las prácticas." Tesis, Universidad Autónoma Metropolitana, Unidad Xochimilco, Departmento de Sociología.

——. 1982. "Trabajo y vida cotidiana de empleadas domésticas en la cuidad de México: Un estudio cualitativo." In Magdalena León, ed., *Sociedad, subordinación y femenismo*, vol. 3, *Debate sobre la mujer en América Latina y el Caribe*, pp. 167–81. Bogotá: Asociación Colombiana para el Estudio de la Población.

Grossman, Allyson Sherman. 1980. "Women in Domestic Work: Yesterday and Today." *Monthly Labor Review* 103, no. 8:17–21.

Grosvenor, Verta Mae. 1972. *Thursdays and Every Other Sunday Off: A Domestic Rap by Verta Mae*. New York: Doubleday.

Guiral, Pierre, and Guy Thullier. 1978. *La vie quotidienne des domestiques en France au XIXe siècle*. Paris: Hachette.

——. 1979. "Les sources de l'histoire régionale des domestiques au XIXe siècle." *Revue Historique* 259, no. 2:441–52.

Gutiérrez, Ana. 1983. *Se necesita muchacha*. México, D.F.: Fondo de Cultura Económica.

Gutton, Jean-Pierre. 1981. *Domestiques et serviteurs dans la France de l'Ancien régime*. Paris: Aubier Montaigne.

Gyani, Gabor. 1983. "A Budapesti Hazicseled-Munkapiac Mukodesi Mechanizmusai, 1890–1941." *Szazadok* 117, no. 2:401–33.

Haims, Lynne Faye. 1981. "In Their Place: Domestic Servants in English Country Houses, 1850–1870." Ph.D. diss., Johns Hopkins University, Baltimore.

Haines, J. W. 1960. "Unethical Practices in Bringing Domestic Servants into U.S. Deplored." *Bulletin, U.S. Department of State* 43:365.

Hamada, Tomoko. 1985. "Apartheid and Maid." Paper presented at the annual meeting of the American Anthropological Association, Symposium on Domestic Workers.

Hamburger, Robert. 1977. "A Stranger in the House." *Southern Exposure* 5, no. 1:22–31.

——. 1978. *A Stranger in the House*. New York: Macmillan.

Hamermesh, Mira. 1985. *Maids and Madams: Apartheid Begins in the Home*. New York: Filmakers Library. Videorecording. Based on the book by Jacklyn Cock.

Hammond, María Elena Mujica de. 1985. "Women in Peru: Domestic Individuals and Domestic Service." Master's thesis, University of Birmingham, England.

Hansen, Karen Tranberg. 1983. "Men Servants and Women Bosses: The Domestic Service Institution in Colonial Zambia." In *Sex/Gender Division of Labor: Feminist Perspectives*, pp. 117–38. Minneapolis: University of Minnesota, Center for Advanced Feminist Studies.

———. 1984. "Members of the Family? Paid Servants and Kept Relatives in Urban Zambian Households." Paper presented at the annual meeting of the American Anthropological Association.

———. 1984. "Continuity and Change in Domestic Service in Zambia." Paper presented at the meeting of the African Studies Association.

Harris, Trudier. 1982. *From Mammies to Militants: Domestics in Black American Literature*. Philadelphia: Temple University Press.

Harrison, Rosina. 1975. *Rose: My Life in Service*. New York: Viking.

Hawks, Joanne V., and Sheila L. Skemp. 1983. *Sex, Race, and the Role of Women in the South*. Jackson: University Press of Mississippi.

Haynes, Elizabeth Ross. 1923. "Negroes in Domestic Service in the United States." *Journal of Negro History* 8, no. 4:384–442.

Hecht, J. Jean. 1949. "The Domestic Servant Class in Eighteenth-Century England." Ph.D. diss., Harvard University, Cambridge, Mass.

———. 1954. *Continental and Colonial Servants in Eighteenth-Century England*. Northampton, Mass.: Smith College Studies in History.

———. 1956. *The Domestic Servant Class in Eighteenth-Century England*. London: Routledge & Kegan Paul; rpt. Westport, Conn.: Hyperion Press, 1981.

Helfer, Ruth. 1966. "El problema social de la empleada doméstica." Tesis, Escuela Normal Superior de Mujeres San Pedro-Monterrico, Lima.

Henry, Frances. 1968. "The West Indian Domestic Scheme in Canada." *Social and Economic Studies* 17, no. 1:83–91.

———. 1982. "A Note on Caribbean Migration to Canada." *Caribbean Review* 11, no. 1:38–41.

Herold, Joan Mildred. 1982. "Socioeconomic and Demographic Aspects of Female Labor Force Participation in Urban Chile." Ph.D. diss., University of Pennsylvania, Philadelphia.

Hewett, Valerie. 1974. "Migrant Female Labour in Colombia: An Analysis of Urban Employment in Domestic Service." Interim report, Corporación Centro Regional de Población, Bogotá.

Higgs, Edward. 1979. "Per la stòria dei servi domèstici: Un' anàlisi quantitativa." *Guarderni Stòrici* 14, no. 1:284–301.

———. 1982. "The Tabulation of Occupations in the Nineteenth-Century Census, with Special Reference to Domestic Servants." *Local Population Studies* 28:58–66.

———. 1982. *Domestic Servants and Households in Rochdale, 1851–1871*. New York: Garland.

———. 1983. "Domestic Servants and Households in Victorian England." *Social History* 8, no. 2:201–10.

Horn, Pamela. 1975. *The Rise and Fall of the Victorian Servant.* Dublin: Gill and Macmillan; New York: St. Martin's Press.

Hoskins, Frank Lawrence. 1955. "Master Servant Relations in Tudor and Early Stuart Literature, with Special Reference to the Drama of Shakespeare and His Contemporaries." Thesis, Columbia University, New York.

Huggett, Frank Edward. 1977. *Life below Stairs: Domestic Servants in England from Victorian Times.* New York: Scribner.

Hunt, Annie Mae. n.d. *I Am Annie Mae.* Austin, Tex.: Rosegarden Press.

Ibarra, Teresita E. 1979. "Women Migrants: Focus on Domestic Helpers." *Philippine Sociological Review* 27, no. 2:77–92.

Instituto Joaquim Nabuco de Pesquisas Sociais, Recife. 1970. "Empregadas domésticas do Recife, suas condições e aspirações." Boletim do Instituto 18:42–106.

Instituto Sindical María Cano, Bogotá. 1972. "Servicio doméstico." I S M A C Publicación No. 1. Mimeo.

International Labour Office (I LO, Geneva). 1970. "Situación y condiciones del empleo de los trabajadores domésticos en los hogares privados." *Revista Internacional de Trabajo* 82, no. 4:433–55.

———. 1970. "The Employment and Conditions of Domestic Workers in Private Households: An I LO Survey." *International Labour Review* 102, no. 4:391–401.

———. 1970. "Belgium: Contracts of Domestic Employment." *International Labour Review* 102, no. 6:617–18.

———. 1970. *The Employment and Conditions of Domestic Workers in Private Households.* Geneva: I LO.

Iturralde, Mariana. 1980/81. "No siempre las víctimas." *FEM* 4, no. 16:71–72.

Jarlin, Françoise. 1969. *Les domestiques à Bordeaux en 1872.* Bordeaux: Université du Bordeaux, Faculté des Lettrés et Sciences Humaines.

Jelin, Elizabeth. 1976. *Migración a las ciudades y participación en la fuerza de trabajo de las mujeres latinoamericanas: El caso del servicio doméstico.* Buenos Aires: Centro de Estudios de Estado y Sociedad.

———. 1977. "Migration and Labor Force Participation of Latin American Women: The Domestic Servants in the Cities." *Signs* 3, no. 1:129–41.

Johnson, Eleanor. 1933. *Household Employment in Chicago.* Bulletin No. 106. Washington, D.C.: U.S. Women's Bureau.

Jung, Reinhardt. 1983. *Muchacha: Die Unsichtbaren Dienerinnen Lateinamerikas.* Borheim, Merten: Lamur Verlag.

Juventud Obrera Católica. 1978. "Informe 'Trabajadoras del hogar,' Perú." Paper prepared for the Encuentro Latinoamericano, Colombia.

——. 1979. *Informe empleadas de hogar Arequipa.* Arequipa: JOC.

——. 1980. "Empleadas del hogar." JOC, Baranquilla, Colombia. Photocopy.

Kamau [Botscharow], Lucy Jayne. 1974. "Domestic Service in Nairobi, Kenya." Unpublished paper, photocopy.

Katz, Paul. 1941. *Situation économique et sociale des domestiques en France, en Allemagne et en Suisse.* Paris: Montpellier.

Katzman, David M. 1978. *Seven Days a Week: Women and Domestic Service in Industrializing America.* New York: Oxford University Press.

——. 1978. "Domestic Service; Woman's Work." In Ann Stromberg and Shirley Harkess, eds., *Women Working: Theories and Facts in Perspective,* pp. 377–91. Palo Alto, Calif.: Mayfield.

Keckley, Elizabeth [Hobbs]. 1868. *Behind the Scenes. Or, Thirty Years a Slave, and Four Years in the White House.* New York: C. W. Carlton; rpt. New York: Arno, 1968.

Kline, Ruth Fifield. 1980. "Domestic Servants on the New York and London Stages, 1800–1920, with an Emphasis on Costume." Ph.D. diss., University of Illinois, Urbana.

Kofes de Almeida, Maria Suely. 1982. "Entre nos mulheres, elas as patrōas e elas as empregadas." In Maria Suely Kofes de Almeida, Antonio Augusto Arantes, Carlos Rodrigues Brandão, Nariza Correa, Bela Feldemann Bianco, Verena Stolhke, and Alba Zaluar, eds., *Colcha de Retalhos.* São Paulo: Editora Brasiliense.

Kussmaul, Ann S. 1978. "Servants in Husbandry in Early Modern England." Ph.D. diss., University of Toronto.

——. 1981. *Servants in Husbandry in Early Modern England.* New York: Cambridge University Press.

——. 1981. "The Ambiguous Mobility of Farm Servants." *Economic History Review* 34, no. 2:222–35.

Kyrk, Hazel. 1932. "The Household Worker." *American Federationist* 39, no. 1:36.

Kytle, Elizabeth Larisey. 1958. *Willie Mae.* New York: Knopf.

Lacelle, Claudette. 1982. "Les domestiques dans les villes canadiènnes au XIXe siècle: Effectifs et conditions de vie." *Social History* 15, no. 29:181–207.

Laguerre, Michel. 1985. "Domestic Servants in Fort-de-France, Martinique." Paper presented at the annual meeting of the American Anthropological Association, Symposium on Domestic Workers.

Langhorne, Orra. 1901. "Domestic Service in the South." *Journal of Social Science* 39:169–75.

Lanz, Gregorio. 1969. "Servicio doméstico: Una esclavitud?" *Estudios Sociales* 2, no. 4:197–201.

Laslett, Peter. 1977. *Family Life and Illicit Love in Earlier Generations.* New York: Cambridge University Press.

Lasser, Carol S. 1978. "Lifecycle and Class: Domestic Service and the 'Girls' of the Salem Female Charitable Society." Paper presented at the fourth Berkshire Conference on the History of Women.

———. 1980. "A 'Pleasingly Oppressive' Burden: The Transformation of Domestic Service and Female Charity in Salem, 1800–1840." *Essex Institute Historical Collections* 116, no. 1:156–75.

———. 1981. "Mistress, Maid and Market: The Transformation of Domestic Service in New England, 1790–1870." Ph.D. diss., Harvard University, Cambridge, Mass.

———. 1984. "The 'Golden Age of Domestic Service': A Re-Evaluation." Paper presented at the sixth Berkshire Conference on the History of Women.

———. 1987. " 'The World's Dread Laugh': Singlehood and Service in Nineteenth-Century Boston." In Herbert G. Gutman and Donald H. Bell, eds., *The New England Working Class and the New Labor History,* pp. 72–88. Urbana: University of Illinois Press.

Lawson, Lesley. 1986. *Working Women: A Portrait of South Africa's Women Workers.* Johannesburg: Ravan Press.

Lázaro, G., and M. Bayon. 1976. *Empleadas de hogar—trabajadoras de tercera clase.* Madrid: Col. Z.

Leashore, Bogart R. 1984. "Black Female Workers: Live-in Domestics in Detroit, Michigan (1860–1880)." *Phylon* 45, no. 2:111–20.

Leff, Gloria. 1974. "Algunos aspectos del servicio doméstico en la área metropolitana de la ciudad de México." Tesis, Universidad Nacional Autónoma de México, Facultad de Ciencias Políticas y Sociales.

Lenskyj, Helen. 1981. "A 'Servant Problem' or a 'Servant-Mistress Problem'? Domestic Service in Canada, 1890–1930." *Atlantis* 7, no. 1:3–11.

León, Magdalena. 1985. "The Program for Domestic Servants in Colombia/El programa de servicio doméstico de Colombia." Paper presented at the twelfth Congress of the Latin American Studies Association.

Leslie, Genevieve. 1974. "Domestic Service in Canada, 1880–1920." In Janice Acton, Penny Goldsmith, and Bonnie Shepard, eds., *Women at Work, Ontario 1850–1930,* pp. 71–125. Toronto: Canadian Women's Educational Press.

Llinas, Mario Alberto de. 1974. "Introducción al servicio doméstico en Colombia." Tesis, Universidad de los Andes, Bogotá, Facultad de Ingeniería.

Losey, Joseph, and James Fox. 1963. *The Servant.* Videorecording, based on the novel by Robin Maugham. London: Thorn EMI Video/Springfield Films, Ltd.

Luna Clara, C. 1966. "Situación socioeconomica de la servidumbre en la ciudad de México." Tesis, Universidad Nacional Autónoma de México.

McBride, Theresa Marie. 1973. "Rural Tradition and the Process of Modernization: Domestic Servants in Nineteenth-Century France." Ph.D. diss., Rutgers University, New Brunswick, N.J.

———. 1974. "Social Mobility for the Lower Classes: Domestic Servants in France." *Journal of Social History* 8:63–78.

———. 1975. " 'Women's Work': Mistress and Servant in the Nineteenth Century." *Proceedings of the Annual Meeting of the Western Society for French History* 3:390–97.

———. 1976. *The Domestic Revolution: The Modernisation of Household Service in England and France, 1820–1920.* New York: Holmes & Meier; London: Croom-Helm.

———. 1978. " 'As the Twig Is Bent': The Victorian Nanny." In Anthony S. Wohl, ed., *The Victorian Family: Structure and Stresses*, pp. 44–58. New York: St. Martin's Press; London: Croom Helm.

McGrew, Lilian Culbertoon, and J. R. Hawke. n.d. "A Study of Household Employment in Omaha, Nebraska." Amey E. Watson Papers, Cornell University, Ithaca, N.Y.

Mack, Beverly. 1985. "Service and Status: Slaves and Concubines in Kano, Nigeria." Paper presented at the annual meeting of the American Anthropological Association, Symposium on Domestic Workers.

McKinley, Blaine Edward. 1969. " 'The Stranger in the Gates': Employer Reactions toward Domestic Servants in America, 1825–1975." Ph.D. diss., Michigan State University, East Lansing.

Macpherson, C. B. 1973. "Servants and Labourers in Seventeenth Century England." In *Democratic Theory: Essays in Retrieval*, pp. 207–23. Oxford: Clarendon Press.

Malcolmson, Patricia E. 1986. *English Laundresses: A Social History, 1850–1930.* Urbana: University of Illinois Press.

Marshall, Dorothy. 1949. *The English Domestic Servant in History.* London: Historical Association.

Martin, Linda, and Kerry Seagrove. 1985. *The Servant Problem: Domestic Workers in North America.* Jefferson, N.C.: McFarland.

Martin-Fugier, Anne. 1979. *La place de bonnes: La domesticité feminine à Paris en 1900.* Paris: Grasset & Fasquelle.

Mattila, J. Peter. 1971. *The Impact of Extending Minimum Wages to Private Household Workers.* Washington, D.C.: U.S. Department of Labor.

Maza, Sarah Crawford. 1978. "Domestic Service in Eighteenth Century France." Ph.D. diss., Princeton University.

———. 1983. *Servants and Masters in Eighteenth-Century France: The Uses of Loyalty.* Princeton, N.J.: Princeton University Press.

Medina N., Martha, and Julieta Romero. 1977. "La mujer en el servicio doméstico." Tesis, Universidad Nacional, Bogotá.

Mehta, Aban B. 1960. *The Domestic Servant Class.* Bombay: Popular Book Depot.

Mejia Duque, Jaime. 1975. "Femineidad y servidumbre." *Casa de las Américas* 15, no. 88:93–95.

Melosh, Barbara. 1983. "Historians and The Servant Problem." *Reviews in American History* 11, no. 1:55–58.

Mena, María. n.d. "Estudio sociológico sobre la marginalidad de la trabajadora doméstica chocana en Medellín." Tesis, Pontificia Universidad Bolivariana, Medellín.

Méndez, Martha. 1980. "Participation of Women in the Labour Force in Colombia: Domestic Service, 1951–1976." Thesis, Ontario Institute for Studies in Education, Toronto.

Mercado, Isabel. 1970. "Trabajadoras auxiliares del hogar en México." *Boletín Documental de CIDHAL* 1:51–57.

Moreira, Rita, and Maria Luisa Leal. 1981. *The Lady of Pacaembu: A Portrait of Brazil.* Film. Produced in Brazil as *A dama do Pacaembu.* São Paulo: Tecnovideo e Engevideo.

National Committee on Household Employment. 1978–82. *Household Employment News,* vols. 10–13 (continues *NCHE News,* vols. 1–9).

Nava, Gregory, and Anna Thomas. 1984. *El Norte.* Videorecording. Farmington Hills, Mich.: CBS/Fox Video.

Neff, Wanda Fraiken. 1966. "The Governess." In *Victorian Working Women: An Historical and Literary Study of Women in British Industries and Professions 1832–1850,* pp. 151–85. New York: AMS Press.

Nett, Emily M. 1966. "The Servant Class in a Developing Country: Ecuador." *Journal of Inter-American Studies* 8, no. 3:437–52.

Neu, Peter. 1968. "Die Gesindemarkte der Sudeifel." *Rheinische Vierteljahrsblatter* 32:498–522.

Noble, Jeanne L. 1967. "An Exploratory Study of Domestics' View of Their Working World." New York University, School of Education. Mimeo.

Norris, William P. 1984. "Patron-Client Relationships in the Urban Social Structure: A Brazilian Case Study." *Human Organization* 43, no. 1:16–26.

Oliver, L. 1911. *Domestic Service and Citizenship.* London.

Orlansky, Dora, and Silvia Dubrovsky. 1978. *The Effects of Rural-Urban Migration on Women's Role and Status in Latin America.* Paris: UNESCO.

Orrego, C. A. 1972. *Legislación del trabajador doméstico: Derechos y obligaciones de empleador e del doméstico.* Lima: Los Rotarios.

Overs, Robert P. 1970. *Paid Domestic Work for the Trainable Retarded Girl: A Pilot Project.* Milwaukee, Wis.: Curative Workshop of Milwaukee.

Palmer, Phyllis. 1984. "Household and Service Work: The Racial Division of Women's Work and Workers." Paper presented at the sixth Berkshire Conference on the History of Women.

Parkinson, C. Northcote. 1981. *Jeeves: A Gentleman's Personal Gentleman.* New York: St. Martin's Press.

Pascual Badiola, María Pilar. 1968. "Diagnosis ético-social de las empleadas domésticas." Tesis, Pontificia Universidad Católica del Perú, Lima.

Perelli, C. 1983. *La mujer en el sector informal: El caso de las empleadas domésticas en Montevideo.* Montevideo: Editorial A L C A L I.

Pérez Alcantara, Gloria Haydee. 1969. "El problema social de la empleada doméstica en Lima." Tesis, Universidad Nacional Federico Villarreal, Lima.

Pérez Fuentes, Ana. n.d. "Investigación del problema socio-educativo de la doméstica." Tesis, Pontificia Universidad Católica del Perú, Lima.

Perry, Ronald Dennis. 1975. "History of Domestic Servants in London, 1850–1900." Ph.D. diss., University of Washington, Seattle.

Peters-Joffre, Ruth. 1984. "Estudio de las condiciones de empleo de las trabajadoras domésticas en México realizado en base a la situación de la mujer trabajadora doméstica de Cuernavaca, Morelos." Thesis, Academia Social "De Horst," Driebergen, Netherlands.

Peterson, J. Jeanine. 1972. "The Victorian Governess: Status Incongruity in Family and Society." In Martha Vicinus, ed., *Suffer and Be Still,* pp. 3–19. Bloomington: Indiana University Press.

Pettengill, Lillian. 1903. *Toilers of the Home: A Report of a College Woman's Experience as a Domestic Servant.* New York: Doubleday.

Pike, E. Royston. 1967. "Domestic Service in the 1860s." In *Golden Times: Human Documents of the Victorian Golden Age,* pp. 157–68. New York: Praeger.

Poelstra, J. 1981. "Dienstboden tussen arbeiders en burgerstand." *Tijdschrift voor Vrouwenstudies* 5, no. 2:45–68.

Porter, Susan L. 1978. "Mother/Mistress, Servant/Child: The Orphan as Indentured Servant in the Early Victorian Family." Paper presented at the fourth Berkshire Conference on the History of Women.

———. 1984. "The Benevolent Asylum—Image and Reality: The Care and Training of Female Orphans in Boston, 1800–1840." Ph.D. diss., Boston University.

Preston-Whyte, Eleanor. 1976. "Race Attitudes and Behavior: The Case of Domestic Employment in White South African Homes." *African Studies* 35, no. 2:71–89.

Prochaska, F. K. 1981. "Female Philanthropy and Domestic Service in Victorian England." *Bulletin of the Institute of Historical Research* 54, no. 129:78–85.

Pruitt, Ida. 1967. *A Daughter of Han: The Autobiography of a Chinese Working Woman.* Stanford, Calif.: Stanford University Press.

Renard, Roland. 1974. "Servides domestiques et garde des enfants." *Population et Famille* 2, no. 32:95–137.

Rennie, Jean. 1982. *Every Other Sunday.* New York: St. Martin's Press.

Richardson, Sheila J. 1967. "'The Servant Question': A Study of the Domestic Labor Market, 1851–1911." Master's thesis, University of London.

Rivera, Olga. 1979. "Situación de la trabajadora del hogar en Lima metropolitana." *Tareas para el Trabajo Social.* Mimeo.

Robinson, Mary V. 1924. *Domestic Workers.* Washington, D.C.: Government Printing Office.

Rodríguez-Luis, Julio. 1983. "Guzmán, criado inpenitente, criado perfecto: El servicio doméstico en la picaresca." *Revista Internacional de Sociología* 41, no. 46:273–93.

Roffiel, Rosa María. 1980–81. "Informe de Managua." *FEM* 4, no. 16:93–97.

Rollins, Judith. 1983. "The Social Psychology of the Relationship between Black Female Domestic Servants and Their White Female Employers." Ph.D. diss., Brandeis University, Waltham, Mass.

———. 1985. "Ideology and Servitude." Paper presented at the annual meeting of the American Anthropological Association, Symposium on Domestic Workers.

———. 1985. *Between Women: Domestics and Their Employers.* Philadelphia: Temple University Press.

Romero, Mary. 1984. "Domestic Service in Rural to Urban Migration: The Case of the Chicana." Paper presented at the Illinois Conference of Latin Americanists.

———. 1984. "Domestic Work among Chicanas: A Transitional or Ghetto Occupation?" Paper presented at the meeting of the National Association for Chicano Studies.

———. 1985. "Day Work in the Suburbs: The Work Experience of Chicana Private Housekeepers." Paper presented at the Wingspread Conference on Integrating Qualitative Research.

———. 1986. "Chicana and Mexican Domestics in the United States." Paper presented at International Congress of the Latin American Studies Association.

———. 1986. "Domestics and the Struggle for Harmony: The Case of Chicana 'Cleaning Ladies.'" Paper presented at the annual meeting of the National Association for Chicano Studies.

———. 1986. "Domestic Work in Transition from Rural to Urban Life: The Case of La Chicana." *Women's Studies* 13, no. 3.

———. 1988. "Day Work in the Suburbs: The Work Experience of Chicana Private Housekeepers." In Anne Statham, Eleanor M. Miller, and Hans O. Mauksch, eds., *The Worth of Women's Work: A Qualitative Synthesis.* Albany: State University of New York Press.

Root, Amanda. 1984. "The Return of the Nanny." *New Socialist,* December.

Rubbo, Anna, and Michael Taussig. 1978. "Up Off Their Knees: Servanthood in Southwest Colombia." In *Female Servants and Economic Development,* pp. 5–29. Occasional Papers in Women's Studies No. 1. Ann Arbor: University of Michigan.

———. 1981. "El servicio doméstico en el suroeste de Colombia." *América Indígena* 41, no. 1:85–112.

Rubinow, I. M. 1906. "The Problem of Domestic Service." *Journal of Political Economy* 14:502–19.

Rueda Sánchez, G. 1980. *Nueva legislación del trabajador doméstico.* 4th ed. Lima: Ediciones Jurídicas.

Ruíz Gaytan F., Beatriz, et al. 1979. "Un grupo trabajador importante no incluído en la historia laboral mexicana (trabajadoras domésticas)." In *El trabajo y los trabajadores en la historia de México,* pp. 419–55. México, D.F.: El Colegio de México.

Ruíz, Vicki L. 1987. "By the Day or Week: Mexicana Domestic Workers in El Paso." In Vicki L. Ruíz and Susan Tiano, eds., *Women on the U.S.–Mexico Border: Responses to Change,* pp. 61–76. Winchester, Mass.: Allen & Unwin.

Rutté García, Alberto. 1976. *Simplemente explotadas: El mundo de las empleadas domésticas en Lima.* 2d ed. Lima: Centro de Estudios y Promoción del Desarrollo (DESCO).

Safiotti, Heleieth Iara Bongiovani. 1978. *Emprego doméstico e capitalismo.* Petrópolis, Brasil: Editora Vozes.

———. 1978. "Domestic Employment and Capitalism." Paper presented at the International Sociological Association.

Salaff, Janet W. 1981. "Ci-li: From Domestic Service to Government Service." In *Working Daughters of Hong Kong: Filial Piety or Power in the Family?,* pp. 156–76. Cambridge: Cambridge University Press.

Salazar, F. 1978. "Los sirvientes domésticos." In *Ciudad de México: Ensayo de construcción de una historia,* pp. 124–37. Colección Científica No. 61. Mexico: INAH.

———. 1979. "Los trabajadores del servicio doméstico en la ciudad de México en el siglo XIX," pp. 184–93. Cuadernos de Trabajo No. 29. México: INAH.

Salmon, Lucy Maynard. 1897. *Domestic Service.* New York: Macmillan; rpt., New York: Arno Press, 1972.

Sanjek, Roger. 1985. "Maid Servants and Market Women's Apprentices in Adabraka." Paper presented at the annual meeting of the American Anthropological Association, Symposium on Domestic Workers.

Sankar, Andrea P. 1978. "Female Domestic Service in Hong Kong." In *Female Servants and Economic Development,* pp. 51–62. Occasional Papers in Women's Studies No. 1. Ann Arbor: University of Michigan.

———. 1981. "The Conquest of Solitude: Singlehood and Old Age in Traditional Chinese Society." In Christine Fry, ed., *Dimensions: Aging, Culture and Health,* pp. 65–83. New York: Praeger Special Studies.

———. 1984. "Spinster Sisterhoods," In Mary Sheridan and Janet W. Salaff, eds., *Lives: Chinese Working Women,* pp. 51–70. Bloomington: Indiana University Press.

Schellekens, Thea, and Anja van der Schoot. 1984. "Todos me dicen que soy muchachita . . . trabajo y organización de las trabajadoras del hogar en

Lima, Perú." Doctoral thesis, Catholic University of Nijmegen, Netherlands.

Schwickert, Pauline. 1950. "Concepts of Domestic Service in German Legal Sources from the Middle Ages to 1919." Ph.D. diss., New School for Social Research, New York.

Sejourne, Laurette. 1980. "Escuela para domésticas." In *La mujer cubana en el quehacer de la historia,* pp. 139–49. Mexico: Siglo XXI.

Silvera, Makeda. 1983. *Silenced: Talking with Working Class West Indian Women about Their Lives and Struggles as Domestic Workers in Canada.* Toronto: Williams-Wallace.

Sindicato de Trabajadoras del Hogar, Cusco. 1982. *Basta: Testimonios.* Cusco: Centro de Estudios Rurales Andinos "Bartolomé de las Casas."

Sindicato Nacional de Trabajadoras del Servicio Doméstico. 1972. *Reivindicaciones.* Bogotá: SINTRASEDOM.

Smith, Charles. 1980. *Lord Mountbatten: His Butler's Story.* New York: Stein & Day.

Smith, Margo L. 1971. "Institutionalized Servitude: Female Domestic Service in Lima, Peru." Ph.D. diss., Indiana University, Bloomington.

———. 1973. "Domestic Service as a Channel of Upward Mobility for the Lower-Class Woman: The Lima Case." In Ann Pescatello, ed., *Female and Male in Latin America,* pp. 191–207. Pittsburgh: University of Pittsburgh Press.

———. 1975. "The Female Domestic Servant and Social Change: Lima, Peru." In Ruby Rohrlich-Leavitt, ed., *Women Cross-Culturally: Change and Challenge,* pp. 163–80. The Hague: Mouton.

———. 1977. "Construcción residencial y posición social del servicio doméstico en el Perú contemporáneo." In Jorge E. Hardoy and Richard P. Schaedel, eds., *Asentamientos urbanos y organización socioproductiva en la historia de América Latina,* pp. 363–85. Buenos Aires: Ediciones SIAP.

———. 1977. "El servicio doméstico como medio de movilidad ascendente para la mujer de clase baja: el caso de Lima." In Ann Pescatello, ed., *Hembra y macho en Latinoamérica,* pp. 233–52. México, D.F.: Editorial Diana.

———. 1978. "The Female Domestic Servant and Social Change: Lima, Peru." In Richard P. Schaedel, Jorge E. Hardoy, and Nora Scott Kinzer, eds., *Urbanization in the Americas from Its Beginnings to the Present,* pp. 569–85. The Hague: Mouton.

———. 1980. "Women's Careers in Lima, Peru: Domestic Service and Street Vending." Paper presented at the annual meeting of the American Anthropological Association.

———. 1982. "El servicio doméstico—reflexiones posteriores." Paper presented at the Congreso de Investigación acerca de la Mujer en la Región Andina, Lima.

Só a gente que vive é que sabe: Depoimento de uma doméstica. 1982. *Cadernos de Educação Popular* 4. Petrópolis, Brasil: Editora Vozes.

Solberg-Ladd, Helena. 1975. *The Double Day* (film). UNIFILM, San Francisco.
South Africa, Non-European Affairs Department. 1971. *Your Bantu Servant and You: A Few Suggestions to Facilitate Happier Relations between Employer and Employee.* Johannesburg: Non-European Affairs Department.
Souza da Silva, Francisca. 1983. *Ai de vos: Diario de uma dómestica.* Rio de Janeiro: Editorial Civilização Brasileira.
Souza, Julia Filet-Abreu de. 1979. *Paid Domestic Service in Brazil.* Amsterdam.
———. 1980. "Paid Domestic Service in Brazil." *Latin American Perspectives* 7, no. 1:35–63.
Souza, Paulo R., and Victor E. Tokeman. 1976. "The Informal Urban Sector in Latin America." *International Labour Review* 114:355–65.
Spalter-Roth, Roberta M. 1977. "Organizing Private Household Workers: An Exploration of Necessary Conditions." Paper presented at a meeting of the Southern Sociological Society.
Spofford, Harriet Elizabeth Prescott. 1881. *The Servant Girl Question.* Boston: Houghton, Mifflin. Rpt. New York: Arno Press, 1977.
Stekl, Hannes. 1975. "Hausrechtliche Abhangigkeit in der Industriellen Gesellschaft: Das Hausliche Personal vom 18. bis ins 20. Jahrhundert." *Wiener Geschichtsblatter* 30, no. 4:301–13.
Stigler, George J. 1946. *Domestic Servants in the United States, 1900–1940.* Occasional Paper No. 24. New York: National Bureau of Economic Research.
Stillinger, Martha. 1966. "Domestic Service in Lima, Peru." Mimeo.
Strasser, Susan M. 1978. "Mistress and Maid, Employer and Employee: Domestic Service Reform in the United States, 1892–1920." *Marxist Perspectives* 1, no. 1:52–67.
———. 1982. *Never Done: A History of American Housework.* New York: Pantheon.
Sutherland, Daniel Ellyson. 1976. "Americans and Their Servants, 1800–1921: Being an Inquiry into the Origins and Progress of the American Servant Problem." Ph.D. dissertation, Wayne State University, Detroit.
———. 1979. "The Servant Problem: An Index of Antebellum Americanism." *Southern Studies* 18, no. 4:488–503.
———. 1981. "A Special Kind of Problem: The Response of Household Slaves and Their Masters to Freedom." *Southern Studies* 20, no. 2:151–66.
———. 1981. *Americans and Their Servants: Domestic Service in the United States from 1800 to 1920.* Baton Rouge: Louisiana State University Press.
Taylor, Pam. 1978. "Domestic Service in Britain between the Wars." M.A. thesis, University of Birmingham, England.
———. 1979. "Daughters and Mothers—Maids and Mistresses: Domestic Service between the Wars." In J. Clarke, C. Crichter, and R. Johnson, eds., *Working Class Culture: Studies in History and Theory,* pp. 121–39. London: Centre for Contemporary Cultural Studies/Hutchinson Publishing Group; New York: St. Martin's Press.

——. 1979. *Women Domestic Servants, 1919–1939.* Centre for Contemporary Cultural Studies, Paper No. 40. Birmingham, Eng.: University of Birmingham.

Tellis-Nayak, V. 1983. "Power and Solidarity: Clientage in Domestic Service." *Current Anthropology* 24, no. 1:67–79.

Tilly, Louise A., et al. 1978. "Introduction and Overview." In *Female Servants and Economic Development,* pp. 1–4. Occasional Papers in Women's Studies No. 1. Ann Arbor: University of Michigan.

Todaro, Rosalba, and Thelma Gálvez. 1987. *Trabajo doméstico remunerado: Conceptos, hechos, datos.* Santiago de Chile: Centro de Estudios de la Mujer.

Tokeman, Victor. 1979. *Informal-Formal Sector Interrelationships.* Santiago de Chile: Comisión Económica para América Latina (CEPAL).

Toussaint, Florence. 1980–81. "Otro mito de la televisión." *FEM* 4, no. 16:67–68.

Towner, Lawrence W. 1962. "'A Fondness of Freedom': Servant Protest in Puritan Society." *William and Mary Quarterly* 19, no. 2:201–19.

——. 1981. "Trabajo doméstico y la doble explotación de la mujer." *Desarrollo Indoamericano* 16, no. 71:33–40.

Turković, Robert J. 1981. "Race Relations in the Province of Córdoba, Argentina, 1800–1853." Ph.D. diss., University of Florida, Gainesville.

Turner, Ernest Sackville. 1963. *What the Butler Saw: Two Hundred and Fifty Years of the Servant Problem.* New York: St. Martin's Press.

Turritin, J. S. 1976. "Networks and Mobility: The Case of West Indian Domestics from Montserrat." *Canadian Review of Sociology and Anthropology* 13, no. 3:305–20.

United Nations, Economic Commission for Latin America (ECLA/CEPAL). 1983. "Housemaids." In *Five Studies on the Situation of Women in Latin America,* pp. 106–8. Santiago de Chile: Estudios e Informes de la CEPAL.

United States, Department of Labor. 1971. *Three on a Single Theme: There Can be Career Opportunities in Household Employment.* Annandale, Va.: MK Trimble.

——. 1974. *Upward Mobility for Private Household Workers.* Washington, D.C.: Government Printing Office.

——. 1978. *Private Household Workers: A Statistical and Legislative Profile.* Washington, D.C.: Government Printing Office.

——. 1979. *Domestic Service Employment.* Washington, D.C.: Government Printing Office.

United States, Department of Labor, Bureau of Labor Statistics. 1967. *Employment Outlook for Private Household Workers.* Bulletin No. 1450–39. Washington, D.C.: U.S. Department of Labor.

——. 1981. *Women in Domestic Work: Yesterday and Today.* Special Labor Force Report No. 242. Washington, D. C.: U.S. Department of Labor.

United States Employment Service. 1941. *Job Descriptions for Domestic Service and Personal Service Occupations.* Washington, D.C.: Government Printing Office.

Upstairs Downstairs. 1973. London: British Broadcasting Co., BBC-TV.

Urrútia, Elena. 1980–81. "Experiencias de organización." *FEM* 4, no. 16:37–39.

Useem, Ruth Hill. 1972. "The Servant Problem." In *The American Family in India,* pp. B1–B34. Studies of Third Cultures No. 7. East Lansing: Michigan State University, Institute for International Studies in Education.

Vallejo, Nancy. 1982. "Situación socio-jurídica del servicio doméstico en Colombia." Tesis, Facultad de Derecho, Universidad de los Andes, Bogotá.

Van Noord, Carl. 1983. "The Decline in Employment of Young Single Women in Service Occupations, England and Wales, 1871–1961" Ph.D. diss., New School for Social Research, New York.

Van Onselen, Charles. 1982. "The Witches of Suburbia: Domestic Service on the Witwatersrand, 1890–1914." In Van Onselen, ed., *Studies in the Social and Economic History of the Witwatersrand, 1886–1914,* vol. 2, pp. 1–73. Essex, Eng.: Harlow; New York: Longman.

Van Raaphorst, Donna. 1983. "The Unionization Movement among Domestic Workers in the United States, 1870 to 1940." Ph.D. diss., Kent State University, Ohio.

Vázquez, Jesús María. 1960. *El servicio doméstico en España.* Madrid: Ministerio de Trabajo, Instituto Nacional de Previsión.

———. 1969. "Estudio sobre la situación del servicio doméstico en Lima." Misión Conciliar, Lima. Mimeo.

———. 1970. *El servicio doméstico en Lima.* Lima: Centro Arquidiocesano de Pastoral.

Waggoman, Mary. 1945. "Wartime Job Opportunities for Women Household Workers in Washington, D.C." *Monthly Labor Review* 60, no. 3:575–84.

Waterson, Merlin. 1980. *The Servants' Hall: A "Downstairs" History of a British Country House.* New York: Pantheon.

Watson, Amey E. 1931. "Domestic Service." *Encyclopedia of the Social Sciences* 5:198–202.

———. 1932. *Household Employment in Philadelphia.* U.S. Women's Bureau, Bulletin No. 93. Washington, D.C.: Government Printing Office.

Watson, Rubie. 1985. "Wives, Concubines, and Maidservants: Domestic Workers in Chinese Society." Paper presented at the annual meeting of the American Anthropological Society, Symposium on Domestic Workers.

Weinrich, A. K. H. 1976. *Mucheke: Race, Status, and Politics in a Rhodesian Community.* New York: Holmes & Meier.

Whisson, Michael G., and William Weil. 1971. *Domestic Servants: A Microcosm of the "Race Problem."* Johannesburg: South African Institute of Race Relations.

Wierling, Dorothee. 1980. "Living Conditions and Life Histories of Female Domestic Servants at the Turn of the Century." in *Proceedings of the International Oral History Conference* 2:307–23.

———. 1982. "Vom Mädchen zum Dienstmädchen: Kindliche Sozialisation und Beruf im Kaiserreich." In Klaus Bergmann and Rolf Schorken, eds., *Geschichte im Alltag, Alltag in der Geschichte,* pp. 57–87. Dusseldorf.

———. 1982. "Women Domestic Servants in Germany at the Turn of the Century." *Oral History* (Autumn), no. 2:47–57.

———. 1983. "Indirect Rule and Resistance: Housewife and Servant in the German Middle Class." Paper presented at the International Conference on Oral History and Women's History.

Wilcox, Penelope. 1982. "Marriage, Mobility, and Domestic Service in Victorian Cambridge." *Local Population Studies* 29:19–34.

Willer, Katheryn. 1940. *Women Domestic Workers in Washington, D.C.* Washington, D.C.: Government Printing Office.

Woodson, C. G. 1930. "The Negro Washerwoman, A Vanishing Figure." *Journal of Negro History* 15, no. 3:269–77.

Young, Grace Ester. 1985. "The Myth of Being 'Like a Daughter': Domestic Service in Lima, Peru." Master's thesis, University of Chicago.

Zarnowska, Anna. 1977. "La famille et le statut familial de souvriers et des domestiques dans le royaume de Pologne au déclin du XIX siècle." *Acta Poloniase Historica* 35:113–44.

Zurita, Carlos. 1983. "El servicio doméstico en Argentina: El caso de Santiago de Estero." Instituto Central de Investigaciones Científicas, Universidad Católica de Santiago del Estero, Santiago del Estero.

About the Contributors

ELSA M. CHANEY is an independent researcher, with extensive publications on women in politics and the workforce. She is the author of *Supermadre: Women in Politics in Peru and Chile* (1980) and, with Ximena Bunster, of *Sellers and Servants: Working Women in Lima, Peru* (1985).

MARY GARCIA CASTRO has carried out various studies with the International Labor Office on the conditions of working women in Latin America, including an extensive study in Colombia on domestics. She teaches sociology at the Universidade Federal de Bahia in Brazil.

SHELLEE COLEN teaches in the Metropolitan Studies program at New York University. The article in this book is based on her doctoral dissertation in anthropology at the New School for Social Research.

ODETE MARIA DA CONCEIÇÃO is the founder of the domestic workers' movement in Brazil. She has finished her primary education, is single, and does not have any children.

ADELINDA DÍAZ URIARTE for over twenty years has labored in many capacities as an organizer of domestic workers.

ISIS DUARTE is professor and researcher at the Autonomous University of Santo Domingo. She is co-author of *Azucar y política en R.D.* (1976) and *Capitalismo y superpoblación en Santo Domingo* (1980). Her newest work, *Trabajadores urbanos en República Domincana,* is about to appear.

CORNELIA BUTLER FLORA is professor of sociology at Kansas State University. Her major publications have dealt with popular culture and the structure of agriculture, in both the U.S. and Latin America.

THELMA GÁLVEZ is a researcher with the Centro de Estudios de la Mujer in Santiago, Chile. She is coauthor (with Rosalba Todaro) of *Yo trabajo así . . . en casa particular* (1985).

ELENA GIL IZQUIERDO (1906–85), active all her life on behalf of working women and a leader in the Federation of Cuban Women, organized the retraining of household workers in Cuba.

MÓNICA GOGNA is a fellow of the Consejo Nacional de Investigaciones Científicas y Técnicas in the Centro de Estudios de Estado y Sociedad of Buenos Aires.

MARY GOLDSMITH is completing work on her dissertation on domestic service in Mexico City. She is associated with the Interdisciplinary Women's Studies Program at the Colegio de México.

SANDRA LAUDERDALE GRAHAM teaches and does research at the Institute of Latin American Studies, University of Texas (Austin), and has also taught Latin American history under the Five College Program at Mount Holyoke College. She is completing a book about domestic servants in nineteenth-century Rio de Janeiro.

B. W. HIGMAN is professor of history at the University of the West Indies, Mona, Jamaica, and the author of *Slave Population and Economy in Jamaica, 1807–1834* (1976) and *Slave Populations of the British Caribbean, 1807–1834* (1984).

ELIZABETH KUZNESOF is associate professor of history at the University of Kansas, Lawrence. She has published *Household Economy and Urban Development: São Paulo 1765 to 1836* (1985) and is completing a social and political history of the family in Latin America from 1492 to 1930.

MAGDALENA LEÓN has carried out numerous investigations and consultations with international agencies dealing with the female labor force, rural women, and domestic service. She has published (with Carmen Diana Deere) *Women in Andean Agriculture* and edited a three-volume collection, *Debate sobre la mujer en America Latina y el Caribe* (both 1982).

PATRICIA MOHAMMED is attached to the Institute for Social and Economic Research, University of the West Indies, Trinidad. She has served on the faculty of the Institute for Development Studies, University of Sussex, and at present is Coordinator of the Rape Crisis Centre in Port of Spain.

ANAZIR MARIA DE OLIVEIRA (Zica) was president of the Associação Profissional dos Empregos Domésticos (Domestic Workers Professional Association) of Rio de Janeiro when this article was written. She had completed her secondary education and has six children and eight grandchildren.

AÍDA MORENO VALENZUELA has worked for many years with the Sindicato Nacional de Trabajadoras de Casa Particular (SINTRACAP) In Chile. She manages Servicios Quillay, a venture of a group of SINTRACAP members to operate a professional cleaning service, the proceeds of which will finance union activities.

HILDETE PEREIRA DE MELO is adjunct professor and coordinator of the economics course at the Universidade Federal Fluminense, Niterói, Rio de Janeiro, and counselor to the National Commision on Women's Rights in Brazil. She is the author of several works on energy and development, as well as *Sequelas do Aborto: Custos e Implicações Sociais (1982)* and (with Maria Valeria Pena Junho) *A Teoria Económica e a Condição Feminina* (1985).

SUZANA PRATES (1940–1988) directed the Grupo de Estudios sobre la Condición de la Mujer (Study Group on Women's Condition) in the Centro de Información y Estudios, Montevideo, Uruguay. Her published work includes *Estratégia exportadora y la búsqueda de trabajo barato: Trabajo visible e invisible de la mujer en la industria del calzado en el Uruguay* (1983) and (with Graciela Taglioretti) *Participación de la mujer en el mercado de trabajo uruguay: Características básicas y evolución reciente* (1980).

THEA SCHELLEKENS and ANJA VAN DER SCHOOT are cultural anthropologists of the Netherlands. After completing work on a joint doctoral thesis, they spent a year in Peru with the Asociación Peru-Mujer as part of a training project for household workers.

MARGO L. SMITH is professor and chair of the anthropology department, Northeastern Illinois University. In addition to her publications on domestic service in Peru, she has published reference materials in anthropology and, most recently, an article on the applications of anthropology in the private sector.

ROSALBA TODARO is coauthor (with Thelma Gálvez) of *Yo trabajo así . . . en casa particular.* She directs the Centro de Estudios de La Mujer (Women's Studies Center) in Santiago, Chile.

ISABEL MIGNONE (who translated Díaz Uriarte, Gálvez and Todaro, Gil Izquierdo, Gogna, and Moreno Valenzuela) is currently a research assistant at the World Bank. She was assisted in her translations by her husband, MARIO DEL CARRIL, a journalist and teacher.

MANUEL GONZÁLEZ PINEIRO (Pereira de Melo, and Oliveira and Conceição) is finishing his doctoral work at the University of Florida, Gainesville, where he specializes in Spanish and linguistics.

KATHERINE PETTUS (Duarte, Garcia Castro, León, Prates, and Schellekens and van der Schoot) is a professional translator who "works to bring the voices of Latin American women in struggle to the English-speaking feminist movement." She currently directs Latin American Scholarly Services, which does translation, bibliography, and editing.